ISAIAH

ISAIAH

HIS TIMES & HIS PREACHING

The Eighth-century Prophet

JOHN H. HAYES and STUART A. IRVINE

Abingdon Press
Nashville

ISAIAH
THE EIGHTH-CENTURY PROPHET: HIS TIMES AND HIS PREACHING

Copyright © 1987 by John H. Hayes and Stuart A. Irvine

Library of Congress Cataloging-in-Publication Data

Hayes, John Haralson, 1934-
  Isaiah, the eighth-century prophet : his times and his preaching /
John H. Hayes, Stuart A. Irvine.
    p. cm.
    Bibliography: p.
    Includes index.
    ISBN 0-687-19705-8 (alk. paper)
    1. Bible. O.T. Isaiah I-XXXIX—Commentaries. 2. Isaiah (Biblical
prophet)   I. Irvine, Stuart A.   II. Title.
BS1515.3.H39 1987
224'.107—dc 19   87-17834
                                                                      CIP

This book is printed on acid-free paper.

All scripture quotations, unless otherwise noted, are the authors'
translations.

Those marked NEB are from The New English Bible. Copyright © the
Delegates of the Oxford University Press and the Syndics of the Cambridge
University Press, 1961, 1970. Reprinted by permission.

Those marked NJPSV are from *The Prophets (Nevi'im)* and *The Writings
(Kethubim)*. Copyright © 1978 *(Nevi'im)* and © 1982 *(Kethubim)* by the Jewish
Publication Society of America.

Those marked RSV are from the Revised Standard Version of the Bible,
copyrighted 1946, 1952, © 1971, 1973 by the Division of Christian Education
of the National Council of the Churches of Christ in the U.S.A., and are used
by permission.

Manufactured by the Parthenon Press at
Nashville, Tennessee, United States of America

Contents

Abbreviations

AASOR	*Annual of the American Schools of Oriental Research*
ABC	*Assyrian and Babylonian Chronicles*, by A. K. Grayson (Locust Valley, NY: J. J. Augustin, 1975)
AEL	*Ancient Egyptian Literature: A Book of Readings*, by M. Lichtheim (3 vols.; Berkeley/London: University of California Press, 1973–1980)
AJSL	*American Journal of Semitic Languages and Literature*
AJT	*American Journal of Theology*
ALUOS	*Annual of Leeds University Oriental Society*
ANEP	*The Ancient Near East in Pictures Relating to the Old Testament*, by J. B. Pritchard (2d ed.; Princeton: Princeton University Press, 1969)
ANET	*Ancient Near Eastern Texts Relating to the Old Testament* (ed. J. B. Pritchard; 3rd ed.; Princeton: Princeton University Press, 1969)
Ant	*Jewish Antiquities*, by Josephus
AO	*Acta Orientalia*
ARAB	*Ancient Records of Assyria and Babylonia*, by D. D. Luckenbill (2 vols.; Chicago: University of Chicago Press, 1926–1927)
ARI	*Assyrian Royal Inscriptions*, by A. K. Grayson (2 vols.; Wiesbaden: Otto Harrassowitz, 1972–1976)
AS	*The Annals of Sennacherib*, by D. D. Luckenbill (Chicago: University of Chicago Press, 1924)
ASTI	*Annual of the Swedish Theological Institute*
ATR	*Anglican Theological Review*
AUSS	*Andrews University Seminary Studies*
BA	*Biblical Archaeologist*

BAR	*Biblical Archaeologist Reader*
BASOR	*Bulletin of the American Schools of Oriental Research*
Bib	*Biblica*
BJRL	*Bulletin of the John Rylands Library*
BR	*Biblical Research*
BS	*Bibliotheca sacra*
BSOAS	*Bulletin of the School of Oriental and African Studies*
BT	*The Bible Translator*
BTB	*Biblical Theology Bulletin*
BZ	*Biblische Zeitschrift*
BZAW	*Beihefte zur Zeitschrift für altestamentliche Wissenschaft*
CB	*Cultura biblica*
CBL	*A Cyclopaedia of Biblical Literature* (ed. J. Kitto; New York/Cincinnati: Mark H. Newman/William H. Moore & Co., 1846)
CBQ	*Catholic Biblical Quarterly*
CHJ	*Cambridge History of Judaism*, vol. 1: *Introduction: The Persian Period* (ed. W. D. Davies and L. Finkelstein; Cambridge/New York: Cambridge University Press, 1984)
CJ	*Conservation Judaism*
CQR	*Church Quarterly Review*
DTT	*Dansk Teologisk Tidsskrift*
EB	*Encyclopedia Britannica*
EglT	*Église et Théologie*
EI	*Eretz Israel*
EstEc	*Estudios eclesiasticos*
ET	*Expository Times*
ETL	*Ephemerides theologicae lovanienses*
EvTh	*Evangelische Theologie*
GS	*Gesammelte Studien*
HBD	*A Dictionary of the Bible* (5 vols.; ed. J. Hastings; Edinburgh/New York: T. & T. Clark/Charles Scribner's Sons, 1900–1904)
HTR	*Harvard Theological Review*
HUCA	*Hebrew Union College Annual*
IA	*Die Inschriften Asarhaddons, Königs von Assyrien*, by R. Borger (Graz: Im Selbstverlags des Herausgebers, 1956)
IEJ	*Israel Exploration Journal*

Int	*Interpretation*
IR	*Iliff Review*
JANESCU	*Journal of the Ancient Near Eastern Society of Columbia University*
JAOS	*Journal of the American Oriental Society*
JARCE	*Journal of the American Research Center in Egypt*
JB	Jerusalem Bible
JBL	*Journal of Biblical Literature*
JCS	*Journal of Cuneiform Studies*
JNES	*Journal of Near Eastern Studies*
JNSL	*Journal of Northwest Semitic Languages*
JQR	*Jewish Quarterly Review*
JR	*Journal of Religion*
JSOT	*Journal for the Study of the Old Testament*
JSS	*Journal of Semitic Studies*
JTS	*Journal of Theological Studies*
KS	*Kleine Schriften*
LQ	*Lutheran Quarterly*
LR	*Lutherische Rundblick*
MT	Masoretic Text
NEASB	*Near East Archaeological Society Bulletin*
NEB	New English Bible
NJPSV	New Jewish Publication Society Version
NTT	*Norsk Teologisk Tidsskrift*
OLZ	*Orientalische Literaturzeitung*
OTS	*Oudtestamentische Studiën*
OTWSA	*Die Ou Testamentiese Werkgemeenskap in Suid-Afrika*
PEQ	*Palestine Exploration Quarterly*
PSB	*Princeton Seminary Bulletin*
RB	*Revue biblique*
RHPR	*Revue d'histoire et de philosophie religieuses*
RHR	*Revue de l'histoire des religions*
RGG	*Religion in Geschichte und Gegenwart*
RivB	*Rivista biblica*
RSR	*Recherches de science religieuse*
RSV	Revised Standard Version
SAT	*Die Schriften des Alten Testaments*
SDB	*Supplements Dictionaire de la Bible*
SEA	*Svensk exegetisk årsbok*
SH	*Scripta Hierosolymitana*

SJT	*Scottish Journal of Theology*
ST	*Studia theologica*
SVT	*Supplements to Vetus Testamentum*
SZDMG	*Supplements to Zeitschrift der deutschen morgenländischen Gesellschaft*
TA	*Tel Aviv*
TB	*Tyndale Bulletin*
ThEv	*Theologia Evangelica*
TLZ	*Theologische Literaturzeitung*
TSBA	*Transactions of the Society of Biblical Archaeology*
TSK	*Theologische Studien und Kritiken*
TUAT	*Texte aus dem Umwelt des Alten Testaments* (ed. O. Kaiser; Gutersloh: Gerd Mohn, 1982—)
TZ	*Theologische Zeitschrift*
UF	*Ugaritische Forschungen*
VT	*Vetus Testamentum*
WD	*Wort und Dienst*
WO	*Die Welt des Orients*
ZAW	*Zeitschrift für die alttestamentliche Wissenschaft*
ZDMG	*Zeitschrift der deutschen morgenländischen Gesellschaft*
ZDPV	*Zeitschrift des deutschen Palästina-Vereins*
ZKT	*Zeitschrift für katholische Theologie*
ZTK	*Zeitschrift für Theologie und Kirche*

Preface

The present volume is based on a number of rather simple conclusions about the work of the prophet Isaiah and about the biblical texts that are attributed to him. Practically none of these conclusions is currently shared by scholars working in the field, and all of them will have to be demonstrated in the course of our interpretation. At this point, we will enumerate these conclusions so that the reader may have them in mind when beginning the book.

(1) With the exception of Isaiah 34–35, practically all of the prophetic speech material in what is traditionally called First Isaiah—that is Isaiah 1–39—derives from the eighth-century ⊥ B.C.E. prophet. Isaiah 34–35 has many affinities with the remainder of the book (Isaiah 40–66) and probably derives from ⊥⊏ a period later than the eighth century. (2) The prophetic speeches and narratives about the prophet in Isaiah 1–27 are arranged in general chronological order. As we shall see, chapters 7–12, all related to a single historical crisis, contain biographical, autobiographical, and sermonic material that is as much parallel as it is sequential. (3) Isaiah 28–33, concerned with the final years of the state of Israel and the city of Samaria, either once comprised a separate prophetic booklet or were shifted from their original chronological ordering. These chapters had the years and events of 728–725 B.C.E. as their original historical background. Chronologically, they belong between chapters 18 and 19. Chapters 28–33 were given their present "non-chronological" placement in order to prepare the reader for the Assyrian crisis described in Isaiah 36–37. (4) The prophetic legends in chapters 38–39 concern events of the years 713–711 B.C.E. and belong to the same general historical context as chapters 20–22. These legends in their present form

have been shaped and literarily located to anticipate the exile and the preaching of Second Isaiah. (5) The prophetic speeches in Isaiah 1–33 can be related to events and conditions in ancient Near Eastern and Judean history of the second half of the eighth century, events in which Israel and Judah were directly involved or in which they were vitally interested. Chapters 1–6 come from the reign of Uzziah/Jotham, 7–14 from the period of Ahaz (742–727), and 15–33 (+ 36–39) from the days of Hezekiah (727–698). (6) The relationships among the city of Jerusalem, the state of Israel, and the state of Judah during the ministry of Isaiah were highly complex and varied from period to period. Thus the internal history and interplay of these three political entities must constantly be given consideration. (7) Isaiah 6 is not an autobiographical narrative account of how Isaiah first became a prophet, but rather a narrative of how Isaiah moved into a new phase of his ministry, a phase reflecting a new set of historical circumstances. (8) The prophetic speeches in Isaiah range from short units of a few verses (Isa. 14:28-32) to long units extending over two or more chapters (Isa. 10:27d–12:6). Such an assumption differs from current form-critical approaches, which subdivide the material into numerous small units. (9) Very few editorial additions were made to the Isaianic speeches, and these consist primarily of glosses inserted into texts here and there. (10) Isaiah must not be understood as either a preacher of only judgment or as a proclaimer of only salvation. Both elements were held together in the prophetic proclamation and worked together as components of a theological message that transcended both.

A few specifics about the present volume are in order. (1) Although written in commentary form, the present volume is by no means an exhaustive commentary. Many philological, textual, and theological matters have been ignored. (2) The primary concerns of the book focus on the demarcation of the prophetic speeches, their historical and social contexts, their internal structure and cohesion, and their basic content. (3) Since historical issues are involved in practically every speech, we have prefaced the volume with a rather lengthy reconstruction of the history of the last half of the eighth century. (4) Because the theories about the content of Isaiah

1–39 are legion and the literature voluminous, we have made no effort to describe and refute specific theories and positions. (5) Selective and relevant bibliograpy is given at the heading of each section for those who wish to explore topics and passages further. (6) In transliteration of Hebrew words, diacritical marks have been omitted to simplify the typesetting. (7) Our translations of passages are given primarily only where we felt widely used existing translations, especially the RSV, were misleading or in need of correction. (8) The user may wish to read the material on chapters 28–33 following that on chapter 18.

We are deeply indebted to the stimulus of articles on Isaiah by H. L. Ginsberg and Jacob Milgrom and to the work of Yehoshua Gitay, who has pioneered in the rhetorical analysis of prophetic speeches and whose commentary on Isaiah 1–12 will soon be published by Indiana University Press. Thanks are due to two Emory University graduate students, Julie Galambush and Dennis Livingston, for assistance on the manuscript and to Dorcas Doward for typing the work.

Further volumes, on Hosea, Amos, and Micah, along the lines of the present investigation, are planned.

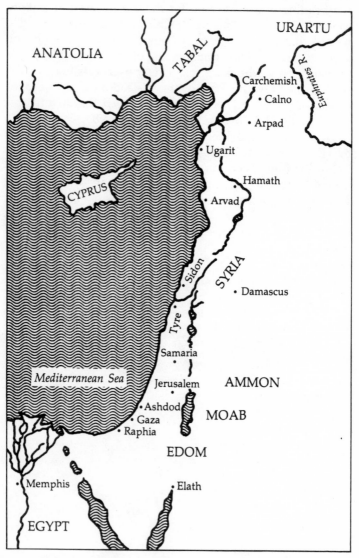

The Eastern Mediterranean Seaboard in the Eighth Century B.C.E.

I

The Historical Background—750–700 B.C.E.

The states of Israel and Judah were small kingdoms nestled in the mountainous heartland of Palestine, a narrow land bridge lying between the Mediterranean Sea to the west and the Arabian Desert to the east. Across this bridge, travelers, merchants, and soldiers moved between the civilization centers of Asia to the north and Africa to the south.

As part of the eastern Mediterranean seaboard and lying adjacent to the Arabian Desert, Palestine was very much involved in ancient Near Eastern commerce, politics, and warfare. Three features ensured such involvement. (1) Major overland trade routes between Mesopotamia and Asia Minor to the north and Egypt to the south passed through Palestine. (2) The eastern Mediterranean coast was dotted with bustling seaports. To the north, Phoenician harbors—Tyre, Sidon, Byblos, and Arvad—and to the south, Philistine ports— Gaza, Ashkelon, and Ashdod—served as channels for cargo moving throughout the Mediterranean world. (3) A main caravan route from Arabia funneled goods through southern Palestine and from there, via the Philistine ports, to the entire Mediterranean world.

A dominant issue in the international politics of the eighth century was control over the land and sea trade of the eastern Mediterranean seaboard. Indigenous states in the region sought to defend their own interests against the encroachment and dominance of Assyria and Egypt, the two major powers in the area at the time.

1. ASSYRIAN RELATIONS WITH SYRIA-PALESTINE

A. **Alt**, "Das System der assyrischen Provinzen auf dem Boden des Reiches Israel," *ZDPV* 52(1929)220-42 = his *KS*

(Munich: C. H. Beck, 1953)II, 188-205; **Alt**, "Neue assyrische Nachrichten über Palästina," *ZDPV* 67(1945)128-46 = his *KS* II(1953)226-41; **Alt**, "Tiglathpilesers III. erster Feldzug nach Palästina," in his *KS* II(1953)150-62; J. M. **Asurmendi**, *La Guerra Siro-Efraimita: Historia y Profetas* (Valencia/Jerusalem: Institución San Jerónimo, 1982); J. **Begrich**, "Der syrisch-emphraimitische Krieg und seine weltpolitischen Zusammenhänge," *ZDMG* 83(1929)213-37 = his *GS* (Munich: Chr. Kaiser, 1964)99-120; R. **Borger** and H. **Tadmor**, "Zwei Beiträge zur alttestamentlichen Wissenschaft aufgrund der Inschriften Tiglatpilesers III," *ZAW* 94(1982)244-51; H. **Cazelles,** "Problèmes de la guerre Syro-Ephraimite," *EI* 14(1978)70-78; M. **Cogan**, "Tyre and Tiglath-pileser III: Chronological Notes," *JCS* 25(1973)96-99; M. **Elat**, "The Economic Relations of the Neo-Assyrian Empire with Egypt," *JAOS* 98(1978)20-34; W. W. **Hallo**, "From Qarqar to Carchemish: Assyria and Israel in the Light of New Discoveries," *BA* 23(1960)34-61 = *BAR* II(Garden City: Anchor Books, 1964)152-88; L. D. **Levine**, *Two Neo-Assyrian Stelae from Iran* (Toronto: Royal Ontario Museum, 1972); **Levine**, "Menahem and Tiglath-Pileser: A New Synchronism," *BASOR* 206(1972)40-42; **Levine**, "Sennacherib's Southern Front: 704-689," *JCS* 34(1982)28-58; G. L. **Mattingly**, "An Archaeological Analysis of Sargon's 712 Campaign Against Ashdod," *NEASB* 17(1981)47-64; A. R. **Millard**, "Sennacherib's Attack on Hezekiah," *TB* 36(1985)61-77; N. **Na'aman**, "Sennacherib's 'Letter to God' on His Campaign to Judah," *BASOR* 214(1974)25-39; **Na'aman**, "The Brook of Egypt and Assyrian Policy on the Border of Egypt," *TA* 6(1979)68-90; B. **Oded**, "The Historical Background of the Syro-Ephraimite War Reconsidered," *CBQ* 34(1972)153-65; **Oded**, "The Phoenician Cities and the Assyrian Empire in the Time of Tiglath-pileser III," *ZDPV* 90(1974)38-49; A. T. **Olmstead**, "The Assyrian Chronicle," *JAOS* 34(1915)344-68; J. E. **Reade**, "Sargon's Campaigns of 720, 716, and 715 B.C.: Evidence from the Sculptures," *JNES* 35(1976)95-104; R. **Reich**, "The Identification of the 'Sealed *karu* of Egypt,'" *IEJ* 34(1984)32-38; H. W. F. **Saggs**, *The Might That Was Assyria* (London: Sidgwick & Jackson, 1984); G. **Smith**, "On a New Fragment of the Assyrian Canon Belonging to the Reigns of Tiglath-pileser and Shalmaneser,"

TSBA 2(1873)321-32; H **Tadmor**, "The Campaigns of Sargon II of Assur: A Chronological-Historical Study," *JCS* 12(1958)22-40, 77-100; **Tadmor**, "Azriyau of Yaudi," *SH* 8(1961)232-71; **Tadmor**, "The Southern Border of Aram," *IEJ* 12(1962)114-22; **Tadmor**, "Philistia under Assyrian Rule," *BA* 29(1966)86-102; **Tadmor**, "Introductory Remarks to a New Edition of the Annals of Tiglath-Pileser III," *Proceedings of the Israel Academy of Sciences and Humanities*, II/9(1967)168-87; E. **Vogt**, "Die Texte Tiglat-Pilesers III. über die Eroberung Palästinas," *Bib* 45(1964)348-54; M. **Weippert**, "Menahem von Israel und seine Zeitgenossen in einer Steleninschrift des assyrischen Königs Tiglathpileser III. aus dem Iran," *ZDPV* 89(1973)26-53. D. J. **Wiseman**, "Two Historical Inscriptions from Nimrud," *Iraq* 13(1951)21-27; **Wiseman**, "A Fragmentary Inscription of Tiglath-pileser III. from Nimrud," *Iraq* 18(1956)117-29.

The accession of Tiglath-pileser III (745–727) to the throne of Assyria inaugurated a new era in Near Eastern politics. He inherited a kingdom that had grown progressively weaker during the four-decade rule of his two immediate predecessors—a kingdom torn by internal insurrection, dominated by provincial governors who acted as if they were independent monarchs, and troubled by disgruntled subjects annoyed over the growing shortages of certain goods and supplies. Part of this trouble was produced by pressure from the Urartian kingdom to the north of Assyria. The Urartian king, Sarduri II (c. 764–734), along with a coalition of allied kingdoms, was encroaching on Assyrian territory and strangling trade routes in both the northwest and the northeast.

To counter this external pressure, Tiglath-pileser revived and expanded practices employed by his illustrious predecessors—routine aggressive military campaigns beyond the borders of Mesopotamian "greater Assyria," the extraction of tribute from both cooperative and defeated states, a sophisticated system of espionage and informants to keep abreast of possible anti-Assyrian activity, the support of pro-Assyrian factions and rulers in other countries, and the application of military strength to ensure the flow of trade and commerce into Assyria.

Earlier kings had pursued such practices with great success

and ensured the flow into the homeland of luxury and exotic goods, essential raw materials, and transplanted laborers. Ashur-nasir-pal II (883–859), for example, had conducted campaigns west of the Euphrates and into the eastern Mediterranean seaboard. The following is the king's description of one such visit:

At this time I made my way to the slopes of Mount Lebanon and went to the Great [Mediterranean] Sea of the land Amurru. I cleansed my weapons in the Great Sea and made sacrifices to the gods. I received tribute from the kings of the sea coast, from the lands of the men of Tyre, Sidon, Byblos, Mahallatu, Maizu, Kaizu, Amurru, and the city Arvad which is (on an island) in the sea—silver, gold, tin, bronze, a bronze casserole, linen garments with multi-coloured trim, a large female ape, a small female ape, ebony, box-wood, ivory. . . . I climbed up to Mount Amanus and cut down logs of cedar, cypress. . . . I transported cedar logs from Mount Amanus and brought them to Eshara for my house. . . a joyful house, to the temple of the gods Sin and Shamash, the holy gods. (*ARI* II § 586)

Ashur-nasir-pal's son and successor, Shalmaneser III (858–824), conducted nineteen major campaigns west of the Euphrates during his thirty-four year reign.

The needs of the Assyrians were not limited to material goods. The demand for laborers to work on building projects and for settlers to occupy newly acquired or decimated areas meant that humans were deported to Assyrian territory. Presently known texts indicate that between the years 881 and 815 B.C.E., 193,000 people were uprooted from their homelands and resettled in Assyrian territories.

Assyrian court life involved conspicuous consumption and lavish entertainment. When Ashur-nasir-pal dedicated his new capital at Calah, an inscription was made noting the amounts of foodstuffs required and the numbers of guests who attended. Among the menu demands were the following:

1,000 fat oxen, 1,000 calves and sheep of the stable, 14,000 . . . sheep which belonged to the goddess Ishtar my mistress, 2,000 oxen which belonged to the goddess Ishtar my mistress, 1,000 . . . sheep, . . . 1,000 spring lambs, 500 *ayalu*-deer, 500 deer, 1,000 ducks. . . . (*ARI* II § 682)

The list goes on and on, noting how much beer, wine, eggs, bread, onions, and other foodstuffs were required for the inaugural banquet. The inscription concludes with a note about the guests:

When I consecrated the palace at Calah, 47,074 men and women who were invited from every part of my land, 5,000 dignitaries and envoys of the people of the lands Suhu, Hindanu, Patinu, Hatti, Tyre, Sidon, Gurgummu, Malidu, Hubushkia, Gilzanu, Kumu, and Musasiru, 16,000 people of Calah, and 1,500 *zariqu* of my palace, all of them—altogether 69,574 including those summoned from all lands and the people of Calah—for ten days I gave them food, I gave them drink, I had them bathed, I had them anointed. Thus did I honour them and send them back to their lands in peace and joy. (*ARI* II § 682)

Assyrian military campaigns, in their search for material and laborers, often met with opposition. Coalitions of kingdoms were frequently formed to oppose Assyrian intrusions and to protect local and regional interests. When Shalmaneser, for example, moved into Syria in 853, he confronted a military coalition of twelve states headed by Kings Hadadezer of Damascus, Irhuleni of Hamath, and Ahab of Israel, but including contingents of troops from as far away as Egypt to the south, Arabia to the east, and eastern Asia Minor (Anatolia) to the northwest. This alliance had opposed Shalmaneser on several occasions, remaining intact for over a decade.

Assyrian practices and policies, which had proven their worth under Ashur-nasir-pal and Shalmaneser, were rigorously executed by Tiglath-pileser, who added a new dimension to the Assyrian program. He became the first to transform territory west of the Euphrates into Assyrian-governed provinces.

A. Tiglath-pileser III (745–727 B.C.E.)

After stabilizing affairs in Mesopotamia and conducting his first campaign against Babylon, Tiglath-pileser turned his attention to the Urartian-inspired anti-Assyrian coalition in the west. The local leading power in the coalition was the city of Arpad, ruled by King Mati'ilu, whose father (or grandfather), Atarshumki, had headed an anti-Assyrian group in 805–796. Tiglath-pileser campaigned for three years along the eastern Mediterranean seaboard (743–740) while Arpad was laid under siege. The Urartians were defeated in the region of Kummukhu. It was probably during these years that Menahem, the Israelite king, first paid tribute to the Assyrians (II Kings 15:19-20), as had two of his predecessors, Jehu (in 841) and Joash (in 796).

After the fall of Arpad, Tiglath-pileser moved out of Syria and campaigned on the eastern frontier of the empire (739). In his absence, the north Syrian coalition regrouped, led by King Tutammu of Unqi, whose capital was at Kullani (Calneh/Calno—Amos 6:2; Isa. 10:9). Other members of the coalition were the "nineteen districts of Hamath" and the coastal region headed by an otherwise unknown Azriyau (*TUAT* I 370-73). Upon Tiglath-pileser's return to the west in 738, the rebellious kingdoms were defeated, provinces organized, and populations exchanged.

During this second western campaign, the Assyrian king received homage and gifts from a number of eastern Mediterranean and Anatolian rulers. Among the tributaries mentioned in his annals were Rezin of Damascus, Menahem of Samaria, Hiram of Tyre, and Queen Zabibe of Arabia (*ANET* 283; *TUAT* I 371). A second list, apparently from a time shortly previous, notes the king of Tyre as Tubail (see Levine 18-19). The presence of Anatolian kings in these lists might indicate that Tiglath-pileser had previously campaigned in this area also, probably in 743–740.

From 737 to 735, Tiglath-pileser was in the eastern portion of the empire, fighting, among others, the Urartians. During these years, Rezin, who had nominally displayed loyalty to the Assyrians in 738, was strengthening an anti-Assyrian coalition in southern Syria-Palestine. When Rezin had become king of Syria is uncertain; the last known ruler in Damascus before him was Khadianu (attested as ruler in 773). As we shall see below (in section 3C), evidence suggests that Rezin had been on the throne since the 750s and had increasingly encroached on Israelite and Judean territory, as had his counterpart, Hazael, a century earlier (see II Kings 10:32-33; 12:17-18; 13:1-4; see Isa. 9:1; 9:11-12). Most southern kingdoms seem to have cooperated with Rezin. Israel, however, continued its century-long policy and took a pro-Assyrian attitude, refusing to support the coalition until Pekah, probably a stooge of Rezin, seized the throne in Samaria in 736/5. Judah, throughout the subsequent fracas, refused to join the anti-Assyrian fellowship (Isa. 7-12).

Tiglath-pileser took action against the coalition in 734. Moving down the eastern Mediterranean seaboard, he apparently encountered only moderate opposition from the north Syrian states. He moved south into Philistia to subdue the rebel Philistines and to block any movement of Egyptian forces into Syria-Palestine. Hanunu, the king of Gaza, fled to Egypt. The Meunites, known from isolated references in the Bible (I Chron. 4:41; II Chron. 20:1; 26:7), were defeated and a royal stela expressing Assyrian authority in the area was erected at the Brook of Egypt (Wadi Besor, just south of Gaza). Apparently, while on this campaign, Tiglath-pileser received tribute from a number of kingdoms from as far away as Anatolia. Among the southern Syro-Palestinian monarchs offering tribute were Sanipu of Bit-Ammon, Salamanu of Moab, Mitinti of Ashkelon, Jehoahaz (Ahaz) of Judah, Kaushmalaku of Edom, and Hanunu of Gaza (*ANET* 282; *ARAB* I §§ 800-801, 803; *TUAT* I 374-75). Either at this time or in the course of the two subsequent campaigns against Damascus, Tiglath-pileser assigned the Arab tribe of Idi-bi'li (see Adbeel in Gen. 25:13) to special duty on the border of Egypt. Security of the area and trade supervision may have become their responsibilities. In text ND 4301 + 4305, Tiglath-pileser refers to a "trading center of Assyria" (*bit ka-a-ri sha (mat) ashshur*), presumably in the Gaza region (*TUAT* I 376-78; Wiseman, 1956, 126). Whether he established this center or referred to an existing complex is unknown.

In 733 and 732, Tiglath-pileser moved against Damascus. Hiram of Tyre continued to support Rezin, who was also joined by Queen Samsi of Arabia. Assyrian accounts of her defeat have been preserved as well as a report on the defeat of Rezin, although not on the destruction of Damascus. The Bible reports that Damascus was taken, people exiled, and Rezin killed (II Kings 16:9). Tiglath-pileser provincialized the sixteen districts of Damascus, or the "widespread land of Hazael." Part of this territory—Gilead, Galilee, and the coastal plain—had previously been claimed and periodically ruled by Israel (see II Kings 15:29; Isa. 9:1), but now became part of the Assyrian empire in its confiscation of Syrian territory (*ANET* 283-84; *ARAB* I §§ 777-79, 815-19; *TUAT* I 376-78).

Israel, unlike Judah, had joined the 734–732 anti-Assyrian coalition. Apparently, before Tiglath-pileser marched against Samaria, the capital city, the Israelite King Pekah was assassinated by Hoshea, who then reigned in his stead (II Kings 15:29-30). The Assyrian king recognized Hoshea as the new Israelite monarch (*ANET* 284; *ARAB* I § 816; *TUAT* I 373-74) and left him holding the Israelite territory, which had not previously been annexed by Syria. This consisted only of the central hill country between Judah in the south and the Valley of Jezreel in the north—that is, the Ephraimite and Manassite hill country west of the Jordan Valley.

In 731, Tiglath-pileser marched against Babylon in southern Mesopotamia (Isa. 13). Eventually in 729, Tiglath-pileser ascended the throne in Babylon. For two years, he reigned as king over and lived in Babylon (*ABC* 72-73; Isa. 14:1-27).

While Tiglath-pileser was engaged in Babylon, the old anti-Assyrian coalition was revived in Syria-Palestine. Assyrian references to the last years of Tiglath-pileser—who died in 727, the same year as Ahaz king of Judah (Isa. 14:28-32)—appear in an eponym, or year list (see Smith). For the year 728, the broken text has the beginning of the word *Damascus*. The entry for the next year indicates an expedition, but the text is broken where the name of the destination would appear. Probably the province of Damascus had rebelled in 728 and was the object of the 727 expedition (see below, chap. 4, sects. 19 and 28). Presumably Tiglath-pileser died (Isa. 14:1-27) while engaged in suppressing the new revolt in the west (Isa. 15-17). Israel and other kingdoms and Assyrian provinces were involved in the uprising (Isa. 15–16; 17:3-6; Josephus, *Ant* IX 283-87).

B. Shalmaneser V (727–722 B.C.E.)

Shalmaneser V, Tiglath-pileser's son and successor, carried on the campaign to suppress this latest revolt.

Unfortunately, no Assyrian historical texts from his reign have been excavated. Josephus reports, quoting Menander, who is said to be dependent on the state archives of Tyre, that the Assyrian King Shalmaneser came with an army and invaded Phoenicia (*Ant* IX 283). Assyrian forces also marched into Transjordan (Hos. 10:14) and harassed Moab probably at the same time as the Phoenician campaign (Isa. 15–16). Some form of military action was taken against Israel (Isa. 17), but King Hoshea apparently submitted quickly, satisfied Shalmaneser with treaty oaths and tribute (II Kings 17:3), and was allowed to remain on the throne. Apparently Samaria was not attacked or laid siege to at this time (727).

In 726, Shalmaneser remained in Mesopotamia, according to the eponym list. King Hoshea, under popular pressure, took the occasion to appeal to Egypt for help (Isa. 30-31). When Shalmaneser returned to Syria-Palestine the following year, he took Hoshea prisoner and later placed Samaria under attack. The city fell after a three year siege (*ABC* 73; II Kings 17:6). According to Josephus, Tyre was blockaded, probably also in 725, but held out against Assyrian pressure for five years (see *Ant* IX 287; and below, chap. 4, sect. 19).

C. Sargon II (722–705 B.C.E.)

Sargon came to the throne in Assyria after a dynastic crisis that involved insurrection in the old capital city of Assur. Almost simultaneous with Sargon's accession to the Assyrian throne, the sagacious and scheming Marduk-apla-iddinna (the biblical Merodach-baladan) ascended the throne in Babylon (*ABC* 73). In the eastern highlands, Elam flexed its muscle and thus, for about two years, Sargon was occupied in the east of the empire. The Babylonian Chronicles report the following:

The second year of Marduk-apla-iddina [721/20], Humban-nikash king of Elam did battle against Sargon, king of Assyria, in the district of Der, effected an Assyrian retreat and inflicted a major defeat upon them. Marduk-apla-iddinna and his army, who had gone to the aid of the king of Elam, did not reach the battle in time so he withdrew. (*ABC* 73-74)

This diversion in the east allowed time for the anti-Assyrian coalition to re-form in the west. Assyrian provinces and vassal kingdoms rebelled. In one text, Sargon describes the situation as follows:

Ia'ubidi from Hamath, a commoner without claim to the throne, a cursed Hittite, schemed to become king of Hamath, induced the cities Arvad, Simirra, Damascus, and Samaria to desert me, made them collaborate and fitted out an army. I called up the masses of the soldiers of Ashur and besieged him and his warriors in Qarqar, his favorite city. I conquered it and burnt it. Himself I flayed; the rebels I killed in their cities and established again peace and harmony. (*ANET* 285)

Sargon then moved down the Mediterranean coast after taking Samaria. Hanunu of Gaza, along with an Egyptian general sent to his assistance by some ruler in the Delta, was defeated. The city of Raphia was taken and Hanunu captured (*ANET* 285; *TUAT* I 383-85). The support offered by the Egyptians seems to have been more token than substantive.

After the battle of Raphia, Sargon took actions to establish amicable relations with the Egyptian rulers in the Delta, at the time nominally under the rule of the Ethiopians (Isa. 18). Sargon's conciliatory actions toward northern Egypt were evident in his references to having "opened the closed trading center (or borders) of Egypt" and "caused the Assyrians and Egyptians to mingle together and engage in trade" (*TUAT* I 382). The Assyrian king thus sought to establish a cooperative alliance between the Egyptians and the Assyrians, an alliance obviously viewing the Ethiopians as a common enemy. (Egyptians and Ethiopians are distinguished in Assyrian texts.) In Judah, Hezekiah was allowed to expand his territory in the southwest (I Chron. 4:34-43). Isaiah viewed this new state of affairs with enthusiasm and proclaimed Sargon Egypt's savior (Isa. 19).

With the passage of time, Sargon became increasingly involved with matters in western Anatolia. Here Mita of Mushku (the legendary King Midas of Phrygia in Greek tradition) was operating to stir up opposition to the Assyrians. In 717, Sargon attacked Carchemish, accusing King Pisiri of breaking treaty oaths under the influence of

Midas (*ANET* 285; *ARAB* II § 8; *TUAT* I 379). The year following (716), Sargon campaigned against a number of Arab tribes, settling some of his captives in the city of Samaria (*ANET* 286; *ARAB* II §§ 17-18). During this same year, he was presented with a dozen large horses by an Egyptian ruler, called Shilkanni by Sargon (*ANET* 286). Such a gift suggests continuing good relations between Sargon and the Delta rulers.

In 715, Sargon again moved into western Anatolia against Midas. It was perhaps at this time that rebellion was again fomented in southern Palestine (Isa. 20). Azuri, king of Ashdod, showed signs of disloyalty and was deposed from office, probably by local Assyrian officials stationed in the area. He was replaced on the throne by Ahimiti, a younger brother. The new king was soon deposed by the local citizens and replaced by a certain Yamani, who secured the cooperation of other Philistine cities, of Judah, Edom, Moab, and "those who live on islands" (Cyprus?). The group made a joint appeal to Egyptian and Ethiopian rulers for help (*ANET* 286-87; *ARAB* II §§ 30, 62, 193-95; *TUAT* I 381; Isa 20:3-5). By 712/11, when the Assyrians moved to take actions against this southern coalition, Sargon's forces were engaged on several fronts—in Anatolia as well as Babylonia—while Sargon himself remained in Assyria (*ABC* 75). When Assyrian troops moved against Ashdod, Yamani fled to Egypt where he received no help; in fact, the Ethiopian king returned him to Assyria (*ANET* 286). Sargon's inscriptions imply that he headed the forces that fought against Ashdod, but Isaiah 20:1 indicates otherwise. Judah suffered reprisals while Assyrian troops were in the area (Isa. 22:1-15).

By 710, Sargon had invaded southern Mesopotamia in force. Marduk-apla-iddinna fled Babylon to take refuge in Elam. In the following year, Sargon "took the hand of Bel,"—that is, ascended the throne of Babylon (*ABC* 75). This year also saw two other events of great significance. In Anatolia, Sargon's forces had turned the tide against Midas, who, now also pressured by the nomadic Cimmerians, made peace with Sargon. Perhaps as a response to this new development, as well as to Assyrian military pressure, rulers on Cyprus submitted to Assyrian authority and sent gifts to Sargon in Babylon (*ANET* 284; *ARAB* II § 118, 186; *TUAT* I

385-86; see below, chap. 4, sect. 26). This move gave Assyria dominance over eastern Mediterranean commerce and at the same time intensified the anti-Assyrian feelings of the Ethiopians, now firmly in command in the Egyptian Delta (Isa. 23).

In 705, shortly after Sargon had inaugurated his new capital at Dur-Sharrukin, he led his troops to the east Anatolian province of Tabal, apparently in an attempt to halt the movement of Cimmerians into the empire. The last Assyrian notice about Sargon's reign states: "King killed, camp of the king of Assyria [taken]." Sargon's death was the occasion of previously planned widespread revolt and celebration. In Jerusalem, the prophet Isaiah led the community in rebellion and rejoicing (Isa. 24–27).

D. Sennacherib (704–681 B.C.E.)

In spite of hopes and expectations, the death of Sargon did not mean the demise of Assyria. The new king, Sennacherib, in restoring order to his empire, was confronted with a herculean task. His first step, after establishing his authority at home, was a campaign against Marduk-apla-iddinna, who had reestablished himself as king in Babylon. After forcing Marduk-apla-iddinna's retreat and placing Bel-ibni on the throne in Babylon, Sennacherib waged war east of the Tigris before turning, in his third campaign (701), against the revolt in Syria-Palestine. Sennacherib seems to have suppressed this revolt sufficiently (this will be further discussed in our treatment of Isaiah 36–37). Apparently while on campaign in the west, Sargon was confronted with renewed troubles in Babylon, which may have hastened his move out of Syria-Palestine. The Babylonian Chronicles report:

The third year of Bel-ibni: Sennacherib went down to Akkad and plundered Akkad. He led away to Assyria Bel-ibni and his officers. For three years Bel-ibni ruled Babylon. Sennacherib put Ashur-nadin-shumi, his son, on the throne in Babylon. (*ABC* 77)

Since Sennacherib's campaign to the west is the last noted event in the ministry of Isaiah, we can conclude our survey of Assyrian history at this point.

2. EGYPT DURING THE SECOND HALF OF THE EIGHTH CENTURY

K. **Baer**, "The Libyan and Nubian Kings of Egypt: Notes on the Chronology of Dynasties XXII to XXVI," *JNES* 32(1973)4-25; R. **Borger**, "Das Ende des ägyptischen Feldherrn Sib'e = Sô'," *JNES* 19(1960)49-53; H. **Goedicke**, "The End of 'So, King of Egypt,'" *BASOR* 171(1963)64-66; K. A. **Kitchen**, *The Third Intermediate Period in Egypt (1100-650 B.C.)* (Warminister: Aris & Phillips, 1973); **Kitchen**, "Late-Egyptian Chronology and the Hebrew Monarchy," *JANESCU* 5(1973)225-33; D. B. **Redford**, "The Relations Between Egypt and Israel from El-Amarna to the Babylonian Conquest," *Biblical Archaeology Today: Proceedings of the International Congress on Biblical Archaeology Jerusalem, April 1984* (ed. J. Amitai; Jerusalem: Israel Exploration Society, 1985) 192-206; A. **Spalinger**, "The Year 712 B.C. and Its Implications for Egyptian History," *JARCE* 10(1973)95-101; F. J. **Yurco**, "Sennacherib's Third Campaign and the Coregency of Shabaka and Shebitku," *Serapis* 6(1980)221-40.

In his twenty-first year, the Ethiopian king Piye (often given as Piankhi) set out from his capital at Napata, just down river from the fourth cataract, sailing down the Nile to extinguish growing opposition to his authority in Upper and Lower Egypt (see *AEL* II 66-84). The exact date of this military campaign remains uncertain. If Piye ruled for forty years (753–713), as is now widely assumed, but not proven, the date would have been about 732. In describing his Egyptian opposition, Piye refers to two rulers of Upper Egypt and two rulers of Lower Egypt (the four kings Namart, Peftuaubast, Iuput II, and Osorkon IV). In addition, he mentions numerous chiefs and counts. The most powerful of his opponents was Tefnakht, who bore the title "Great Chief of the West."

After severe fighting, Piye forced into submission and received tribute from most of his opponents. The four kings offered their obeisance, although only one was allowed into the presence of Piye—the others being uncircumcised and fish eaters and, therefore, unclean to an Ethiopian. After his successful expedition, Piye returned upstream to his homeland with ships "loaded with silver, gold, copper, and clothing; everything of Lower Egypt, every product of Syria, and all plants of god's land" (*AEL* III 80).

From Piye's account of his invasion, we can learn a number of things about Egypt in the third quarter of the eighth century. (1) Lower Egypt, that is, the Delta region, at the time was a patchwork of competing states and kingdoms with virtually constant rivalry and civil warfare (see Isa. 19:1-3). (2) The Ethiopians had earlier asserted their authority throughout Egypt, but, as Piye's invasion demonstrated, they were not able to do so very effectively while ruling from a distance. At least nominally, all Egyptians were under the authority of the Ethiopians (note the latter's role in Isaiah 18; 19:4). (3) The fact that Piye notes that his tributary gifts included every product of Syria indicates how important trade with the eastern Mediterranean seaboard must have been for Egypt.

In the light of Egypt's long-standing commercial relationship with the eastern Mediterranean seaboard, it was inevitable that tension would develop between Egypt/Ethiopia and Assyria, once the latter moved to dominate the commerce in the area, unless the Egyptian/Ethiopian rulers were willing to take a secondary role. Early evidence illustrating this potential for tension can be seen in a letter, most probably from the reign of Tiglath-pileser III, written by an Assyrian official stationed in Phoenicia to the Assyrian royal court (see *Iraq* 17 [1955] 127-28). After reporting on several local matters touching on Assyrian interests, the writer notes that timber from Lebanon was not being sold to the Egyptians or to the Philistines. Thus at this time a deliberate effort was being made by the Assyrians to curtail Phoenician trade with Egypt.

With Tiglath-pileser's assertion of his authority to the Brook of Egypt, in 734, a new international situation came into being—Assyrian claims extended to the traditional border of Egypt. Piye's campaign to assert his authority in the Delta probably followed shortly after Tiglath-pileser's move against Philistia, a region with traditional ties to Egypt. The chronological correlation of these two events would suggest that Piye's invasion was at least indirectly related to the westward movement of Assyria's influence and the latter's increasing control of trade in the area.

What role the Egyptians and Ethiopians may have had in the formation of anti-Assyrian coalitions in Syria-Palestine during Tiglath-pileser's reign remains unknown. Over a century earlier, Egypt had sent troops to join forces against Shalmaneser III, at the battle of Qarqar (*ANET* 278-79; *ARAB* I § 610; *TUAT* I 360-62). The fact that Tiglath-pileser began his operation in 734 by moving down the seacoast to the border of Egypt would indicate that a response from Egypt was expected.

When Sargon moved into Philistine territory in 720, he encountered an Egyptian force (*ANET* 285; *ARAB* II § 5; *TUAT* I 378-79). The commander of the Egyptian army is called Re'e (a better reading than the older transliteration Sib'e) and is described as a *turtan*, indicating that he was not a pharaoh. Little military activity occurred since the Egyptian commander apparently left the field quickly. As we have noted, Sargon took two actions in 720 that were both symbolic and significant for Assyrian-Egyptian relations: (1) He reactivated the Assyrian trading center in the region of the Brook of Egypt. (2) Sargon claims to have made the Assyrians and Egyptians mingle together and trade. These two actions indicate that Sargon took a very conciliatory attitude toward the Egyptians and made positive steps toward international rapprochement between the two peoples. At the same time, his actions indicate a less than friendly attitude toward the Ethiopians. Sargon thus began a long history of cooperation between Egyptians and Assyrians that lasted throughout the reign of the Sargonids in Assyria, that is, until the end of the Assyrian empire.

In Israel's final days, King Hoshea is said to have "sent messengers to So, king of Egypt" (II Kings 17:4; see Isa. 30:1-7; 31:1-3). This Egyptian ruler must have been reigning in the Delta (see, chap. 4, sect. 30). Whether any aid was forthcoming from Egypt is unknown; at least, Hoshea and Israel hoped for Egyptian help, even if it had not been promised.

When Sargon was again in southern Syria-Palestine, in 716, an Egyptian pharaoh, Shilkanni, presented him with twelve fine horses unmatched in Assyria. This Shilkanni was probably Osorkon IV or, perhaps, Tefnakht (see further, below, chap. 4, sect. 28).

When a southern anti-Assyrian coalition formed sometime after 715, the group spearheaded by Ashdod made appeals to both Egyptians and Ethiopians (Isa. 20; see *ANET* 286, where Sargon mentions appeals only to Pir'u [pharaoh] king of Musru [Egypt]). Neither seems to have responded. When Yamani, king of Ashdod, sought refuge in Egypt, he eventually made his way to the border of Ethiopia. Even here he received no favorable treatment. The Ethiopians returned him to Assyria in fetters, shackles, and iron bands (*ANET* 286; *ARAB* II § 62; *TUAT* I 385).

By about 713/12, a new state of affairs had developed in Egypt. The Ethiopian pharaoh, Piye, died and was succeeded by his brother Shabako (713–698, the dates are still somewhat uncertain). The new Ethiopian ruler invaded Egypt shortly after ascending the throne and established his authority throughout the Delta. By the time he reached the Delta, Osorkon IV had died. Bocchoris, who had succeeded his father, Tefnakht, as the "great Chief of the West" and assumed the title of pharaoh, was killed by Shabako (see further, below, chap. 4, sect. 21). With Shabako's conquest of and settlement in Egypt, the XXVth (the Ethiopian) Dynasty was firmly in control of the country.

The increased Assyrian control over the eastern Mediterranean seaboard and its commerce must have strained relationships between the Ethiopians and the Assyrians. Isaiah 18:1-2 indicates that the Ethiopians were aggressively initiating contact with Mediterranean states even before Shabako's invasion of the Delta.

Assyria's dominance over Cyprus and Phoenician trade in 709, and thus its unchallenged control of maritime commerce in the eastern Mediterranean, must have been a severe and costly blow to the Ethiopians. In commenting on this new situation, Isaiah notes:

> When the report comes to Egypt,
> they will be in anguish over the
> report about Tyre.
>
> Isaiah 23:5

It is thus no wonder that when general revolt broke out at the death of Sargon, in 705, the Ethiopians were deeply involved. When the southern coalition in 701 fought to ward off the attack of Sennacherib, the kings of Egypt (the Delta princes under Ethiopian control) and the Ethiopian king himself sent help—"an army beyond counting." Although Sennacherib claims to have enjoyed an overwhelming victory at Eltekeh over these troops from the Nile Valley, he may have been greatly overstating the case (*ANET* 287-88; *ARAB* II §§ 233-40; *TUAT* I 388-91).

3. HISTORICAL DEVELOPMENTS WITHIN ISRAEL AND JUDAH

P. R. **Ackroyd**, "The Biblical Interpretation of the Reigns of Ahaz and Hezekiah," *In the Shelter of Elyon: Essays on Ancient Palestinian Life and Literature in Honor of G. W. Ahlström* (ed. by W. B. Barrick and J. R. Spencer; Sheffield, England: JSOT Press, 1984) 247-59; R. **Borger** and H. **Tadmor**, "Zwei Beiträge zur alttestamentliche Wissenschaft aufgrund der Inschriften Tiglatpilesers III," *ZAW* 94(1982)244-51; M. **Broshi**, "The Expansion of Jerusalem in the Reigns of Hezekiah and Manasseh," *IEJ* 24(1974)21-26; M. **Cogan**, *Imperialism and Religion: Assyria, Judah and Israel in the Eighth and Seventh Centuries B.C.E.* (Missoula: Scholars Press, 1974); **Cogan**, "Tyre and Tiglath-pileser III: Chronological Notes," *JCS* 25(1973)96-99; H. J. **Cook**, "Pekah," *VT* 14(1964)121-35; M. **Haran**, "The Rise and Decline of the Empire of Jeroboam ben Joash," *VT* 17(1967) 266-97; L. D. **Levine**, *Two Neo-Assyrian Stelae from Iran* (Toronto: Royal Ontario Museum, 1972); **Levine**, "Menahem and Tiglath-Pileser: A New Synchronism," *BASOR* 206(1972)40-42; J. W. **McKay**, *Religion in Judah under the Assyrians, 732-609 BC* (London: SCM Press, 1973); H. **Mommsen** et al. "The Provenience of the *lmlk* Jars," *IEJ* 34(1984)89-113; F. L. **Moriarty**, "The Chronicler's Account of Hezekiah's Reform," *CBQ* 27(1965)399-406; N. **Na'aman**, "Sennacherib's Campaign to Judah and the Date of the *LMLK* Stamps," *VT* 29(1979)61-86; **Na'aman**, "Hezekiah's Fortified Cities and the *LMLK* Stamps," *BASOR* 261(1986)5-21; **Na'aman**, "Historical and Chronological

Notes on the Kingdoms of Israel and Judah in the Eighth Century B.C.," *VT* 36(1986)71-92; B. **Otzen**, "Israel under the Assyrians: Reflections on the Imperial Policy in Palestine," *ASTI* 11(1977)96-110 = *Power and Propaganda: A Symposium on Ancient Empires* (ed. M. T. Larsen; Copenhagen: Akademisk Forlag, 1979)251-61; J. **Rosenbaum**, "Hezekiah's Reform and the Deuteronomistic Tradition," *HTR* 72(1979)23-43; S. **Stohlmann**, "The Judean Exile After 701 B.C.E.", *Scripture in Context II: More Essays on The Comparative Method* (ed. W. W. Hallo et al.; Winona Lake: Eisenbrauns, 1983)147-75; E. **Strachey**, *Jewish History and Politics in the Times of Sargon and Sennacherib: An Inquiry into the Historical Meaning and Purpose of the Prophecies of Isaiah* (2nd ed.; London: W. Isbister & Co., 1874 [1st ed. 1853]); H. **Tadmor**, "Azriyau of Yaudi," *SH* 8(1961)232-71; **Tadmor** and M. **Cogan**, "Ahaz and Tiglath-Pileser in the Book of Kings: Historiographic Considerations," *Bib* 60(1979)491-508.

A. The Chronological Problems

The superscription to the book of Isaiah relates his ministry to four kings: Uzziah, Jotham, Ahaz, and Hezekiah. In spite of both biblical and non-biblical sources and chronological data, it is, unfortunately, still impossible to produce a universally accepted chronology for Israelite and Judean kings. Some of the greatest problems are related to the reigns of the kings under whom Isaiah worked. Thus, in contemporary treatments of Israelite and Judean history, dates that scholars assign these kings may vary as much as a decade or more.

At this point, we cannot discuss in detail the intricate and, perhaps, insolvable problems of biblical chronology. Dates and chronology, however, are important, especially in relating Judean history and Isaiah's preaching to other Near Eastern events.

One certain date in Judean history is the occasion of Nebuchadrezzar's first capture of the city of Jerusalem (II Kings 24:10-12). The Babylonian texts (*ANET* 564; *ABC* 102; *TUAT* I 403-4) provide an exact date for this event, which corresponds to 16 March 597 B.C.E. By calculating backwards from this date, when Jehoiachin surrendered to the

Babylonian king, the following chronology can be assigned the Judean kings on the basis of their lengths of reign:

Jehoiachin	(3 months; II Kings 24:8)	598–597
Jehoiakim	(11 years; II Kings 23:36)	608–598
Jehoahaz II	(3 months; II Kings 23:31)	609
Josiah	(31 years; II Kings 22:1)	639–609
Amon	(2 years; II Kings 21:19)	642–640
Manasseh	(55 years; II Kings 21:1)	697–642
Hezekiah	(29 years; II Kings 18:2)	727–698
Ahaz (Jehoahaz I)	(16 years; II Kings 16:2)	742–727

Once we move to the Judean predecessors of Ahaz, namely to Jotham and Uzziah (also called Azariah), matters become more difficult. Jotham is assigned sixteen years (II Kings 15:33; but see II Kings 15:30 which speaks of his twentieth year) and Uzziah fifty-two years (II Kings 15:2). However, we are told that Uzziah was stricken with leprosy and that Jotham governed the country while Uzziah was still alive (II Kings 15:5). Thus the years of Jotham and Uzziah may have overlapped. In fact, since there is no mention of Jotham in the book of Isaiah, which does refer to the death of Uzziah (Isa. 6:1), it may have been that Jotham actually died before his father Uzziah. At any rate, the dates for Judean kings from Ahaz forward seem reasonably secure, although even here it is impossible to reconcile all the cross-referencing synchronisms in the text. For example, II Kings 18:13 correlates the fourteenth year of Hezekiah with the year of Sennacherib's invasion (701). This synchronism, however, may be the result of editorial miscalculation (see below, chap. 4, sect. 34).

The chronological issues become even more complex when one turns to the Israelite kings who ruled from about 750 until the fall of Samaria and the end of the state of Israel in 722. Assyrian texts are of some value in establishing absolute dates. Two of Tiglath-pileser's inscriptions, which can be dated to about 738, mention the payment of tribute by King Menahem of Israel (see *ANET* 283; Levine; *TUAT* I 371, 378). Another of his inscriptions reports the placement of Hoshea on the throne in Samaria (*ANET* 284; *TUAT* I 374) probably in 732. Thus in any tabulation of Israelite kings, Menahem must be on the throne in 738 and Hoshea by 732. However, the Israelite king, Pekah, who preceded Hoshea on the throne, is assigned a reign of twenty years (II Kings 15:27). Since it is impossible to have a reign of twenty years between 738 and 732, it is obvious that Pekah's reign must either be drastically shortened, or else his twenty-year reign must have overlapped with those of other Israelite kings. As a rival king, Pekah probably dated his reign from the time he initially assumed power. When the biblical editors produced their chronology, they assumed that all reigns were sequential and successive and did the best they could on that basis to make synchronisms and connections between Judean and Israelite kings.

Having raised some of the chronological issues, we will explore these further in discussing the course of Israelite-Judean history in the following sections.

B. *Jeroboam II of Israel and Uzziah/Jotham of Judah*

In 750, Jeroboam II of the Jehu dynasty was probably still reigning in the Israelite capital city of Samaria. (The most likely dates for his reign are 785–745.) Uzziah/Jotham were ruling in Jerusalem. If Pekah had ruled for twenty years when he was assassinated in 732, then he, too, must have been claiming and exercising authority over some territory at the time.

The reign of Jeroboam II is discussed in II Kings 14:23-29. Very few facts are provided about his rule, since the biblical editors are primarily interested in discoursing on theological factors related to his reign. We are told in II Kings 14:25, however, that "he restored the border of Israel from the entrance of Hamath [the southern entry of the Bekaa Valley] as far as the Sea of the Arabah [the Dead Sea]." Jeroboam thus must have continued the Israelite revival that had begun under his predecessors, Joash (800–785) and Jehoahaz (816–800). Under Jehu (843–816) and most of the reign of Jehoahaz, Israel had been dominated by the Syrians led by Hazael. The latter practically ruled Israel and had overrun Israelite-claimed territory in Transjordan, Galilee, and along the coast, even threatening Jerusalem (II Kings 10:32-33; 12:17-18). At the time, Syria seems to have divided up portions or all of Israelite territory into administrative districts under the authority of governors (I Kings 20:14). The tide had turned near the end of Jehoahaz's reign, and under Joash conditions for Israel improved enormously, thanks to the attack on Damascus by Assyria to whom Joash paid tribute in 796 (II Kings 13:3-25; *TUAT* I 368).

In the struggle between Syria and Assyria, Joash, as had Jehu earlier, sided with Assyria. This policy of cooperation with Assyria characterized Israelite politics until Pekah's takeover of the throne in Samaria (probably in 736/5). During the early part of Jeroboam II's reign, when Assyrian pressure was still strong west of the Euphrates, Israel again ruled over the northern Transjordan, Galilee, and the central coastal region (II Kings 14:25). Judah also benefitted from the reign of Jeroboam, according to II Kings 14:28, which should be understood as follows: "he (Jeroboam) restored (territory claimed by) Damascus [Elath and part of Transjordan; see II Kings 14:22 and I Chron. 5:1-22] and (territory claimed by) Hamath [along the Mediterranean coast; see II Chron. 26:6-8] to Judah in Israel." Assyrian records speak of sixteen districts belonging to Damascus and nineteen to Hamath in the 730s. The territory ruled over by the former was mostly in inland Syria-Palestine, while the latter's extended along the Mediterranean coast. Thus Israel/Judah's expansion under Jeroboam was primarily into territory dominated by these two powers.

Before the end of Jeroboam's reign and the beginning of Isaiah's ministry, Israel was again being hard pressed. In the years before Tiglath-pileser seized the Assyrian throne, Assyrian influence in the west had weakened considerably (after 772). Israel had begun again to feel the pressure of opponents in the region, opponents who soon joined together, with the encouragement and support of the vigorous Urartian king Sarduri II (c. 764–734) to form an anti-Assyrian coalition in southern Syria-Palestine.

Several factors indicate that military and other action against Israel by members of the anti-Assyrian group had already been taken before the death of Jeroboam II. (1) The prophet Amos, who apparently functioned during the final year(s) of Jeroboam (Amos 1:1; 7:10-11), proclaimed judgment on several Palestinian states for various atrocities committed against Amos' Israelite and Judean contemporaries—Damascus for war atrocities in Gilead (Amos 1:3-5), the Philistines for selling a whole people (the total population of a town) to Edom (or Aram = Syria; "Edom" may represent a changed reading or a scribal mistake) and thus into exile (Amos 1:6-8), Tyre for the same crime as Philistia (Amos 1:9-10), and the Ammonites for war atrocities in Gilead (Amos 1:13-15). It is significant that in the later anti-Assyrian coalition, Syria (Damascus), Phoenicia, and Philistia played leading roles (see Isa. 9:11-12). The leaders of the coalition were already active against Israel (and Judah) in the days of Amos. (2) Pekah, who appears in the biblical texts as a "stooge" or subordinate associate of the Syrian king, Rezin, had apparently either led a portion of Israel (probably in Gilead; see II Kings 15:25) to break away and recognize him as king or had been made ruler over a portion of Israel taken over by Rezin. (3) Before the death of Jotham, which may have been after the death of Jeroboam II, Pekah and Rezin are said to have been harassing Judah (II Kings 15:37).

Syria reclaimed large portions of Palestinian territory that the Israelites had regained under Jeroboam II. The old tribal territories of Zebulun and Naphtali, which lay along the major highway joining Damascus and the southern Mediterranean seacoast, are noted by Isaiah as having been "brought into contempt" (Isa. 9:1, so the RSV). Rezin probably reconquered these areas early in his efforts to reestablish the boundaries of the earlier "Greater Syria," which had existed under Hazael and his successor, Ben-hadad, during the preceding century. At the time of Amos, near the end of the reign of Jeroboam II, the northern Transjordan (Gilead) had become a battleground between Syrian and Israelite forces, as it had a century earlier (Amos 1:3; 6:13-14; II Kings 8:28-29). Hosea 1:5 probably anticipates the defeat of Israel at the hands of Syria in the valley of Jezreel and thus the loss of all of Galilee.

The II Kings account provides little information on Uzziah (II Kings 15:1-7) and Jotham (II Kings 15:32-38), who ruled Judah contemporaneously with Jeroboam in the north. The two factors noted are Uzziah's having been stricken by Yahweh with leprosy (some skin ailment, but not Hansen's disease, which required isolation; II Kings 15:5) and Jotham's harassment by Pekah and Rezin (II Kings 15:37). The II Chronicles account adds considerably more to the depiction of the monarch.

The description of Uzziah's reign in II Chronicles 26 reports the following about his rule. (1) He rebuilt the seaport at Elath (v. 2; II Kings 14:22 implies that it was during the reign of Uzziah's father, Amaziah, that the port was resecured. More likely, this text should be understood as a statement about Jeroboam's reconquest of Elath on behalf of Judah [see II Kings 14:28].) (2) Uzziah fought against the Philistines, breaking down "the wall of Gath and the wall of Jabneh and the wall of Ashdod; and he built cities in the territory of Ashdod and elsewhere among the Philistines" (v. 6). (3) He fought against the Arabs and the Meunites (vv. 7-8; *Ammonites*, in v. 8, should probably be read *Meunites*). (4) The defenses of Jerusalem were strengthened (vv. 9, 15). (5) Defense towers were constructed in the land and animal husbandry and viticulture developed on royal lands (v. 10). (6) A large, well-equipped military was developed (vv. 11-15).

It is reported that Jotham carried out construction projects in Jerusalem and other cities building "forts and towers on the wooded hills." He is said to have fought against the Ammonites and received tribute from them for three years, but, again, probably Meunites should be read rather than Ammonites (II Kings 17:3-5).

Probably at the time, Uzziah and Jotham were acting as vassals or subjects of the Israelite monarch, as Judean kings had from the time of Omri (885–873) and Ahab (873–851). I Chronicles 5:11-17 recalls the cooperative activity of Jotham and Jeroboam II in Transjordan (in Gilead and Bashan), involving a census in these territories under their control, apparently in some sort of joint administration. II Kings 14:28 indicates that Jeroboam resecured territory for Judah (see above). Judean prosperity and expansion were thus carried out under the protective umbrella of Jeroboam's strength.

As in Israel, however, so also in Judah. Just as Israelite territory in the late 750s and 740s was being taken over by nations in the vicinity, especially Syria, so Judean territory was being lost. Under Jotham, Rezin and Pekah are said to have been sent against Judah (II Kings 15:37), perhaps taking territory claimed by Jotham in Transjordan (see I Chron. 5:11-17).

Although the historical books make no reference to its occurrence, a massive earthquake struck Palestine in the days of Uzziah. The superscription to the book of Amos notes that the prophet was active in the days of Uzziah, "two years before the earthquake." Zechariah 14:1-5 speaks of the future, when the Mount of Olives will be split asunder and people will flee from the movements of the earth "as you fled from the earthquake in the days of Uzziah king of Judah" (v. 5).

C. Israelite Civil War

Zechariah succeeded his father, Jeroboam II, on the throne of Israel but was assassinated by Shallum after only six months (II Kings 15:8). The prophets Hosea and Amos had both denounced the reigning dynasty in the north, proclaiming its destruction (Hos. 1:4-5; Amos 7:9-13). Such announcements of judgment probably functioned as calls for the assassination of the royal family (see I Kings 14:10-11; 16:1-4; 21:20-24). To insure the end of a dynasty, all males of the royal line and pregnant females who might be carrying a male child would have been killed. (Note Hosea's judgment on the "house of Jehu," the entire royal house, rather than just the immediate family of Jeroboam II.) Shallum's conspiracy succeeded in removing the dynasty of Jehu from the throne but was not capable of keeping Shallum in power. After a month, he was struck down by a counter coup headed by Menahem of Gadi.

The biblical text offers no explanation for the overthrow of the house of Jeroboam. The prophetic condemnations of the dynasty by Hosea and Amos may have been significant. If one speculates on the international factors that may have been involved, then a feasible scenario comes easily to mind. From the time Jehu submitted to Assyrian authority in 841, a submission enshrined on the Black Obelisk of Shalmaneser III (see *ANET* 281; *TUAT* I 362-63; *ANEP* Nos 351-55), Israel had apparently refused to participate in any anti-Assyrian movement. The years prior to the overthrow of the Jehu dynasty, however, were years of increasing Urartian influence and anti-Assyrian fervor in the eastern Mediterranean seaborad. The movement had grown so strong that Tiglath-pileser had to spend three years putting down its north Syrian supporters in 743–740. No doubt, in 745, Shallum and his supporters felt the time was ripe for Israel to cast its lot with the anti-Assyrian forces.

When Menahem and his supporters put down the Shallum conspiracy, Israel seems to have been thrown into a state of virtual civil war. In seizing the throne, Menahem took vicious action against Israelite citizens. The town of Tappuah, a city in Ephraim, perhaps near Shallum's home (if son of Jabesh, in describing Shallum, refers to his place of origin rather than his parentage), was sacked and all its inhabitants slaughtered, including the pregnant women (II Kings 15:13-16). Isaiah later spoke of this strife as a time when the people were like fuel for the fire; no man spared his brother (see Isa. 9:19). Other groups in addition to the Shallum and Menahem factions may have been part of the general civil strife. Pekah and his supporters were certainly somewhere in the background. Other pretenders to the throne may have arisen, but since they, unlike Menahem and Pekah, never made it to the throne in Samaria, no record of their exploits has survived.

Menahem (745–736) solidified his hold on the throne in Samaria by offering tribute to, and perhaps securing assistance from, Tiglath-pileser. II Kings 15:19-20 reports that Pul (Tiglath-pileser) came up against the land and that Menahem made the Assyrians a heavy gift so "the king of Assyria turned back, and did not stay there in the land" (v. 20). Such a scene is most apt to have occurred when Tiglath-pileser first moved into the eastern Mediterranean seaboard in power, namely in 743, a time when Menahem was still struggling to secure a firm base of support.

During his reign, Menahem was apparently able to retain control of only the central hill country of the old Israelite state:

> The Syrians on the east and the
> Philistines on the west
> devoured Israel with open mouth.
>
> Isaiah 9:12

Transjordan, Galilee, and the coastal plain were taken from Israelite control and absorbed into Rezin's "Greater Syria" (Isa. 9:1).

D. *Ahaz and the Syro-Ephraimitic Crisis*

The editors of II Kings were not very gentle with Ahaz, the successor to Uzziah/Jotham in Jerusalem. Their account of his reign in II Kings 16 opens with specifics about the king—father's name, age, and length of reign (vv. 1-2*a*). Oddly, no mention is made of his mother's name, as is the case with practically every Judean king. The editors immediately charge him with great wrongs: "He did not do what was right in the eyes of [Yahweh]. . . but he walked in the way of the kings of Israel" (16:2*b*-3*a*). After this general charge against Ahaz, there follows a list of specific "sins" (vv. 3*b*-4).

After this initial evaluation of Ahaz, the editors provide a description of events in his reign. All, however, are related by the editors to the siege of Jerusalem by Pekah and Rezin and its aftermath. About Ahaz and his reign, we are told the following: (1) Rezin, the king of Syria, recovered Elath for Syria, drove the men of Judah from Elath, and allowed Edomites to move into the city (v. 6; note the marginal readings in the RSV). (2) Ahaz sent messengers with presents to Tiglath-pileser, asking for his help. It was given, resulting in the destruction of Damascus, exile for its people, and death for its king (vv. 7-9). (3) While in Damascus to meet with Tiglath-pileser, Ahaz saw an altar and had a model of it sent to Jerusalem with orders that the priest Uriah should construct one for the Jerusalem temple following this pattern. Upon returning home, Ahaz offered sacrifice on the new altar and removed the old bronze altar to the northern side of the new altar (vv. 10-16). (4) Finally, Ahaz made some changes in the architecture of the temple and palace (the Hebrew is obscure), which are associated with the king of Assyria (vv. 17-20).

The chronicler's account of Ahaz's reign (II Chronicles 28) reports the following, after giving him a general negative evaluation (vv. 1-4). (1) Yahweh gave him into the hand of the king of Syria, who carried great numbers of Judeans to

Damascus (v. 5*a*). (2) The king of Israel, Pekah, defeated Ahaz and killed 120,000 of his troops (vv. 5*b*-6). (3) A son of Ahaz, the commander of the king's palace, and the official next in authority to Ahaz were killed by Zichri, a mighty man of Ephraim (v. 7). (4) Israelites carried 200,000 Judeans and much spoil to Samaria, but, on the insistence of Oded the prophet and certain Ephraimite leaders, released the captives and restored the spoil in Jericho (vv. 8-15). (4) Ahaz sent to the Assyrian kings for help because the Edomites and Philistines were attacking Judah and seizing territory (vv. 16-19). (5) The Assyrian king, Til-gath-pilneser (Tiglath-pileser), came against Ahaz and afflicted him, requiring Ahaz to pay tribute (vv. 20-21). (6) Ahaz sacrificed to Syrian gods (vv. 22-23). (7) Ahaz carried out various acts of apostasy (vv. 24-25).

Both II Kings and II Chronicles present Ahaz as a very bad king. Two major charges are leveled against him: (1) He was guilty of apostasy and false worship, and (2) he was responsible for inviting the Assyrians into the life and affairs of Judah.

Neither of these charges appears to be historical for a number of reasons. (1) The prophet Isaiah, functioning in Jerusalem and intimately involved in royal affairs, never accuses Ahaz of apostasy and never refers to any appeal to the Assyrians for military assistance. (2) In the Assyrian inscriptions, Tiglath-pileser never makes any reference to a special appeal from Ahaz and, in fact, treats him just as if he were any other of the western kings. Ahaz paid tribute; this Tiglath-pileser acknowledges, but notes his tribute along with others in a list that includes even states that took an anti-Assyrian posture (*ANET* 282). (3) The terminology in Ahaz's supposed appeal to the Assyrian king utilizes terms—"your son" and "bribe"—that would not have been used in official communications, especially not if Ahaz, as seems likely, had never before personally submitted to Assyrian authority. (4) Ahaz is presented by the biblical editors as a negative counterpart to Hezekiah, the righteous king, who fought apostasy and rebelled against the Assyrians. Ahaz thus functions as II Kings' evil foil to the good Hezekiah.

The editors of the II Kings material apparently had evidence concerning Ahaz's payment of tribute. (Note that the chronicler, however, does not connect the payment of tribute with the Syro-Ephraimitic crisis.) They then composed an account of the payment, drawing upon the pattern of crisis–appeal–rescue already present in the Baasha–Asa–Ben-hadad story (I Kings 15:17-18).

The following picture of the historical Ahaz and his reign seems plausible. First of all, Ahaz assumed the throne when Judah still had strong vassal ties to Israel and commitment to Israel's long-standing policy of not opposing the Assyrians. Ahaz's father, Jotham, and Ahaz himself probably had intermarried into the northern ruling house, the dynasty of Jehu, as had been the case earlier in the Omride era. Nothing is said in the biblical texts about Ahaz's mother. The only other Judean king whose mother's name is not given in his accession data is Jehoram, whose wife was Athaliah, the daughter of Jezebel (see II Kings 8:16-19). Moreover, Ahaz is said to have walked in the way of the kings of Israel, a charge leveled against Jehoram as well (II Kings 8:18). Ahaziah, the son of Athaliah, is also said to have walked in the way of Ahab (II Kings 8:25-27). All of these kings were condemned for their association with the Israelite royal house.

Second, Ahaz assumed the throne when there may have been questions about the status of the Davidic family and its relationship to Yahweh. Uzziah had developed leprosy— "Yahweh smote the king" (II Kings 15:5)—and the land had suffered from an earthquake so severe as to imprint itself for generations in the memory of a people accustomed to earthquakes. These two events could have been seen as ill omens on the house of David. (The earthquake may have been read as fulfillment of Amos' prophecy; see Amos 9:1.) In addition, three of the last five Judean rulers had been assassinated in office—Athaliah (II Kings 11:13-16), Jehoash (II Kings 12:20), and Amaziah (II Kings 14:19).

Third, Judean people and territory were being ravished from several directions. (a) Pekah and Rezin were encroaching on Judean territory even before the death of Jotham (II Kings 15:37). (b) Under either Jotham or Ahaz, Rezin seized the port of Elath in cooperation with the Edomites (II Kings 16:6.) The term *recovered* may have been used in describing Rezin's action because under Hazael a century earlier Syria perhaps had gained control of the port. (c) The Edomites had invaded Judean territory and carried away captives (II Chron. 28:17; see Amos 1:11-12). (d) One can imagine the Meunites taking vengeance on Judah as the state weakened. (Note that II Chronicles 27:5 assigns Jotham only three years of tribute from the Meunites [so read for Ammonites].) (e) The Philistines are said to have raided "the cities in the Shephelah and the Negeb of Judah, and had taken Beth-shemesh, Aijalon, Gederoth, Soco with its villages, Timnah with its villages, and Gimzo with its villages; and they settled there" (II Chron. 28:18). (f) Amos spoke of the Philistines and Phoenicians as selling on the slave market, probably captives that were Israelites and Judeans (Amos 1:6-10). Damascus may have been the destination for such exiles in addition to those Syria herself carried away (see II Chron. 29:5).

Fourth, Ahaz was confronted with a lack of support among his own Judean subjects (see Isa. 8 and below, chap. 4, sect. 10). The cities condemned by Micah in the opening chapter of his book were apparently Judean towns in the Shephelah, just north of those seized by the Philistines, which had rebelled against Jerusalem and the Davidic family, just as had Libnah earlier at the time of Jehoram and apparently in concert with Edom (II Kings 8:22). As we shall see, this Judean opposition to the house of David forms an important element in the background to Isaiah's activity (especially Isa. 6-8).

Fifth, Ahaz was under increasing pressure to cooperate with the anti-Assyrian forces in the west. Although it cannot be clearly demonstrated, several forms of pressure must have been asserted to persuade Judah and Ahaz to participate. (Similar pressure was applied to the north.) (a) Diplomatic negotiations must have been tried over a long period of time. Strong Urartian pressure was asserted in much of Syria in the 750s and 740s. At a time when Assyrian presence was weak in the west, Judah and Israel would surely have been targets of diplomatic influence. (b) A further level of pressure took the form of territorial harassment, a factor already noted. (c) When Ahaz continued to be uncooperative, an effort was apparently made to assassinate him. II Chronicles 28:7 notes that Zichri from Ephraim killed three persons closely associated with Ahaz—his son, the palace commander, and a "second" to the king. Such a slaughter can hardly refer to anything other than an unsuccessful attempt to assassinate Ahaz himself. In the north, of course, such an assassination attempt succeeded when Pekah slew Pekahiah, the son of Menahem (II Kings 15:25). Had Zichri succeeded, he might have laid claim to the Judean throne. (d) Once Pekah secured the throne of Samaria, he, with Rezin's support, marched to Jerusalem to depose Ahaz as a renegade vassal who refused to go along with Israel's new political alignment. Ahaz was to be removed from power and, no doubt, he and the dynasty's males and pregnant women slaughtered. In his place, a son of Tabeel was to be enthroned in Jerusalem (Isa. 7:6). This Tabeel is probably King Tubail (Ittoba`al) of Tyre, who paid tribute to Tiglath-pileser in or before 738/7 (Levine; *TUAT* I 378).

As we shall see in examining Isaiah 7–12, Ahaz asserted Judean independence from Israel (Isa. 9:2), was encouraged by Isaiah, and continued to follow an independent political course, in spite of the Syro-Ephraimite attempt to remove him from power. Of his reign, we know little more. Presumably he made, at some indeterminable point in his rule, some radical changes in the Jerusalem cult. These have all been condemned by the biblical editors. Such changes, however, seem not to have offended either Isaiah or the high priest Uriah. A more favorably disposed editor might have presented Ahaz in a positive light as a significant reformer of cultic life.

E. *The Reign of Hezekiah*

Ahaz and Tiglath-pileser both died in 727 (Isa. 14:28-29). After living in and reigning as king over Babylon (*ABC* 73; Isa. 14:1-27) for two years, Tiglath-pileser died, apparently while on a campaign against Damascus and an anti-Assyrian coalition in the west (see above, p. 24, and below, chap. 4, sects. 19 and 28). Nothing is noted in Assyrian texts about the nature of his demise or about the outcome of his campaign against Damascus (see Isa. 14:1-27). Historical texts for his successor, Shalmaneser V (727–722), do not exist or have not been discovered. An eponym list notes that Shalmaneser spent the year of 726 at home. One could hypothesize that the campaign against the west, in which Tiglath-pileser died or was killed, did not achieve complete success, and Shalmaneser returned home to rebuild his forces. At any rate, Shalmaneser spent much of his reign in the west fighting anti-Assyrian forces, including Damascus, Israel, Moab, and Phoenicia (Isa. 15–16; 17; 28–33; Hos. 10:14; Josephus *ANT* IX 283-87).

The biblical narratives about Hezekiah, excluding II Kings 18:13–20:21, which we will examine below in discussing Isaiah 36–39, are found in II Kings 18:1-12 and II Chronicles 29–32. II Kings notes the following items about Hezekiah's reign, not necessarily in chronological order, but in the order of their significance as understood by the editors. (1) He took action to close places of worship outside Jerusalem (II Kings 18:4a; note II Kings 18:22 and Isa. 27:9). (2) Some materials used in worship, even in the Jerusalem temple, were outlawed and destroyed (II Kings 18:4b). (3) He rebelled against the Assyrians (v. 7b). (4) He fought against the Philistines (v. 8; and other groups in the southwest, according to I Chron. 4:34-43).

Second Chronicles depicts Hezekiah as a great religious reformer who began purifying the temple and Jerusalem worship in the first month of his reign (29:3-36). He invited Israelites from the northern tribes, from Beersheba to Dan, to a Passover celebration in Jerusalem, the likes of which had not been seen since the days of Solomon (chap. 30). The festival was followed by the destruction of cultic sites and furniture throughout the land and by the reorganization of the clergy, the temple and clergy funds, and the temple administration (chap. 31). Second Chronicles 32 describes Hezekiah's preparations for war with the Assyrians and notes, in 32:3-8, some of the steps taken for national defense.

In the light of the biblical and extra-biblical texts, the following may be set out as features of Hezekiah's reign. (1) On four occasions in his reign, the Assyrians took action against anti-Assyrian coalitions in the area: (a) Shalmaneser continued his father's campaign against western rebels throughout his reign. Early in his rule (727), Shalmaneser was in Transjordan (Isa. 15–16; Hos. 10:14), moved against Damascus, with whom Israel was in cooperation (Isa. 17), and received the submission of Hoshea (II Kings 17:3). Hezekiah, now on the throne (see Isa. 16:5), seems not to have cooperated in the efforts of the coalition. (b) In 725–720, first Shalmaneser and then Sargon fought the anti-Assyrian coalition and each captured Samaria (II Kings 17:4-6; *ABC* 73; *ANET* 284-85; *TUAT* I 378-79, 382). Hezekiah and Judah-Jerusalem probably offered some informal assistance to Israel early in the period (Isa. 28:14-22), at least allowing Israelite messengers to pass through Judah on their way to appeal for help from Egypt in 726 (Isa. 30:6-7). Isaiah seems to have believed that Jerusalem would be placed under siege as a consequence (Isa. 29), although he spoke of Hezekiah, who may have been less cooperative than Judah generally, as "He who stands firm will not be in haste" (Isa. 28:16). In Samaria's last days, Judah and Jerusalem seem to have offered the north no support. (c) In 712/11, Assyrian troops moved against an Ashdod-led coalition that had formed over several years (Isa. 20) and took action against Judah for its support of the coalition (Isa. 22:1-14). Hezekiah's role in this revolt remains uncertain; he may have been ill at the time (II Kings 20:1-19/Isa. 38), with Shebna as second in command—"over the household" (Isa. 22:15-19; see II Kings 15:5*b*)—running the country. (d) In 705 and the years following, Hezekiah, with Isaiah's support (Isa. 24-27), was a ringleader in a western revolt.

(2) Hezekiah had expansionist goals for his kingdom. These included not only Judah but also dominion over the whole of Israel, "from Beersheba to Dan" (II Chron. 30:5) or "from the river Euphrates to the Brook of Egypt" (Isa. 27:12). Several matters attest to this aspect of his reign. (a) The preaching of Isaiah held out such a possibility of a new Israel under Davidic rule (Isa. 7:17; 11:13-14; 19:24-25; 26:15). (b) Hezekiah expanded his territorial holdings in the south (II Kings 18:8; I Chron. 4:34-43). (c) Northern Yahwists were invited to participate in Jerusalem festivals (II Chron. 30). (d) His son and successor, Manasseh, born about 710/709, was given the name of a northern tribe.

(3) Hezekiah took steps to centralize religious and political matters in Judah. No doubt these steps were taken partially to prevent Judean disaffection from the house of David and Jerusalem, which had manifested itself in the disloyalty of much of Judah during the reign of Ahaz. Included in this move toward centralization were the steps taken to

reorganize Jerusalem worship and to close cultic centers outside Jerusalem (II Kings 18:4, 22; II Chron. 31; Isa. 27:9). Politically and militarily, to judge from jar handles stamped *lmlk* ("belonging to the king") plus a place name, Hezekiah divided Judah into four main districts, with regional capitals at Hebron, Ziph, Socoh, and *Mmst*, the last being Jerusalem or a site nearby.

(4) Military strength and siege preparations were important elements of his reign. Second Chronicles 32:3-6 speaks of some of his activities, including strengthening Jerusalem's defenses, placing military commanders over the people, increasing the supply of arms, and regulating water supplies. No doubt the last included plans for construction of the famous tunnel in Jerusalem to bring water inside the city for protection during a siege (see II Kings 20:20; Isa. 22:8*b*-11).

II

The Religious and Theological Backgrounds of Isaiah's Ministry

J. **Barton**, "Ethics in Isaiah of Jerusalem," *JTS* 32(1981)1-18; R. E. **Clements**, *God and Temple: The Idea of the Divine Presence in Ancient Israel* (Oxford: B. H. Blackwell, 1965); R. J. **Clifford**, *The Cosmic Mountain in Canaan and the Old Testament* (Cambridge: Harvard University Press, 1972); E. W. **Davies**, *Prophecy and Ethics: Isaiah and the Ethical Traditions of Israel* (Sheffield: JSOT Press, 1981); J. H. **Eaton**, *Kingship and the Psalms* (2d ed.; Sheffield: JSOT Press, 1986); H. **Gese**, "Der Davidsbund und die Zionserwählung," *ZTK* 61(1964)10-26 = his *Vom Sinai zum Zion* (Munich: Chr. Kaiser, 1974)113-29; H. L. **Ginsberg**, *The Supernatural in the Prophets with Special Reference to Isaiah* (Cincinnati: Hebrew Union College Press, 1979); R. **Gordis**, "Isaiah—Prophet, Thinker, World Statesman," in his *Poets, Prophets, and Sages: Essays in Biblical Interpretation* (Bloomington/London: Indiana University Press, 1971)255-67; B. **Halpern**, *The Constitution of the Monarchy in Israel* (Chico: Scholars Press, 1981); E. **Hammershaimb**, "On the Ethics of the Prophets," in his *Some Aspects of Old Testament Prophecy from Isaiah to Malachi* (Copenhagen: Rosenkilde og Bagger, 1966)63-90; J. **Jensen**, "Weal and Woe in Isaiah: Consistency and Continuity," *CBQ* 43(1981)167-87; A. R. **Johnson**, *Sacral Kingship in Ancient Israel* (2d ed.; Cardiff: University of Wales Press, 1967); J. D. **Levenson**, "The Davidic Covenant and Its Modern Interpreters," *CBQ* 41(1979)205-19; **Levenson**, *Sinai and Zion: An Entry into the Jewish Bible* (Minneapolis: Winston-Seabury, 1985); H. M. **Lutz**, *Jahwe, Jerusalem und die Völker: Zur Vorgeschichten von Sach. 12, 1-8 und 14, 1-5* (Neukirchen-Vluyn: Neukirchener Verlag, 1968); T. N. D. **Mettinger**, *King and Messiah: The Civil* *and Sacral Legitimation of the Israelite Kings* (Lund: CWK Gleerup, 1976); P. D. **Miller**, *The Divine Warrior in Ancient Israel* (Cambridge: Harvard University Press, 1973); S. **Mowinckel**, *He That Cometh* (Oxford/Nashville: B. H. Blackwell/Abingdon Press, 1956); B. C. **Ollenburger**, *Zion, the City of the Great King: A Theological Symbol of the Jerusalem Cult* (Sheffield: JSOT Press, 1987); N. **Poulssen**, *König und Tempel im Glaubenszeugnis des Alten Testamentes* (Stuttgart: Katholisches Bibelwerk, 1967); G. **von Rad**, *Old Testament Theology*, vol. 2: *The Theology of Israel's Prophetic Traditions* (Edinburgh/New York: Oliver and Boyd/Harper and Row, 1965)147-75; J. J. M. **Roberts**, "The Davidic Origin of the Zion Tradition," *JBL* 92(1973)329-44; **Roberts**, "Zion in the Theology of the Davidic-Solomonic Empire," *Studies in the Period of David and Solomon and Other Essays* (ed. T. Ishida; Winona Lake, Ind.: Eisenbrauns, 1982)93-108; **Roberts**, "The Divine King and the Human Community in Isaiah's Vision of the Future," *The Quest for the Kingdom of God: Essays in Honor of George E. Mendenhall* (ed. H. B. Huffmon et al.; Winona Lake: Eisenbrauns, 1983)127-36; J. **Schreiner**, *Sion-Jerusalem. Jahwes Königssitz. Theologie der Heiligen Stadt im Alten Testament* (Munich: Kösel Verlag, 1963); K. **Seybold,** *Das davidische Königtum im Zeugnis der Propheten* (Göttingen: Vandenhoeck und Ruprecht, 1972); F. **Stolz**, *Strukturen und Figuren im Kult von Jerusalem: Studien zur altorientalischen vor- und frühisraeli-tischen Religion* (Berlin: Walter de Gruyter, 1970); T. C. **Vriezen**, "Essentials of the Theology of Isaiah," *Israel's Prophetic Heritage: Essays in Honor of James Muilenburg* (ed. B. W. Anderson and W. Harrelson; New York: Harper Brothers, 1962)128-46; K. W. **Whitelam**, *The Just King: Monarchical Judicial Authority in Ancient Israel* (Sheffield: JSOT Press, 1979).

In the preceding chapter, we outlined the national and international political and military contexts of Isaiah's career and preaching. There is no doubt that the prophet's preaching was shaped by and reflective of his assessment of these political conditions and the options available to Judean and Israelite monarchs. His evaluation of these conditions and of the potential for success or failure of particular policies influenced his thought and his proclamation—that is, he was a realistic political analyst. Nonetheless, other factors and considerations were of far greater impact and overshadowed matters of contextual expediency.

Before examining some of the specific content and characteristics of his thought and preaching, we must note one particular feature of his career. This is reflected in the radical difference between chapters 1–5 and 7–33.

In the first five chapters of the book, Isaiah focuses fundamentally on internal social and religious issues. Significant statements on ethical, moral, and social concerns are found in these opening addresses and are practically nonexistent in the remainder of the book. Likewise, his harsh condemnations and judgments of Judah and Jerusalem for their social and religious shortcomings are virtually limited to chapters 1–5. Simultaneously, it is particularly in these chapters that the prophet exhorts his audience to accept certain dire conditions as the work and judgment of Yahweh and admonishes the population about particular actions, ethical stances, and faith postures.

In chapters 7–33, on the other hand, Isaiah focuses almost exclusively on political and international affairs and events. He addresses the question of Israel's, Judah's, and other nations' relationship with Assyria, the issue of Assyria's role in human affairs *vis à vis* Yahweh, and the conditions that will prevail in the future in Israel, Judah, and the world at large.

The difference between the orientations of these two blocks of material may be partially accounted for by political and military considerations. In the early years of Isaiah's career, the international scene was relatively quiet in comparison to later times. Nonetheless, with Assyrian strength in remission and most Syro-Palestinian powers cooperating with Urartu, political and limited military pressure was certainly being exerted on pro-Assyrian powers in the area even during Isaiah's early years. Israel was already under assault before the death of Jeroboam II (see Amos 1-2; Hos. 1:4-5).

If Isaiah's earliest preaching (Isa. 1:2-20) has as its background the earthquake during Uzziah's reign (see Amos 1:1; Zech. 14:5), Isaiah probably began his prophetic ministry about 745 or 744 B.C.E. (this assumes that Amos's short ministry belongs to the last years of Jeroboam II's reign, about

747 or 746 B.C.E.). At that time, Judah and Jerusalem were certainly not in a grave political or military crisis. With the outbreak of civil war over the Israelite throne (II Kings 15:8-16), the growing Judean anti-Assyrianism and disaffection with the Davidic monarchy and its policies, and the presence of Assyrian forces in the west, Isaiah shifted his attention almost entirely to the political arena. Jerusalem, the Davidic dynasty, state policies, and international affairs became the focus of his proclamation. Social issues and other internal matters were considered, if at all, only when they impinged on the political sphere. Isaiah 6 gives autobiographical expression to the transition from one phase to the other.

In his preaching, the prophet based his argumentation on several ethical and theological considerations and traditions. Frequently, Isaiah argues a case or draws a conclusion on the basis of common sense or universal human experience. These common sense deductions about life are then applied theologically to divine-human relationships. Several examples can be noted. In the opening verses of the book, the nation's behavior is contrasted unfavorably with that of ordinary domesticated animals, the ox and the ass (1:2-3). In 3:10-11, folk wisdom asserting that one gets what one's labors produce is used to clinch the argument. The failure of a viticulturist's efforts illustrates God's disappointment with Israel and Judah (5:1-7). That a tool does not use but rather is used by its manufacturer describes relations between Yahweh and Assyria (10:15-19; see 29:16). Metaphors about crop production and processing are used to draw theological conclusions (28:23-29).

Isaiah also appears to rely on common Near Eastern ethical ideals, which he proclaims as the demands of Yahweh. The exhortation to defend the fatherless and to plead for the widow (1:17b, 23b; 9:17; 10:2b) occurs in the literature of so many ancient cultures as to appear to be a moralizing cliché or a universal standard. Judgment by this standard served to test one's capacity to act beyond self-interest.

Nowhere does Isaiah explicitly draw on anything comparable to a law code or a body of covenant stipulations such as we find in the Pentateuch (the apparent allusion to Exod. 22:22-24 in Isa. 10:1-4 may be an exception). The term *torah* is used by the prophet without much precision, almost as a synonym for *word* or prophetic statement (see 1:10*b*; 8:16). Had Isaiah based his preaching on some legal code, one would expect this to be most evident in chapters 1–5, where most of the moral denunciations and exhortations appear. (See below concerning Isaiah's dependence on "priestly" theological concerns.)

Central to the views and preaching of Isaiah were the ideologies of the Zion/Jerusalem and Davidic traditions. Although the beliefs about the city of Zion/Jerusalem and the Davidic monarchy were interconnected and mutually supportive (see Pss. 2:6; 78:67-72; 132:11-18), such beliefs may be discussed individually. Since Isaiah's use of these traditions will be noted throughout the commentary, here we will provide only an outline of their contents.

The clearest expressions of the Zion/Jerusalem ideology are found in various psalms that were apparently used in festival celebrations. In the Judean capital city and cult, Jerusalem was proclaimed the city chosen by Yahweh for his dwelling place, being the site of his temple.

> but he chose the tribe of Judah,
>   Mount Zion, which he loves.
> He built his sanctuary like the high
>   heavens, like the earth, which he has
>   founded for ever.
>   Psalm 78:68-69 RSV

> For the Lord has chosen Zion;
>   he has desired it for his
>   habitation:
> "This is my resting place for ever;
>   here I will dwell, for I have
>   desired it. . . ."
>   Psalm 132:13-14 RSV

Jerusalem was thus the "dwelling place for the Mighty One of Jacob" (Ps. 132:5; see Pss. 9:11; 74:2; 135:21). Fundamental to Isaiah's thought is the belief that Yahweh dwells on Mt. Zion, that Jerusalem is the Deity's special abode (Isa. 8:18; 18:4).

As the dwelling place of Yahweh and the site where he reigned as king, Mt. Zion was understood as the cosmic mountain, the center of the world, the link between the earthly and the heavenly worlds, the meeting place of the divine council, the source of a stream(s) whose waters nourished the land, and a "garden of Eden." These components of the Zion theology, best seen in Psalms 2, 46, 48, 76, 82, and 132, are reflected in Isaiah's preaching:

Zion the cosmic mountain, the center of the world (Pss. 46:2-3; 48:1-2; Isa. 2:2)

Zion as the meeting place of the divine council (Pss. 82; 89:5-7; Isa. 6:8)

Zion as the source of divine decrees (Pss. 2:4-6; 50; 93:5; Isa. 2:3; 14:24-27)

Zion as the source of special streams (Pss. 46:4; 48:7; Isa. 33:21; see Isa. 8:6; Ezek. 47:1-12)

Zion as the "garden of Eden," the embodiment of plenty and perfection (Pss. 36:8-10; 50:2; 132:15-16; Isa. 11:6-9)

To be counted among those who dwell in Zion was a special status recognized by both psalmist and prophet (Ps. 87:5-6; Isa. 4:3; 14:32; see 23:18; 33:24).

Zion/Jerusalem enjoyed special divine protection. This protection is frequently described in the psalms in terms of an assault of forces or nations against the city, which is repelled by divine action (see Pss. 2:1-3; 46:5-9; 48:4-8; 76:3, 5-9). This motif is often appealed to by Isaiah in his argument that Yahweh would guard Jerusalem and not allow it to fall into enemy hands, even though he might bring an enemy against the city as an act of judgment (Isa. 8:8b-10, 14-15; 10:16-19, 26-27, 33-34; 14:24-27; 17:12-14; 26:20-27:1; 29:1-8; 30:27-33; 31:4-5).

Isaiah makes varied use of the Zion traditions depending on the rhetorical situation (on rhetorical situation, see below, chapter 3). In his speech in 1:21-2:5, he focuses on the city in terms of its righteousness and its role in mediating the ways and teachings of Yahweh. He alludes to the ideal times of the past (1:21a, 26) as well as the anticipated glorious days of the future (2:2-4). The views of an idealized Zion of past history and a utopian Zion of the future were probably part of the Jerusalemite world view. The prophet drew on both to address and to admonish the Zion of his own day. As Zion became threatened by invaders, first by the Syrians and the Israelites and later by the Assyrians, Isaiah appealed to a different set of traditions—namely those describing the city under attack by enemy hordes, but rescued by divine intervention.

Isaiah also makes extensive use of the Davidic theology. This ideology finds expression in numerous royal psalms (2; 20–21; 45; 72; 89; 101; 110; 132) as well as in Nathan's dynastic promise to David (II Sam. 7:8-16). Such traditions declared that Yahweh had chosen David, the son of Jesse, just as he had chosen Jerusalem, and that David's descendants would rule perpetually in Jerusalem, enjoying divine favor and protection.

The Davidic theology was at home in the Jerusalem court, rehearsed and proclaimed on state occasions, such as coronations, royal anniversaries, and festival observances. In the coronation, the new king was declared reborn as the son of Yahweh (Pss. 2:6; 89:26) and was promised a great and extensive kingdom (Pss. 2:8-12; 72:8-11; 89:25, 29). As indicative of the king's new status, the monarch was supplied with "throne names" or coronation titles. The new king's reign was celebrated as the beginning or as the promise of a new era (Ps. 72:1-7, 15–17) and divine protection was promised the king (Pss. 89:19-24; 110:5-6; 132:18). Righteousness and justice were expected to characterize the rule of the Davidic monarch (Pss. 72:1-4; 101).

Isaiah draws extensively on the Davidic theology and appeals to the kings in Jerusalem to act on the basis of its promises (Isa. 7:1-17; 9:6-7; 11:1-5). He does not argue a case for the validity and truthfulness of the Davidic ideology; he assumes these and alludes to the sacred traditions as being well known and worthy of confidence.

In addition to the Zion and Davidic traditions, allusions in Isaiah's speeches indicate that he was familiar with other traditions and themes related to Israelite history and that he used these as examples and illustrations. References are made to Sodom and Gomorrah (1:9-10; 3:9; 13:19) as examples of complete destruction and unabashed sinfulness (see Gen. 19). The Israelite triumph over the Midianites (at great numerical odds) is used as an example of Yahweh's great deliverance (9:4; 10:26; see Judg. 7). Similarly, his allusions to Mount Perazim and the valley of Gibeon (28:21) presuppose acquaintance with stories presumably like the present narratives in II Samuel 5:17-25 and Joshua 10:6-14.

Only one clear and explicit reference is made by the prophet to the Hebrew exodus from Egypt. In promising the return of Israelite exiles from Assyria, Isaiah describes their crossing of the Euphrates and return to the homeland as analogous to the crossing of the sea and the journey from Egypt.

> [Yahweh] will wave his hand over the River
>   with his scorching wind,
> and smite it into seven channels
>   that men may cross dryshod.
> And there will be a highway from
>   Assyria
>   for the remnant which is left of
>   his people,
> as there was for Israel
>   when they came up from the land
>   of Egypt.
>   11:15*ab*-16 RSV

Although the allusion to the exodus is clear, what Isaiah says about the event shares only general, and not special, parallels to the narrative in Exodus. (Isa. 4:5; 10:24-25; and 26:20-21 share some parallels with terminology found in the exodus story, but do not explicitly mention the exodus. See the discussion of these texts in the commentary below.)

Isaiah also shows an acquaintance with what might be called priestly theology—that is, the theology undergirding the cult in the Jerusalem temple. He makes use of this theology in a number of ways. First, the concepts of impurity/defilement and purity/cleanliness appear in the description of his temple vision (6:5-7), in the context of statements about the cleansing and purgation of Jerusalem (4:4), and in the description of the earth's pollution by its inhabitants (24:4-5).

Second, Isaiah alludes to the belief that sin and wrong-doing contaminate and that their pollutant must be purged. In concluding his denunciation of the Jerusalemite leaders' participation in the Ashdod-led revolt, he declares that God has whispered in his ears an oath that the rebels' iniquity would never be purged (22:14). Again, he associates the destruction of the altars throughout the land with the purgation of the people's sin (27:9).

Third, in his depiction of Yahweh's recreation of world orders in chapter 24, Isaiah's language has numerous parallels to the opening chapters of Genesis. The similarity is not so close as to indicate Isaiah's dependence on a literary form of the priestly primeval history; general knowledge of the thought world out of which the Genesis material evolved could explain the parallels.

Fourth, in Isaiah 24:5, the prophet refers to the breaking of the "everlasting covenant." His reference occurs within a discussion of the pollution of the earth. The pollution has resulted from the transgression of laws and statutes and has brought the world under a curse; the transgression involved violates the eternal covenant. The context and content of this statement points to a connection with what are called the Noachic laws of Genesis 9:1-7. In Genesis 9, the "eternal covenant" does not refer to the laws and commandments. This expression is used, instead, to denote the divine promise that the world would not again be destroyed by a flood, a covenant of which the rainbow is the sign (Gen. 9:8-17). Isaiah, however, must be alluding to the Noachic laws, and particularly to the regulation about bloodshed (see Gen. 4:10), since "blood pollutes" (Num. 35:33). Again, Isaiah seems familiar with the thought world of certain pentateuchal texts but not necessarily with their present formulation.

Fifth, Isaiah's concern with holiness (4:3; 6:13; 11:9; 23:18; 27:13; 30:29) and his designation of Yahweh as the Holy One (1:4; 5:16, 19, 24; 6:3; 10:17, 20; 12:6; 17:7; 29:19, 23; 30:11, 12, 15; 31:1; 37:23) share concerns with the priestly material of the Pentateuch (see Lev. 19:1-2, for example).

A final feature of Isaiah's thought is his nationalism. He supported, perhaps orginated, the strong nationalistic movement that characterized the age of Hezekiah. Texts such as 7:17; 9:7; 11:14; 19:24-25; 27:12-13 promise an Israelite state as extensive as that described in the Pentateuch.

III

The Nature and Function of Prophetic Speech in Isaiah

R. **Alter**, *The Art of Hebrew Poetry* (New York: Basic Books, 1985)137-62; K. **Baltzer**, *Die Biographie der Propheten* (Neukirchen-Vluyn: Neukirchener Verlag, 1975); L. F. **Bitzer**, "The Rhetorical Situation," *Philosophy and Rhetoric* 1(1968)1-14 = *Rhetoric: A Tradition in Transition* (ed. W. R. Fisher; Ann Arbor: Michigan State University, 1974)247-60; M. **Buss**, "The Social Psychology of Prophecy," *Prophecy: Essays Presented to Georg Fohrer* (ed. J. A. Emerton; Berlin/New York: Walter de Gruyter, 1980)1-11; **Buss**, "An Anthropological Perspective Upon Prophetic Call Narratives," *Semeia* 21(1981)9-30; E. P. J. **Corbett**, *Classical Rhetoric for the Modern Student* (2d ed.; New York: Oxford University Press, 1971); H. **Donner**, *Israel unter den Völkern: Die Stellung der klassischen Propheten des 8. Jh. v. Chr. zur Aussenpolitik der Könige von Israel und Juda* (Leiden: E. J. Brill, 1964); G. **Fohrer**, "Remarks on Modern Interpretation of the Prophets," *JBL* 80(1961)309-19; D. N. **Freedman**, "Discourse on Prophetic Discourse," *The Quest for the Kingdom of God: Essays in Honor of George E. Mendenhall* (ed. H. B. Huffmon et al.; Winona Lake: Eisenbrauns, 1983)141-58; S. A. **Geller**, "Were the Prophets Poets?" *Prooftexts* 3(1983)211-21; Y. **Gitay**, "Reflections on the Study of the Prophetic Discourse: The Question of Isaiah I:2-20," *VT* 33(1983)207-21; **Gitay**, "Isaiah and His Audience," *Prooftexts* 3(1983)223-30; N. K. **Gottwald**, *All the Kingdoms of the Earth: Israelite Prophecy and International Relations in the Ancient Near East* (New York/London: Harper & Row, 1964); H. **Gunkel**, "The Israelite Prophecy from the Time of Amos," *Twentieth Century Theology in the Making* (ed. J. Pelikan; New York: Harper & Row, 1969)48-75; J. L. **Mays** and P. J. **Achtemeier** (eds.), *Interpreting the Prophets* (Philadelphia: Fortress Press, 1987); D. L. **Petersen**, *The Roles of Israel's Prophets* (Sheffield: JSOT Press, 1981); **Petersen**, "The Prophetic Process Reconsidered," *IR* 41(1984)13-19; **Petersen** (ed.), *Prophecy in Israel: Search for an Identity* (London/Philadelphia: SPCK/Fortress Press, 1987); R. B. Y. **Scott**, "The Literary Structure of Isaiah's Oracles," *Studies in Old Testament Prophecy Presented to Theodore H. Robinson* (ed. H. H. Rowley; Edinburgh: T. & T. Clark, 1957) 175-86; G. M. **Tucker**, "Prophetic Speech," *Int* 32(1978)31-45; **Tucker**, "From Oral Tradition to Prophetic Books," *The Hebrew Bible and Its Modern Interpreters* (ed. D. A. Knight and G. M. Tucker; Chico/Philadelphia: Scholars Press/Fortress Press, 1985)335-45; C. **Westermann**, *Basic Forms of Prophetic Speech* (Philadelphia: Westminster Press, 1967); R. R. **Wilson**, "Form-critical Investigation of the Prophetic Literature: The Present Situation," *SBL 1973 Seminar Papers* (ed. G. W. McRae; Cambridge: Society of Biblical Literature, 1973), vol. 1, 100-27.

The prophet Isaiah was an orator, a rhetorician who presented his insights through the medium of the spoken word. This sweeping generalization must be understood in the light of certain modifying factors. First, we probably possess only a selective representation of material either about or by the prophet. Isaiah's career and ministry were obviously more comprehensive than the material in First Isaiah would now indicate. Some features of his career, such as the significance of naming one of his sons Shear-jashub, were probably made clear by the prophet, but such clarifications have not survived. Thus we have no detailed, comprehensive portrait of the prophet.

Second, the written word may have been highly important in his career. References to the writing down of the prophet's words, apparently both for their present communication and as a record of the prophet's predictions for future verification, appear in 8:1, 16 and 30:8. As we shall note in several places throughout the study, speeches and proclamations by Isaiah were probably officially recorded and preserved; some may have been recorded by the prophet himself. Such a work as chapters 24–27 was the result of deliberate composition; it was intended as a written text for public use in a complex national celebration.

Third, in addition to proclamation, public actions in which Isaiah acted out his thoughts and convictions are illustrated in chapter 20 and by the naming of his children. While these appear unique, other similar, but unrecorded, actions may have been employed to draw public attention to the prophet's proclamation or to illustrate its content.

Because Isaiah was a preacher and spokesperson to his generation, his ministry may be understood in terms of general speech or rhetorical theory. The prophet's preaching ministry occurred within particular contexts, which may be called rhetorical situations. A rhetorical situation involves an audience, a speaker, a topic or issue of mutual concern, a shared world of meaning, and an occasion for communication. The speech or oral presentation is the means for the speaker to impress the audience, to entertain, or to influence the listeners. (In dramatic symbolic actions, the communication is more indirect and less verbal.) In a rhetorical situation where more than entertainment is involved, the speaker—in this case the prophet—tries to convince, console, convict, and/or persuade the audience. Often the speaker's goal is to create a disposition or attitude in the audience that will lead to a specific action or to the adoption and pursuit of a particular policy. That the audience and the speaker share a world of values and meaning makes communication possible. Isaiah drew on shared moral and political values and commitments as well as inherited theological beliefs and traditions (as we noted in chap. 2).

Like any good orator, Isaiah varied his material and approach according to the nature of the rhetorical situation and the inclination and character of the audience. At different times, he employed invective and denunciation, rebuke and reproof, satire and sarcasm, assurance and encouragement, poetry and prose, depending apparently on the needs of the situation, the goal at hand, and the response to be evoked.

Any speaker, to communicate effectively, must attract and engage the attention of the audience. Various devices relying on form or content or both serve to gain the attention of the hearers, to stimulate their minds and emotions, and to ensure an authoritative hearing.

The appeal and authority of a speaker are dependent on a number of circumstances. Obviously, if the speaker occupies a communal position or the status of authority by virtue of an office, the audience is apt to grant the speaker an inherent authority. Unfortunately, we have no direct knowledge of Isaiah's status or profession. Whether he was a priest or other cultic authority, court official, or member of the royal family remains unknown, but he clearly seems to have assumed and to have been granted authoritative standing both in the community at large and at the royal court in particular. (The autobiographical chapter 6 is not an explanation of the basis of his authority in a vocational call, but rather an explanation of the particular cast and content that his work and preaching acquired in the course of his prophetic ministry.)

One factor in the audience's concession of authority to a speaker is the power and impact of the spoken words themselves. (The manner of their delivery is, of course, a significant factor in this regard, but for the ancients we unfortunately possess only texts in written form.) Through-out this commentary, we will note how Isaiah's word choice, turn of phrase, and selection of similes and metaphors give his words an arresting effect. In addition to emotionally based appeals, Isaiah used rational argumentation to drive his point home more forcefully.

In the course of Isaiah's long career, the changing international scene created a number of different rhetorical situations for the prophet. His audience and the goal of the prophet's addresses varied with the changes in the rhetorical situation.

In the earliest phase of his career, to which chapters 1–5 belong, his audience was primarily the people at large, but with a focus on the inhabitants of Jerusalem. In the speeches from this period, Isaiah sought to convince his listeners that the recent catastrophic earthquake was the work of Yahweh and that the people's response to that event was not what Yahweh demanded (1:2-20). The earthquake had been, in fact, a "day of Yahweh" and thus a time of judgment exposing the futility of trusting in anything human (2:6-22). During this period, Isaiah cajoled the Jerusalem population, comparing its present status with that of an ideal past, promised that a divine purification of the city lay ahead, and called on his contemporaries to walk in the light of their beliefs about the Zion of the future (1:21–2:5). He castigated segments of Jerusalem's leadership and proclaimed a significant role for Zion in the future (3:1-15; 3:16–4:6). Finally, as the war clouds thickened over the eastern Mediterranean world, Isaiah addressed the recent turn of events, describing and interpreting the present and future trampling of the people of Yahweh, the vineyard of the Lord (5:1-30).

In the 730s, Isaiah confronted a different rhetorical situation. His audience came to consist primarily of the Davidic court and its supporters in Jerusalem (Isa. 7–12). With Syria and Israel allied against King Ahaz and the Davidic dynasty threatened with sedition from within and invasion from without, it was no time for social denunciations or discussion of general issues. Isaiah's rhetorical goal at the time was to encourage and to solidify the Davidic house in its policy of non-alignment with the Syrian-led anti-Assyrian coalition (7:2–8:20). The prophet held out hope and promise to the Davidic supporters and citizens of Jerusalem (8:21–9:7; 10:27d–12:6), declared a continuation of troubles for the Northern Kingdom (9:8–10:4), and offered an interpretation of Assyria's role in history (10:5-27c).

Immediately following Tiglath-pileser's third campaign against the western anti-Assyrian coalition came a short period of military respite in Syro-Palestine (731–729), thus presenting Isaiah with a new rhetorical situation. At the time, the Assyrians were fighting the Babylonians in southern Mesopotamia. The prophet offered commentary on this warfare in a speech describing Babylon's downfall (Isa. 13). With Israel recently humiliated, and for a moment unengaged in conspiratorial activity, Isaiah spoke a word of encouragement and consolation to the people, parodying the form of a memorial inscription (14:1-27).

Throughout the next two decades, Isaiah's preaching was almost totally conducted in an environment of anti-Assyrian activity. His preaching revolved around two foci—condemnation of the untimely revolts and encouragement of southern fidelity to the policy of non-participation amid the rampant anti-Assyrianism. Thus early in the reign of Shalmaneser (in 727), he denounced Moab (chaps. 15–16), Damascus, and Israel (chap. 17) for rebellion and the Ethiopians for stirring up trouble in the region (chap. 18). Later, he again denounced the northern rebels and Jerusalemite sympathizers (28:1-29; 29:1-24). Ephraim's involvement with and appeal to Egypt met with prophetic condemnation, but Jerusalem's non-involvement evoked encouragement and consolation (chaps. 30–31). Further deterioration in the north was greeted with both calls for lamenting and promises of a better tomorrow (chap. 32). Refugees from the north were greeted with enthusiasm (chap. 33).

Changes in the international situation in 720 and immediately following, characterized by Assyrian-Egyptian cooperation and by a momentary surge in Judah's self-esteem and international standing, led the prophet to deliver a speech of unparalleled ecumenism, probably because Assyria was one of the intended audiences (chap. 19).

Isaiah was confronted with a new rhetorical situation with the outbreak of renewed western anti-Assyrianism, Ashdod-led and encouraged by Babylonia (see chap. 39). Temporarily deprived of one of his traditional audiences, the royal court and the reigning monarch, Isaiah drastically altered the form of his proclamation, resorting to public symbolic actions (chap. 20). His denunciation of Babylon and its allies (chap. 21) and of the leadership of Jerusalem (chap. 22) reflect the failed revolt and the larger rhetorical situation.

Always sensitive to international affairs, Isaiah offered an analysis of Tyre's new status in 709, using the address to express Judean nationalism (chap. 23).

The latest material deriving from the prophet, chapters 24–27 and the prophetic proclamations in chapter 37, belongs to yet another rhetorical situation (705–701). The situation was again characterized by strong anti-Assyrianism and revolt, this time, however, condoned and encouraged by Isaiah.

In addressing this kaleidoscope of changing situations, Isaiah constructed speeches that frequently draw on a rich diversity of genres, images, and theological-historical traditions. For example, the long speech in 10:27*d*–12:6 contains materials and genres reflecting military contexts, coronation rituals, and cultic celebrations. Such a speech should be analyzed as an original whole and interpreted in the light of its rhetorical situation, rather than broken down into a multiplicity of genres and forms that have supposedly been linked together only secondarily by the work of a redactor.

Among Isaiah's speeches are instances of reported divine speech—that is, Isaiah, like most other prophets, quotes what is described as divine speech. The prophet frequently says, "Thus says Yahweh" or "Hear the word of Yahweh" and then gives what purports to be divine speech in which the Deity "speaks" in the first person. Sometimes the prophet apparently presents statements as divine speech without clearly labeling them as such and without noting where the divine speech begins and ends. For example, in 3:4 Isaiah seems to be quoting divine speech, but nothing indicates this except that the "I" in the text seems best understood as a divine self-reference. If 3:4 is presented as divine speech, where does it end? In 3:16-17, what is introduced and begins clearly as a divine word (v. 16) shifts quickly into speech *about* God (v. 17). The two verses, however, obviously belong together. Verse 16 states the case against the women of Jerusalem, and verse 17 pronounces the judgment. Such cases indicate that the prophet was conscious of presenting material as divine speech, but often took no special care to indicate the fact or to differentiate between divine and human address.

On the basis of a generous assignment of material to this category, about 20 percent of Isaiah 1–33 falls into the category of reported divine speech. The manner in which this divine speech is employed varies within the different speeches. The use, however, is sufficiently clear to exclude two rather common approaches to the prophetic use of divine address. First, Isaiah does not appear to have considered himself as simply an intermediary between the divine and human worlds, nor does he principally understand his function as that of a messenger of God. Second, there is little evidence in the text that Isaiah received such divine speech as auditory communications while in a state of ecstasy or that his task was to transmit the words received in such auditions. (Only Isaiah's account of his temple vision, and perhaps 8:11, point to any experience of ecstasy in the prophet's career.)

The interpretation of the reported divine speech in Isaiah should not be influenced by any preconceived theory of the nature of prophecy and the prophetic office in ancient Israel. Instead, such speech should be understood in terms of its rhetorical function within the individual passages. For example, the divine word in 1:2b-3, in which the prophet has Yahweh speak as the father of rebellious sons is a more powerful and empathy-creating form of expression than is a prophetic description of the situation in the third person. Nothing, however, would indicate that the prophet is here a messenger delivering some divine oracle. Similarly, the formulation of the material in 1:11-20 as a divine speech is rhetorically more engaging than third person statements, since it has the recipient of the sacrifices responding personally to the barrage of cultic expressions.

Obviously, speech formulated as direct divine address had a higher claim to authority than prophetic speech about the Deity in third person address. Thus the prophet could use direct divine speech to conclude a presentation (16:14), to introduce a speech authoritatively (30:1), to confront the audience with the necessity of decision (5:14b-15), and to authenticate the validity of a declaration (5:9b-10; 7:3-6; 22:15). At times, to provide a statement or conviction with special authority, divine speech was proclaimed in oath form (5:9-10; 14:24-25; 22:14), a more binding category than regular speech.

Finally, Isaiah, like all the prophets, spoke of ordinary, mundane, historical events and affairs in poetic, cosmic, hyperbolic, and mythological terms. This gives the material a highly evocative and suggestive quality. It occasionally makes recovery of the original referent an ominous task, but the resultant high level of generality and the transgression of historical boundaries have allowed Isaiah's prophecies to be appreciated and appropriated by readers over the centuries who had no connection with the original rhetorical situations.

IV

Isaiah's Preaching and the Isaianic Narratives

1. THE SUPERSCRIPTION (1:1)

H. M. I. **Gevaryahu**, "Biblical Colophons: A Source for the 'Biography' of Authors, Texts and Books," *SVT* 28(1975)42-59; H. L. **Ginsberg**, "Isaiah in the Light of History," *CJ* 22(1967)1-18; J. **Milgrom**, "Did Isaiah Prophesy During the Reign of Uzziah?" *VT* 14(1964)164-82; G. M. **Tucker**, "Prophetic Superscriptions and the Growth of a Canon," *Canon and Authority: Essays in Old Testament Religion and Theology* (ed. G. W. Coats and B. O. Long; Philadelphia: Fortress Press, 1977)56-70.

The opening verse of the book of Isaiah was obviously written not by the prophet himself but by the editors of the Isaianic materials. Whether composed originally to form the heading for what would today be called "First Isaiah" (Isaiah 1–33 or Isaiah 1–39 minus 34–35) or for the entire book of Isaiah cannot be determined with absolute certainty. The former appears more likely.

As the heading for the book, it shows many of the features found in the superscriptions of other prophetic books.

The title of the book: "The vision of Isaiah." The term *vision*, from the word *haza*, meaning "to see," is a bit unusual. The more frequent term in the headings for prophetic books is "the words" or "the word" of such and such a prophet. The use of the noun *vision* and the infinitive *to see*, however, would not have been out of keeping in describing the function of a prophet or the content of a prophetic message.

Information about the prophet. Isaiah is identified only in terms of his father—"the son of Amoz." Some of the prophetic books provide a little more, but still skimpy, information about the prophets. For example, Jeremiah is identified as "the son of Hilkiah, of the priests who were in Anathoth in the land of Benjamin" (Jer. 1:1), while Amos, whose father is not named, "was among the shepherds of Tekoa" (Amos 1:1). Lack of information about Isaiah could, but does not necessarily, mean that he and/or his father were well-known figures in the people's life, thus requiring no further description.

A statement about the contents: "which he saw concerning Judah and Jerusalem." The reference to both Judah and Jerusalem gives recognition to the fact that Jerusalem and Judah were actually two different political entities. Jerusalem was the special city-state of the Davidic family, perhaps even royal property. Judah was the old territorial state with roots going back to the older tribal structures. As we shall again note, the importance of the Judah-Jerusalem distinction is highly important for interpreting Isaiah's preaching.

Information about the dating of the contents: "in the days of Uzziah, Jotham, Ahaz, Hezekiah, kings of Judah." The chronological framework given for Isaiah's preaching is to be taken seriously; that is, the prophet was active during the reigns of four Judean kings. That Isaiah had already begun his career during the reign of Uzziah is assumed by II Chronicles 26:22, which reports that "the rest of the acts of Uzziah, from first to last, Isaiah the prophet the son of Amoz wrote."

The common tendency to view Isaiah's ministry only within the context of the reigns of Ahaz and Hezekiah and to deny that he functioned under Uzziah/Jotham is based on several wrong hypotheses. (1) The assumption that Isaiah 6 is a narrative about the inaugural call of Isaiah to become a prophet at the time of Uzziah's death means that all the materials attributable to the prophet, including chapters 1–5, must come from a time after Uzziah's reign. (2) The tendency to interpret Isaiah 1, and especially 1:7-9, in terms of a military catastrophe has forced scholars to relate this material to either the Syro-Ephraimitic crisis or to some invasion by the Assyrians. Once Isaiah 1 is moved to this later period—that is, to the reign of either Ahaz or Hezekiah, it becomes easy to transfer the rest of chapters 1–5 to the same periods. (3) The argument that the original Isaianic materials were subjected to extensive and radical redaction and editorial additions for decades or even centuries after Isaiah's time has created the impression that First Isaiah is a conglomerate anthology of literature from varied historical periods that must be reordered.

The present work is based on the assumptions that Isaiah was active during the reigns of the four Judean kings (Uzziah to Hezekiah mentioned in the superscription; that the material in the book has been ordered along general chronological lines (except for the collection of speeches in 28–33, which belongs to the early, rather than the final, years of Hezekiah, and the legends of 38–39, which report events related to the middle of Hezekiah's reign); and that few redactional additions have been made to Isaiah's speeches and addresses.

2. AN EARTHQUAKE AND ITS AFTERMATH
(1:2-20)

J. **Begrich**, "Die priesterliche Tora," *BZAW* 66(1936)63-88 = his *GS* (1964)232-60; W. T. **Classen**, "Linguistic Arguments and the Dating of Isaiah 1:4-9," *JNSL* 3(1974)1-18; E. W. **Davies**, *Prophecy and Ethics: Isaiah and the Ethical Traditions of Israel* (Sheffield, England: JSOT Press, 1981)40-64; F. C. **Fensham**, "Widow, Orphan, and the Poor in Ancient Near Eastern Legal and Wisdom Literature," *JNES* 21(1962) 129-39; G. **Fohrer**, "Jesaja 1 als Zusammenfassung der Verkündigung Jesajas," *ZAW* 74(1962)251-68; K. **Fullerton**, "The Rhythmical Analysis of Is 1, 10–20," *JBL* 38(1919)53-63; Y. **Gitay**, "Reflections on the Study of the Prophetic Discourse: The Question of Isaiah I 2–20," *VT* 33(1983)207-21;E. **Hammershaimb**, "On the Ethics of the Old Testament Prophets," *SVT* 7(1960)75-101 = his *Some Aspects of Old Testament Prophecy from Isaiah to Malachi* (Copenhagen: Rosenkilde og Bagger, 1966)63-90; H. B. **Huffmon**, "The Covenant Lawsuit in the Prophets," *JBL* 78(1959)285-95; J. **Jensen**, *The Use of tora by Isaiah: His Debate with the Wisdom Tradition* (Washington: Catholic Biblical Association, 1973); D. R. **Jones**, "Expositions of Isaiah 1," *SJT* 17(1964)463-77; 18(1965)457-71; 19(1966)319-27; I. **von Loewenclau**, "Zur

Auslegung von Jesaja 1, 2-3," *EvTh* 26(1966)294-308; A. **Mattioli**, "Due schemi letterari negli oracoli d'introduzione al libro d'Isaia: Is. 1, 1-31," *RivB* 14(1966)345-64; J. **Milgrom**, "Concerning Jeremiah's Repudiation of Sacrifice," *ZAW* 89(1977)273-75 = his *Studies in Cultic Theology and Terminology* (Leiden, Holland: E. J. Brill, 1983)119-21; S. **Niditch**, "The Composition of Isaiah 1," *Bib* 61(1980)509-29; L. G. **Rignell**, "Isaiah Chapter I: Some Exegetical Remarks with Special Reference to the Relationship Between the Text and the Book of Deuteronomy," *ST* 11(1957)140-58; J. J. M. **Roberts**, "Form, Syntax and Redaction in Isaiah 1:2-20," *PSB* 3(1982)293-306; J. **Schoneveld**, "Jesaia I 18-20," *VT* 13(1963)342-44; N. A. **van Uchelen**," Isaiah I 9—Text and Context," *OTS* 21(1981)154-63; J. T. **Willis**, "The First Pericope in the Book of Isaiah," *VT* 34(1984)63-77; **Willis**, "An Important Passage for Determining the Historical Setting of a Prophetic Oracle—Isaiah 1.7-8," *ST* 39(1985) 151-69.

The opening speech of Isaiah has as its background the devastating earthquake that struck Palestine during Uzziah's reign (Amos 1:1; Zech. 14:5) and the cultic activities that were performed in the Jerusalem temple celebrating the city's survival. Isaiah used the occasion to accuse the people of a lack of understanding and of misplaced devotion and to appeal to his audience for fidelity to Yahweh, for redirection of its devotion, for aid to the poor and suffering, and for a proper understanding of the correlation between obedience and reward. In interpreting the catastrophe that had wreaked havoc in the land, the prophet viewed the event as God's judgment on the people.

In the speech, one finds the following elements:

(1) An accusation addressed to the people in an indirect form (2-3)
(2) Direct address, confronting the people with their condition (4-9)
(3) Divine instruction and divine admonition (10-17)
(4) A divine invitation to proper understanding (18-20)

Isaiah 1:2-3

The speech opens not with a direct address to the people, but with an appeal to the heavens and earth to give attention. The reason for such an approach was probably to attract a favorable initial response. The quotation of the divine oracle, spoken as a lamenting father about his wayward sons, would have evoked a sympathetic ear by referring to an issue of universal interest—parental problems with children. "Heavens" and "earth" are addressed, not because they play any special role, but because they represent disinterested and ever-present phenomena (for other similar addresses to heavens and earth, see Deut. 32:1; Mic. 6:1-2; Ps. 50:4). Indirect address allows the audience to listen in, as if it were a third party, only subsequently to become the object of accusation in the application.

According to Deuteronomy 21:18-21, an obstinate son, such as Isaiah describes, could be turned over to a city's elders and stoned, a law probably intended more to instill sibling obedience than to be applied in actuality.

The people are compared unfavorably to animals; therefore, Isaiah has Yahweh argue on the principle "if the lesser (in this case the dumber), then how much more the greater (the smarter)." The dumb ox knows its owner's stable, and the ass knows the master's crib—they are smart enough to show up for food and thus acknowledge their dependence—but Yahweh's children are without such discipline or learning. Isaiah's entire argument in this section was based on an appeal to common sense and to natural phenomena. At the same time, the use of the parent-child example was a way of drawing on a universal and emotional relationship.

Isaiah 1:4-9

In verse 4, the prophet moves toward direct second-person confrontation with his audience, but no second person verbs appear until verse 5 in the Hebrew text. Verse 4, no longer spoken as a divine oracle, is introduced by an attention getting particle (*hoy*), which here functions somewhat like our "hey." Then follow four descriptive phrases and three plural verbal forms that, although unsignified grammatically, are to be read together.

> Hey, O sinful nation,
>> people weighed-down with iniquity,
>>> wickedly acting offspring,
>>>> corruptly behaving children,
>> who have forsaken Yahweh,
>>> who have deserted the Holy One of Israel,
>>> who have turned back.

After this seven-fold stacatto sequence of epithets, which the audience probably increasingly recognized as applying to themselves even without a single second-person pronoun or verbal form, Isaiah shifts to direct address in verse 5. The people's miserable plight is described, first in terms of "medical diagnosis" (drawing on the condition of a severely punished son who has been harshly beaten) and, second, in terms of the direct consequences of the earthquake.

5. Would you continue to be beaten,
     would you go on being obstinate?
   The whole head is suffering,
     and the whole heart is hurting;
6. from the sole of the foot to (the top of) the head,
     there is no health in it:
   Bruises and blows and fresh wounds;
   they are neither squeezed out nor bandaged up,
     nor soothed with oil.
7. Your country is ransacked,
     your cities burned with fire;
   in your very presence your farmland
     is being devoured by trespassers;
   and ransacked like something scavenged by trespassers.
8. And daughter–Zion is left like a lean-to in a vineyard,
     a shed in a cucumber patch,
       like a city under surveillance.
9. If Yahweh of hosts had not left us a few survivors
     we would have been like Sodom and become like Gomorrah!

                                                    Isaiah 1:5-9

This section (vv. 4-9), unlike what precedes and follows, is not given as an oracle of Yahweh but as the prophet's description of his people's condition. One would have to assume that the prophet expected his hearers to connect his characterization of the people (v. 4) with their present condition, although verses 5-9 are intended as much to stress the desperation of the situation as to create a sense of guilt. The descriptions and metaphors are emotion-filled and, in verse 9, the prophet empathizes with his listeners and places himself among the suffering survivors of the calamity.

A few particulars require comment. The sores and wounds referred to in verses 5-6a can be seen as referring to the injuries people received in the earthquake but interpreted in terms of a parental beating. Verses 7-8 depict the earthquake-devastated area. The countryside has been turned topsy-turvy; evidence of conflagration abounds; looters plunder; and the whole land looks like it has been ransacked by roving outsiders (v. 7; on *zar*, see Exod. 29:33; 30:33). Zion has survived but sits isolated amid the surrounding countryside (v. 8).

The comparison of the situation with that of Sodom and Gomorrah (Gen. 19) is here dependent only on the analogy of the two great natural disasters. Deuteronomy 29:22-23 and 32:23-33, like Isaiah 1:5-9, join together references about sickness, afflictions, various other disasters, and statements about Sodom and Gomorrah. To speak of Sodom and Gomorrah was to speak of the most disastrous of calamities.

Isaiah 1:10-17

In verse 10, Isaiah identifies his audience—both the leaders and the people—with the inhabitants of ancient Sodom and Gomorrah. His oratorical artistry can be seen in the juxtaposition of verses 9 and 10 and their use of the Sodom and Gomorrah motif. In verse 9, the prophet uses these two cities to illustrate the state of his audience and to allow the people to feel momentarily how bad off they are, how desperate their condition is, and how pitifully they stand there, in need of consolation, solace, and sympathy. In verse 10, he immediately pulls that protective blanket from the hearers and identifies them with the residents of ancient Sodom and Gomorrah, who everyone in his audience would have believed got what they deserved!

The audience is now called to hear a message from God, which is then "quoted" in verses 11-17. Two phrases, presumably employed synonymously, are used to denote what God says—"the word of Yahweh" and "the torah of our God." *Torah* and *word* are identified, suggesting that *torah* may have had a more inclusive reference than our word *law*, which is usually used to translate *torah* (see below on 8:16). The torah was especially associated with the priests and their rulings concerning sacrifices, purity, and uncleanness given in the name of God (see Hag. 2:11-13; Deut. 33:8-10; Lev. 10:8-11). Perhaps Isaiah is here imitating the priestly practice of giving verdicts, rulings, and instruction in the name of the Deity. (Could Isaiah himself have had priestly lineage or even been a priest?) What follows in verses 11-15 is a series of rulings about the people's cultic worship and sacrificial services. Thus Isaiah is "giving torah" like the priests, but his torah is a series of rulings that is critical of the cultic practices he presently observed being performed.

A broad spectrum of cultic events and occasions, as well as a variety of sacrifices, is referred to in this section and all are denounced. Among the sacrifices noted are the *zebah* (v. 11*a*), the `*oloth* (v. 11*b*), and the *minhah* (v. 13*a*). Other terms associated with the disposition of animal offerings are *fat* (which was burned on the altar), *blood* (ritually splattered on the altar), and *incense* (or perhaps more broadly, the sacrificial odors).

Other activities connected with worship are prayer and the associated spreading of the hands (v. 15). The last part of verse 13, which the RSV translates as "iniquity and solemn assembly," should probably be read and translated "fasting (so the Greek texts) and time of ritual preparation" (see II Kings 10:20; Deut. 16:8; Lev. 23:36; Num. 29:35). In ancient times, rituals and routines were used to mark the move from normal time (everyday life) across the boundary to sacred time (worship occasions), and these included such things as fasting, washing one's clothes, and abstinence from sex before attending worship (see Exod. 19:10-15). This seems to be what is referred to in the last part of verse 13. Such a reading makes better sense of the text than "iniquity and solemn assembly"; all references in verses 12-15 can then be seen as related to some aspect of worship. No one would ever have argued that iniquity and solemn assembly go together!

The text also piles up terms denoting times and occasions of worship. "New moon," "sabbath," "called assemblies," "time of preparation," "new moons," and "appointed feasts." All are depicted, like the other acts of worship noted, as wearisome and burdensome to God.

This text (vv. 11-15) is often read as if Isaiah were advocating a total repudiation of cultic worship. Verse 16 is then read as the demands of true devotion to God in lieu of temple worship. Such conclusions, however, are unwarranted by the text.

First of all, the condemned sacrifices all fall into the category of voluntary sacrifices, that is, those offered on the initiative of the worshipers (these are discussed in Leviticus 1–3). The *zebah* (or *zebah shelamim*) was a well-being offering (translated as "peace offering" in the RSV), made when things were going well. These offerings were primarily eaten by the donors and were part of celebrative occasions involving conspicuous consumption at cultic meals (see Lev. 3; 7:11-18). The `*oloth*, or burnt offerings, were totally burned on the altar and were the means of expressing extravagance in one's devotion or thanksgiving (see Lev. 1; 6:9-13). *Minhah* was a voluntary cereal offering (see Lev. 2; 6:14-18). Isaiah thus makes no reference to mandatory animal offerings that were demanded by God. The *hatta'* ("sin offering" RSV), or purgation offering (Lev. 4; 6:24-30), and the *'asham* ("guilt offering" RSV), or reparation offering, were required by God for purging the temple sancta of the contamination of sins and impurities and for making reparation to God for transgression on divine sancta. Isaiah certainly does not declare these two mandatory sacrifices abhorrent to God; in fact, he does not mention them.

Second, Isaiah here, as the prophets did frequently, engages in overstatement and exaggeration in order to make a point. The Judeans and Jerusalemites apparently were responding in only one way to their survival of the earthquake—by an outpouring of worship and sacrifice in thanksgiving to and celebration before God. Maybe they understood their good fortune as special divine protection rather than the earthquake as divine judgment. Isaiah protested against this, having Yahweh declare their voluntary religious rituals and festivals excessive, unnecessary, and representative of misplaced devotion.

Following the divine verdict (vv. 11-15), one finds a series of divine admonitions or commands (vv. 16-17). Verses 16-17 contain nine imperatives; the tenth appears in verses 18-20, which contain the third quotation of God employed by the prophet in this speech.

The first two demands call for changes in the hearers: "wash yourselves, make yourselves clean." This call for personal cleansing follows immediately on the description of the people as having their hands full of blood (v. 15; note how the prophet had earlier used the terms *hands*, in v. 12*b* ["who requires this from your hand"] and *blood* in 11*c*). *Blood*, in the last line of verse 15, a plural form, generally refers to violence. Bloody hands require cleansing. Further, biblical texts frequently describe sin as a pollutant or contaminant, as something dirty that stains and soils (note the cleansing and purging terminology in Psalm 51). If sin is pollution, then movement away from sin and wrongdoing can be expressed in terms of washing and cleansing. Probably, rituals in the temple in which innocence was claimed by a worshiper or declared by a priest could involve bathing or washing (see Ps. 26:6-7).

It is uncertain whether the prophet, in having God admonish the audience to "remove the evil of your doings from before my eyes," was simply reiterating what was said previously or was adding a new dimension. Was "the evil of your doings" a reference to the abundance of the people's religious services and sacrifices?

The couplet—"cease to do evil, learn to do good"—gives two sides of the same coin. If the choice of words was deliberate and expressive of some anthropological judgment, then this couplet would imply that doing evil is understood as almost a natural tendency, whereas to do the good is something that must be learned, something acquired.

The final four admonitions—"seek justice, relieve oppression, defend the fatherless, plead for the widow"—appear as the ideals of ethical behavior throughout the ancient Near East and in slightly varying forms are embodied in diverse types of literature from the area. God himself (see Ps. 68:5) and the Hebrew kings especially (Ps. 72:4, 12-14) were responsible for acting on such ideals. To seek justice was probably a way of saying "try to establish in society the orders of life that should properly exist" (which, of course, presupposes a theological view of right order). To relieve oppression meant to act to correct cases of misjustice. The last couplet was a way of calling society to defend its powerless members. The fatherless (perhaps children of illegitimate and irregular parentage) had no claim to a heritage or status. The widow had no right of inheritance (see Num. 27:8-11, where the widow is not even mentioned as a possible inheritor) nor frequently any male to defend her and to intervene on her behalf in a patriarchal and male-dominated culture.

Although Isaiah does not repudiate all cultic worship and animal offerings in this text, he does confront his contemporaries with ethical and moral demands. Perhaps under the circumstances produced by the earthquake, in which homes had been ruined, lives lost, and possessions destroyed, Isaiah felt that the hour was at hand to call for the old charitable and legal ideals—a just order in society, and a helping, defending hand for the powerless at the bottom levels of humanity. The times did not call for sacrifice but social service, not for prayer but repentance. If the devastating earthquake was God's way of dealing with his people, his way of punishing a stubborn, rebellious child, then he certainly was not asking the community to continue as it had, except for the addition of a few more religious services.

Isaiah 1:18-20

The final section of the speech (vv. 18-20) contains the third quotation of divine address and extends to the audience an invitation and a promise.

18 "Come now, let's get things straight," says Yahweh,
   "if your sins are as scarlet, they can be as white as snow;
   if they are as red as crimson, they can be as wool.
19 If you acquiesce and take heed, the good of the land you can eat:
20 but if you disagree and are obstinate, you can be eaten by the sword," because the mouth of Yahweh has spoken.

The meaning of these verses has been widely debated. Some interpret lines two and three of verse 18 as questions: "If your sins are as scarlet, shall they become white like snow?" Others take the statements as sarcastic: "Though your sins are as scarlet, they can be (you know how to make yourselves) white as snow!" Our interpretation is based on the assumptions that this text is an appeal for change and an offer of forgiveness; that it reflects a use of language related, perhaps, to the making of agreements, if not actual court terminology (see Lev. 17:19); and that one should read the second and third lines of verse 18 as signifying something like, "if you admit (recognize) your sins are. . . ." Verse 19 promises that if the people admit they are sinners and take appropriate action (v. 16) then life in the land will return to normal. Verse 20 counterpoises the opposite proposition: If the people do not agree, then not only will they not eat the good of the land, but also they shall themselves be eaten up.

3. JERUSALEM: PAST, PRESENT, AND FUTURE (1:21–2:5)

P. R. **Ackroyd**, "A Note on Isaiah 2:1," *ZAW* 75(1963)320-21; E. **Cannawurf**, "The Authenticity of Micah IV 1-4," *VT* 13(1963)26-33; H. **Cazelles**, "Qui aurait visé, à l'origine, Isaïe II 2-5?" *VT* 30(1980)409-20; R. J. **Clifford**, *The Cosmic Mountain in Canaan and the Old Testament* (Cambridge, Mass.: Harvard University Press, 1972); M. **Dahood**, "'Weaker than Water': Comparative beth in Isaiah," *Bib* 59(1978)91-92; E. W. **Davies**, *Prophecy and Ethics: Isaiah and the Ethical Tradition of Israel* (Sheffield, England: JSOT Press, 1981)90-112; F. E. **Diest**, "Notes on the Structure of Isa. 2:2-22," *ThEv* 10/2-3(1977)1-6; H. **Junker**, "Sancta Civitas Jerusalem Nova: Eine formkritische und überlieferungsgeschichtliche Studie zu Is. 2," *Ekklesia* (Festschrift M. Wehr; ed. H. Gross; Trier: Paulinus Verlag, 1962) 17-33; J. D. **Levenson**, *Sinai and Zion: An Entry into the Jewish Bible* (Minneapolis: Winston Press, 1985); L. M. **von Pakozdy**, "Jes. 2:2ff.: Geschichte–Utopie–Verkündigung," *Vom Herrengeheimnis der Wahrheit* (Festschrift H. Vogel; Berlin: Walter de Gruyter, 1962)416-26; J. **Schreiner**, *Sion-Jerusalem. Jahwes Königssitz. Theologie der*

heilgen Stadt im Alten Testament (Munich: Kösel Verlag, 1963);
F. **Stolz**, *Strukturen und Figuren im Kult von Jerusalem* (Berlin:
Alfred Töpelmann, 1970); B. **Wiklander**, *Prophecy as Litera-
ture: A Text-linguistic and Rhetorical Approach to Isaiah 2–4*
(Malmo: CWK Gleerup, 1984); H. **Wildberger**, "Die Völker-
wallfahrt zum Zion: Jes. II 1-5," *VT* 7(1957)62-81; J. T. **Willis**,
"Lament Reversed—Isaiah 1, 21ff.," *ZAW* 98(1986)236-48.

The speech that begins in Isaiah 1:21 and extends to 2:5
revolves around the subject and status of Zion. The prophet
denounces the present ruling class in the city, reminding the
people of Zion's previous character and calling on them to
live and act in the light of the claims made about the city in its
own confession of faith.

Although 2:1 duplicates many of the features of a
superscription, it is best understood as an editorial gloss
added to the text at some point in transmission. Since Isaiah
2:2-4 also appears as Micah 4:1-3, the gloss was added in
Isaiah to claim the passage as an Isaianic composition. As we
shall note, when we discuss this passage below, Isaiah 2:2-4
and Micah 4:1-3 are best understood as an older text
expressive of beliefs held about Jerusalem/Zion, which both
prophets incorporated into their preaching.

The speech may be divided into the following sections:

(1) An accusation against present conditions in the light of
the city's past (1:21-23)
(2) The proclamation of coming divine judgment to purify
the city (1:24-31)
(3) A description of the ideal Zion and a call for the people
to live in the light of this vision (2:2-5)

Isaiah 1:21-23

The speech opens with the prophet drawing a contrast
between the Zion of the present and the Zion of the past. The
opening ("how she has become a whore") and closing ("but
now murderers") phrases of the verse describe the prophet's
evaluation of present conditions. In between appear a title or
slogan ("faithful city") and two descriptions of the old ideal,
"she was filled with justice: righteousness lodged in her."

Justice and righteousness refer to proper order in society. Both negative assessments represent harsh, emotion laden accusations. To call the city a whore was to call into question the town's fidelity, honesty, and devotion. To make this charge against a woman, that she had become a harlot, could have been a way to initiate legal proceedings (see Gen. 38:24). To label one a murderer would have had the same effect in ancient as in modern societies. Speaking of murderers as now lodging in Jerusalem may have been Isaiah's way of alluding to the assassinations of three previous rulers of Jerusalem. Athaliah was killed in a coup headed by the high priest and aided by royal mercenaries (II Kings 11:1-16). King Jehoash was killed by two of his officials (II Kings 12:20-21), and his son Amaziah was the object of a general conspiracy hatched in Jerusalem but was killed by the conspirators in Lachish, where he had tried to find refuge (II Kings 14:19-21). Given Isaiah's high regard for the monarchy and his devotion to the house of David, the prophet probably looked with horror on such acts of regicide.

With verse 22, Isaiah turns to direct address. The city's fine qualities, like silver and wine (the rare Hebrew term *sabe´* probably referred to an unusual, choice beverage), have become adulterated, bearing only a resemblance to the real thing. The leaders, responsible for the order of society, have become contumacious embodiments of disorder, the associates of thieves. They are described as not only passively taking bribes, but also as actually running after pay-offs (v. 23*a-b*). Such overstatements, which exaggerate the actuality, were intended to drive home the point. The leaders make no effort to measure up to social ideals to defend the fatherless and plead for the widow (v. 23*c*).

Behind such charges against the city fathers ("the princes" in the RSV) may have lain a legal system in which those who were in need of legal adjudication paid those who functioned as judges or as adjudicators. The impovished—the fatherless and the widows—who could not afford such legal expenses were being ignored and their cases left unheard. At least during much of Uzziah and Jotham's reign, Judean society must have been reasonably economically well-off. The city's leaders were accused by Isaiah of catering to those who could pay to the disregard of those who could not.

Isaiah 1:24-31

Isaiah's proclamation of coming judgment on and re-vamping of the city and its legal authorities is two-pronged: He pronounces first a divine oracle of judgment (vv. 24-26), then his own description of the process (vv. 27-31).

In his introduction to the divine oracle, the prophet piles up a series of titles and names for the Deity: "the Lord, Yahweh of hosts, the Mighty One of Israel" (v. 24*b*). At least the last two were probably titles associated with Yahweh in military contexts. The last part of verse 24 may, in fact, have been an old Yahweh saying that functioned as a military motto or pre-battle acclamation: "Take note, I will get satisfaction from my adversaries, and I will take vengeance on my enemies." Now, however, the enemy is the city and its leading citizens.

The divine action against the city involves a reversal of the immediate past and a return to the better conditions of by-gone days. Jerusalem will undergo a time of purification (v. 25), and judges and counselors as of old will be returned (v. 26*a*). Whether "as of old" refers only to some ideal time in the past or actually alludes to some particular legal changes cannot be determined. When the situation "as at the first" changed is not alluded to. Two possibilities suggest themselves. According to II Chronicles 19:5-11, Jehoshaphat instituted radical legal reforms involving judicial functions in the city of Jerusalem. Had this system gone bad, or had changes been made that perverted it? Under more recent rule—Athaliah, Jehoash, and Amaziah—government officials apparently had become much more powerful in Judean affairs, sometimes asserting their power in assassinations. Under Uzziah, with the king's quarantine, this tendency may have continued, if not accelerated.

At any rate, Isaiah has Yahweh declare that after the purification the city will be able to reassume its old names: "city of righteousness," "faithful town" (v. 26*b*).

In verses 27-31, the prophet seems to reaffirm in different terminology, and not as a divine oracle, the theme and the content of verses 24-26 with a slightly different emphasis. In verses 27-31, the judgment seems to be directed more against certain groups in the city than against the city as a whole (see

v. 25). Verse 27 seems to envision a coming realignment of Zion and drastic change among its people, while verse 28 affirms that rebels, sinners, and those forsaking God will be dealt with severely.

Verse 29 declares that the citizens of Jerusalem shall be ashamed of and embarrassed at the town's officials and leaders, here described as oak trees and gardens (metaphors for males and females), in whom they have delighted and whom they have chosen to hold high position and to rule over them. In their disillusionment with the current Jerusalem leadership, the people are described as becoming like an oak that has lost its leaves or a garden without water (v. 30). That is, the people (or the leaders?) will lose their attractiveness and thus cease to be objects of adulation and respect. The strong (the leaders, or a particular leader?) will become kindling and the work of the strong will be a spark; both the strong and their work will be destroyed as in an unquenchable conflagration (v. 31).

Isaiah 2:2-5

In 2:2-5, Isaiah recites an old confession, probably part of a Zion psalm, regarding the role of the ideal Zion of the future and then challenges his audience to walk in the light of that vision. The parallel version of this text in Micah 4:1-4 is almost identical, although the Micah version contains a verse not found in Isaiah. (Mic. 4:4 may be a "rural addition" to express an aspect of the peasant's idealized future!). Rather than seeing one prophet's use of this text as dependent on the other or both as some later redactional addition, the most logical treatment is to see both prophets as using an older text that was part of Jerusalem's theological view of the city's future role.

The poem is dependent on the widespread ancient Near Eastern myth of the cosmic mountain at the center of the world (see above, chap. 2). The following elements are found in this rendition of Zion as the cosmic mountain. (1) The significance of Zion will be manifest in that the temple mount will become the highest of the mountains, elevated above the surrounding hills. (2) Zion will be the destination of a great pilgrimage of the nations and peoples of the world.

(3) The goal of such a pilgrimage will be to learn of God's will in order to live according to that will. (4) Out of Zion shall go forth the torah and the word of Yahweh (see 1:10). (5) Yahweh (through the Davidic king?) will function as the judge among nations and arbitrate international disputes. (6) Military implements, designed to destroy life, will be refashioned into agricultural tools, designed to sustain life, and war will be neither practiced nor studied any more.

Isaiah nowhere builds a case for accepting this mythology of Zion's future status and role. Presumably he could assume a familiarity on the part of his audience. He simply quotes the depiction of the ideal Zion and concludes by challenging his audience to walk in the light of Yahweh and thus live in the light of the vision's judgment on the present and in hopes of its ultimate realization.

4. YAHWEH HAD A DAY (2:6-22)

J. **Blenkinsopp**, "Fragments of Ancient Exegesis in an Isaian Poem (Jes 2:6-22)," *ZAW* 93(1981)51-62; K. J. **Cathcart**, "Kingship and the 'Day of YHWH' In Isaiah 2:6-22," *Hermathena* 125(1978)48-59; R. **Davidson**, "The Interpretation of Isaiah II:6ff.," *VT* 16(1966)1-7; A. J. **Everson**, "The Days of Yahweh," *JBL* 93(1974)329-37; J. **Gray**, "The Day of Yahweh in Cultic Experience and Eschatological Prospect," *SEA* 39(1974)12-16; Y. **Hoffmann**, "The Day of the Lord as a Concept and a Term in the Prophetic Literature," *ZAW* 93(1981)37-50; J. **Milgrom**, "Did Isaiah Prophesy During the Reign of Uzziah?" *VT* 14(1964)164-82; G. **von Rad**, "The Origin of the Concept of the Day of Yahweh," *JSS* 4(1959)97-108; K. **Seybold**, "Die anthropologischen Beiträge aus Jesaja 2," *ZTK* 74(1977)401-15; M. **Weiss**, "The Origin of the 'Day of the Lord'—Reconsidered," *HUCA* 37(1966)29-72.

One of the most problematic texts in the entire book of Isaiah, this passage bristles with both translational and interpretive difficulties. The text should be interpreted as describing a past catastrophic day of Yahweh, namely the earthquake under Uzziah, rather than as predicting a future day of destruction. The speech is more of a theological discourse on the frailty of humanity than a prediction about the future. Its central thrust is to argue that the earthquake was Yahweh's work and that when Yahweh acts, as in the earthquake disaster, all human efforts pale in significance.

Because the text presents unusual textual problems, and one's translation depends so much on one's overall view of the passage, we offer a translation before analyzing the text's structure and content.

6. Surely, you [Yahweh] have left unattended your people, the house of Jacob,
   even though they were filled with diviners from the east,
      and foretellers like the Philistines,
      and with the children of foreigners they slapped hands;
7. even though his [Jacob's] land was filled with silver and gold,
      and there was no limit to his treasures;
   even though his land was filled with horses,
      and there was no limit to his chariots;
8. even though his land was filled with images—
      to the work of his hands he would bow down,
      to what his fingers had fashioned—
9. yet the human race was brought low
      and humanity was humbled,
         and there was no relief for them.
10. "Go into the rock [caverns] and burrow in the ground,
      from before the terror of Yahweh, and from the
      awesomeness of his might."
11. The arrogant look of mankind was humbled,
      and brought low was human pride;
         and only Yahweh was exalted on that day.
12. Surely Yahweh of hosts had a day,
      against all the proud and arrogant,
      and against everything high and low,
13.   and against all the cedars of Lebanon, the tall and lofty,
      and against all the oaks of Bashan,
14.   and against all the high mountains,
      and against all the lofty hills,
15.   and against every high defense tower,
      and against every fortified wall,
16.   and against all the ships of Tarshish,
      and against all the cherished seacraft;

17. then the arrogance of mankind was humbled,
    and human pride was brought low,
    and only Yahweh was exalted on that day.
18. For the images are totally useless,
19. when people enter the caverns of the rocks and the caves of the
    ground,
    from before the terror of Yahweh, and from the awesomeness
    of his might,
    when he stands up to shake the earth.
20. On that day, humans cast aside their silver images and their
    gold images—
    which they make for themselves to bow down to—
    to the beetles and the bats:
21. When they enter the fissures of the rocks and the clefts of the
    cliffs,
    from before the terror of Yahweh, and from the awesomeness
    of his might,
    when he stands up to shake the earth.
22. Call it quits with humanity,
    the one with breath in its nostrils;
    for of what value is it?

This translation is based on a text that has been amended in two places. The first part of verse 6b reads "even though they were filled from the east." Probably *qosemim* ("diviners") was omitted before the similar looking word *miqqedem* ("from the east"). The last phrase in verse 9 actually reads "and do not raise them up" (or "forgive them").

The following appears to be the structure of the passage:

(1) An introductory comment addressed to Yahweh (6a)
(2) A statement demonstrating that human planning means nothing before the awesome power of Yahweh (6b-11).
(3) A description of the recent earthquake as the day of Yahweh (12-17)
(4) A general declaration of the futility of human effort before Yahweh's power (18-21)
(5) An appeal to give up confidence in humans and human achievement (22)

This text, with its intricate, but artistic, repetition, draws upon the destructiveness of the earthquake that shook

Palestine during Uzziah's reign to expound anthropological considerations. It presupposes the general prosperity of the area, which characterized the reigns of Uzziah/Jotham and Jeroboam II.

Isaiah 2:6a

The speech opens with the prophet making what appears to be an accusation or complaint against God. The divine is charged with "neglect" for his own people. The verb that we have translated "left unattended" is used with reference to letting land lie fallow during a sabbatical year (see Exod. 23:11). Thus the meaning is not that Yahweh has abandoned, forsaken, or rejected his people, he simply did not look after and care for them. When land was left fallow, fields were not farmed or planted, and vineyards were not pruned, but the land was not forsaken; it merely went for a period without care and cultivation.

The form and content of this opening remark would have accomplished two things. By expressing the feeling that undeserved disaster had struck, the statement would have immediately grasped the hearers' attention. The opening statement would have led the audience to expect an ensuing complaint against the Deity. Thus Isaiah had his audience poised to hear a further address, but not for the one he was about to give.

Isaiah 2:6b-11

Verses 6b-8 describe the conditions in the land, which would have led one to expect a good future. None of these should be taken as items that Isaiah condemns in and of themselves. The land was adequately supplied with prognosticators (6b-c). The last line of this verse remains obscure. Presumably "to slap hands," or whatever is signified, meant something like "making agreements"—our shaking hands. Thus Isaiah seems to be saying that international relationships were in good order, or at least certain relationships were intact.

Neither economic wealth nor military power nor religious preparedness meant anything when disaster struck (vv. 7-8).

(The images or religious paraphernalia do not seem here to be referred to in any special pejorative manner.) The earthquake's destruction brought low any sense of human security. In the midst of the earth's tremors, neither images nor war machines nor wealth made a difference (v. 9). In verse 10, the prophet appears to be quoting the cries of distress and calls to seek shelter that greeted the disaster. But on the day of destruction, only Yahweh and his power were exalted (v. 11). The earthquake and its destruction had not occurred because Yahweh had left the people unattended; it was his doing.

Isaiah 2:12-17

The destructive power of the earthquake is described in verses 12-17. Against the earthquake's forces, nothing, no matter how lofty or fortified, remained secure. Even the prized naval forces and cargo ships in the port of Elath were demolished, probably by the tidal waves that accompanied the quake (see II Chron. 26:9-10; 27:4; II Kings 14:22).

Isaiah 2:18-21

Verses 18-21 present Isaiah's theological evaluation of how humanity stands when confronted with the raw power of divine action. Even one's religious symbols and cultic furniture are useless when Yahweh stands up to shake the earth.

Isaiah 2:22

The speech concludes with Isaiah's appeal to his audience: Give up your trust and faith in humanity and its achievements.

5. A SOCIETY TOPSY-TURVY (3:1-15)

J. A. **Dearman**, *Property Rights in the Eighth-Century Prophets: The Conflict and Its Background* (dissertation, Emory University, 1981); M. **DeRoche**, "Yahweh's *rib* Against Israel: A

Reassessment of the So-called 'Prophetic Lawsuit' in the Preexilic Prophets," *JBL* 102(1983)563-74; H. **Gamoran**, "The Biblical La   Against Loans on Interest," *JNES* 30(1971)127-34; R. **Gnuse**, *You Shall Not Steal: Community and Property in the Biblical Tradition* (Maryknoll: Orbis Books, 1985); W. L. **Holladay**, "Isa. III 10–11: An Archaic Wisdom Passage," *VT* 18(1968)481-87; R. P. **Maloney**, "Usury and Restrictions on Interest–Taking in the Ancient Near East," *CBQ* 36(1974)1-20; E. **Neufeld**, "The Prohibitions Against Loans at Interest in Ancient Hebrew Laws," *HUCA* 26(1955)355-412; H. M. **Weil**, "Exégèse d'Isaïe III, 1-15," *RB* 49(1940)76-85.

In this speech, Isaiah draws upon the imagery and actions of a children's game—"playing ruler"—and uses them to describe the anarchic conditions that would result if children actually became the people's rulers. The conditions of such a make-believe world, the imagined reality, are then claimed to be the real conditions existing at the time in Judean and Jerusalemite society, the actual reality. The prophet has his audience imagine a ridiculous situation, a world ruled over by youngsters, and then he satirizes the present situation by declaring it to be just as absurd. Against this backdrop, he then describes Yahweh as ready to bring charges against society's leaders, who are responsible for abuses as bad as those in an imaginary world ruled by children.

The following outline of the speech can serve as the basis for discussion.

    (1) A description of an imaginary state of anarchy and oppression (1-7)
    (2) The actual state of affairs (8-12)
    (3) The judgment of Yahweh upon the leaders (13-15)

Isaiah 3:1-7

Isaiah opens the speech with the announcement that Yahweh is removing from Jerusalem and Judah the mainstays of life (v. 1)—that is, the social and institutional leaders, the pillars of society (vv. 2-3) on whom the normal operations of life depended and who were responsible for the ongoing health and welfare of the people. Eleven different categories, or classes, of people are noted. Here Isaiah again displays his tendency to utilize lists to press home his point (see 2:12-16; 3:18-23). Conspicuously absent from this list are the king and the priest whose status and functions were founded on divine covenants (II Sam. 7:11*b*-16; Num. 25:12-13). The eleven types mentioned cover a broad spectrum of public leaders, both military and civilian, both professional and amateur. Some, like the elder, probably had status based on social rank rather than on official governmental position. Some of the leaders in this list, such as the diviner (*qosem*) in verse 2, are condemned in other biblical texts as irregular and illicit functionaries (see Deut. 18:10). Isaiah here, and probably also in 2:6, mentions such figures as normal functionaries in Judean/Jerusalemite society and makes no negative judgment about their status.

In verse 4, Isaiah slips momentarily into first person and apparently divine speech ("I will make"), although there is no indication that he is giving a divine oracle. The terms used to denote those taking over the reins of leadership and becoming princes ("leaders") in this verse refer not so much to infants (note the RSV's "boys" and "babes") as to unskilled, untrained persons, those who play at or make sport of being something. Under such leadership, anarchy would result and social classes and distinctions would disappear; in such a condition, the "princes" would have neither the ability nor the inclination to rule effectively (v. 5). Oppression would result; citizens would be at one another's throats; neighbor would be against neighbor; youths would bully the elders; and persons of lower class would abuse the honored citizens. It would be, in other words, a topsy-turvy world characterized by disorder and uncivil behavior.

Things would eventually become so bad that when one brother tried to coax the other into assuming leadership, not even a relative could be talked into taking the job. (Note that Isaiah implies this would take place in "the father's house" but that it is the sons, not the father, as in normal society, who are the decision makers.) Eventually no one would want to play ruler and lord over "this tottering mess" (v. 6). Who would want to attempt to hold together and bind up such a situation (v. 7)?

Isaiah 3:8-12

With verse 8, Isaiah moves into an accusation against the Jerusalem and Judah of his own day. No longer describing an imaginary situation, he now deals with the actual situation, but the actual situation he declares is as bad as the imagined.

In verse 6, Isaiah had spoken of a society ruled by neophytes and pretenders as a "tottering mess," employing a participial form of the verb *kashal*. Now in verse 8 he opens his accusation using a verbal form of the same word: "Surely, Jerusalem has tottered and Judah is fallen!"

The charges or accusations against the city and the state occur in verses 8*b*-9*a* and 12. Their speech and their deeds (everything about them) are against Yahweh to defy the eyes of his glory. The obstinacy of their faces (probably the people's unashamedness) condemns them, since they, like ancient Sodom, make no effort to conceal their sins. Isaiah, even in his accusations, does not address the accused directly. He has moved from a hypothetical situation, Jerusalem ruled by neophytes (vv. 4-7), to an indirect condemnation of his audience beginning in verse 9. Only in quoting the divine oracle does he shift to direct second person address (vv. 13-15).

On the behavior specified in the accusations, Isaiah pronounces a woe (v. 9*b*) declaring that the people will get what they deserve since they have brought their fate upon themselves. To illustrate his point and prove his argument, Isaiah resorts to proverbial wisdom. The present Hebrew text reads the opening word of verse 10 as an imperative ("say"), but it should probably be vocalized as a Hebrew perfect ("they say" or "one says"). Isaiah thus quotes a proverb expressive of what his audience would have universally assented to: "As they say, 'for the righteous, it is good because they eat the fruits of their deeds, for the wicked, it is bad because the rendering of his hands shall be done unto him.'" The proverb, also stated in "woe" form, reiterates the central thrust of Isaiah's woe (the end of v. 9*b* shares parallels in terminology with v. 11*b*).

Having clinched his point that Jerusalem and Judah could expect evil to overtake them just as the people had been taught all their lives, Isaiah returns to his accusation before closing his speech with a divine oracle. Two major shifts in Isaiah's speech are evident in verse 12. First of all, Isaiah identifies himself with the audience—"my people, my people"—thus giving a more sympathetic tone to his speech and inviting his audience to identify with him and his position. Second, Isaiah distinguishes between the general population—the people—and the leaders. The leaders, as has been implied throughout the speech, are depicted as the real problem and the villains.

The translation of verse 12*a* is a problem. The present form of the Hebrew text is vocalized so as to continue the depiction of the leaders in terms of the earlier satire (see v. 4). Isaiah here, however, was probably playing on the earlier used imagery but not repeating it. Merely revocalizing the consonants gives a more sensible reading (also reflected in the Greek and Aramaic versions): "My people, its oppressors deal cruelly, and moneylenders (or usurers) rule over them." Such a translation brings the passage into parallelism with 12*b*: "My people, your guides are leading you astray, and the course of your paths they are confusing."

Isaiah 3:13-15

In the conclusion of his speech, Isaiah describes Yahweh as entering into judgment with the elders and princes (the social and governmental leaders) and the people. Verse 13 affirms the nature of Yahweh as judge: "Yahweh is the one who sets himself to contend, and is the one stationing himself to judge." The "contending" (*rib*) refers to the pre-trial statements of the case and the effort to settle matters before taking them to court; "judging" denotes the actual rendering of a decision once cases had gone to court. Isaiah, in verse 13 and with the use of participial forms, could simply have been affirming what his audience would have acknowledged, namely, Yahweh is a God who brings cases and who judges his people.

Verses 14-15 describe Yahweh entering into judgment against the leaders of Judean/Jerusalemite society and presents the divine accusations and evidence against the oppressors and usurers. The charges open sharply and pointedly:

GREAT ASSIZE

". . .You have burned to acquire vineyards;
the exploitation of the poor is in your houses.
What are you doing when you crush my people,
and grind (into the ground) the faces of the poor?. . ."

The evil Isaiah condemns among the leaders of the day is
their exploitation of their own people, probably through
excessive interest, land foreclosures, debt slavery, and the
use of the apparatus of government to fill their own coffers. It
was worse than a society run by neophytes. Those in office to
uphold and establish justice and righteousness were
themselves the perverters of the system. Society's order was
topsy-turvy!

6. THE DAUGHTERS OF JERUSALEM (3:16–4:6)

J. G. **Baldwin**, "ṣemaḥ as a Technical Term in the Prophets,"
VT 14(1964)93-97; J. **Buda**, "ṣemaḥ Jahweh," *Bib* 20(1939) 10-26;
H. F. B. **Compston**, "Ladies' Finery in Isaiah III 18–23," *CQR*
103(1926-27)316-30; S. Daiches, "Der Schmuch der Töchter
Zions und die Tracht Istars," *OLZ* 14(1911)390-91; K.
Galling, "Die Ausrufung des Namens als Rechtsakt in
Israel," *TLZ* 81(1956)65-70; E. E. **Platt**, "Jewelry of Bible
Times and the Catalog of Isa. 3:18-23," *AUSS* 17(1979)71-84,
189-201; W. **Plautz**, "Monogamie und Polygamie im Alten
Testament," *ZAW* 75(1963)3-27.

In this speech, Isaiah uses a pattern of preaching similar to
that employed in 1:21–2:5. The conditions that Yahweh
condemns are laid out (1:21-23; 3:16), then follow a
description of the judgment of God and the purification of
the people (or remnant) in that judgment (1:24-25, 27-31;
3:17–4:1), after which the prophet announces how matters
will be in the redeemed times beyond the judgment (2:2-4;
4:2-6).

Evidence in the text, as well as the speech's location in the
book (before the death of Uzziah, noted in 6:1), points to a
general historical period for the speech's deliverance.
Jerusalem and its female citizens seem to be or have recently
been prosperous, and the city does not appear to be facing

any external threat. The reference to the "fugitives of Israel" in 4:2, who take refuge in Jerusalem, points to the period after the outbreak of civil war in Israel. About 745, Shallum led a conspiracy that wiped out the dynasty of Jehu, but he and his supporters were opposed by Menahem, who, after a period of bloody civil strife, was able to ascend and secure the throne in Samaria (see II Kings 15:8-16).

The appearance of both prose and poetic material in this speech certainly does not automatically mean that an original poetic text has been redacted by the editorial insertions of prose material. (The NJPSV of Isaiah prints only verses 3:18-23 and 4:5-6 as prose.) There is certainly no reason why a prophet could not vary the form in which material was delivered, moving back and forth between poetry and prose. Certain material may naturally have lent itself to prose expression.

Two other features in the speech are worth noting. First, the speech opens with the quotation of a divine oracle (3:16), but before the oracle is completed, the quotation form is abandoned and the Deity is referred to in the third person (3:17). Why this is the case is unknown. The accusation against the women is given as a word of Yahweh, and the description of the coming judgment as a word of the prophet. Second, in the speech, sometimes the women of Jerusalem seem to be talked about (3:16-17; 4:1) while in other places, it appears to be Jerusalem who is addressed or spoken about (3:25-26). Perhaps the prophet addresses both (see 4:4) and deliberately moves between singular and plural address.

The following is an outline of the speech's content.

(1) The accusation against the daughters of Zion (3:16)
(2) A description of the coming judgment against them (3:17–4:1)
(3) A description of the future state beyond the judgment (4:2-6)

Isaiah 3:16

It is possible to read verse 16*a* as the charge against the women of Jerusalem. The rest of the verse would be the supporting evidence substantiating the charge. The women are "haughty" (RSV) or "vain" (NJPSV). The term used to describe the attitude of these Jerusalemites was employed by Isaiah in 2:6-22 (see especially vv. 11, 17). There we translated the term "arrogant" and "arrogance." The haughtiness/arrogance/vanity of the women of Jerusalem is manifested in their decorum and demeanor.

The general behavior of the women, or at least Isaiah's description of it, which may have been greatly exaggerated, seems quite clear. The question is whether their walking posture, blinking of the eyes and clanking of jewelry, were merely their normal mode of carriage and stride or whether they were sauntering the streets of the city so as to be deliberately seductively enticing. The text is too ambiguous to decide the matter, and the prophet probably intended it to be. The activity of the women, perhaps wives and daughters of the city's leaders and princes, should be compared with the activities of the princes denounced at the end of the last speech (see 3:14-16 and compare Amos 4:1-3). The tinkling jewelry adorning some upper class ankle may have been purchased with the skin off some peasant's back.

Isaiah 3:17–4:1

In comparison to the brief exposition of the accusation, the descriptions of the coming punishment are extensive and variegated. These include physical affliction (3:17, 24c), removal of luxuries (vv. 18-24), and deprivation of menfolk (3:25–4:1).

The physical ailment and abuse are described as being smitten with scabs on the head, which probably would render one unclean (see Lev. 13), and exposure (3:17). It is uncertain whether the humiliation implied in the exposure was of the total person (RSV: "secret parts"; compare Ezek. 23:26) or only of the female's head (so the NJPSV). The latter interpretation is as old as the Middle Ages and is founded on a story in the Mishnah (*Baba Kamma* 8:6), which indicates that the female's failure to cover her head in public was highly socially unacceptable. Such a sentiment, however, may not have been as old as Isaiah. At any rate, Isaiah announces that the women will undergo a radical reversal of status.

The luxury items to be lost are such as a people might have to give up to pay tribute in time of national emergency. (Menahem probably drew on the resources of Judah to pay his tribute to Tiglath-pileser, and this may be the background of the speech; see II Kings 15:17-20.) The jaw-breaking list of one-and-twenty items (some masculine attire) impresses the reader by its thoroughness, almost to the point of monotony. The ancient audience, no doubt, had similar sentiments.

Verse 24 is structured around the scheme of "now this . . . but then that": perfume-musk (or pus), girdle-rope, coiffured hair-baldness, rich robe-sackcloth, beauty-shame (the last following a reading found in the Qumran Scrolls).

In 3:25–4:1, the manifestations of the judgment against the women are the slaughter of the people's males in war and the resultant shortage of men/husbands this would create in the society. The alternation of person and number in the verses is peculiar but may have been employed for emphasis—second person feminine singular in verse 25, third person singular in verse 26, and feminine plural in 4:1. Jerusalem/Zion is undoubtedly the addressee and referent in verses 25-26. Without men, the gates would lament and mourn, since the traffic through them would be slowed, and they would become a place to express public laments and the emptied city would "sit upon the ground" (as a sign of mourning).

Conditions are described as so desperate that there would be many women for each man (4:1). Isaiah describes the conditions produced by such a situation: Women would initiate "marriage" proposals, try to force responses, and even offer to provide their own necessities (food and clothing; see Exod. 21:10-11) if the male would have them. The "marriage formula" is here expressed by the phrase "Let your name be called over us." To call the name over something was a way of saying "take control over" or "become master over" (see Amos 9:11 for a similar expression). Isaiah may be indicating in this text that men would be so scarce that women would volunteer to become secondary wives or concubines if only they could have the status of some legal sexual relationship to a man (see Exod. 21:7-9, where the relationship is based on the man's purchase of the woman).

Isaiah 4:2-6

In 4:2-6, Isaiah describes the status and role of Jerusalem "in that day." The expression "in that day" can and frequently does have a future reference, but this is not absolutely necessary. In describing the day of Yahweh—that is, the day of the earthquake—Isaiah uses "in that day" in referring to the past (see 2:11, 17 and our earlier discussion of 2:6-22). In fact, Isaiah may be describing some aspects of life in 4:2-3 which already exist. Fugitives of Israel may have already moved south into Judah, and some may have taken up residence in Jerusalem. If "in that day" has a future reference, then Isaiah is here advocating a position that would allow some Israelites to settle in the Judean capital.

A number of expressions and titles in 4:2-6 require definition and discussion, and as to the referents of some, no absolute certainty can be claimed. The "branch (or sprout) of Yahweh" and the "fruit of the land" are probably the prophet's way of referring to the Davidic King and to Jerusalem. Use of the term *ṣemaḥ* to refer to a ruler is common in later texts (see Jer. 23:5; 33:15; Zech. 3:8; 6:12). The use of an agricultural image in speaking of Judah is clear in Gen. 49:11-12. (If this song has reference to David in its images, then Jerusalem may be the "choice vine.") Isaiah here declares that Jerusalem and its reigning Davidic monarch will be viewed as beautiful and glorious and the pride and glory of the fugitives coming there from the horrible conditions in Israel.

Probably verse 3 should be translated as "the remnant in Zion and the survivors in Jerusalem will be called holy, everyone written down to live in Jerusalem." Three singular collective nouns—"fugitives, remnant, survivors"—are used to refer to the same group, namely, the people from the north, who have made it to Jerusalem and have been granted the right to live there and be enrolled as citizens. Isaiah declares that living there, the group can be called holy.

In verse 4, the prophet speaks of the "new Jerusalem" itself, which will exist after God will have washed away and cleansed the city of the filth of the daughters of Zion and the town's blood. Again, the prophet speaks of sin as a pollutant and of forgiveness or purification in terms of washing and cleansing (see 1:15c-16a). Isaiah is here expressing his thoughts in terms and concepts that reflect cultic and purity beliefs and practices—that is, the cultic theology of the Jerusalem priesthood. The association of "filth" with females and menstrual periods would have been clearly perceived by his audience (see Lev. 12; 15:19-30). The cleansing and purification of the city are to be achieved by Yahweh through the means of a spirit/wind of justice/judgment and a spirit/wind of burning (4:4). Here, as earlier in 1:27-28, the new comes through justice (the righting of the wrong) and through purgation.

After Jerusalem is purged, Yahweh, the prophet says, will create special conditions for the city. "Then Yahweh will create over the whole site of Mount Zion and over its places of assembly a cloud by day and smoke and the glow of flaming fire by night. Indeed, over all the glory shall be a canopy. And it will be a booth, for a shade by day from the heat and a shelter and a refuge from the storm and rain" (4:5-6).

The cloud by day and fire by night have parallels in the exodus story, in which these were considered God's way of guiding the people through the wilderness (see Exod. 14:19-24). Isaiah, and the exodus imagery as well, draws upon the appearance of the temple site as viewed from a distance during the offering of sacrifices. As the altar wood and the sacrifices burn, they give the appearance in the daytime of a cloud and at night of flaming fire.

The canopy, a term used elsewhere of a bridal chamber (Joel 2:16; Ps. 19:6), and here obviously spoken of metaphorically by Isaiah, is depicted as a covering enclosing and protecting Mount Zion, the mount of the temple, and the temple courtyards where worshipers and pilgrims assembled. The canopy is to function as a shade and shelter from the elements of the weather. In speaking of the "booth" or "lean-to" (*sukkah*, under which people found shade and shelter while resting from work in the fields), Isaiah picks up a term he had already used in speaking of Jerusalem (1:8). The term was also at home in the temple cult of Jerusalem. A worshiper could speak of being hidden in God's *sukkah* (Ps. 27:5), and worshipers could confess that Yahweh had established his *sukkah* in Zion.

7. A VINEYARD GONE BAD (5:1-30)

B. S. **Childs**, "The Enemy from the North and the Chaos Tradition," *JBL* 78(1959)187-98; R. B. **Chisholm**, "Structure, Style, and the Prophetic Message: An Analysis of Isaiah 5:8-30," *BS* 143(1986)46-60; R. J. **Clifford**, "The Use of HOY in the Prophets," *CBQ* 28(1966)458-64; E. W. **Davies**, *Prophecy and Ethics: Isaiah and the Ethical Traditions of Israel* (Sheffield, England: JSOT Press, 1981)65-89; H. **Donner**, "Der Feind aus dem Norden," *ZDPV* 84(1968)46-54; J. A. **Emerton**, "The Textual Problems of Isaiah V 14," *VT* 17(1967)135-42; E. **Gerstenberger**, "The Woe-Oracles of the Prophets," *JBL* 81(1962)249-63; A. **Graffy**, "The Literary Genre of Isaiah 5, 1-7," *Bib* 60(1979)400-409; D. R. **Hillers**, "Hoy and Hoy-Oracles: A Neglected Syntactic Aspect," *The Word of the Lord Shall Go Forth: Essays in Honor of David Noel Freedman* (ed. C. L. Meyers and M. O'Connor; Winona Lake: Eisenbrauns/American Schools of Oriental Research, 1983)185-88; W. **Janzen**, *Mourning Cry and Woe Oracle* (Berlin/New York: Walter de Gruyter, 1972); H. **Junker**, "Die literarische Art von Is. 5:1-7," *Bib* 40(1959)259-66; H.-J. **Krause**, "*Hoj* als prophetische Leichenklage über das eigene Volk im 8. Jahrhundert," *ZAW* 85(1973)15-46; C. E. **L'Heureux**, "The Redactional History of Isaiah 5.1–10.4," *In the Shelter of Elyon: Essays on Ancient Palestinian Life and Literature in Honor of G. W. Ahlström* (ed. W. B. Barrick and J. R. Spencer; Sheffield, England: JSOT Press, 1984)99-119; O. **Loretz**, "Weinberglied und prophetische Deutung im Protest-Song Jes. 5:1-7," *UF* 7(1975)573-76; D. **Lys**, "La vigne et le double je. Exercice de style sur Esa`ïa V:1-7," *SVT* 26(1974)1-16; T. **de Orbiso**, "El cantico a la viña del amado (Is. 5:1-7)," *Est Ec* 34(1960)715-31; W. **Schottroff**, "Das Weinberglied Jesajas (Jes 5.1-7): Ein Beitrag zur Geschichte der Parabel," *ZAW* 82(1970) 68-91; G. T. **Sheppard**, "More on Isaiah 5:1-7 as a Juridical Parable," *CBQ* 44(1982)45-47; J. W. **Whedbee**, *Isaiah and Wisdom* (Nashville: Abingdon Press, 1971); G. R. **Williams**, "Frustrated Expectations in Isaiah v 1–7: A Literary Interpretation," *VT* 35(1985)459-65; J. G. **Williams**, "The Alas-oracles of the Eighth Century Prophets," *HUCA* 38(1967) 75-91; J. T. **Willis**, "The Genre of Isaiah 5:1-7," *JBL* 96(1977) 337-62; G. A.

Yee, "A Form Critical Study of Isaiah 5:1-7 as a Song and a Juridical Parable," *CBQ* 43(1981)30-40.

Isaiah uses a song about a vineyard to introduce this lengthy speech containing a number of genre forms. If the speeches of Isaiah are generally arranged in chronological order, then this unit should belong to the period after civil strife had come to characterize Israelite society. This assumes that the preceding speech (3:16–4:6) contains references to the potential or actual flight to Jerusalem of fugitives from the north (4:2). These fugitives would have been fleeing the terrors associated with the political struggles, regicide, and open warfare attendant upon the Zechariah-Shallum-Menahem struggle as well as the encroachment of neighboring peoples on Israelite territory (see II Kings 15:8-16; and above chap. 1, sect. 3C).

Several details in this speech point to the period of Menahem's rule as its historical context and background. (1) In the description of the treatment of the vineyard (i.e., Israel and Judah), the vineyard's walls have been demolished, and the vineyard is being trampled. This parallels the treatment that Israel and Judah were beginning to receive during the days of Menahem. (2) The fact that some of the people had already been taken into captivity (5:13) fits the period of Menahem, when anti-Assyrian states in Syria-Palestine had taken over Israelite and perhaps some Judean territory and carried off Israelites and Judeans (Amos 1–2, and see below on Isa. 9:1). (3) In 5:26-30, Isaiah speaks of "a nation afar off" who will come against the land. The identity of this nation is not specified. Isaiah may have thought of either Urartu or Assyria, for the international situation was such that it was not clear that Assyria would emerge from the present struggle as the dominant power. This was the state of affairs early in the reign of Menahem, when Tiglath-pileser was moving to break Urartian influence in the eastern Mediterranean seaboard. (4) The devastation of the earthquake is still sufficiently recent and memory of it vivid enough for Isaiah to appeal to this as an act of Yahweh's recent judgment and as illustrative of matters to come (vv. 14-17, 25).

The following is an outline of the speech.

Isaiah 5:1-7

Isaiah opens his song about a vineyard with words that must have reminded his hearers of David and Solomon. The latter also bore the name Jedidiah or Yedidiah ("Beloved of Yahweh"), given him by the prophet Nathan (II Sam. 12:25). Both the names, David and Jedidiah, have a nickname quality about them, expressing endearment and/or benefi-cence, and may have been applied this way to later members of the house of David. The root for both names, *dwd*, was used to speak of a lover or a close, actual or "assumed," kinship relationship (such as our [rich] "uncle," "sugar daddy," or "godfather"). If we write out the consonants of the line introducing the song, it is easy to see the possibility of associating the imagery with David (*dwd*) and Yedidiah (*ydydyh*):

'shyrh   n'   lydydy   shyrt   dwdy   lkrmw

One can imagine that this line may have once read, or at least have been understood (with only slightly different vocaliza-tion), as: "Let me sing for Yedidiah a song of my David about his vineyard." The audience probably expected to hear some song with erotic content similar to those found in the Song of Solomon, where the young male lover is spoken of not only as a *dwd*, but also as a *mlk* ("king"). Even the term "vineyard" carried female sexual overtones.

The content of the song, which is limited to verses 1*b*-2, appears on the surface to be merely the depiction of what one would normally do in preparing land and establishing a vineyard, as must have been very widespread at the time of Uzziah, who was recalled in tradition as a proponent of viniculture, one "who loved the soil" (II Chron. 26:10). Having a choice site, the owner prepared the soil, removed the stones, set out the choicest vines, built a watchtower to guard his property, and prepared equipment for transforming the grapes into wine. But, the abnormal factor, the unexpected feature, is that the farmer, anticipating a good yield, harvested only inedible grapes unsuited for winemaking. The conclusion of the song describes the disappointing results that attended the hard work of a farmer whose vineyard produced what he had not planted.

At a deeper, allegorical level, Isaiah has here presented a theological overview of his people's history. The enterprising farmer (David-Solomon and/or Yahweh) establishes a vineyard (Israel) on a promising site and provides it with all that is required, but the people produce bad fruit. They turn out to be very disappointing (see Ps. 80:8-11 for a similar picture and compare Isa. 4:2). Probably by the time the prophet had finished verse 2, the audience had clearly made the connection between themselves and the vineyard, its history and theirs.

In verses 3-6, Isaiah assumes the role of the vineyard owner. He first asks his audience, Jerusalemites and Judeans but stated in the singular ("you inhabitant of Jerusalem, you Judean"), to judge where the fault in the enterprise lay (vv. 3-4). Obviously, as he has presented the case, only one verdict is possible. It was not the owner's fault. Isaiah and all his hearers know that, so he is really not asking them for a juridical decision.

Before his audience has a chance to do the natural—namely, offer advice about what to do ("Maybe you should use a different fertilizer", "Another type of grape would probably solve the problem")—the owner announces an unexpected course of action. The protective walls are to be torn down and the vineyard left unworked to return to the wild like the grapes it bore. With the last statement of verse 6, Isaiah moves in his presentation to what no human owner could do, namely, control the clouds and the rainfall. Thus he prepares for verse 7 in which he drives home his point without ambiguity. The vineyard and the vines are the house of Israel and the people of Judah, and the owner is Yahweh. When Yahweh sought to gather the fruits of his labor,

> he looked for justice [*mishpat*],
>   and there was bloodshed *mispah*];
> for righteousness [*ṣedaqah*],
>   and there was outcry [*ṣeʿaqah*]!

Isaiah 5:8-24a

In verses 8-24*a*, Isaiah seeks to make clear and to illustrate two points. On the one hand, his goal is to demonstrate his contention that Israel and Judah, as the vineyard of Yahweh, have yielded bad fruit. He does this with a series of seven woe sections (assuming that originally verse 23 began with a "woe"). On the other hand, he sought to show that, like the vineyard owner, Yahweh already had begun and would continue to tear apart the defenses of the vineyard, opening it to be devoured and trampled and leaving it uncared for and neglected to return to a "wild" state. This the prophet does primarily with three sections beginning with "therefore," which describe consequences brought about by God. The woe sections are verses 8, 11-12, 18-19, 20, 21, 22, 23. The "therefore" sections, which describe actions and results sometimes past and sometimes future, are verses 13, 14-17, and 24*a*. Verses 9-10 functionally parallel the "therefore" sections and are presented as a word of Yahweh. The actions described in the "therefore" sections include both events already past and events yet to come.

Although textual and translation problems plague the first woe section, its overall thrust is clear. The prophet condemns those accumulating immovable property (v. 8). Beyond this, difficulties cloud understanding. First of all, it is difficult to know the full impact of and exactly how to translate the opening expression *hoy*. Suggestions range from seeing it as only an attention-getting device (like beginning a hymn with "O") to viewing it as a form of curse that already anticipates death/judgment on the ones noted in the following phrases. In the woe sections of Isaiah 5 and elsewhere, the woe is followed by participial forms. Following the *hoy* and the participial construction, the verbs and pronouns may be either second person (v. 8*b*), which would suggest a translation like "*Hey*, you who join house to house. . . ," or third person (v. 11), which would suggest a translation like "*Woe* to (*shame on* or *doom to*) those who rise. . . ." Perhaps there was no single pattern of use for this expression except for its employment to call to attention or to call attention to (generally in a negative, reproachful manner) some particular group or condition. Second, the translation of the last half of verse 8 is uncertain. The verse appears to denounce those whose ambition is to acquire property, house after house and field after field, "until there is no more space and you (pl.) dwell alone in the midst of the land." If the people being condemned here are the same as those in 3:14-15, then Isaiah is denouncing the government officials and social leaders who, through money-lending, land foreclosures, and their status as political administrators, are amassing enormous wealth from the peasant and small landowning classes. Isaiah here obviously satirizes these shrewd businessmen by caricaturing their ultimate goal—owning everything.

The opening of verse 9 may have suffered from scribal error in transmission. The Hebrew text now reads, "in my ears (or "in the ears of") Yahweh Sebaoth," which certainly suggests something is lacking. Had this line once begun with a phrase opening with "therefore," then verses 8-24a would have even greater symmetry than is now the case. There would have been the following pattern:

woe-section (v. 8)
therefore section (vv. 9-10)
woe section (vv. 11-12)
therefore sections (vv. 13-17)
five woe sections (vv. 18-23)
therefore section (v. 24a)

After the opening of verse 9a follows a pronouncement in oath form about some aspects of Yahweh's judgment: Numerous homes, big and beautiful, will be ravaged and without inhabitant; vineyards will yield only a gallon of wine per acre; and cereal crops will produce only one-tenth of the seed required to plant them (vv. 9b-10). The envisioned distress matches the offense, the punishment fits the crime; as houses and fields were objects of acquisition, so houses and fields shall be cursed. If verse 9 once began with something like, "therefore, Yahweh Sebaoth swore in my ears," then the judgment announced could refer to events that had already occurred. The homes were those destroyed in the earthquake, and the poor harvests were those attendant on the disaster.

103

The second woe (vv. 11-12) singles out those said to drink from early morning to late evening, to spend their time at parties and feasts, and thus to be oblivious to the work of Yahweh going on around them. The "deed of Yahweh and the work of his hands" should be understood as a reference to what was going on in international affairs in the area. Isaiah claims that the ravaging of the population of Israelite and, perhaps, Judean territories was the work of Yahweh. The drinking and partying crowd was incapable of discerning this work of Yahweh in the events around them.

Verses 13-17 expound upon and develop the claim of verse 12*b*, namely, that the ills befalling the people were the work of Yahweh. All of verses 13-17 in the Hebrew are in the perfect (past) tense and thus Isaiah is describing events already past as the deeds of Yahweh and the work of his hands. Two events are seen as Yahweh's acts of judgment: the exile of some of the people (v. 13) and the devastation of the recent earthquake (vv. 14-17). Earlier, Isaiah had described the earthquake as a time when the pride and arrogance of human beings were brought low and Yahweh was exalted (2:6-22). Now he adds another dimension to God's judgment: the carrying away of his people into exile.

As we noted in the introductory historical survey (see above, chap. 1, sect. 3*B*), portions of Israelite territory were being attacked and annexed to Syria and neighboring states already under Jeroboam II. The Gilead area in Transjordan, lying along the main north-south highway in the region, and the tribal areas of Zebulun and Naphtali, lying along the main highway route connecting Damascus with the southern Mediterranean coast, were the first areas affected (Amos 1-2; Isa. 9:1). Israel's struggles to hold these areas gradually collapsed, and they were incorporated into Syria during the reign of Menahem. Even Judean territory was probably already being encroached on (II Kings 15:37). Israelite and Judean towns in these areas were being devastated and ransacked (Isa. 5:13) and populations deported or placed on the slave market (Amos 1:6-12).

Isaiah says little about the deportation of his fellow citizens in verse 13 except to associate it with lack of understanding and to allude to the hunger and thirst associated with being captive. He is much more descriptive in speaking of the effects of the earthquake.

14. Therefore Sheol enlarged its throat,
    and opened its mouth unbelievably wide;
    and her [Jerusalem's? Sheol's?] nobility and her masses went down,
    her throng and whoever exulted in her.
15. And the human race was brought low,
    and arrogant looks were humbled;
16. And Yahweh Sebaoth was justly exalted,
    and El the Holy righteously showed himself holy.
17. And lambs grazed as they wished,
    and among the ruins [foreign] settlers are eating the fatlings.

The consequences of the earthquake are described in several ways in this section. Verse 14 notes the huge loss of life which resulted but describes this as Sheol, the underworld, consuming the people. The humiliation of humanity in verse 15 reiterates the theme of an earlier speech (see 2:9, 11, 17). The earthquake, which abased humanity, exalted the Deity, here referred to under the titles Yahweh of Hosts and El the Holy. As a consequence of the quake, sheep now graze where previously one would not have expected to see them (in the farmlands and town sites) and foreigners (*gerim*), or "squatters," who have occupied Israelite territory eat from flocks not their own.

Woes three to five are given without any predicted or correlated calamity. Most interpreters see the people singled out in woe three (vv. 18-19) as persons who deny the reality of God's moral judgment of the world—that is, they mockingly declare that God will not execute his judgment and punish their wrongdoing. In fact, they challenge the belief in divine action. This may be the meaning of the text. On the other hand, the passage could be taken in a more straightforward sense. The people Isaiah condemns are those who want a quick manifestation of the purpose of God and immediate divine action to make sense of the international situation that seems to become more and more complex with the passage of time. The refusal of Israel and

Judah to join anti-Assyrian coalitions had been a policy for a century, and under that policy things had gone well. Now international anarchy seemed to have broken out, and the very existence of Israel and Judah was being challenged. In such circumstances, one can see how people would become impatient and anxious to see God make known his work and purpose. Isaiah, however, senses that there will be no quick resolution of matters, that the people must live for a time in the pain and turmoil of unclarified issues when God and his work seem hidden (or, as he later argues, alien and strange; 28:21). Those who demand haste and probably advocate a change in present policies, Isaiah describes as people who drag and pull their iniquity behind them like animals pulling carts.

Woes four through seven (vv. 20-23) make good sense if given merely a surface reading. The opinions they express would be right at home in the book of Proverbs. However, in the form Isaiah has cast them, as woe sayings, he is probably accusing his hearers, at least indirectly, of the wrongs embodied in the sayings. To agree with general principles is one thing; to be accused of the actions condemned is another matter.

In verse 24*a*, Isaiah issues a summarizing pronouncement to the woes, opening with a "therefore":

> Therefore, as surely as a tongue of fire consumes stubble,
>   and dry grass collapses in the flame;
> so their root shall be as rot,
>   and their growth rise up like soot.

Isaiah 5:24b-30

In his conclusion to this powerful speech, Isaiah gives a summarizing statement condemning the people (v. 24*b*) and then declares the people's wrongdoing to be the basis for God's acts of judgment, one past (v. 25) and one future (vv. 26-30). The condemnation accuses the people in terms already encountered in 1:10: "Because they have rejected the torah of Yahweh Sebaoth and the word of the Holy One of Israel they have despised."

The past action of Yahweh against his people was the devastation of the earthquake.

> For this reason, the anger of Yahweh was kindled against his people,
>> and he stretched out his hand against them and smote them;
>> and the mountains quaked and their corpses were as refuse in the streets;
>>> in all this his anger was not abated and his hand is outstretched still.

> Isaiah 5:25

The past judgment of God was severe and widespread. The earthquake demolished much of the country. But Yahweh was not yet through. His anger was unabated and his hand was still stretched out—to strike again. The second blow was yet to come but was already on the horizon. Isaiah spoke of the coming calamity in terms of a nation from afar ("distant nations" appears to be a scribal error). The nation is unidentified. Its forces are described in frighteningly idealized terms. The army moves swiftly; none of its troops falter or grow faint; its military dress is impeccable; its weapons are ready and menacing; its horses and chariots dart like a whirlwind; its prey is without mercy; and like the roaring of the sea or the darkening of the day, it brings gloom and distress in its wake. When it comes, or when Yahweh brings it into the land, that day will be a day of judgment, a day the vineyard is trampled and devoured.

Undoubtedly, Isaiah's depiction of the army Yahweh will bring against his vineyard draws on stereotypical terminology and paints the coming enemy with the colors of the traditional and legendary "foe from the north."

8. A NEW TASK AND A NEW MESSAGE (6:1-13)

K. **Budde**, *Jesaja's Erleben. Eine gemeinverständliche Auslegung der Denkschrift des Propheten (Kap. 6, 1-9, 6)* (Gotha: L. Klotz, 1928); H. **Cazelles**, "La vocation d'Isaïe (ch. 6) et les rites royaux," *Homenaje a Juan Prado* (ed. L. Alvarez Verdes and E. J. Alonso Hernandez; Madrid: Consejo Superior de Investigaciones Cientificios, 1975)89-108; G. R. **Driver**, "Isaiah 6:1 'his train filled the temple,'" *Near Eastern Studies in Honor of William Foxwell Albright* (ed. H. Goedicke; Baltimore/London: Johns Hopkins Press, 1971)87-96; J. A. **Emerton**, "The Translation and Interpretation of Isaiah vi. 13," *Interpreting the Hebrew Bible: Essays in Honour of E. I. J. Rosenthal* (ed. J. A. Emerton and S. C. Reif; Cambridge/New York: Cambridge University Press, 1982)85-118; I. **Engnell**, *The Call of Isaiah: An Exegetical and Comparative Study* (Uppsala/Leipzig: A.–B. Lundequistska/Otto Harrassowitz, 1949); C. A. **Evans**, "The Text of Isaiah 6:9-10," *ZAW* 94(1982)415-18; C. **Hardmeier**, "Jesajas Verkündigungsahsicht und Jahwes Verstrockungsauftrag in Jes 6," *Die Botschaft und die Boten* (Festschrift H. W. Wolff; ed. J. Jeremias and L. Perlitt; Neukirchen-Vluyn: Neukirchener Verlag, 1981)235-51; E. **Jenni**, "Jesajas Berufung in der neueren Forschung," *TZ* 15(1959)321-39; K. R. **Joines**, "Winged Serpents in Isaiah's Inaugural Vision," *JBL* 86(1967)410-15; M. M. **Kaplan**, "Isaiah 6:1-11," *JBL* 45(1926)251-59; R. **Knierim**, "The Vocation of Isaiah," *VT* 18(1968)47-68; T. **Lescow**, "Jesajas Denkschrift aus der Zeit des syrisch-emphraimitischen Krieges," *ZAW* 85(1973)315-31; L. J. **Liebreich**, "The Position of Chapter Six in the Book of Isaiah," *HUCA* 25(1954)37-40; H.-P. **Müller**, "Glauben und Bleiben: Zur Denkschrift Jesajas Kapitel vi 1-viii 18," *SVT* 26(1974)25-54; J. M. **Schmidt**, "Gedanken zum Verstockungsauftrag Jesaja (Is. VI)," *VT* 21(1971)68-90; A. **Schoors**, "Isaiah, the Minister of Royal Anointment?" *OTS*20(1977) 85-107; O. H. **Steck**, "Bemerkungen zu Jesaja 6," *BZ* 16(1972)188-206; U. F. C. **Worschech**, "The Problem of Isaiah 6:13," *AUSS* 12(1974)126-38; A. **Zeron**, "Die Anmassung des Königs Usia im Lichte von Jesajas Berufung: Zu 2. Chr. 26, 16-22 und Jes. 6,1ff.," *TZ* 33 (1977)65-68.

Chapter 6 of Isaiah is one of the most discussed and debated texts in the whole of scripture. Few passages have proved as difficult for scholars to agree on a translation as 6:13. The following interpretation of the chapter and our translation of 6:13 are based on the following considerations.

(1) Isaiah had been a prophet for some time and his preaching, prior to the experience of chapter six, is contained in chapters 1–5. That Isaiah 6 is not an account of the prophet's initial call is indicated by the following factors. (a) The placement of the text suggests that the preceding

material in chapters 1–5 comes from an earlier period. A vocational call narrative would be more normal at the beginning of the book (see Jeremiah 1 and Ezekiel 1–3). (b) The content of the speeches in chapters 1–5 is best interpreted in the light of events and conditions during the period of Uzziah/Jotham rather than later. (c) After chapter 6, Isaiah's preaching focuses almost totally on political affairs, whereas in chapters 1–5, the concern is with social issues and criticisms. This indicates that the experience of Isaiah 6 marked a shift in Isaiah's ministry rather than an inaugural call. (d) The calls to repentance and change in chapters 1–5 contrast strongly with the command to harden the people's hearts in 6:9-10, making it difficult to see these earlier chapters as fulfillment of the commission of chapter 6. (e) In Isaiah 6, the prophet is not called; he volunteers. There is no hesitancy or resistance to the commission as is common in other call narratives.

(2) This autobiographical narrative was formulated by the prophet to justify and support the new political stance and role taken by Isaiah following the death of Uzziah.

(3) Isaiah had preached that the purification and purgation of Jerusalem were to be carried out by Yahweh as preparation for the city's new life (1:24-31; 4:4). Isaiah 6 has, as one of its purposes, to demonstrate that the prophet had already passed through the purification process, been admitted and was privy to the deliberations of the divine, and thus could speak with special status and authority.

(4) The experiences of the prophet reported in the chapter are probably dependent in their imagery on rites associated with the coronation ritual for a new king—in this case, probably Ahaz. Isaiah may, himself, have participated in the coronation service, perhaps in the anointment ritual.

(5) At least verse 12*a* is to be considered a later scribal gloss, not so much because its content is out of keeping with the context, but because it refers to Yahweh in the third person in the midst of a Yahweh oracle.

(6) By the time Isaiah reported this vision, Judean society had become thoroughly polarized. The two entities, Judah and Jerusalem, and their counterparts, the general Judean population and the house of David and its supporters, were greatly estranged. This becomes more evident in Isaiah 7–8

but seems presupposed in Isaiah 6 as well. Isaiah's allegiance was to the house of David and its supporters. The "this people" whom Isaiah sees as his task to solidify in their waywardness (6:9) are primarily the Judeans who had adopted an anti-Davidic attitude and who would soon lend support to the Syrian-led anti-Assyrian coalition (see the discussion of 8:5-15 below). "This people" would thus refer to the whole population except for the remnant loyal to the house of David and the Davidic family itself.

The material in this chapter can be discussed in terms of the following outline:

(1) The prophet's vision of God (1–4)
(2) The prophet's purification (5–7)
(3) The prophet's commission (8–13)

Isaiah 6:1-4

Reporting this visionary experience, Isaiah dated it to the year of Uzziah's death. That a past date is given in an autobiographical narrative would indicate that the experience was cited by Isaiah to justify the character of his prophetic role and function and his deep involvement in the politics and fate of the house of David. The experience is not reported merely for its own sake, but was appealed to by the prophet himself to authenticate his task and message.

The occasion for the vision and its imagery have been much discussed and may have been closely connected with some event "in the year that King Uzziah died." Was it the death of the old king himself, who, in spite of his leprosy and the questions this raised about his status with Yahweh, who had "smote" him, had been a major factor in Judean life for over half a century (see II Kings 15:1-7), that helped trigger the event? Was it the coronation of a new king at the next autumn New Year festival and all the associated ritual that such events entailed? Was the experience and the new role that Isaiah saw himself assuming connected with the growing unrest in the north, the increasing disaffection from the house of David, and the swelling pressure to join the anti-Assyrian forces in the region that were intensified at the time of a change in leadership in Jerusalem? Was it necessary for Isaiah to reaffirm his prophetic role in the context of a new administration? Of the particulars we have no knowledge. When the prophet related the experience, three things seemed of particular importance: his vision of the heavenly world, his purification, and his commission to be an instrument in hardening the hearts of the people.

Yahweh is described as sitting on a throne with the skirts of his robe filling the temple or heavenly palace. Attendant upon the Deity were the six-winged seraphim, who proclaimed the holiness of God and the universality of his glory. The voices of the seraphim made the structure shake, and smoke filled the house. All of this imagery no doubt drew on the theology and iconography of the Jerusalem temple. Here God sat enthroned and ruled over the world as king. The seraphim were the heavenly counterparts to the bronze seraph that graced the temple (see II Kings 18:4; Num. 21:6-9). This seraph and the seraphim probably draw upon Egyptian inconography, where the *uraeus*, or cobra, was associated with the monarch, adorning the royal headdress and the throne.

Isaiah 6:5-7

Isaiah describes his reaction to the vision as a sense of unworthiness and sinfulness in the presence of the absolutely holy. The prophet's words of self-description are cast in purity terminology: "my lips are unclean (*ṭame'*, the opposite of holy) and I dwell in the midst of a people of unclean lips."

The purification of the prophet's lips, which results in the removal of his guilt and the forgiveness of his sins and thus the purgation of his uncleanness, probably draws on the purification ritual and imagery used in preparing the new king for his coronation. Such mouth purification rituals were known in both Egyptian and Mesopotamian cultures. Here Isaiah applies the imagery to himself. As purified and cleansed, he now stands on the side of God, the holy. He is, like the king, a true representative of the divine, having stood in the divine council.

Isaiah 6:8-13

The account of Isaiah's commissioning, like the description of his vision of Yahweh, shares parallels with the account of Micaiah's vision in I Kings 22:19-23. In the latter, however, it is a heavenly being, not an earthly prophet, who is commissioned by God to bring about the downfall of the Israelite army. In Isaiah 6, the prophet volunteers to serve as the agent of God. His task with regard to "this people" is a negative one, to ensure that the people (the non-supporters of the Davidic house) get the punishment they deserve (vv. 9-10). References in chapter 8 to "this people" clearly indicate that this phrase refers to Ahaz's subjects, who favored an anti-Assyrian policy of state. In 8:6, "this people" has given up its support of the Davidic house and its political stance and rejoices over the anti-Assyrian policy of Syria and Israel. In 8:12, "this people" has levelled a charge of conspiracy and treason against Ahaz and the house of David for failure to continue its support of Israelite politics.

In response to the question of how long such preaching should go on, the prophet is told:

11. "Until cities lie waste without inhabitant,
    and houses without occupants;
   and the land lies completely desolate . . .
12*b*. and deserted sites are many in the land.
13. And though a tenth [is left] in it (the land),
    yet it (the tenth) shall remain and be for burning (or ravaging).
   As an oak and a terebinth when felled,
    a stump [is left] in them [as the source of new growth];
   the holy seed [the house of David] is its (the land's) stump."

The content of verse 11 is clear, specifying the conditions expected to prevail in the land as a consequence of coming events—desolation and depopulation. A similar depiction is found in 7:21-25 and 8:6-10.

As we have noted, even the translation of verse 13 is a matter of controversy. Interpretations of the passage are wide ranging and divergent. Our interpretation assumes the authenticity of the received text and is based on the following considerations. (1) The coming devastation of the land of

Judah is to be the consequence of divine judgment on "this people" for their lack of support for the Davidic house. (2) The imagery of verses 11 and 13a parallels the descriptions of the earlier speech on the "vineyard gone bad" in 5:1-30 (see especially 5:5, 9). (3) The reference to the fallen tree is used to indicate that matters will not be totally hopeless, since certain varieties of even fallen trees are capable of rejuvenation from the roots or stump (see Job 14:7-9). Although Judah may be laid waste, survival will occur. (4) The stump from which new life will grow is the house of David, the holy seed. While "holy seed" is used nowhere else with reference to the house of David (see Ezra 9:2), that seems to be its most obvious referent in this passage, especially when considered in the light of other Isaianic texts, such as chapter 7. The prophet may have deliberately chosen the term *maṣṣebah*, since it could be understood not only with reference to the standing remains of a toppled tree, but also with reference to pillars of various sorts and diverse use in ancient Israel. Such *maṣṣeboth* served as cultic furnishings (Gen. 35:14), memorial stones (Gen. 35:20; II Sam. 18:18), and territorial markers (I Sam. 15:12; Isa. 19:19). It has been proposed that a dynastic stela (*maṣṣebah*) stood in the temple (see I Kings 7:15; II Kings 11:14; 23:3, although these texts use the term `ammud*). Such a stela would have served as a sign of the perpetuity of the dynasty similar to the Djed pillar in Egyptian royal rituals. If this were the case, and the evidence is very slight, then Isaiah's allusion would have been even clearer to his audience. The land of Judah might be devastated, but the Davidic family (and its supporters) would be the source of continuing existence and new life.

9. DELIVERANCE FOR THE HOUSE OF DAVID—DISASTER FOR JUDAH (7:1-25)

W. F. **Albright**, "The Son of Tabeel (Isaiah 7:6)," *BASOR* 140(1955)34-35; J. M. **Asurmendi**, *La Guerra Siro-Efraimita: Historia y Profetas* (Valencia/Jerusalem: Institución San Jerónimo, 1982); R. **Bartelmus,** "Jes 7:1-17 und das Stilprinzip des Kontrastes. Syntaktisch-stilistische und traditionsgeschichtliche Anmerkungen zur 'Immanuel-Perikope,' " *ZAW*

96(1984)50-66; S. H. **Blank**, "The Current Misunderstanding of Isaiah's She'ar Yashub," *JBL* 67(1948)211-15; **Blank**, "Immanuel and which Isaiah?" *JNES* 13(1954)83-86; G. W. **Buchanan**, "The Old Testament Meaning of the Knowledge of Good and Evil," *JBL* 75(1956)114-20; K. **Budde**, "Isaiah vii. 1 and 2 Kings xvi. 5," *ET* 11(1899/1900)327-30; **Budde**, *Jesaja's Erleben. Eine gemeinverständliche Auslegung der Denkschrift des Propheten (Kap. 6, 1–9, 6)* (Gotha: L. Klotz, 1928); **Budde**, "Jesaja und Aḥas," *ZDMG* 84(1930)125-38; **Budde**, "Das Immanuelzeichen und die Ahaz-Begegnung Jesaja 7," *JBL* 52(1933)22-54; M. **Burrows**, "The Conduit of the Upper Pool," *ZAW* 70(1958)221-27; W. **Dietrich**, *Jesaja und die Politik* (Munich: Chr. Kaiser Verlag, 1976); G. **Fohrer**, "Zu Jesaja 7, 14 im Zusammenhang von Jesaja 7, 10-22," *ZAW* 68(1956)54-56 (= *BZAW* 99[1967]167-69; **Fohrer**, *Die symbolischen Handlungen der Propheten* (Zurich/ Stuttgart: Zwingli Verlag, 1967); N. K. **Gottwald**, "Immanuel as the Prophet's Son," *VT* 8(1958)36-47; W. C. **Graham**, "Isaiah's Part in the Syro-Ephraimite Crisis," *AJSL* 50(1934)201-16; A. H. J. **Gunneweg**, "Heils-und Unheilsverkündigung in Jesaja 7," *VT* 15(1965)27-34; E. **Hammershaimb**, "The Immanuel Sign," *ST* 3(1949)124-42 = his *Some Aspects of Old Testament Prophecy from Isaiah to Malachi* (Copenhagen: Rosenkilde og Bagger, 1966)11-28; C. **Hardmeier**, "Gesichtspunkte pragmatischer Erzahlteranalyse: 'Glaubt ihr nicht, so bleibt ihr nicht'—ein Glaubensappell an schwachende Anhänger Jesajas," *WD* 15(1979)33-54; P. **Höffken**, "Notizen zum Textcharakter von Jesaja 7, 1-17," *TZ* 36(1980)321-37; J. **Jensen**, "The Age of Immanuel," *CBQ* 41(1979)220-39; R. **Kilian**, *Die Verheissung Immanuels Jes 7, 14* (Stuttgart: Katholisches Bibelwerk, 1968); E. J. **Kissane**, "Butter and Honey Shall He eat (Isaiah 7:15)," *Orientalia et Biblica Louvaniensia* 1(1957)169-73; E. G. **Kraeling**, "The Immanuel Prophecy," *JBL* 50(1931)277-97; J. **Lindblom**, *A Study on the Immanuel Section in Isaiah (Is 7:1-9:6)* (Lund: CWK Gleerup, 1958); W. **McKane**, "The Interpretation of Isaiah VII 14-25," *VT* 17(1967)208-19; F. L. **Moriarty**, "The Immanuel Prophecies," *CBQ* 19(1957)226-33; S. **Mowinckel**, *He that Cometh* (Oxford/Nashville: Blackwells/Abingdon Press, 1956); W. E. **Müller**, *Die Vorstellung vom Rest* (Leipzig: W. Hoppe, 1939); S. **Porúbčan**, "The Word 'OT in Isaiah 7, 14," *CBQ* 22(1960)144-59; G. **Rice**, "A Neglected Interpretation of the Immanuel Prophecy," *ZAW* 90(1978)220-27; **Rice**, "The Interpretation of Isaiah 7:15-17," *JBL* 96(1977)363-69; L. G. **Rignell**, "Das Immanuelszeichen: Einige Gesichtspunkte zu Jes. 7," *ST* 11(1957)99-119; J. J. M. **Roberts**, "Isaiah and His Children," *Biblical and Related Studies Presented to Samuel Iwry* (ed. A. Kort and S. Morschauser; Winona Lake: Eisenbrauns, 1985)193-203; M. **Saebø**, "Formgeschichtliche Erwägungen zu Jes. 7:3-9," *ST* 14(1960)54-69; J. J. **Scullion**, "An Approach to the Understanding of Isaiah 7:10-17," *JBL* 87(1968)288-300; J. J. **Stamm**, "La prophétie d'Emmanuel," *RTP* 32(1944)97-123; **Stamm**, "Neuere Arbeiten zum Immanuel-Problem," *ZAW* 68(1956)46-53; **Stamm**, "Die Immanuel-Perikope im Lichhte neuerer Veröffenlichungen," *SZDMG* 1(1969)281-90; **Stamm**, "Die Immanuel-Perikope. Eine Nachlese," *TZ* 30(1974)11-22; O. H. **Steck**, "Beitrage zum Verständnis von Jesaja 7, 10-17 und 8,1-4," *TZ* 29(1973)161-78; **Steck**, "Rettung und Verstockung: Exegetische Bermerkungen zu Jesaja 7,3-9," *EvTh* 33(1973)77-90; U. **Stegemann**, "Der Restgedanke bei Isaias," *BZ* 13(1969)161-86; M. E. W. **Thompson**, *Situation and Theology: Old Testament Interpretations of the Syro–Ephraimitic War* (Sheffield: Almond Press, 1982); **Thompson**, "Isaiah's Sign of Immanuel," *ET* 95(1983-84)67-71; A. **Vanel**, "Ṭâbe 'él en Is. VII 6 et le roi Tubail de Tyr," *SVT* 26(1974)17-24; W. **Vischer**, *Die Immanuel-Botschaft im Rahmen des königlichen Zionsfestes* (Zollikon-Zurich: Evangelische Verlag, 1955); E. **Vogt**, "Filius Tab'el (Isa. 7:6)," *Bib* 37(1956)263-64; M. **Weiss**, "The Contribution of Literary Theory to Biblical Research: Illustrated by the Problem of She'ar-Yashub," *SH* 31(1986) 373-86; H. W. **Wolff**, *Frieden ohne Ende. Eine Auslegung von Jes. 7:1-7 und 9:1-6* (Neukirchen-Vluyn: Neukirchener Verlag, 1962); E. **Würthwein**, "Jesaja 7:1-9. Ein Beitrag zu dem Thema: Prophetie und Politik," in his *Wort und Existenz: Studien zum Alten Testament* (Göttingen: Vandenhoeck & Ruprecht, 1970)127-43.

Scholars frequently view Isaiah 7:1-17, if not the whole of the chapter, as an integral part of the prophet's *Denkschrift*, or memoirs. This larger work allegedly extends from 6:1 to 8:18 (or 9:7) and supposedly represents Isaiah's written record of speeches, which he had delivered primarily during the Syro-Ephraimitic crisis. The purpose of the memoirs, so it is argued, was to demonstrate that the opposition that Isaiah's message had met during the crisis had been foreseen by Yahweh and announced to the prophet as early as the death year of Uzziah (6:9-10). The memoirs were thus Isaiah's attempt at self-vindication in the face of his failed ministry.

The interpretation of Isaiah 7:1-17 as part of a larger *Denkschrift* is problematic for several reasons. First, while Isaiah 6 and 8 are autobiographical in form (6:1, 5, 7, 11; 8:1-4, 5, 11, 16-18), Isaiah 7 is essentially a narrative about the prophet, referring to him throughout in third-person style (vv. 3 and 11, and originally v. 10 also). This discrepancy has not been lost on scholars but has often been handled by emending the third-person references to Isaiah to first-person forms. There is, however, no textual evidence to support these changes; all Hebrew manuscripts, as well as the versions, agree with the third-person usage of the Masoretic text. We concede that this fact alone is not decisive; the conversion of an originally autobiographical account to a report about the prophet may simply have preceded the phases of textual transmission represented by the versions and Hebrew manuscript traditions. It remains difficult to see, however, why only a portion of the prophet's memoirs, 7:1-17, would have been converted to a third-person account. If the references to Isaiah in this material arose as explanatory glosses, we would expect to see similar glossing in chapters 6 and 8, where the first-person forms would seem to demand clarification as well. In short, the interpretation of Isaiah 7:1-17 as part of the prophet's memoirs rests on circular reasoning: The first-person forms in 6:1–8:18 (or 9:7) attest to the existence of a *Denkschrift*; the *Denkschrift* hypothesis serves as the basis for arguing that the third-person references to Isaiah in chapter 7 are secondary.

Second, it is questionable whether Isaiah 7:1-17 really functions as the concrete portrayal of the hardening of heart that 6:9-10 anticipates. In the former text, the prophet's words are directed against "this people"—that is, the Judeans alone (see 8:6, 11-12). It is the general population, not the Davidic house, from whom Isaiah expects opposition and against whom he threatens disaster (8:11-20). Isaiah 7:1-17 focuses, in contrast, on Ahaz and the royal court, and at least at the outset (vv. 1-9) assumes that the prophet can influence their political behavior. To see in this material the realization of the "hardening of the heart" theme rests on the interpretation of the Immanuel sign (vv. 14-17) as a word of judgment against not only Syria and Israel, but also Ahaz and Judah. As we will argue, however, the Immanuel sign is best taken as a promise to Ahaz and the whole Davidic house, despite the apparent altercation between the king and prophet in verses 10-13. Only with the redactional addition of "the king of Assyria" at the end of verse 17 does the narrative appear to depict Isaiah's rejection of Ahaz.

The above considerations justify taking Isaiah 7 as an originally independent unit, which collectors of the book of Isaiah placed after chapter 6 because its content followed more or less chronologically. A full history of the material's composition is difficult to sketch with certainty, but two stages of the chapter's growth do seem probable. With the exception of a few glosses, 7:1-17 circulated as a separate narrative about Isaiah's encounter(s) with the house of David prior to the Syro-Ephraimitic attack on Jerusalem. The account exhibits a legendizing tendency, particularly in verses 10-17, in which the prophet is depicted as wonder-worker. The intention of the whole is to document that Isaiah correctly predicted that the Davidic house would survive the Syro-Ephraimitic threat.

To this account was subsequently appended a series of genuinely Isaianic threats originally directed against the Judeans at large (vv. 18-25). Precisely when the prophet uttered these words is difficult to say. It is reasonable, however, to assume that they derive from the general period of the Syro-Ephraimitic crisis when Isaiah, though remaining a steadfast supporter of Ahaz, vigorously condemned the Judean population at large (see 8:6-8*a*).

The editorial combining of verses 1-17 and verses 18-25 resulted in a reinterpretation of the former. By attaching the threats against Judah to what originally was a word of promise to the Davidic house, the redactors led the reader to construe that promise as a judgment as well. They emphasized the point also by inserting "the king of Assyria" at the end of verse 17 as a kind of linchpin between the two blocks of material (see v. 20*a*). The coming days of salvation announced in verse 17 were, likewise, linked with the "that day" of judgment in verses 18-25. Yahweh then appeared to be bringing disaster upon both the Davidic house and the Judeans in the form of an Assyrian invasion. This view, as we will argue, departs widely from the attitude of the historical Isaiah, representing an early attempt to cast Ahaz in a negative light and as such anticipating the later Deuteronomistic denunciation of the king in II Kings 16.

Isaiah 7:1-17

Isaiah 7:1-17 is formally a narrative about the prophet, but the bulk of the material consists of Isaiah's words to the house of David. Structurally, the account divides into three parts:

(1) Summary of the Syro-Ephraimitic crisis (1)
(2) Commissioning of Isaiah with a speech for Ahaz, with a narrative introduction (2-9)
(3) A dispute between king and prophet, climaxing in the Immanuel prophecy (10-17)

These fit together in a prophecy-fulfillment scheme: verse 1 reports the failure of Rezin and Pekah to capture Jerusalem, while verses 2-8 and 10-17 document two parallel messages of prophetic encouragement to Ahaz, predicting the failure of the Syro-Ephraimitic plan and the survival of the Davidic house. (A similar narrative strategy is seen in 20:1-6, where the outcome of a historical scenario is set forth at the beginning and then a previous word and sign-act by the prophet is related, which anticipate that outcome and the accompanying circumstances.)

Verse 1

Isaiah 7:1 consists of an introductory temporal clause and a terse statement about the Syro-Ephraimitic crisis: "In the days of Ahaz the son of Jotham the son of Uzziah, the king of Judah, Rezin the king of Aram came up with Pekah the son of Remaliah the king of Israel to Jerusalem to wage war against it, but he was unable to conquer it." The reference here is to the Syrian-Israelite invasion of Judah in late 735 or early 734, the purpose of which was to replace Ahaz with a more pliant non-Davidic leader who would support Rezin, Pekah, and others in a revolt against Assyria (see vv. 5-6). The same episode is narrated in II Kings 16:5-9 and II Chronicles 28:5-21, albeit in forms that greatly distort the historical event in order to derogate Ahaz. Significantly in all three accounts, however, Rezin/Syria is always mentioned before Pekah of Israel. The order probably reflects Rezin's role as ringleader of the alliance. The conclusion finds support in the singular form of the verb that concludes Isaiah 7:1—"he [Rezin] was unable" to take the city.

The wording of II Kings 16:5 parallels closely that of Isaiah 7:1—"Then Rezin the king of Syria went up with Pekah the son of Remaliah the king of Israel to Jerusalem for battle and they besieged Ahaz but were unable to conquer." The difference between the two verses is clear: In the Isaiah text, the Syro-Ephraimitic attack is aimed against Jerusalem; in the II Kings text, it is Ahaz who is principally threatened. The precise literary relationship between the two texts is difficult to determine with certainty. Earlier scholars have argued that Isaiah 7:1 was borrowed from II Kings 16:5 but altered to deemphasize the threat to Ahaz personally and, thereby, to highlight his lack of faith. The direction of literary dependence could very well have been just the opposite—that is, the Deuteronomistic editors of II Kings 16 had before them a notice similar, if not identical, to Isaiah 7:1 but modified it so as to denounce Ahaz. In their view, the king suffered the attack as a consequence of his religious apostasy.

The events recounted in 7:1 chronologically follow the prophet's words recorded in verses 3-17 (in fact, all of chapters 7–12). Properly speaking then, 7:1 provides not so much the historical background of the speeches that follow, but rather a proleptic summary of the entire episode, giving the dénouement toward which Isaiah's messages to the king point. Its function is not to emphasize that Ahaz had no reason to fear Rezin and Pekah, but rather to affirm that the prophet's predictions about the failure of the campaign had come true.

Verses 2-9

The commissioning of the prophet with a speech of encouragement for Ahaz follows in verses 3-9. Verse 2 introduces the report, describing the disposition of the Davidic house prior to the Syro-Ephraimitic invasion: "Now when it had been told to the house of David, 'Syria has descended upon Ephraim,' its (the house of David's) resolve and the resolve of its people wavered as the trees of the forest waver before the wind." In relation to verse 1, verse 2 functions as a kind of flashback: It takes the reader back to the eve of the impending crisis. It recounts the uncertain courage of the Davidic house and its supporters in order to explain why a word of prophetic encouragement was especially needed at this moment.

The report to the Davidic house in verse 2*a* merits further attention. Scholars have long wrestled with the verb *naḥah*, emending it in various ways or deriving it from unusual roots, all in order to arrive at the meaning, "Syria has fallen in league with Ephraim." The verbal form, however, should be retained as it is and translated according to the normal sense of *nwḥ*, "to rest or settle upon." What the text has in mind here is not altogether clear. It may refer to the movement of Syrian troops into Israel for the purpose of joining Pekah's forces in an attack on Judah. More likely, however, Syria's "descent" upon Ephraim is a vivid metaphorical expression for Pekah's coup in Samaria in 736/5 and with it the effective takeover of the whole of the northern kingdom by Syria. It should be remembered that in previous years Rezin had annexed the northern Transjordan and Galilee and possibly also the coastal Plain of Sharon. As early as the 740s, Pekah had been ruling, perhaps in Gilead as a Syrian puppet. All that was left of the Israelite kingdom, by the middle 730s was the Ephraimite hill country. When Pekah then in 736/5 assassinated Pekahiah and ascended the throne in Samaria, Rezin's control of Israel was effectively complete: Syria had "descended upon Ephraim."

Verse 2*b* mentions not only the house of David, but also "its people." The latter reference is usually understood as the Judean population. As we will see later, however, 8:6*b* indicates that most of the Judeans were favorably disposed toward the Israelite and Syrian kings and supported their anti-Assyrian cause. "Its people" in 7:2*b* accordingly should be taken in a more restrictive sense—that is, as a reference to the few supporters of the Davidic regime and its policies.

These were likely limited to residents of Jerusalem and its environs and members of the standing army.

The text speaks literally of the "heart" of the Davidic house and its supporters. The Hebrew term here is *lebab*, which in the Hebrew Bible exhibits a wide semantic range—the inner person, mind, knowledge, memory, conscience, desire, heart, and so forth. The word in Isaiah 7:2 is usually taken in the sense of courage: The Syro-Ephraimitic threat caused great alarm and fear within the Davidic house. *Lebab*, however, can also mean "resolution, will, or determination." We render the term in this sense and suggest that the text has in mind the wavering resolve of the Davidic leadership to persist in its former course of neutrality. A quick review of Palestinian politics leading up to the Syro-Ephraimitic crisis supports this interpretation.

As early as the reigns of Uzziah and Jotham, Rezin of Damascus had probably been soliciting Davidic support for a coalition of regional states that could check Assyrian expansion. His overtures met with no success. The aloofness of the Davidides, however, only prompted the Syrian king to apply additional pressure (II Kings 15:37). He returned control of Elath and the surrounding region from Judean to Edomite hands (II Kings 16:6) and probably encouraged his Philistine and Meunite allies to encroach upon the western Shephelah area (II Chron. 28:18; *TUAT* I 376). Until 735, Judah proper was not directly threatened by Syria. The Ephraimite hill country ruled by the pro-Assyrian Menahem and Pekahiah served as a buffer between the two countries. With Pekah's coup in Samaria, however, Syria had "descended upon Ephraim." Syrian hegemony now extended to the very border of Judah. Moreover, the Syrian-supported coup demonstrated clearly that Rezin was willing to take decisive steps in handling recalcitrant monarchs. The Davidic house had every reason to expect that Syria would pursue whatever measures necessary to insure a cooperative leadership in Jerusalem.

In this situation, the Davidic house was forced to reevaluate its previous policy of neutrality. Resistance to Syria had already cost Judah a significant amount of territory and cut off the country's access to major trade routes. Syrian pressure had begun to take its toll on the public mood; most

Judeans now favored joining league with Rezin and Pekah (8:6*b*). In the face then of internal and external opposition, the national leadership had to reconsider whether it should capitulate to Rezin's demands and join the anti-Assyrian coalition. Heated debate within the administration undoubtedly ensued, some arguing for a reconciliation with Syria, others advocating Judah's continuing neutrality. It is this controversy that Isaiah 7:2*b* refers to when it reports that the "resolve" of the house of David and its supporters "wavered as trees of the forest waver before the wind."

In verses 3-9 follows Yahweh's commissioning of Isaiah. The unit consists of two parts: (a) The prophet is commanded to go forth with his son, Shear-jashub, to meet Ahaz (v. 3); and (b) Isaiah is ordered to deliver to the king a divinely-dictated speech (vv. 4-9). That speech, in turn, is composed of two parts: an exhortation to Ahaz (v. 4) and a word of assurance and warning to the house of David (vv. 5-9).

The significance of Shear-jashub, mentioned in verse 3, is widely debated. The name is unique in the Bible and undoubtedly carries symbolic meaning (see 7:14-17; 8:3-4; Hos. 1:2-9). Grammatically, it is a short sentence, consisting of a subject, *Shear*, and a verbal predicate, *jashub*. The former derives from a Hebrew verb meaning "to remain or be left over" and in Isaiah is generally translated as "remnant." The term frequently refers to those who survive a divinely wrought destruction (10:19, 22; 17:3, 21:17). The predicate is an inflected form of a Hebrew verb, the base meaning of which is "to turn back, to return." The term exhibits a broad semantic range. Two specific meanings, however, are relevant to the interpretation of the name of Isaiah's son. The word frequently has a religious sense—one turns to Yahweh (9:13; 19:22; see 1:27; 6:10; and 30:15). It can also carry a political-military meaning, referring to a return from battle and thus to one's survival in war (10:22; see I Kings 22:28).

The inversion of the normal Hebrew word order in Shear-jashub is significant. The subject precedes the verb and thereby receives emphasis. Two quite different interpretations, however, are grammatically possible. The emphasis may convey an asseverative meaning—"A remnant surely . . ."—or a restrictive sense—"Only a remnant. . . ."

These grammatical and lexical remarks can be summarized by listing the possible translations of Shear-jashub. They are:

(1) A remnant will surely turn (to Yahweh).
(2) A remnant will surely return (i.e., survive).
(3) Only a remnant will turn (to Yahweh).
(4) Only a remnant will return (i.e., survive).

The first and second of these are both hopeful declarations. They focus respectively, however, on the repentance of a remnant and on its political survival. The third and fourth translations are both pessimistic, but differ from each other in their concern, with a religious turning to Yahweh or with political survival.

Which of these meanings the prophet intended when the child was named and when he and Shear-jashub met with Ahaz is not clear. Nowhere in the pericope is the name explained. Two interpretations of Shear-jashub appear in 10:21 and 22, but these do not necessarily reflect the significance of the name in 7:3. The sense here can only be inferred from the immediate context. This, we will see, is one in which Isaiah was principally concerned to encourage Ahaz, predicting the failure of Rezin's plan to topple the Davidic regime. Accordingly, Shear-jashub in this instance probably expressed a hopeful message, announcing the sure survival of a remnant. A religious connotation was possibly intended as well: the remnant that turns to Yahweh will return (survive).

Scholars disagree over the identity of the remnant. The traditional suggestions include Judah (as opposed to the northern kingdom), the prophet and his few disciples, or any who turn to Yahweh for protection against Syria and Ephraim. We suggest, however, the house of David, with which the whole of 7:1-17 is principally concerned (vv. 2 and 13), as the likeliest candidate. Facing opposition from the Judean population as well as from the Syrian king, the Davidic regime had cause to fear for its continuing existence. By means of the symbolic naming of his son, Isaiah affirmed that Ahaz and the Davidic dynasty would survive the crisis, if they would retain their confidence in Yahweh's promise to safeguard Jerusalem and his anointed. The Judeans at large might suffer catastrophe, but a remnant would survive—the house of David and its supporters.

Isaiah and Shear-jashub were to meet Ahaz at "the end of the conduit to the upper pool, along the Fuller's Field road." The location was undoubtedly outside the walls of Jerusalem (see II Kings 18:17 = Isa. 36:2), probably toward the south of the city in the vicinity of the Kidron spring. The text does not explain why Ahaz was there, but it seems likely that he was inspecting the city's fortification and water supply in anticipation of a Syro-Ephraimitic attack. Apparently the king himself was inclined, though not finally committed, to hold out against the demands of the coalition, despite pressure from the Judean population and, perhaps, from some of his own advisors within the royal court. When Isaiah accosted Ahaz, his aim was to encourage the king in this direction.

The speech of the prophet opens in verse 4 with a string of imperatives: "Remain aloof and stay calm; don't panic and let your resolve not weaken on account of these two smoldering stubs of fire-wood, that is, the burning anger of Rezin and Syria and the son of Remaliah." Scholars have often seen here Isaiah's imitation of the priestly address to troops before battle, which belonged to the sacred features of ancient warfare (see Deut. 20:2-4). In fact, however, only the last two commands— "don't panic and let your resolve not weaken" —have verbal parallels in the war address. These alone do not warrant our reading into the text the entire ideology of holy war. We note, too, that the priestly war address was directed to Israel at large, or at least to all its able warriors, while Isaiah 7:4-9 is meant for Ahaz and the royal court only. Isaiah's exhortations to fearlessness should be viewed simply as part and parcel of a typical oracle of deliverance to a king, the elect of God, in the face of military danger. The ancient Near East affords numerous examples of the genre, in which similar exhortations play a prominent role (see *ANET* 451, 655).

The first of the prophetic imperatives merits further attention. It derives from the Hebrew root *shamar* and is generally translated "take heed" or "be careful." Elsewhere in the Hebrew scriptures, the command is normally accompanied by some stipulation as to what one is to do or is not to do (for example, Gen. 24:6, 31:24, Exod. 10:28, 34:12,

Deut. 12:13; 15:9; 24:8; II Kings 6:9, and so on; see however I Sam. 19:2). Isaiah's meaning in 7:4, however, is not explicit. Was he warning against all defense measures, as for example the king's securing the city's water supply? Isaiah was not so politically naive as to advocate such a radical position. Or was the prophet concerned with preventing Ahaz from appealing to Assyria for military aid? The conclusion has no basis in the text and rests on an uncritical reading of II Kings 16:5-9 as the historical background of Isaiah 7 and 8.

The simplest interpretation of the prophet's command would view it in relation to the concrete issue that Ahaz and the royal court were facing at the moment; namely, whether to agree finally to join the Syrian-led coalition or to hold out, trusting that Jerusalem could withstand an attack. Isaiah advocated the latter option: Ahaz should "remain aloof"— that is, from the coalition. The house of David should abide by its long-standing policy of political neutrality *vis-à-vis* anti-Assyrian movements.

The prophet speaks of the "two smoldering stumps of firewood" before whom Ahaz should not be afraid, referring to the Syrian and Israelite kings. (Verse 4*b* is a glossator's sarcastic explanation of the allusion.) Isaiah carefully chose the image to express his estimation of the threat they posed to Ahaz. Just as the "ends" of firebrands only smoke and, if left alone, soon go out, so also the plans of Rezin and Pekah would come to naught. In the short run, Yahweh, Israel's "light" and "flame" (see 10:17), would protect Jerusalem and his anointed. In the long run, the Syrian-led coalition would probably collapse. (The alliance, in fact, did begin to fold in 734: both Samsi, queen of Arabia, and several Philistine cities temporarily submitted to Tiglath-pileser. Resistance to the Assyrians, however, continued another two years, longer than Isaiah perhaps expected.)

In verses 5-9 follows a word of assurance and warning to Ahaz and the Davidic court. Though structurally complex, it seems to divide into three parts. (1) Verses 5-6 are formally an extended causal clause which introduces the divine oracle in verses 7-9. Isaiah here describes the plan of Rezin, which calls for a divine response. (2) Verses 7, 8*a*, and 9*a* present Yahweh's answer to the Syrian king's scheme. (Verse 8*b* is correctly taken by most scholars as a gloss.) The oracle consists of a predictive pronouncement against the success of the plot (v. 7) and an explanation of this prediction (8*a*, 9*a*). (3) Verse 9*b* is a warning to the Davidic court, apparently reiterating the position called for in the imperatives in verse 4.

The text through verse 4 has said little about the precise nature of the Syro-Ephraimitic threat to the Davidic regime. This changes in verses 5-6, in which we are expressly told the scheme of the coalition: "Because Syria has plotted against you, (in league with) Ephraim and the son of Remaliah, saying, 'Let's go up into Judah and terrify it and split it open for ourselves and set up the son of Tabeel as king in its midst.' " In the present form of the text, Syria and Israel appear as equal members of the alliance. The reference to Ephraim and the son of Remaliah, however, seems tacked on and is generally viewed as a gloss. If the text then spoke originally only of Syria's plotting, this would again reflect Rezin's role as the moving force behind the coalition.

The plan to invade Judah was the final step on a long series of Syrian efforts to secure the country as a coalition partner. Earlier diplomatic overtures had failed; action against Judean territory, and with it economic pressure, had not worked; even an attempted coup within Jerusalem had come to naught (II Chron. 28:7). Rezin must have felt that time had finally run out for the Davidides. If they were still unwilling to join the cause with him, the Syrian king would have to invade and forcibly replace them with a more cooperative regime.

The quotation in verse 6 speaks of the coalition's "terrifying" and "splitting open" Judah. The latter verb derives from the Hebrew root *baqa`*, the basic sense of which is "to divide, cleave, break open." Elsewhere in the Hebrew scriptures, the term frequently refers to the capture of cities. The pronominal suffix on the verb in 7:6, however, likely refers to Judah, though Jerusalem certainly was the ultimate objective of the invasion. The RSV translates the whole phrase, "Let us go conquer it for ourselves," but this wrongly gives the impression that the coalition was undertaking full-scale military action against the entire country. Rezin was probably not interested in actually annexing Judah, but simply in establishing his effective control over it. This he could do merely by replacing the ruling dynasty with a new regime, just as he had managed in the northern kingdom by means of Pekah's coup.

"Splitting open" Judah is best understood as a vivid reference to a *Blitzkrieg*, which the Syrian king was planning and which Isaiah 10:27d-32 describes. The coalition forces would march southward from Samaria along the watershed route as far as Bethel and from there thrust suddenly into Judean territory, detouring around the fortress at Mizpah by means of the rougher, less-traveled road through Michmash and the Geba Pass. The aim was to besiege the capital city as quickly as possible, avoiding any points of possible resistance *en route* and terrifying all opposition that might have lain in their path.

The reference to the son of Tabeel merits special attention. Numerous suggestions have been made as to the identity of this figure, including that he was an Aramean from somewhere in the Transjordan region or a Judean prince whose "mother-house" was the land of Tabeel to the north of Gilead or even an ancestor of the later-known Tobiads. A recently found Assyrian tributary list from about 738, however, probably provides the solution. The inscription mentions Tubail, king of Tyre, among other rulers of Anatolia and Syria-Palestine who had earlier paid tribute to Tiglath-pileser. The Hebrew *Tabe'al* in 7:6 is likely a deliberate misspelling of the name of the Tyrian royal house, expressing either Isaiah's or later copyists' pejorative attitude toward the intended replacement of Ahaz, the Davidic king. (*Tabe'al* means "good-for-nothing.")

It was then a *Tubailide*, a prince of the Tyrian royal house, whom Rezin planned to install as king in Jerusalem. Possibly many Judeans supported the scheme, having grown increasingly disgruntled with the Davidic rule since the latter half of Uzziah's reign. There was good precedent for a member of the Tyrian royal house occupying the Judean throne: Athaliah, a granddaughter of a Tyrian monarch, ruled as queen of Judah for six years during the previous century. Rezin certainly could count on the cooperation of his intended appointee, since the present king of Tyre was a strong ally of the Syrian king.

In verses 7, 8a and 9a, Isaiah gives the divine response to the Syrian scheme: "Thus says the Lord Yahweh, 'It shall not arise nor shall it come to pass, for the head of Syria is (only) Damascus and the head of Damascus (only) Rezin; and the head of Ephraim is (only) Samaria and the head of Samaria (only) the son of Remaliah.'" The opening verbs of the pronouncement reach back to verses 5-6 for their subject; "it"—that is, the plot of Syria against the Davidic house—will not succeed. Yahweh alone decides the fates of nations and rulers. Not as the Syrian "plans" but as God "plans" do things "arise" (see 14:24-27; 19:12, 17; 30:1).

The logic of the explanation of the divine pronouncement in verses 8*a* and 9*a* is not altogether clear. Is the meaning here that Syria and Ephraim and their respective kings have their own separate spheres of influence that do not include Judah and Jerusalem? This interpretation is possible, but not likely, for the wording of the text seems to emphasize who the "heads" in question are, not the limited domains over which they are "head." A likelier view is that the series is elliptical, to be completed by the prophet's audience: "But the head of Judah is Jerusalem, and the head of Jerusalem the son of David." The prophet's aim here is to remind Ahaz of his elected status and of the divine commitment to Jerusalem. While the capitals of Syria and Ephraim are *only* Damascus and Samaria, and the rulers of these cities *only* Rezin and the son of Remaliah, the head of Judah is Zion, Yahweh's chosen city and the place where he has installed his anointed, the Davidic king. The divine legitimation and protection of the royal city and leadership had long been celebrated during national festivals and made the centerpiece of theological claims emanating from the royal court (Pss. 2, 89, and 132; I Sam. 4-6; II Sam. 6; I Sam. 16–II Sam. 7). In Isaiah 7:7-9*a*, Isaiah urges Ahaz to take these ancient traditions seriously.

In verse 9*b* follows the warning to the entire Davidic court (the verb forms are plural): "If you don't stand firm, you won't stand at all." The two verbs of the sentence derive from the same Hebrew root, *'mn*, so that it is clear that the prophet is engaged here in a word-play. The sense of the second verb is clear; it refers to the political survival of the house of David. The meaning of the first verb, however, is debated. Scholars have generally translated the term as "believe" or "have faith," but have disagreed over the prophet's application of the word here. Is Isaiah simply urging the Davidides to have confidence, to remain calm in the face of the present crisis, to trust in their own security? Or is there an implied object to the verb, be it the ancient divine promises regarding Zion and the Davidic king or the divine oracle specifically, which precedes in verses 7-9*a*? Further, how was the "belief" of the Davidic house to manifest itself concretely? By leaving off all defense measures? The above suggestions read too much of a psychological and theological meaning into the text. The verb can carry a profane sense and, when used without an object, can mean simply, "to be firm, stand still, or hold steady" (see Job 39:24). This is the import of Isaiah's words in 7:9*b*. He is warning the Davidides to be firm, refraining from hasty decisions or policy changes (see 28:16), and, specifically, to maintain the Judean position of political neutrality, which the Davidic house had long maintained *vis-à-vis* the Syrian-led coalition. As we have noted repeatedly, the royal court in Jerusalem was under tremendous pressure to join the cause with Rezin and Pekah. The prophet's advice is that the Davidic house resist this pressure, "standing firm" and abiding by its past policy of political neutrality.

Verse 7:9*b* thus reinforces the imperatives of verse 4: "Remain aloof and stay calm; don't panic, and let your resolve not weaken. . . ." Through its conditional form, however, verse 9*b* does more than simply repeat the earlier exhortations; it states the consequence of non-compliance: "You won't stand at all" (literally, "You won't be made firm"). By use of the verb form *te'amenu*, Isaiah here alludes to the Nathan oracle in which Yahweh vouchsafed the endurance of the Davidic house (II Sam. 7:16). There David is assured, "Your house and your kingdom will be established (*ne'eman*) forever; your throne will be sure for all time." In Isaiah 7:9*b*, the prophet warns the royal court that this divine promise will be forfeited if Judah's political neutrality *vis-à-vis* Syria is not maintained. Isaiah astutely saw that Assyria would take tough action not only against the Syrian and Israelite leadership, but also against the Davidides should they join the coalition.

Verses 10-17

Verses 10-17 present a dispute between the king and the prophet. Isaiah instructs Ahaz to request a divine sign, the latter refuses, the prophet chides the king, and on Yahweh's behalf, proclaims the Immanuel "sign." Some scholars have considered the link between this material and verses 1-9 redactional, but the two blocks cannot in fact be literarily separated. Verses 10-17 assume what precedes and, apart from it, cannot be understood. Noteworthy, too, is the linguistic connection. The coalition intends to "terrify" Judah (v. 6); Ahaz is "terrified" of Rezin and Pekah (v. 16). A kind of narrative gap does occur between verses 9 and 10 in that the text does not recount but simply assumes the prophet's actual deliverance of the speech dictated in verses 3-9. Such foreshortening, however, is a common technique in Hebrew narrative and provides no basis for redaction-critical conclusions.

Two other features of the text reflect a degree of tension between verses 1-9 and verses 10-17 and so require our close attention. First, in its present form verse 10 states, "And Yahweh continued speaking (or "spoke again") to Ahaz." In verses 3-9, however, Yahweh speaks directly to the prophet and only through him to the king. Such is the case also in verse 11, in which the prophet addresses Ahaz in his own voice, referring to Yahweh in the third-person ("Yahweh your god"; see v. 12, "Yahweh"; v. 13, "my God"; v. 14, "the Lord"; and v. 17, "Yahweh"). The contradiction is best handled by the text-critical assumption that verse 10 orginally read only, "And he (Isaiah) spoke again to Ahaz" (see the Targum). A glossator mistakenly assumed that Yahweh was the subject of the sentence, perhaps under the influence of 8:5 (see 8:1 and 11) and also because what precedes in verses 7-9 is divine speech.

Second, the scene of action seems to change in the course of the narrative. The first encounter between the king and the prophet occurs outside the city walls "at the end of the conduit to the upper pool, along the Fuller's Field road" (v. 3). If, as we will argue, the "young woman" mentioned in v. 14*b* is a Davidic princess, the second exchange between Isaiah and Ahaz would seem to have taken place within the royal palace. The question now is whether one can assign the two scenes to separate literary sources and understand their conflation as redactional. Our answer is negative for the reason set forth above: The intelligibility of 7:10-17 depends entirely on what is said about Rezin and Pekah in verses 5 and 6 and on the divine oracle in verses 7-9. Although historically distinct, the two encounters were fused in popular memory at an early stage of their tradition history.

Verses 10-17 exhibit a legendary character insofar as they depict Isaiah as a wonder-worker. At the outset, he instructs the king to "ask a sign from Yahweh your God." A prophetic sign in ancient Israel usually functioned as a vivid illustration of a word about the future, as the concrete embodiment of the content of a prophetic prediction. This is the way Isaiah himself seems to have understood the term; the symbolic names of his children, and perhaps his own name as well, were "signs and portents in Israel," illustrating what he had predicted during the Syro-Ephraimitic crisis (8:18). A similar understanding of "sign" emerges in Isaiah 20. The prophet's walking about Jerusalem naked or partly clad for three years amounts to a kind of street drama that vividly illustrates his prediction about the fate of Egypt and Ethiopia and/or the Palestinian rebels. He thereby underscores his warning against Judah's involvement with these two countries during the revolt of Ashdod.

In 7:11, the sign offered to Ahaz is of a different sort. It is not intended to illustrate the content of a prediction. Rather, it is to confirm the veracity of the divine promise given in verses 7-9*a*. Such a sign need not necessarily be a miraculous occurrence, but certainly it must be something unusual or unexpected. The choice given to the king—"Let it be as deep as Sheol or as high as heaven" (v. 11*b*)—means to say that Ahaz may ask for any sign whatever, even a miraculous one.

The scene here bears resemblance to the legendary account of Hezekiah's healing in Isaiah 38 (see II Kings 20). There Isaiah declares to the king: "And this will be for you the sign from Yahweh that Yahweh will do this thing which he has promised. Look, I will make the shadow cast by the declining sun on the dial of Ahaz turn back ten steps" (vv. 7 and 8). Both here and in 7:11, the sign bears no conceptual relation to the content of the prophetic prediction. It is arbitrarily chosen as an unusual, if not miraculous, occurrence that vouchsafes God's power and willingness to carry out what he has promised. (See Judg. 6:11-24 for a similar, though not identical, function of a "sign.")

In this connection, a word must be said about the Immanuel saying (vv. 14-17). The narrative characterizes it, too, as a sign: "Therefore my Lord himself will give to you a sign: Look, the young woman is pregnant and is about to bear a son and she will name him Immanuel. Curds and honey will he eat until he knows how to reject evil and choose good." Scholars have long debated not only the import of the "sign," whether salvation or disaster or both, but also the question in what precisely the "sign" consists, whether the child's birth from the "young woman," his name, his diet, or a combination of these. Taken by themselves, however, verses 14b-15 need not be seen as the presentation of a sign at all. They are instead, we will argue, simply an announcement of the imminent birth of a royal child and a prediction of his survival. Certainly the name of the child is symbolic; it expresses Yahweh's saving presence with the Davidic house. Yet of greater consequence than the name is the child himself—his identity as a royal prince and his survival. That he is born of "the young woman" and expresses the likes and dislikes of normal children—is not a sign that illustrates or guarantees the truth of a prediction, but rather it is the concrete fulfillment of the prediction itself. The Syrian and Israelite kings will not succeed in exterminating the Davidic line.

It remains to be explained how the Immanuel saying came to be characterized as a sign. A conclusive answer is probably not possible, but the following traditio-historical development seems plausible. In the context of the Syro-Ephraimitic crisis, Isaiah at some point chided the Davidic house—"Is it of so little significance to you to weary men that you weary my God also?"—and then continued with the Immanuel saying. The cause of the prophet's criticism was the wavering stance of Ahaz and his advisors; they delayed in adopting a final stand either against or for the Syrian-led coalition. This meaning, however, was lost on a later generation which no longer understood the precise political issue originally at play. Popular reflection on verse 13 produced a different explanation of the prophet's agitation. Unlike Hezekiah, who had rightfully requested from Isaiah a sign confirming a divine promise (Isaiah 38 = II Kings 20), Ahaz had refused a sign verifying the truth of Yahweh's pledge to the Davidic house. The legendary portrayal of the prophet as a great sign- or wonder-worker in 7:10-12 arose then as an attempt to understand verse 13. As a corollary of this popular interpretation, the Immanuel saying also was characterized as a "sign," which Yahweh himself would give in lieu of the sign Ahaz refused.

The above discussion has assumed an interpretation of the Immanuel saying as a word of salvation to the house of David. The passage, however, is one of the most debated texts in the Hebrew scriptures, particularly with regard to whether it is hopeful or threatening. We must, accordingly, attend more closely to its details.

The saying is composed of two parts. First, verses 14b and 15 focus exclusively on the Immanuel-child. The prophet draws attention to the pregnancy of "the young woman" and to the fast-approaching birth of her son (v. 14b), gives instructions as to the naming of the child (v. 14b; see II Sam. 12:24-25), and predicts that he will grow up on a diet of curds and honey "until he knows how to reject evil and choose good" (v. 15). Second, verses 16 and 17 are an extended causal clause (introduced by *ki*) that presents a two-part prophetic announcement about future political developments. Isaiah first predicts the devastation of Syria and Ephraim, thereby implying the failure of the plot against the Davidic house (v. 16). (Note that the text refers to the "land" of the two states as though Syria and Ephraim formed a single political entity; see 7:2a) The prophet then announces Yahweh's intentions to restore the northern kingdom to Davidic control: "Yahweh will bring upon you (Ahaz) and upon your people (supporters of the Davidides) and upon your ancestral house (the Davidic dynasty—present and future) days which have not been since the day when Ephraim broke away from Judah" (v. 17). The whole of this two-part announcement is introduced by the temporal condition of verse 16a: "before the child (Immanuel) knows how to reject evil and choose good," the prophet's predictions will be fulfilled.

The passage as a whole bears some resemblance to birth announcements elsewhere in the Hebrew scriptures. In Genesis 16:11, for example, the angel of Yahweh addresses Hagar: "Behold, you are pregnant and will soon bear a son: you are to call his name Ishmael ("God-gives-heed"), for (*ki*) Yahweh has given heed to your affliction" (see Judg. 13:3). The similarity between the vocabulary and syntax of this text and that of Isaiah 7:14-17 is obvious. Two pecularities of the Isaiah text, however, are important. First, the prophet does not stop with the naming of the child but continues to describe how he will grow up (v. 15). Indeed, it is this detail about the child, not his name, that receives emphasis, picked up verbally as it is in verse 16*a*.

Second, although verses 16-17 are formally a causal or explanatory clause, it is unclear how their content "explains" what is said about Immanuel in verses 14-15. They say nothing about the child's mother, nor interpret directly the boy's name ("God-with-us") nor explain the significance of his growing up. An understanding of these matters seems rather to be assumed. The only direct link between the two halves of the passage occurs in verses 15*b* and 16*a*, and even here the relation is not a matter of one thing explaining another. The connection is rather a temporal one; the child will grow up "until it knows how to reject evil and choose good." Before the child reaches that age, Syria and Ephraim will suffer destruction, and the Davidic house will again rule over the northern kingdom.

How then should one account for the causal form of verses 16-17? The verses, we suggest, do offer an "explanation," but one of a peculiar sort. Assuming that the identity of the Immanuel child and the significance of his growing up for the house of David were obvious to his audience, Isaiah here simply lays out as a prediction the political developments that must follow in the near future, "before the child knows how to reject evil and choose good." The prophet's argument is the reverse from what we might expect, but is nonetheless effective. He announces the birth, the naming, and the survival of the child (vv. 14-15) and then predicts the realization of the political conditions on which what has been said of the child is premised (vv. 16-17).

The identity of Immanuel and of his mother are obviously related questions. The text describes the latter as an *'almah*, a term that elsewhere in the Hebrew Bible designates post-pubescent young women of marriageable age (see Gen. 24:43; Exod. 2:8; Ps. 68:26; Song of Sol. 1:3; 6:8; Prov. 30:18). Regarding her precise identity, however, scholarly interpretations differ. The following options have been proposed. (1) The young woman is the wife of the prophet, either identical with the prophetess mentioned in 8:3 or another woman whom Isaiah had married. (2) She is a woman of no particular status, but one who happened to be standing near the prophet as he addressed the royal court. (3) The young woman stands for a collective entity—either the Daughter of Zion or any Judean woman who may be pregnant at the time. (4) She is a mythological figure—the mother-goddess whose pregnancy by the god-king and bearing of a divine child ensure the stability and fertility of the world for the upcoming year. (5) The woman is the Judean queen or a member of the royal harem, i.e., a wife of Ahaz, whose son (perhaps Hezekiah) would represent the future of the Davidic dynasty. (This last position and the mythological interpretation have often been combined.)

If Isaiah 7:14-17 is interpreted in close connection with the political crisis of the moment, the last of these interpretations, with slight modification, appears to make the best sense. We recall that the goal of the Syro-Ephraimitic campaign was to replace the Davidic leadership in Jerusalem and thus ensure Judean cooperation with the anti-Assyrian alliance (vv. 5 and 6). This would have entailed not simply deposing Ahaz, but executing him, along with all possible Davidic heirs to the throne, even those yet unborn. The practice of exterminating the ruling family is attested to in earlier Israelite history. Apparently with encouragement from the prophet Ahijah, Baasha overthrew the house of Jeroboam, executing not only the king, Nadab, but also all members of the royal family (I Kings 14:7-11; 15:27-29). Similarly, Zimri's coup entailed killing "all the house of Baasha: he did not leave a single male of his kinsmen or his friends" (I Kings 16:11; see vv. 1-4).

When Jehu toppled the Omride dynasty, he slaughtered the seventy relatives and descendants of Ahab as well as all other supporters of that regime (II Kings 10:1-11; compare I Kings 16:11-12). The pronouncements of both Amos and Hosea against Jeroboam II call for the extermination of the entire dynastic house (Amos 7:9, 17; Hosea 1:3). (See also II Kings 15:16, which reports Menahem's brutal action against the citizens of Tappuah, including ripping open all the pregnant women. If the assassinated king, Shallum, had had his home-base in the Tappuah region, the slaughter of pregnant women by Menahem may have been intended in part to eliminate descendants of Shallum, who might challenge the new king's reign.) Undoubtedly, the wiping out of the dynastic line was a real threat to Ahaz and the royal court as they anxiously awaited the approach of Syrian and Ephraimite troops.

It is this threat—the extermination of the Davidic house—which Isaiah's words in 7:14-17 seek to counter. The young woman (the Hebrew noun is accompanied by the definite article) is neither a metaphorical image nor a collective entity but a definite person who is in attendance at the court and whose conception and bearing of a child represent in a literal sense the survival of the royal house. Only one conclusion can follow: She is a Davidic princess, and her son to be born is a potential royal heir. (The royal chronology of the period, however, does not allow one to identify the child as Hezekiah.) That the latter will grow up eating "curds and honey" (probably the normal soft diet of young infants) until it "knows how to reject what is bad and choose what is good" (that is, until it begins to express its likes and dislikes) is tantamount to promising the failure of Rezin's plot and the survival of the Davidic regime. It is the fulfillment of the hope that the child's very name expresses for the house of David: "God is with us."

Isaiah 7:18-25

Isaiah 7:18-25 contains words of doom by the prophet. Against whom the disaster is to come, however, is not made explicit. We note that no reference is made to either the Davidic house or Jerusalem—for these Isaiah foresaw deliverance. Rather it is the "land" (vv. 22b and 24b) that is to be affected: Yahweh will reduce the countryside to a wild, uncultivated state (vv. 21-25). The threat was probably aimed against the many non-Jerusalemite Judeans who were supportive of Rezin and Pekah and whose punishment at the hands of the Assyrians Isaiah thus expected (v. 20). The announcement of disaster upon the Judean countryside accords with the prophet's long-standing anticipation of the devastation of "this people" (6:11-12).

The material consists of a series of four predictions about the events of "that day" (vv. 18, 20, 21, and 23)—that is, the day of divine action against Judah. The sayings fall into pairs. First, verses 18-19 and verse 20 announce Yahweh's use of surrogate powers to wreak havoc on the land and its inhabitants. Second, verses 21-22 and verses 23-25 describe the wild condition of the country that will follow in the wake of Yahweh's actions. Both parts of the passage resume the language and motifs of chapter 5, Isaiah's speech from some years earlier about the "vineyard gone bad." The prophet apparently expected to see in the unfolding events of the Syro-Ephraimitic crisis the continuing fulfillment of his previous announcements of doom.

The first prediction, verses 18 and 19, describes Yahweh's bringing insects against the land: "And on that day Yahweh will whistle (*yishroq*) for the fly which is at the source of the rivers of Egypt and for the bee which is in the land of Assyria." The greatness of their number is emphasized; "all of them" will settle on the ravines and rocky clefts, on "all" the rough brushland and "all" the pastures.

It is not altogether clear whether the prophet's intended meaning here is literal or figurative. If the former, Isaiah apparently expected a great plague of insects to befall Judah and viewed their descent upon the countryside as part of the land's reversion to a wild state. More likely, however, Isaiah used the insect imagery metaphorically to refer to the imminent invasion of Judah by foreign powers. Years earlier, the prophet voiced the same expectation, using similar vocabulary: "He [Yahweh] will raise a signal for a nation afar off, and whistle (*sharaq*) for it from the ends of the earth" (5:26). The parallelism of the sentence, as well as the larger context (5:27-30), make amply clear that Yahweh's "whistling" refers figuratively to his enlisting a foreign army against Judah and Israel. That this same sense is operative in 7:18-19 is suggested from the description that follows in verse 20 of the humiliating treatment of prisoners of war. We note also that the imagery is used elsewhere in the Hebrew Bible to describe military enemies (see Deut. 1:44, Ps. 118:12).

In the earlier speech of chapter 5, Isaiah did not name the enemy nation for whom Yahweh would "whistle." This vagueness, we have argued, was probably due to the prophet's own uncertainty as to the identity of the invader. In 735, however, the year to which 7:18-25 probably dates, such uncertainty must surely have been past. Assyria had emerged as the dominant world power, even though still struggling with a troublesome Urartu. Tiglath-pileser was an obvious threat to revolting Palestinian states and one whom Isaiah expected to devastate the Judean countryside in the course of the Syro-Ephraimitic crisis.

Isaiah 7:18 speaks not only of the "bee which is in the land of Assyria," but also of the "fly which is at the source of the rivers of Egypt." The latter appears to allude to Ethiopia, located at the upper reaches of the Nile River and its tributaries. The reference raises a difficult historical problem: Did both Ethiopia and Assyria pose military threats to Judah and other Palestinian states during the second half of the 730s? The vast majority of scholars answer negatively and so view the allusion to Ethiopia in 7:18 as a secondary addition. Whether Isaiah spoke of the fly and bee both or only of the bee, he allegedly had only Assyria in mind.

As attractive as this solution may be, it is not altogether satisfactory. None of the historical settings that scholars propose for the added reference to Ethiopia—for example, 720, 712, or 701—is really suitable. In these later instances, Ethiopia appeared as a potential ally of the Palestinian states, not as an enemy.

We suggest an alternate interpretation of 7:18 that takes the entire verse as genuinely Isaianic. In referring to Ethiopia, the prophet may have been thinking of Pharaoh Piye. The latter pressed northward into Lower Egypt sometime during the late 730s, presumably in response to Assyria's increasing control of the east Mediterranean ports and, thereby, of the region's entire sea trade (see chap. 1, sect. 2). The plans for such Ethiopian expansion, or perhaps even for more far-reaching action, probably did not arise suddenly but were taking shape already during the early or middle 730s, when Assyria had begun to encroach upon Egyptian, and so also Ethiopian, trade.

It is thus possible that Piye came within Isaiah's purview in 735. If the assumption is correct, the prophet apparently realized that Ethiopia might seek to safeguard its economic interests not simply by invading Lower Egypt but by occupying part or all of Palestine as well. (Events did not, however, unfold as the prophet had anticipated. Piye delayed taking action until the late 730s and so allowed Assyria to solidify control of Palestine as far south as the Brook of Egypt.)

In the second prediction, verse 20, the prophet employs a new image to describe Yahweh's use of surrogate powers against Judah. With "the hired razor," Yahweh will shave the head and "hair of the feet" (a euphemism for pubic hair) and the beard. What precisely Isaiah had in mind here is not clear. He may have meant that by means of the "hired razor" Yahweh will impose upon the Judeans harsh conditions of mourning (Deut. 21:10-13; Isa. 22:12; Jer. 41:4-5; 48:37-39). More likely, however, the background of the metaphor is an ancient practice of humiliating slaves and prisoners of war by shaving off their hair (see II Sam. 10:1-5). Isaiah, then, was portraying the ill treatment the Judeans would suffer at the hands of enemy troops.

Who is the "hired razor" Yahweh will use against the land? Isaiah, himself, may not have explained the allusion, but the concluding gloss or glosses (if "beyond the river" is also secondary) likely reflect the prophet's intended meaning. Yahweh will employ the Assyrian army as mercenaries to bring disaster upon the rural Judeans. The sense is similar to that of 10:5-6 and 15—the Assyrian king functions as the instrument of divine wrath.

The third and fourth predictions, verses 21-22 and 23-25, depict conditions in the land that will ensue in the wake of the enemy invasion. The prophet begins by focusing on the diet of the inhabitants (vv. 21-22): Any who survive the Assyrian onslaught will have to live on the natural products of the land, "indeed *only* curds and honey will one be able to eat." (The inverted Hebrew word order in verse 22*b* emphasizes the deprivation of the survivors.) Isaiah then describes at length the uncultivated condition of the land. Briers and thorns will replace the once lush and valuable vines (v. 23). Indeed, the wild growth will be so extensive that portions of the previously cultivated land will be used for hunting only (v. 24). The once carefully hoed hill country will be neglected; no concern will be given to weeding out the briers and thorns that spring up (v. 25*a*). The formerly cultivated fields will be used only for the grazing of livestock (v. 25*b*).

The parallels between this material and the prophet's earlier speech on the "vineyard gone bad" are numerous. In 5:5, Yahweh states that his vineyard will become a "trampling-ground"; in 7:25*b*, the prophet predicts the Judean farmland will become a place where cattle are let loose and a "trampling-ground" for sheep. In 5:6, Yahweh declares that the vineyard shall no longer be pruned or "hoed" and, consequently, "briers and thorns" will be allowed to grow up. In 7:23-25, Isaiah proclaims that the Judean hills, which used to be "hoed," will no longer be tended; there will be no worrying over the "briers and thorns." Indeed, the "briers and thorns" will overgrow the former vineyards (v. 23). The connections between the two texts are too close to be accidental. The prophet appears in 7:18-25 intentionally to have taken predictions from the earlier period and applied them to the imminently unfolding events of 735–732. Assyria, Isaiah expected, would devastate the Judean countryside, reducing Yahweh's vineyard to a desolate land unsuited for agriculture.

10. REFUSING THE WATERS OF SHILOAH (8:1-20)

R. P. **Carroll**, "Translation and Attribution in Isaiah 8.19f.," *BT* 31(1980)126-34; C. A. **Evans**, "An Interpretation of Isa. 8, 11-15 Unemended," *ZAW* 97(1985)112-13; K. **Jeppesen**, "Call and Frustration: A New Understanding of Isaiah VIII 21-22," *VT* 32(1982)145-57; A. **Jepsen**, "Die Nebiah in Jes 8,3," *ZAW* 72(1960)267-68; H. **Klein**, "Freude an Rezin: Ein Versuch, mit dem Text Jes. 8.6 ohne Konjectur auszukommen," *VT* 30(1980)231-33; N. **Lohfink**, "Isaias 8,12-14," *BZ* 7(1963)98-104; P. **Machinist**, "Assyria and Its Image in the First Isaiah,"

JAOS 103(1983)719-37; H.-P. **Müller**, "Das Wort von dem Totengeistern Jes. 8:19f.," *WO* 8(1975)65-76; L. G. **Rignell**, "Das Orakel 'Maher-salal Has-bas.' Jesaja 8," *ST* 10(1957)40-52; J. J. M. **Roberts**, "Isaiah and His Children," *Biblical and Other Studies Presented to Samuel Iwry* (ed. A. Kort and S. Morschauser; Winona Lake: Eisenbrauns, 1985)193-203; M. **Saebø**, "Zur Traditionsgeschichte von Jesaia 8,9-10," *ZAW* 76(1964)132-44; C. F. **Whitley**, "The Language and Exegesis of Isaiah 8:16-23," *ZAW* 90(1978)28-43; W. I. **Wolverton**, "Judgment in Advent: Notes on Isaiah 8:5-15 and 7:14," *ATR* 37(1955)284-91.

Isaiah 8:1-20 is a collection of genuine Isaianic speeches and reports that relate to different phases of the Syro-Ephraimitic crisis. Four originally separate units comprise the material.

(1) A symbolic action report—"Spoil speeds, prey hastens" (1-4)
(2) An announcement of disaster against Judah, coupled with a promise of deliverance to the Davidic house (5-8*a*, 8*b*-10)
(3) Admonition and promise to supporters of the Davidic house (11-15)
(4) A prophetic confession of confidence and admonition to the Davidic supporters to abide by Isaiah's word (16-18, 19-20)

The pieces combine to produce the same picture of the prophet's thought, which we saw in chapter 7: the Syro-Ephraimitic alliance will fail, Judah at large will suffer harsh punishment, Yahweh will protect the Davidides and Jerusalem.

The autobiographical style runs throughout verses 1-20 in their present form. In two instances, however, the prophetic "I" may have been introduced secondarily. The quotation formula of verse 5—"And Yahweh spoke to me again"—leads one to expect divine speech in verses 6ff. What follows, however, is not a word from Yahweh but a prophetic speech that refers to the Lord in the third person (v. 7). The same discrepancy occurs between verses 11 and 12-15.

The evidence indicates that verses 5 and 11 are redactional additions. More difficult to determine is whether they derive from Isaiah himself or from a later editor. We see no compelling reasons against the former assumption, for elsewhere in the book of Isaiah the prophet appears to have been involved in the written preservation of his words (30:8). At some point prior to the denouement of the Syro-Ephraimitic crisis, Isaiah picked up speeches that he had delivered earlier and wove them together into a larger memoir, 8:1-20. His additions in verses 5 and 11 lent coherence to the whole by extending the autobiographical style already present in verses 1-4 and 16-20 and by enforcing the prophet's overarching polemic—namely, that his predictions and advice during the crisis had been divinely dictated and accordingly were reliable.

Isaiah 8:1-20 reflects a picture of the prophet's ministry as it addressed a wide audience. His words and actions here are directed not only to the king and Davidic court, as in 7:1-17, but also to the Jerusalemite public at large. This is particularly evident in 8:1-4, the details of which we will now examine closely.

Isaiah 8:1-4

The symbolic action report in 8:1-4 consists of two parts. First, verses 1 and 2 concern the erection of a public inscription. Here Isaiah receives the divine order, "Take a large tablet and write upon it in common characters, 'Spoil speeds, prey hastens.'" (The Hebrew preposition that introduces the inscribed words is the "lamed inscriptionis." It functions here as little more than a quotation mark.) The narrative does not actually recount the execution of the command but simply assumes it. It adds only that Isaiah secured two reliable witnesses to the event—Uriah the priest (see II Kings 16:10-16) and an otherwise unknown Zechariah, the son of Jeberechiah.

Second, verses 3 and 4 first recount the conception and birth of the prophet's son by "the prophetess" and then relate Yahweh's word concerning the naming of the child. The latter entails two parts: (a) the divine command, "Call his name 'Spoil-Speeds-Prey-Hastens,'" and (b) the explanation of the name— "for before the child knows how to cry 'Daddy' and 'Mommy,' the wealth of Damascus and the spoil of Samaria will be carried away before the king of Assyria." (The reference here to the Assyrian king may be a gloss, but if so it is certainly one that interprets correctly the prophet's intended meaning.)

What connects the two symbolic actions—the inscription and the naming of Isaiah's son—are the words, "Spoil speeds, prey hastens." Is this statement to be taken in both cases as a proper name? Scholars have generally answered positively, but the assumption raises problems. Isaiah would not likely have written the name of his son for use in public preaching at a time when the child had not yet even been conceived. Related to this difficulty is the apparent fact that Yahweh revealed the significance of the name only after the child's birth. The prophet would not have understood the symbolic meaning of the name when he first wrote it down for public perusal. This assumption, however, is most improbable.

These temporal difficulties have frequently been solved by construing the verbal tenses in verse 3*a* as pluperfects: "I *had approached* the prophetess and she *had conceived* and *had borne* a son." The time lapse between the inscription and the naming of the child is thereby eliminated. This interpretation, however, is not convincing, for the series of Hebrew verbal forms in verses 1-4 reflects a simple narrative style in which events are recounted sequentially. The syntax of the passage clearly indicates that the erection of the inscription long preceded the birth and naming of the prophet's son.

A more satisfactory solution is to assume that Isaiah first used the expression, "spoil speeds, prey hastens," not as a proper name but as a kind of motto or slogan. Undoubtedly, he understood by it something quite definite and used it as a basis for more elaborate preaching. Several months later, when his son was born, Isaiah was inspired to name the child symbolically after the earlier used slogan. At a still later point during the Syro-Ephraimitic crisis, the prophet recorded in writing both symbolic actions—the inscription and the naming of the child. For the sake of brevity and style, however, he reported the sense of the slogan/name only once (v. 4).

The slogan itself may have been a war cry. (It has its parallel in Egyptian texts of the Eighteenth Dynasty.) When the prophet inscribed the slogan on a tablet and used it to comment publicly on contemporary politics, he was probably applying a well-known saying to the specific circumstances of his audience—that is, the increasing pressure on Judah to join Syria and Israel in a common front against Assyria.

Precisely at which point in the Syro-Ephraimitic crisis Isaiah first preached "the spoil speeds, the prey hastens" is difficult to say. If, however, his subsequent application of the slogan to his newborn son assumes a context in which Syria and Israel still posed a threat to Jerusalem and the Davidides, a setting before or during their invasion of Judah in 735/4, it would seem that Isaiah erected the inscription as early as 735. This was a time when the overtures of Rezin and Pekah to the Davidic leadership were probably still of a peaceful nature. By means of the slogan, Isaiah expressed his estimation of the revolt's chances of success: Syria and Israel would soon suffer plunder and pillage at the hands of the Assyrians. The implications of the message for Ahaz and Jerusalem were equally clear: They should remain aloof from the coalition.

Verse 2 reports the presence of "reliable witnesses" at the erection of the inscription. That there were two such witnesses accords with standard Israelite law (see Deut. 17:6 and 19:15). The one, Uriah the priest, is known from II Kings 16:10-16. He was charged by Ahaz with implementing an extensive cultic reform within the Jerusalem temple. The other, Zechariah son of Jeberechiah, is mentioned only here. Presumably, he also was a high religious official. The testimony of both would be particularly appropriate if the prophet's inscription was set up somewhere within the temple area. (Hab. 2:2 attests to the custom of cultic prophets writing their oracles on tablets in easily readable script.)

What purpose did the testimony of these witnesses serve? Certainly it did not concern the authorship of the inscription, for Isaiah's prominent profile in Jerusalem during these years would have left the public in little doubt on this question. Rather, Uriah and Zechariah were needed to certify the exact date of the inscription. By means of their official testimony, Isaiah could later protect himself against the skeptical charge of *ex eventum* prophecy. Uriah and Zechariah would confirm that he had announced the demise of Syria and Israel in advance.

Nine or more months after writing the inscription, Isaiah named his newborn son "Spoil-Speeds-Prey–Hastens." The reuse of the slogan in this way can only mean that Assyria had not dealt with Rezin and Pekah as quickly as the prophet had suggested. Throughout 735, Tiglath-pileser was still bogged down in the east with Urartu and had not yet squashed the budding revolt in the west. The coalition's prospects for success, perhaps, looked better than ever in the early part of 734, and the pressure on Judah to join the cause was probably rising. In such circumstances, the Jerusalemite public and the royal court must have wondered whether Isaiah's prediction of the previous year had been correct.

The response of the prophet to such doubt was firm. Boldly he repeated the threat against Syria and Israel, appropriating the slogan for the symbolic naming of his son. Still, perhaps with an eye to quelling increased skepticism over his ability at prediction, Isaiah added this time a temporal limit within which his words would be fulfilled: "before the child knows how to cry 'Daddy' and 'Mommy'"—that is, within a year—Assyria would crush the coalition.

Isaiah 8:5-8a, 8b-10

Isaiah 8:6-10 forms a single speech in two parts: a threat against "this people"—that is, the Judeans at large (vv. 6-8*a*) and a promise of deliverance for Jerusalem and/or the Davidic house (vv. 8*b*-10). These are linked together by the perfect consecutive verbal form that begins verse 8*b*. The force of the conjunction is adversative: Yahweh is bringing disaster against Judah, *but* "us" God will protect.

Historical allusions within 8:6-10 help date the passage. If verses 7-8*a* speak of an Assyrian invasion of Judah as a future event, the speech likely anticipates Tiglath-pileser's 734 campaign "against Philistia." (As events later transpired, the Assyrian king did not penetrate the heartland of Judah.) Furthermore, if the reference to "nations" and "far off lands" and the assertion that their plans will not "arise" (compare 7:7) have as their background the designs of the Syrian-led coalition upon Jerusalem (7:5-6), the passage would date shortly before the Syro-Ephraimitic siege of the capital city. Finally, the address to Immanuel in verse 8*b* and the play on his name at the end of verse 10 may provide an *ante pro quem* for 8:6-10. The birth of the royal child probably inspired the prophet with confidence in the survival of the Davidic house and prompted these verses.

Verses 6-8*a* combine a reproach of "this people" (v. 6) with a threat of divine punishment (vv. 7-8*a*). The two parts are tightly linked not only syntactically ("because . . . there- fore"), but also by means of a single metaphor: The people have spurned the gently flowing waters of Shiloah; Yahweh is about to bring against them the mighty waters of the river (Euphrates).

The interpretation of the verses rests in large part on the text-critical assessment of verse 6*b*. The Hebrew here betrays an unusual syntax; literally, it reads: "and [this people's] gladness with (*umeśoś 'eth*) Rezin and the son of Remaliah." Most scholars consider the line corrupt, not only for linguistic reasons, but also because of its allegedly impossible sense. The Judean population, so it is argued, ought to have feared rather than rejoiced over the Syrian and Israelite kings who were threatening to invade the country.

These considerations have led to a number of textual reconstructions, the more popular of which involve changing *umeśoś* to a verbal form of *mss*, "dissolve, melt (in fear)." For several reasons, however, this proposal and its many variations are not convincing. First, textual evidence for the emendation is altogether lacking. The ancient versions all seem to assume a Hebrew text similar, if not identical, to the MT. Second, emending *umeśoś* to a form of *mss* may be plausible text-critically, but this change alone hardly resolves the difficult syntax of verse 6*b*. Further alterations of the text are usually required, thus weakening the force of the argument.

Third, with one minor adjustment in the pointing of the MT (*umeśoś* to *umaśoś*), it is possible to explain the unusual Hebrew of verse 6*b* as an example of legitimate poetic license. If the syntax of the line were normal, we would see a verbal form of *śuś* followed by the proposition *b* or `*al* ("rejoice in or over someone"). As it stands, verse 6*b* consists of the noun *maśoś* followed by the accusative particle (or preposition) *'eth*.

The phrasing was intentionally chosen in assimilation to the Hebrew of verse 6a, *ma'as . . . 'eth* (this people "rejected"). The deviation from normal syntax in verse 6b skillfully produces verbal assonance, while still conveying the general sense of "this people's rejoicing in Rezin and the son of Remaliah." (Note Isaiah's use of the word *mśś* in 24:8, 11; 32:13, 14.)

Fourth, the alleged senselessness of 8:6b is not a strong basis for emending the text. Only if one assumes that the Judean king and people alike feared the Syrian and Israelite kings (and so appealed to Assyria for help; II Kings 16:5-9) does the meaning of the verse seem impossible. Without textual evidence to the contrary, however, the MT should be retained and the historical background understood accordingly (see chap. 1, sect. 3D above).

Alongside the text-critical issue is the literary-critical question, Does verse 6b form an original part of the prophet's speech? Many scholars believe not, contending that the line disrupts the close connection between the reference to the waters of Shiloah in the first part of verse 6 and the reference to the waters of the River in verse 7. Verse 6a, along with the reference to the king of Assyria and all his glory in verse 7, is consequently set aside as an explanatory gloss.

Again, several considerations weigh against this conclusion. First, compared with some other glosses in Isaiah, the expressions "rejoicing in Rezin and the son of Remaliah" and "the king of Assyria and all his glory" are more elaborate in their phrasing (compare "the king of Assyria" at the end of 7:17 and 20a). They are not the briefly worded notes that characteristically derive from glossators. Second, if we are correct about the verbal and assonantal parallels between verses 6b and 6a, verse 6b again does not look like a simple explanatory note. Glossators do not usually engage in this kind of skillful wordplay. Third, although the expressions do explain "rejecting the waters of the Shiloah" and "the waters of the River," this alone hardly indicates that the lines are secondary. They are, rather, the prophet's deliberate elucidation of the metaphorical imagery he is using. To claim, as some do, that such explanation appears intrusive and stylistically clumsy is at best an overstatement.

The above remarks justify our retaining 8:6b without emendation and all of verse 7 as original parts of Isaiah's speech. The decision is important, for we thereby recover a rare but clear glimpse into the complex political dynamics within Judah on the eve of the Syro-Ephraimitic crisis.

The prophet begins with an accusation against "this people" (v. 6a). The identical reference appears, as we have seen, in 6:9, but also in 8:11-12. In all three passages, the same group is intended—the Judean population at large. The threat "against them" in 8:7-8a makes this identification certain: into Judah will Yahweh bring the mighty and rising waters of the River (v. 8a).

Isaiah charges that the Judeans have rejected the "waters of the Shiloah." The reference is unique in the Hebrew Bible and, for this reason, not altogether clear. Presumably some sort of water canal for Jerusalem is meant. Nehemiah 3:15 mentions a "pool of Shelah at the garden of the king," which may be a later development of a water works system dating back to the time of Ahaz or earlier. Excavations in Jerusalem at the end of the nineteenth century uncovered two canals that, before the construction of the Siloam tunnel, led off the overflowing waters of the Gihon Spring southward along the east side of the city. Isaiah 8:6 probably refers to one of these.

Still unclear is what "rejecting" the waters of Shiloah means. The language is figurative, and its interpretation depends on our rightly seeing the symbolic import of "the waters of Shiloah." This, however, is not easy, for 8:6 is, as we noted above, the sole reference. The Gihon Spring, on the other hand, whose overflow the Shiloah drained, is mentioned elsewhere in the Hebrew Bible and in connection with highly significant events. First Kings 1:33-40 records that Zadok the priest and Nathan the prophet escorted the young Solomon to the Gihon and there privately anointed him as successor to the throne. Although the anointing ritual at the Gihon is described only in this one instance, the ceremony was likely repeated for each new Davidic king.

In view of the Shiloah's connection to the Gihon Spring, it would hardly be surprising if the canal also became in some way associated with the anointment ritual. Traces of this association may appear in Psalm 110, a royal psalm composed for the coronation. Psalm 110:7 seems to describe part of the ritual itself—the new king drinks from the "brook by the road." The allusion here is unlikely to the Gihon, but rather to the Shiloah, which led off from it. Also noteworthy in this regard is the Syriac and Aramaic translations of I Kings 1:33. These locate the anointment of Solomon at the Shiloah. The translations admittedly derive from the early centuries C.E., but they may accurately testify to a genuine ancient association between the canal and the royal ceremony. In Isaiah 8:6*a*, the prophet assumes this association and thus refers to the Davidic kingship metaphorically as the "waters of Shiloah." The interpretation finds support in the Targum's rendering of the verse: "Because this people despised the kingdom of the house of David which leads them gently as the waters of Shiloah that flow gently, and are pleased with Rezin and the son of Remaliah."

The prophet's reproach against "this people" reveals how strong Judean opposition to the Davidic house had grown since the time of Uzziah (see chap. 1, sect. 3 D above). Ahaz had refused to align himself with the anti-Assyrian coalition at high territorial and economic cost, and many of his subjects must have questioned in retrospect the wisdom of his leadership. With Pekah's coup and Ephraim's subsequent alliance with Rezin, the general Judean population probably looked forward to Ahaz's following suit and thus to cooperative relations with the Syrians. However, when the king persisted in an isolationist course, Judean discontent with the Davidic house reached a high. On the eve of the Syro-Ephraimitic invasion, large portions of the country were practically in open revolt, ready to accept a new non-Davidic leadership that would cooperate with the Syrian and Israelite kings. Rezin's plan to replace Ahaz with a Tyrian prince and thereby to secure Judah as an ally held hope of success because the Judeans at large would be willing to fight in Syria's cause against Assyria.

Isaiah staunchly supported Ahaz and encouraged him to hold out against the coalition (7:1-17). He also tried to muster popular support for the Davidic policy; the Syrians and Israelites, the prophet argued, were no match for the Assyrians and would soon suffer defeat and plunder (8:1-4). Isaiah's preaching, however, failed to persuade many of the Judean public; "this people" opposed the Davidic regime and "rejoiced in Rezin and the son of Remaliah."

The prophet's threat against the Judeans follows in verses 7-8a: Yahweh will soon bring against them the "many and mighty waters of the River." The language is again figurative, but Isaiah, himself, explains his meaning clearly: Yahweh is raising against Judah the king of Assyria (Tiglath-pileser III) and "all his glory." The last phrase may pick up the language of the Assyrian royal inscriptions that speak frequently of the "splendor" of Assur, the Assyrian god, overwhelming the enemy in battle (*ANET* 287; *ARAB* I §§ 794-95). Certainly familiar with this kind of boast, Isaiah turns it against the Judeans, qualifying it by naming Yahweh as the hidden will behind events.

In verses 7b-8a the prophet develops further the flood metaphor. The waters of the River will "rise over its channels and run over its banks and sweep into Judah, flooding and passing on; they will reach up to the neck." The image vividly depicts the prophet's anticipation of doom. Should the Judeans actively join in the Syrian cause, the Assyrians would overrun the country, crush the resistance, and impose harsh penalties on the people.

While the emphasis of verses 7-8a is on the severity of the impending disaster, the final line may qualify the threat. The flood will reach "up to the neck" and, by implication, no further, thus leaving the head above water. Is Isaiah suggesting indirectly here that Jerusalem, the "head" of Judah, and Ahaz, the "head" of Jerusalem (see 7:8-9), will not "go under," but survive? If this interpretation is correct, the line serves as a transition to the second part of the prophet's speech, his words concerning the house of David and Jerusalem (vv. 8b-10).

Verses 8b-10 begin as a direct address: "But the outspreading of his [the Lord's] wings will fill the breadth of your realm (*rohab 'arṣeka*), O Immanuel" (8b). Immanuel, as we have seen, is the royal infant whose birth and survival Isaiah had predicted months earlier (7:14-16). The prophet's ostensible address to the infant is only a rhetorical device. In Isaiah's eyes, Immanuel is the embodiment of the Davidic house and the guarantee of its ongoing reign (see chap. 4, sect. 9 above). In addressing the child, the prophet in effect addresses the regime as a whole.

The words to Immanuel depict Yahweh metaphorically as

a great bird. (The possessive pronoun, "his" reaches back to "the Lord" in v. 7a.) The image appears elsewhere in the Hebrew Bible and usually connotes divine protection. Deuteronomy 32:11, for example, speaks of Yahweh's having led Israel in the wilderness

> Like an eagle that stirs up its nest,
> > that flutters over its young,
> spreading out its wings, catching them,
> > bearing them on its pinions. (RSV)

Several psalms refer to a person's taking refuge in "the shadow of Yahweh's wings" (Pss. 17:8; 36:8; 57:2; and 63:8; see 61:5 and 91:4). The language in some of these texts may be more than metaphorical. Persons accused of certain crimes may have sought legal asylum in the sanctuary of the Jerusalem temple, where, in the holy of holies, the outstretched wings of two cherubic figures reached from wall to wall (I Kings 6:23-28). In any case, the temple iconography is probably the source of Isaiah's metaphor. He employs the bird image to describe Yahweh's protection of the Davidic realm (see Isa. 31:5).

The extent of this Davidic realm is not clear from the prophet's words. What precisely did Immanuel's kingdom include? The Hebrew of 8:8b speaks literally of the "width" of the child's "land" (*roḥab 'arṣeka*) and so would seem, on first reading, to refer to the whole of Judah. Certain considerations, however, point toward a different conclusion. We recall that, during the years preceding the Syro-Ephraimitic crisis, the territory over which the Davidides exercised firm control had shrunk considerably. Both the Edomites and Philistines had encroached upon Judah from the south and west, and large parts of the country openly challenged the authority of the Davidic leadership. On the eve of the Syro-Ephraimitic invasion, Ahaz's effective rule was likely limited to the dynasty's essential power base—Jerusalem and its vicinity. When Isaiah spoke of Immanuel's realm, he probably had in mind only the capital city and its surroundings.

This interpretation finds support in the continuation of the prophet's speech (vv. 9-10). Isaiah hypothetically addresses the "peoples" and "far-off countries"; mockingly he summons them to battle: "Gird yourselves and be dismayed, gird yourselves and be dismayed! Hatch a plot and it will come to nothing; contrive a plan and it shall not arise, for God is with us (*immanuel*)." Underlying the taunt is the ancient tradition of Zion's inviolability (see chapter 2 above and Pss. 2; 46; 48; and 76). Zion is where Yahweh resides and is the city he will defend. Enemy nations may conspire to storm the city, but their plans "come to nothing." Yahweh "terrifies them, in his fury" (Ps. 2:5). He "breaks the weapons of war" (Ps. 76:3); the besieging forces panic and take flight (Ps. 48:5). Zion's residents live securely, confident in the claim, "Yahweh of hosts is with us" (Ps 46:7). The belief is clearly echoed in the concluding line of the prophet's speech, "for God is with us" (v. 10b). The phrase, however, is also a play on the name of the royal child addressed in verse 8b. The repeated *immanuel* justifies our taking verses 9-10 as a continuation of the thought of verse 8b: Yahweh's protection of "your land, O Immanuel" is his protection of Jerusalem, the seat of the Davidic house and the city where Yahweh dwells.

Although Isaiah's taunt is framed as a general address to the "peoples" and "far-off countries," it is reasonable to suspect that the prophet had Syria and Israel particularly in mind. Their plan to set aside the Davidic house involved besieging the capital city. Isaiah had already declared against its success, stating, "It shall not arise" (7:7). An echo of the same promise resounds in 8:10: "Contrive a plan, but it will not arise." Repeatedly, then, during the Syro-Ephraimitic crisis, Isaiah showed himself as one who took the Zion-Davidic theology seriously and who urged the royal house to do likewise. Ahaz, he argued, should hold out against Rezin and Pekah, confident in the promise that Yahweh would sustain his reign and protect Jerusalem against enemy attack.

Isaiah 8:11-15

The prophetic speech in verses 12-15 presents several interpretive problems. These include the uncertain identity of the prophet's audience, the unclear meaning of the conspiracy charge in verse 12, the possible corruption of the Hebrew text in verses 13 and 14, and the questionable integrity of verses 12-15 as a single speech of Isaiah. The following analysis argues that, except for one slight emendation at the beginning of verse 14, the Masoretic text should be retained. Verses 12-15 form a single speech, which Isaiah delivered to the Davidic house and its supporters prior to the Syro-Ephraimitic advance against Jerusalem in 735/4. His message reiterates what he had said on other occasions during the same crisis: Ahaz should not capitulate to Rezin and Pekah, for Yahweh would deliver him and the capital city.

The speech exhibits a two-part structure. (a) Isaiah admonishes the Davidides and their supporters to dissent from the political leanings of "this people" (vv. 12-13). (b) The prophet promises that Yahweh will protect Zion against the "two houses of Israel" (Judah and Israel) and safeguard the throne of its king (vv. 14-15). How the admonition and promise relate is not explicit. Isaiah likely understood the former as a pre-condition of the latter. The prophet's logic might thus be paraphrased: If the Davidides revere Yahweh and, accordingly, hold out against the demands of Syria, Israel, and the Judean people, Yahweh will defend Zion and its leadership against all opponents.

The prophetic admonition is first couched in negative terms: "Do not consider conspiracy (*qesher*) all that this people considers conspiracy" (v. 12*a*). Isaiah's meaning here is less than clear and has invited several interpretations. First, the conspiracy charge refers to the plan of Rezin and Pekah to set aside the Davidic regime (see 7:6). Second, the charge alludes to the treasonous schemes of Ahaz's own subjects, eager to install a new pro-Syrian leadership. Third, Isaiah was accused of conspiracy, because he either denounced Ahaz or, in counseling against the king's appeal to Assyria, he seemed to favor Syrian and Israelite interests or, in advising against Judah's cooperation with Rezin and Pekah, he appeared to represent the concerns of Assyria.

None of the above proposals proves fully adequate. "Conspiracy" in the Hebrew Bible normally refers to an internal coup (I Kings 15:27; 16:9; II Kings 9:14; 11:14; 12:20; 14:19; 15:25; 15:30; 21:24; Amos 7:10) but can also describe a king's revolt against his suzerain (II Kings 17:4). The Syro-Ephraimitic invasion does not fit either meaning.

Possibly the charge in Isaiah 8:12 describes plots against the Davidic house arising within Jerusalem itself. In this case, however, it is hard to imagine how someone as politically astute as Isaiah could discard the seriousness of such plots so lightly. At least one attempted coup, reported in II Chronicles 28:7, nearly succeeded.

Interpreting the conspiracy charge as an accusation against Isaiah is also unconvincing for several reasons. (a) There is no clear evidence that the prophet ever broke with Ahaz (see the discussion of 7:13 in chap. 4, sect. 9 above). The Immanuel saying and 8:6-10 point, in fact, to the opposite conclusion—namely, that Isaiah supported the king throughout the Syro-Ephraimitic crisis. (b) The idea of Ahaz's appeal to Assyria is likely a fabrication of the editors of II Kings (II Kings 16:7-9) and so cannot be made the bone of contention between the prophet and "this people." Accordingly, there is little reason to think that Isaiah was suspected of having Syrian and Israelite loyalties. To the contrary, the prophet made his stand against the coalition repeatedly clear (7:7-9, 16; 8:1-4). (c) Isaiah's denouncement of the coalition could have been misconstrued by some Judeans as a pro-Assyrian stand. This hypothesis, at least as it has been framed, still does not adequately explain the conspiracy charge. "Conspirarcy" refers either to an internal coup or to a revolt against one's suzerain. Neither meaning would fit the possible Assyrian leanings of Isaiah.

The conspiracy charge in 8:12 is best understood as an accusation against Ahaz. "This people," we have seen, favored the Syrian-led coalition and advocated Judah's participation. Popular discontent with the neutral stand of Ahaz was growing during the early 730s, and many must have hoped that, with Pekah's coup in 736/5 and Samaria's swing to Rezin's side, Ahaz, too, would change his position. When the king still refused to cooperate with the coalition, the Judeans accused him of conspiracy and insubordination to Israel. The charge makes sense in the light of Judah's long-standing political subordination to Israel.

As early as the Omride era, Judah had become more or less a vassal of the Northern Kingdom. Since Jehoram's mother is not named in II Kings 18:16-19, his father, Jehoshaphat, may have been married to an Israelite princess. Jehoshaphat is certainly depicted as cooperative with, even submissive to, Israel (see I Kings 22:5, 41). In any case, the fact that Shalmanesser III fails to mention Judah in his account of the battle at Qarqar (853) might indicate that Jehoshaphat's forces were counted as part of Ahab's troops. (The assumption would partly explain the strikingly large contribution of the Israelite king to the coalition's forces; see *ANET* 278-79; *TUAT* I 360-62; *ARAB* I § 610.) A similar situation obtained during the reigns of Jehoram and Ahaziah: Both were related to the Omride kings through Athaliah and, at least in the case of Ahaziah, Judah again found itself fighting Israel's wars, this time against the Syrians (II Kings 8:16-19, 25-29).

Israelite domination of Judah continued into the period of the Jehu dynasty. If I Kings 22:1-40, or the events upon which it draws, related originally to the reign of Jehoahaz, a Judean king during the late ninth century (probably Joash) again supported the Northern Kingdom in its conflicts with Syria. Some years later, Amaziah tried to assert his independence from Israel, but the northern king, Jehoash, crushed the revolt and ransacked Jerusalem (II Kings 14:8-14).

The reign of Jeroboam II was initially a period of Israelite political and economic revival (II Kings 14:23-29) and one in which Judah continued as the subordinate member of the alliance. (Note that the Hebrew of II Kings 14:28 speaks of "Judah in Israel" and attributes Judah's acquisition of territory to Jeroboam II.) Judean prosperity during the reign of Uzziah was possible under the umbrella of Israelite strength. His successor, Jotham, possibly was married to an Israelite princess (note that the mother of Ahaz, Jotham's son, is not given by the editors of II Kings in 16:1-4). In any case, he appears to have cooperated closely with Jeroboam II (II Chron. 5:11-17). The marriage of his young son Ahaz to Abi, apparently the daughter of Zechariah the Israelite king (II Kings 18:2), promised to ensure that Judean kings would continue to "walk in the ways of the kings of Israel" (II Kings 16:3; compare 8:18 and 27).

The Israelite-Judean alliance remained intact during the late 740s and early 730s. Uzziah/Jotham and then Ahaz followed Menahem's lead and refused to join the cause with Rezin of Damascus. All this changed, however, with Pekah's coup and the subsequent pro-Syrian policy of Israel. Ahaz's refusal to cooperate with the coalition thus constituted blatant defiance of his Israelite overlord. The significance of this decision cannot be overestimated. Ahaz was the first Judean king since the days of Amaziah to attempt an assertion of independence from the Northern Kingdom. Pekah must have viewed Ahaz as a renegade vassal, and in this opinion most Judeans apparently concurred. They denounced Ahaz's revolt against the Israelite king as "conspiracy."

This interpretation of the conspiracy charge finds support in Isaiah 8:12b. There, Isaiah urges the Davidic house: "and do not revere nor regard with awe the one whom it ("this people") reveres." The first verb, as well as the object, derive from the root *yr'* and usually are translated with the meaning of "fear" or "to be afraid." Frequently in the Hebrew Bible, and particularly in Deuteronomy, *yr'* has the sense of "revere" or "respect" and, furthermore, carries political overtones, expressing the properly obedient attitude of a vassal toward a suzerain. The expression occurs frequently in the diplomatic language of the ancient Near East, in which a suzerain demands the undivided loyalty of a subjugated people or ruler. (See, for example, the vassal treaties of Esarhaddon, where *palahu* is the Akkadian equivalent to *yr'*.) Isaiah 8:12b has this political use as a background. While most Judeans urged Ahaz to honor his obligations to Pekah, his Israelite superior, Isaiah encouraged the king to renounce such claims on his loyalty (see below on 9:2).

The prophet's advice in 8:13 takes the form of positive admonition: "Yahweh of hosts—him you should declare holy and he is the one whom your shall revere and regard with awe." The meaning of the second half of the verse is clear. Yahweh is the one whom the Davidides should respect as sovereign, not Pekah of Israel. Such respect, of course, would entail their following Yahweh's instruction—holding out against Rezin and Pekah.

Less certain is the interpretation of verse 13a. Scholars frequently question the appropriateness of the command in its present context and so change the text to read: "Yahweh of hosts, him shall you regard as a conspiracy." The emendation presumes a corruption of the Hebrew text, which scribally is plausible enough, from *taqshiru* to *taqdishu*. (Alternatively, one might see the corruption as an intentional scribal change. To regard Yahweh as a conspirator presumably struck later tradents as an impious assertion, and so they changed the text.) The proposal falters, however, on the fact that the verb in question does not occur anywhere else in the Hebrew Bible in the form that scholars restore here. (The root *qshr* appears in the qal, niphal, piel, pual, and hithpael, but never in the hiphil.) The proposal thus amounts to emending the Hebrew text only to create a new hapax legomenon. We believe it best to retain the Masoretic text and explore anew its possible meanings.

"To declare Yahweh holy" is an infrequent expression in the Hebrew Bible, occurring only in Numbers 20:12; Numbers 27:14; Isaiah 29:23; and Isaiah 8:13. In the first two instances, the phrase seems to mean the acknowledgment of Yahweh's awesome power. Moses and Aaron are reproached for not having credited Yahweh with the miracle at Meribah. A similar sense is present in Isaiah 29:23. When the Israelites see their children, "the work of my (Yahweh's) hands," they will confess the numinous power of their God. Probably the same meaning is present in 8:13; the prophet urges the Davidides to acknowledge the power of Yahweh on their behalf. The exhortation makes sense alongside Isaiah's promises elsewhere that Yahweh will protect the Davidic house and Zion against the attacks of Rezin and Pekah.

The context of verse 13*a*, however, is one in which the question of Ahaz's loyalties is particularly at issue. The overall sense of verses 12-13 is that the Davidic king should honor Yahweh as suzerain, not Pekah of Israel. Is it possible that "declaring Yahweh holy" also carries political overtones? We suggest that it does and cite Psalm 99 as corroborating evidence. This composition is an enthronement psalm in which the declaration of Yahweh's holiness functions somewhat like a refrain (vv. 3, 5, and 9). Confessing Yahweh's holiness, then, is precisely what one did in the ritual celebration of the divine kingship over Israel and the particular expression, "Yahweh is holy," quite likely carried connotations of Yahweh's sovereignty. Certainly Isaiah and his audiences would have been familiar with this tradition and would have understood 8:13*a* in this light. (See

Isa. 6:1-3, in which Yahweh's kingship and holiness are closely connected. Here, however, it is not the human community but the heavenly seraphim who proclaim the holiness of God.) Interpreted in this way, the line fits well with the meaning of its overall context: The Davidides should acknowledge Yahweh as sole overlord, not Pekah of Israel.

In verses 14 and 15, Isaiah describes the future action of Yahweh. Again, however, text-critical questions come into play in the interpretation of the material. The RSV translates the Hebrew of verse 14: "And he will become a sanctuary [*lemiqdash*], and a stone of offense, and a rock of stumbling to both houses of Israel, a trap and a snare [*ulemoqesh*] to the inhabitants [*leyosheb*] of Jerusalem." A majority of commentators argue that "sanctuary" fits badly here with the other descriptions of Yahweh and so emend the term to either "snare" (*moqesh*) or "conspiracy" (*maqshir*). The force of both proposals is the same; Yahweh's future action is altogether threatening, against both the two houses of Israel and the residents of Jerusalem.

Several considerations weigh against the above translations. (a) Changing "sanctuary" to "snare" appears to be a somewhat capricious emendation. Scribally, the two terms are not very similar. One could justify the textual change only by hypothesizing again that later tradents found offensive the portrayal of Yahweh as a "snare" and so intentionally substituted "sanctuary." (b) "Conspiracy" is textually more plausible than "snare," but the proposed Hebrew term, *maqshir*, is elsewhere unattested. The emendation thus results only in a new hapax legomenon. (c) The versions tend to support the Masoretic text; both the Septuagint and the Vulgate read "sanctuary" in 8:14a. Only the Targum construes the line as a threat: "And his (Yahweh's) Memra will become among you an avenger (*pur`an*)." (d) Elsewhere in Isaiah 7 and 8, the prophet sharply distinguishes between the fate of Zion and that of Judah and Israel. Yahweh is said repeatedly to protect the former and punish the latter. It would be most surprising then if in 8:14 Isaiah predicted disaster for both.

We believe it best to construe verse 14 as a promise of divine protection for Zion and the Davidic house. The verse should be rendered: "Then he (Yahweh) will become for the sake of his holy domain (Zion) a stone of offense and a rock of stumbling to the two houses of Israel (Israel and Judah), a trap and a snare for the sake of the ruler of Jerusalem." This reading rests on four translation decisions. (1) *Miqdash*, in verse 14*a*, does not mean "sanctuary" but more broadly "holy domain" and refers to Zion. (2) The conjunction that now precedes "stone of offense" was originally a third person singular masculine possessive pronoun qualifying "holy domain." The Masoretic text as it now stands is simply a case of incorrect word separation. (3) *Yosheb*, at the end of verse 14, does not mean "inhabitant" but "the one who sits or is enthroned" and refers to the Davidic king. The term has the same sense in Amos 1:8; Isaiah 9:8, and elsewhere. (4) The preposition *le*, which precedes "holy domain" (*lemiqdash*) and "ruler of Jerusalem" (*leyosheb yerushalaim*), does not express a resulting condition, but rather interest or advantage and should be rendered "for the sake of" or "in behalf of."

If this translation is correct, Isaiah pronounced in 8:14-15 the same message as that delivered on other occasions during the same period. If the Davidides honor Yahweh's sovereignty and follow his instructions, holding out against the demands of the coalition as well as those of their Judean subjects, Yahweh will defend Zion, "his holy domain," and its ruler, Ahaz. Verse 15 describes clearly the disaster that will befall Israel and Judah: "many of them will stumble and fall and be shattered and be snared and trapped."

Isaiah 8:16-20

Isaiah 8:16-20 concludes the collection of reports and speeches that began in 8:1. The verses form a single prophetic speech, addressed to the Davidic court prior to the end of the Syro-Ephraimitic crisis. Isaiah calls for the official securing of his earlier words, presumably in a written document to be deposited in royal or temple archives (v. 16) and claims for them an authoritative status (vv. 19-20). His "testimony" and "instruction" should serve as the standard by which Ahaz and the royal court might assess the truth of the oracles of other intermediaries.

Beyond this, several details of the passage remain obscure, including numerous textual and translation uncertainties, particularly in verses 16 and 20. In the analysis below, we must be content at several points with reviewing the various possible interpretations. First, however, it is important to set out for the reader certain positions with which we sharply disagree.

(1) Most scholars have seen in 8:16-18 Isaiah's recognition that his ministry during the Syro-Ephraimitic crisis had failed and his consequent decision to withdraw from public life for a time. This interpretation rests on the assumption that Isaiah and Ahaz were at odds over the issue of an appeal to Assyria. As we have argued all along, Isaiah's primary aim was to encourage the king to hold out against Rezin and Pekah, and the prophet apparently succeeded in this. Further, the prophetic speeches in Isaiah 13–19 and 28–33 can be adequately explained against the background of international events from 731 to 720, and so testify to Isaiah's continued activity in the wake of the Syro-Ephraimitic crisis (see chap. 4, sects. 15-21 and 28-33 below). There is no need to posit a gap of several years in the prophet's career, let alone one that resulted from his failed ministry during the reign of Ahaz.

(2) Scholars generally have seen in verse 16 a clear reference to a small group of the prophet's followers, distinct from the royal court and the Judeans at large. Isaiah requests that his earlier speeches be deposited "among my disciples" (*belimmuday*), as the Hebrew is usually translated, to be preserved for a later time and generation. This interpretation also rests on the assumption that Isaiah broke not only with the Judean people but also with Ahaz and then withdrew from public affairs to a private life within a circle of loyal supporters. Evidence for the existence of this circle elsewhere in the book of Isaiah is lacking; the often-cited speech in 8:11-15 does not in fact address private supporters of the prophet, but rather the royal court. Furthermore, the reading, "among my disciples" (or "in the presence of my disciples") is by no means certain. Among the ancient versions, only the Vulgate gives this translation. The Septuagint, the Targum, and the Syriac vary in their readings, but none of them makes any reference to a distinct prophetic group. Whether the Masoretic text is retained or emended, other renderings and/or interpretations of 8:16 make better sense.

(3) Commentators have often assigned 8:19-20 to an exilic or even post-exilic redactor. The arguments marshalled against the Isaianic authorship of the verses, however, are not convincing. The sequence of the terms *testimony* and *instruction* in verse 16 is reversed in verse 20*a*, but this variation alone hardly proves the hand of a redactor. Neither, as many contend, do the two terms have a new sense in verse 20*a*, referring here to a written law code or to the writings of the pre-exilic prophets.

Scholars have overplayed the echoes of the exilic passage, Isaiah 47:10*b*-12, in interpreting 8:18-20. The verbal similarities are limited to *shaḥrah* in 47:11 and *shaḥar* in 8:20, and even this parallel is not altogether certain (see below the analysis of v. 20). Neither is the content of the two passages particularly close. Isaiah 47:10*b*-12 tells an exilic audience that no "enchantments" and "sorceries" can stay the impending punishment of their sins. In contrast, Isaiah 8:18-20, together with verses 16-18, aims at: (a) reassuring Ahaz and his supporters that the hopeful message given to them earlier by Isaiah was truly from Yahweh and (b) convincing them, accordingly, to adhere to the prophet's word, even when other prognosticators disagree.

The prophet's speech opens in verse 16 with the command, "Bind up the testimony (*te`udah*), seal the instruction (*torah*)." Both nouns refer to Isaiah's earlier speeches during the Syro-Ephraimitic crisis, but the precise nuance of each Hebrew term remains unclear. The first, *te`udah*, occurs elsewhere in the Bible only in Ruth 4:7, where it means "attestation" and describes a specific symbolic act accompanying property transactions. The term in our text appears closer in meaning to the etymologically related nouns `*edah* and `*edut*, both usually translated "testimony." While these, however, generally refer to the divine will as encapsulated in specific laws or law codes, *te`udah* in 8:16 refers to Yahweh's will as expressed through Isaiah's speeches. Perhaps relevant in this connection is the meaning of the verb `*ud* as "protest, warn, charge." This connotation may also be present in 8:16—the prophet's "testimony" reproached and threatened the opponents of the Davidic house while warning the Judean king to hold to a neutralist course.

The second noun, *torah*, frequently means "law" or "law code," but it also describes the divine response to cultic questions, communicated by the priests to the worshipers. Neither sense fits the context of our text. *Torah* can mean "instruction" generally, and in Proverbs describes parental teaching (1:8; 4:1; and 6:20), a wife's advice to her husband (31:26), and the wisdom of the sages (13:14). The term may also refer to the political instruction or advice a counselor gives the king or the people, although clear instances of this meaning are lacking (but see Prov. 28:18). Isaiah uses the verb *yrh* in 28:9, where he questions the political acuity of the northern leaders' plans for rebellion against Assyria (see chap. 4, sect. 28 below). We suggest a similar political connotation for the noun in 8:16, since the prophetic speeches that comprised the "instruction" (*torah*) were essentially political advice to the royal court and its supporters. Certainly, Isaiah regarded such instruction not simply as prudent counsel but as the authoritative will of Yahweh (8:3*b*, 5, 11, and 18; see 1:10).

The verb forms in the Hebrew of verse 16 are singular imperatives. Assuming that these commands are addressed to Isaiah and that the concluding phrase, *belimmuday*, means "with my disciples," it would seem that Yahweh is the speaker. Divine speech in verse 16, however, would be strangely isolated, since the "I" in verses 17 and 18 is clearly Isaiah. To solve the problem, some scholars emend the imperative verbs to infinitive absolutes and translate the line as an indicative statement by the prophet: "I bind [*ṣûr* in place of *ṣôr*] the testimony, I seal [*ḥātôm* in place of *ḥătôm*] the instruction with my disciples."

This proposal is unnecessary, for the question of the speaker in verse 16 arises only if one insists on seeing here a reference to a select group of Isaiah's followers. As we argued above and will explain further, *belimmuday* may be rendered in other ways that obviate the problem.

The plene spellings of the imperative forms is in fact unusual (*ṣōr* and *ḥātōm* are more customary) and the proposed infinitive absolutes involve only slight changes in the Masoretic pointings. However, whether the verbs are taken as imperative or infinitive forms, they have in either case the force of a command. Before the royal court and its supporters, Isaiah calls for the securing of his "testimony."

The precise procedure envisioned here merits further attention. The prophetic speeches are apparently to be written down, although this is not explicitly stated. What then is to be done with the document is not clear. Isaiah may intend simply for it to be deposited for safekeeping in a container of some sort, or more generally in the royal archives. (The Qumran sectarians preserved scrolls in clay vessels, and Jer. 32:14 testifies to the same practice.) Alternatively, the prophet may have in mind a more elaborate procedure for sealing up a papyrus document. The writing would be rolled or folded up, tied with string, and daubed with soft wax or clay, upon which an official seal impression could be made. Once bound in this way, the document might be deposited in a vessel. Examples of sealed writings at Elephantine vividly demonstrate this procedure, and Jeremiah 32:9-15 seems to describe the same practice. A similar picture may be assumed in Isaiah 29:11—the writing that is sealed (*hasseper heḥatum*) cannot be read, even by one who is literate, "for it is sealed *up*" (*ki ḥatum hu'*; compare Job 14:17; Dan. 12:4; Neh. 9:38; 10:1; I Kings 21:8; and Esther 8:8).

The concluding phrase of verse 16, *belimmuday*, allows several interpretations. The Hebrew may mean "with the things taught by me" (compare the Syriac). We would then translate verse 16: "Bind up the testimony, seal the instruction with my teaching." Alternatively, *belimmuday* might be rendered "with my learned ones." The reference in this case would be to court or temple personnel, perhaps Uriah and Zechariah, mentioned in 8:2, who were in charge of securing official documents.

Slight emendations of the Masoretic text yield still other plausible translations. Changing *belimmaday* to *kelimmud*, we might translate verse 16, "Bind the testimony, seal the instruction in accordance with what is customary." (Ancient scribes frequently misread *b* for *k*. The possessive suffix perhaps arose in part through dittography: the *w* that begins v. 17 was written twice and then construed by later scribes as *y*. Note that neither the Septuagint nor the Targum affixes the first person pronoun here.) In this case, the prophet appears to ask that his written speeches be handled in the manner standard for all documents entered into the royal archives.

Alternatively, *belimmuday* may be a corruption of *belimmudyah*, "upon its ties." (The similarity of the *yh* and the *wh* at the beginning of v. 17 might easily have resulted in haplography.) Mishnaic texts attest to this meaning for *limmud*, and biblical examples offer support: "a roped heifer" in Hosea 10:11 (`*eglah melummadah*), "like an unhitched heifer" in Jeremiah 31:18 (*ke`egel lo' lummad*), and "a wild ass bound to the wilderness" in Jeremiah 2:24 (*pereh limmud midbar*). If Isaiah understands the term in this sense, verse 16 graphically describes the handling of his written speeches. The document (presumably papyrus) would first be folded up and tied with string; then "upon its ties" the wax seal would be affixed.

The prophet proceeds in verse 17 to express his confidence: "And I will wait for Yahweh, who is about to hide his face from the house of Jacob, and will hope in him." The words are reminiscent of lament psalms, in which the distressed individual frequently proclaims faith in divine deliverance, "waiting for" and "hoping in" Yahweh (Pss. 25:3, 5, 21; 27:14; 39:8; 69:7-21; 130:5; compare Jer. 14:22). Isaiah here identifies with Jerusalem and the Davidic house, both seriously threatened by Syria and Israel, and by the Judeans as well. He is sure that just as he has predicted all along, Yahweh will deliver Ahaz and his supporters from the present crisis.

Isaiah's profession of confidence thus reflects his belief in the truth of his "testimony" and "instruction." The earlier speeches predicted the demise of Ahaz's enemies, and 8:17 affirms the prediction. Yahweh is about to "turn his face from the house of Jacob." The idiom generally describes Yahweh's giving someone over to terror and distress (Pss. 104:29-30; 143:7; Deut. 32:20; and Mic. 3:4). In our text, it refers to Yahweh's delivering Israel over to its adversaries (compare Ezek. 39:23 and Jer. 33:5). The prophet firmly believes that "the house of Jacob"—perhaps the Northern Kingdom alone, but more probably the Judean countryside as well (see v. 14)—will suffer at the hands of the Assyrians (8:4, 7-8b, 15). The defeat of Israel and the anti-Davidic faction marks Yahweh's salvation of the Davidic house and Jerusalem;

for this the prophet "waits" and "hopes" (compare 8:8*b*-10 and 14).

In verse 18, Isaiah draws special attention to himself and his children: "Look! I and the children whom Yahweh has given me are signs and portents against Israel from Yahweh Sebaoth who resides on Mt. Zion." The logical connection with what precedes is not altogether clear. If the "testimony" were sealed up so that its message was no longer accessible, public signs might be necessary to call it to mind. The symbolic names of the prophet's children, both of which had hopeful import for the Davidic house, and Isaiah's own appearance, if not his name ("Yahweh delivers"), would serve this function. The continuing prominence of the prophet and his children in the public eye would effectively substitute for the open copy of a document normally drawn up for ongoing consultation (see Jer. 32:9-15).

Verse 18 may, however, emphasize not so much the function of Isaiah and his children as signs and portents, but rather the claim that, as signs and portents, they are "from Yahweh Sebaoth." Their message is, therefore, authoritative and certain to come true. In this case, the prophet's reference to himself and the children may be a shorthand way of characterizing the content of the "testimony." (The document's sealed or open status is here left undecided.) The testimony, we have argued above, was directed "against Israel" (the Northern Kingdom and the Judeans together; see v. 14) and Syria, but contained an assurance for Ahaz and Jerusalem. Isaiah's confidence in the testimony is his conviction that he and the children stand in the commission of Yahweh.

The hopeful import of verses 16-18 is clearly expressed by the concluding description of Yahweh as "the one who resides on Mt. Zion." The language is probably formulaic and at home in the liturgy of the Jerusalem temple (see Pss. 74:2; 135:21; Joel 4:17). Isaiah aptly encapsulates the Zion tradition, which in the ears of the Davidic court could only have promising overtones. The God who commissions the prophet and his children as signs and portents protects Zion, his place of residence, against all attacking enemies. Those who live within, particularly the royal house, must stand firm in the ancient promise: If they hold out against the

Syro-Ephraimitic forces and against the pressures of the Judean people, Yahweh will defend them in his holy city.

An admonition to the Davidic court and its supporters follows in verses 19-20: They are to abide by Isaiah's word, now contained in the "testimony" and "instruction," even in the face of differing predictions from other intermediaries. The actual rendering of the verses is difficult, and, accordingly, their interpretation varies among scholars. We suggest the following as a tentative translation:

(19) And if they say to you, "Consult [*dirshu*] the necromancers and wizards who chirp and mutter; should not a people consult its spirits [*'elohayw*], the dead on behalf of the living?" (20) [Look] to the instruction and testimony if they [the mediums and wizards] do not speak according to this word [the instruction and testimony] for which there is no desire.

The verses appear to form a complex conditional sentence. The prodosis (v. 19) hypothetically quotes popular advice to the royal court; they are to confer with other specialists in divination, presumably for help in understanding the present crisis and in charting proper policy. The Hebrew verb here is *drsh* and in context clearly means "to seek an oracle." The named specialists—necromancers (*'obot*) and wizards (*yidde'onim*)—are later proscribed in the Deuteronomic literature (Deut. 18:11) and here already by Isaiah may be derogated as ones who "chirp and mutter." The prophet thus begins his polemic even before the apodosis. The babble of the mediums and wizards hardly deserves equal consideration alongside Isaiah's "testimony."

How far the quotation extends is debatable. The RSV concludes it with verse 19*a*, presenting what follows as the prophet's reply: "Should not a people consult their God? Should they consult the dead on behalf of the living?" The two rhetorical questions presumably are to be answered differently, the first affirmatively, the second negatively. In opposition to the oracles of necromancers and wizards, Isaiah sets forth the word of God, which in verse 20 he identifies with the "instruction" and "testimony."

This interpretation, however, is not convincing. If we grant for the moment that verse 19*b* consists of two questions, the interrogative *halo'* ("should *not*") would likely govern both and so call for an affirmative answer in both cases. We can hardly imagine, though, that Isaiah suggested that a people "consult the dead on behalf of the living." Be that as it may, the most straightforward reading of verse 19*b* would take the line as a single question in which "its spirits" (see I Sam. 28:13 for this rendering of *'elohim*) and "the dead" stand in apposition, both being objects of the verb, "consult." In this way, the impious advice quoted by the prophet continues to the end of verse 19—namely, that a people, particularly its leadership, might legitimately confer with its dead spirits for advice in critical situations. This kind of divination was popularly thought to be the prerogative of the "necromancer" (v. 19*a*), the Hebrew term for which also means "ghost" (*'ob*).

Less certain is whether the quotation of impious advice in verse 19 extends to the end of verse 20*a*. The NEB translates the text in this way: ". . . a nation may surely seek guidance of its gods, of the dead on behalf of the living, for an oracle or a message?" The NJPSV interprets similarly. This reading, however, forces one to construe the *'im-lo'* that immediately follows in an asseverative sense: "Surely they will say. . . ." Isaiah's reply would then take the form of an oath formula in which the principal sentence (e.g., "May Yahweh do harm to me if . . .") has been suppressed. While this interpretation is certainly possible, it is by no means the most straightforward one syntactically. The text makes equally good sense if one begins the prophet's answer in verse 20*a* ("To the instruction and testimony"), taking the *'im* that then follows as the conditional "if." Our translation above follows this decision.

Isaiah does not specify who might urge the Davidides to consult other intermediaries. The opening verb form is left impersonal: "And if they say to you . . . " (or in the passive, "and if it is said to you . . ."). The speakers are probably the many Judeans who opposed Ahaz's neutralist stance and the counsel of Isaiah upon which that policy was based. These might understandably pressure the king and court to consult other specialists, hoping that the latter would support their own political views. The rhetorical style of verse 19*b* fits well with this assumption. Isaiah anticipates the arguments of the Judeans and thereby weakens their force.

The prophet's reply in verse 20 is elliptical. If the implied verb of the line is "consult" (*drsh*, as in v. 19), the prophet's exhortation might be paraphrased, "Refer to the instruction and testimony rather than consulting necromancers and wizards." (It remains unclear whether this inquiry would involve opening a sealed document or simply retrieving the document, presumably in open form, from the royal archives.) The Hebrew preposition *le*, translated above as "to," may also have the sense of "according to," thus setting forth Isaiah's "testimony" as the norm by which the royal court should steer foreign affairs. If this interpretation is correct, we might render v. 20*a*: "Hold to the instruction and testimony. . . ." This fits well with the continuation, "if they [the necromancers and wizards] do not say according to this word [the instruction and testimony]. . . ." The prophet proposes his earlier speeches as the authoritative word of Yahweh (also the firm basis for foreign policy!) by which the advice and prognoses of other specialists should be judged.

The concluding phrase of verse 20, "which [who] has no dawn" (*asher 'en-lo' shaḥar*), has tried the ingenuity of translators. The relative clause could be a gloss originally intended for verse 21*a*: The one who "passes through it [the land?]" has no "dawn"—that is, hope. The metaphor does fit with the darkness motif of verses 22-23, yet we would expect a gloss on verse 21*a* to elucidate the cryptic identity of its subject. The relative clause more likely belongs originally to verse 20*b*, qualifying "this word." Two solutions are then available.

First, the word *dawn* (*shaḥar*) may be a corruption of "bribe" or "payment" (*shoḥad*). The spelling of the two words is very similar (*d* and *r* look alike in Hebrew), and the Septuagint reading, "gifts" (*dora*), assumes the latter. If the emendation is made, the sense of the entire line is that the testimony of the prophet is reliable because it has not been bought. (Compare Micah's charge during the same period that Jerusalem's "prophets divine for money"; 3:11). By implication, the same cannot be said of prognoses that differ from "this word."

Second, the Hebrew *shaḥar* might be retained but rendered "desire" or "longing." Other instances of this meaning for the noun are lacking, but the verb *shḥr* frequently has the sense of "seek eagerly, diligently, or with longing" (see Ps. 78:34, where the term is parallel to "consult," *drsh*; also Hos. 5:15; Ps. 63:2; and Isa. 26:9). Alternatively, we might repoint *shaḥar* as a participle, *shoḥer* (see Prov. 7:15, where it occurs alongside *bqsh* and *drsh*). In either case, however, the prophet's meaning would be the same. His testimony was an unwelcome word, particularly to the Judeans. They, indeed, had no "desire" for it and encouraged their leadership to seek a different message from other sources.

11. AHAZ AND THE THRONE OF DAVID
(8:21–9:7)

A. **Alt**, "Jesaja 8:23-9:6. Befreiungsnacht und Krönungstag," *Festschrift für A. Bertholet* (ed. W. Baumgartner; Tübingen: J. C. B. Mohr [Paul Siebeck], 1950)29-49 = his *KS* II (1953) 206-25; H. **Barth**, *Die Jesaja-Worte in der Josiazeit: Israel und Assur als Thema einer produktiven Neuinterpretation der Jesajaüberlieferung* (Neukirchen-Vluyn: Neukirchener Verlag, 1977) 141-77; R. A. **Carlson**, "The Anti-Assyrian Character of the Oracle in Is. IX 1-6," *VT* 24(1974)130-35; M. B. **Crook**, "A Suggested Occasion for Isa. 9:2-7 and 11:1-9," *JBL* 68(1949) 213-24; G. R. **Driver**, "Isaianic Problems," *Festschrift für Wilhelm Eilers* (ed. G. Wiessner; Wiesbaden: Otto Harrasowitz, 1967)43-49; J. A. **Emerton**, "Some Linguistic and Historical Problems in Isaiah VIII 23," *JSS* 14(1969)151-75; H. L. **Ginsberg**, "An Unrecognized Allusion to Kings Pekah and Hoshea of Israel," *EI* 5(1958)61*-65*; H. **Gressmann**, *Der Messias* (Göttingen: Vandenhoeck & Ruprecht, 1929)242-46; W. **Harrelson**, "Nonroyal Motifs in the Royal Eschatology," *Israel's Prophetic Heritage* (ed. B. W. Anderson and W. Harrelson; New York: Harper & Brothers, 1962)147-65; S. **Mowinckel**, *He That Cometh* (Oxford/Nashville: B. H. Blackwell/Abingdon Press, 1956); H. P. **Müller**, "Uns ist ein Kind geboren. . . ," *EvTh* 21(1961)408-19; J. P. J. **Olivier**, "The Day of Midian and Isaiah 9:3b," *JNSL* 9(1981) 143-49; G. **von Rad**, "The Royal Ritual in Judah," *The Problem of the Hexateuch and Other Essays* (Edinburgh/New York: Oliver and Boyd/McGraw-Hill, 1966)222-31; H. G. **Reventlow**, "A Syncretistic Enthronement Hymn in Isa. 9:1-6," *UF*

3(1971)321-25; L. G. **Rignell**, "A Study of Isaiah 9:2-7," *LQ* 7(1955)31-35; W. H. **Schmidt**, "Die Ohnmacht des Messias," *KD* 15(1969)18-34; K. D. **Schunck**, "Der fünfte Thronname des Messias (Jes. IX 5-6)," *VT* 23(1973)108-10; K. **Seybold**, *Das davidische Königtum im Zeugnis der Propheten* (Göttingen: Vandenhoeck & Ruprecht, 1972); M. E. W. **Thompson**, "Isaiah's Ideal King," *JSOT* 24(1982)79-88; J. **Vollmer**, "Zur Sprache von Jesaja 9:1-6," *ZAW* 80(1968)343-50; C. F. **Whitley**, "The Language and Exegesis of Isaiah 8:16-23," *ZAW* 90(1978)28-43; H. **Wildberger**, "Die Thronnamen des Messias, Jes. 9:5b," *TZ* 16(1960)314-32; H. W. **Wolff**, *Frieden ohne Ende; Jesaja 7, 1-17 und 9, 1-6 ausgelegt* (Neukirchen Kreis Moers: Neukirchener Verlag, 1962); W. **Zimmerli**, "Vier oder fünf Thronnamen des messianischen Herrschers in Jes. IX 5b. 6," *VT* 22(1972)249-52.

Scholarly interpretations of Isaiah 8:21–9:7 disagree widely on several issues. The translation is in doubt at many points, particularly in 9:1 where the Hebrew syntax and meaning of the verbs are unclear. Throughout the material, furthermore, the verb tenses are open to question. Consequently, it is debatable which verses, if any, anticipate future developments and which verses reflect past events.

The compositional unity of 8:21-9:7 is also contested. While most commentators agree on a sharp break between verses 21-22 and 9:1, there is less consensus as to whether 9:1 and verses 2-7 belong together as parts of a single original speech. Related to this issue are questions of authorship and date. Opinions range between two extremes: (1) attributing the whole section to Isaiah, though allowing for a few glosses and (2) assigning the verses to multiple exilic and post-exilic writers.

Finally, there is wide disagreement over the identity of the royal child mentioned in 9:6. The various proposals include a future messianic figure, a newly born prince of the Davidic house, and a contemporary Davidic king who has recently ascended the throne, perhaps Hezekiah or even Josiah. Deciding the matter obviously depends in part on whether one assigns the verses to Isaiah and, if so, on how one assesses Isaiah's attitude toward contemporary Davidic monarchs.

The following interpretation of 8:21-9:7 differs sharply from previous treatments. We argue that the verses constitute a single speech delivered by the eighth-century prophet to a Jerusalemite audience. The historical setting is the recent coup of Pekah in 736/5 and Ahaz's subsequent move to assert independence from the Northern Kingdom. Isaiah's speech celebrates this assertion of independence, predicts the continued well-being of the Davidic Kingdom, and promises divine support. Structurally it divides into three parts:

(1) A description of Pekah's coup in Israel (8:21-22)
(2) A summary statement on the bright future of Jerusalem and/or Judah (9:1*aa*)
(3) The celebration of Ahaz's recently asserted independence from Israel and the promise of eternal security for the Davidic rule (9:1*ab*-7)

Isaiah 8:21-22

Verses 21-22 are usually thought to describe the oppressive conditions prevailing in the land, either in Israel following the Assyrian campaigns in 734–732 or in Judah after the Babylonian destruction of Jerusalem in 586. Our interpretation of the passage against the background of political developments in Israel in 736/5 depends in large part on a specific translation. We, therefore, discuss this translation at the outset.

(21) So he passes over into it [the land], fierce and hungry [for power]. And when he becomes ravenous and works himself into a rage, then he revolts against his king and his God and turns upward [toward Samaria].
(22) And he sets his sights on the land [Israel]. And look, there is distress and darkness, the gloom of oppression and widespread calamity.

The prophet's opening is curiously cryptic: "So he passes over into it [*we`bar bah*]". Neither here nor in what follows does Isaiah identify clearly the subject of the action. Assuming that the material depicts a general situation of hardship, most commentators render the third person verb forms with the impersonal "one" or "they." It is more likely, however, that the repeated "he" refers to a specific figure—namely, Pekah. Pekah had been ruling in Gilead for several years, but in 736/5 he and fifty Gileadite troops managed to assassinate Pekahiah, and Pekah ascended the throne in Samaria (II Kings 15:25). Isaiah 8:21*a* probably alludes to Pekah and his co-conspirators' passage from Transjordan into the Northern Kingdom.

Isaiah characterizes Pekah as "fierce and hungry" (*niqšeh wera`eb*). The first term is the only occurrence of the niphal participle of *qšh* in the Hebrew Bible. The base meaning of the root is "to be hard, severe, fierce." Many translations thus render the participle in 8:21 as "hard-pressed" or "distressed" or some similar expression of hardship. We suggest construing the niphal form in the reflexive sense, "to harden oneself," or by the passive "hardened." Either way, the prophet's meaning is the same: Pekah is "fierce" or "hardened" in purpose, intent on overthrowing Pekahiah's rule.

If this interpretation is correct, the second term must be taken metaphorically: Pekah is "hungry" for power. The same is true for what follows: "he becomes ravenous" (*yir`ab*) for land and power and "works himself into a rage."

The description of the coup continues in verse 21*aa*, "then he revolts against (*weqillel be*) his king and his God [gods?]." The verb is a piel form of the root *qll* and normally means "curse." Most commentators thus render the line, "He will curse his king and his God." This translation, however, does not accurately reflect the Hebrew syntax. If "his king" and "his God" were being cursed, they would normally be introduced as accusatives. Here, in 8:21, they are governed by the preposition *b* and so would seem to be the objects *by* which "he" curses. However, this sense does not fit well in context. Our solution is to understand the verb as parallel to the Akkadian *qullulu*, "to offend or revolt" (compare the NJPSV), and to take the preposition in an adversative sense, "against." The line thus has a clear political meaning, referring to Pekah's conspiracy.

The phrase "his king" merits further comment. The above interpretation assumes that "his king" is Pekahiah. If, however, Pekah has been ruling autonomously in Gilead for several years, it seems odd that Isaiah should call Pekahiah "his king." One solution is to assume that Pekah's authority in Gilead was originally under the auspices of the Israelite king; Jeroboam II had appointed him as a high-ranking officer over the region. At some point toward the end of Jeroboam's rule, Pekah had apparently led a schismatic movement, undoubtedly with Syrian support, and ruled independently in Gilead. Not surprisingly, neither the Israelite royal annals nor Isaiah acknowledge this new status, but continue to view him as a renegade subject of Pekahiah. Second Kings 15:25 thus refers to Pekah as Pekahiah's *šališ* ("captain" RSV). In the same way, Isaiah describes Pekahiah as "his (Pekah's) king."

An alternate interpretation might understand the phrase as a reference to Tiglath-pileser III. Pekah's coup was also an act of rebellion against the Assyrian monarch, suzerain over not only Israel but also most Syro-Palestinian states, beginning in the early 730s, if not earlier. Indeed, Pekah's takeover in Israel was an important development in the anti-Assyrian movement and certainly was a factor that prompted the Assyrian invasion of 734.

If this second solution is correct, the continuation of verse 21*bb* should be translated, "and against his [Tiglath-pileser's] gods [*ube'lohayw*]," the Assyrian deities by whom the oaths of vassals were sworn. In toppling Pekahiah's regime, Pekah revolted against the Assyrian monarch and offended his gods.

The final clause of verse 21 and the opening of verse 22 are frequently interpreted together and translated, and they will "turn their faces upward; and they will look to the earth" (RSV). Given this rendering, two senses would be possible. (1) Distressed inhabitants of the land search the heavens above and the earth below for a sign or omen of an imminent turn of fate. (2) "Upward" and "to the earth" are opposites that together express the idea, "everywhere." The distressed inhabitants look around on all sides.

Both of the above interpretations assume that verse 22*b* states a result: Those who gaze "upward" and "to the earth" see only distress and darkness. Both interpretations, again, construe the subject of the verbs as the impersonal "they." The text allegedly describes hopeless circumstances in the land after a foreign invasion. If we are correct, however, in seeing a reference to Pekah, the text might be translated to express a more political meaning. Two renderings of the final clause in verse 21 are possible. First, "He [Pekah] turns to treachery [*lema`lah*]." This presumes that that Hebrew *ma`lah* derives from the noun *ma`al* ("treachery, transgression") with the directive *h*. Second, "He [Pekah] turns [to go] upward." The first of these readings is the less likely because the verb *m`l* and the related *ma`al* occur predominantly in late texts, the noun usually functioning as a cognate accusative. We adopt the second reading and understand it as an allusion to Pekah's move upward into the central hill country toward Samaria. There, in the capital city, the coup took place (II Kings 15:25).

Verse 22*a* similarly alludes to Pekah's takeover in Israel. The verb in this passage derives from the Hebrew root *nbṭ* and generally means "to look." In certain contexts, however, it has a specific nuance: to look on something with desire or envy (compare Ps. 92:11 and I Sam. 2:32). We suggest a similar sense in 8:22*a*—Pekah looks to "the land" with desire. He sets his "sights" on Israel to acquire it.

In verse 22*b*, Isaiah describes the adverse consequences of Pekah's coup in the Northern Kingdom. The prophet here is probably exaggerating matters, for many of the Israelites undoubtedly favored the change in leadership. Nevertheless, a certain amount of confusion and some oppressive measures would have been inevitable. The new king probably took steps to establish his control over the whole country, perhaps tracking down and executing whatever supporters Pekahiah had once had. Isaiah exaggerates the distress for rhetorical purposes. His ultimate aim is to highlight how favorably the fate of Ahaz and his kingdom compares with that of the former Israelite regime.

A final question demands some comment: Do verses 21 and 22 assume antecedent material that has been lost? The anonymous "he" throughout the verses and the vague reference to "it" (the land of Israel) in verse 21*a* might indicate that we are dealing here with only a fragment. However, elsewhere Isaiah begins a commentary on current political events in a similar way. (Compare Isa. 10:27*d*, in which the prophet opens his description of the invading

Syrian and Israelite army, "He has come up from Samaria.") If the coup of Pekah was quite recent, the prophet could assume his audience's familiarity with it and so could begin simply, "So he passes over into it." The residents of Jerusalem and the Davidic house would easily have sensed whom and what the prophet was describing.

Isaiah 9:1aa

Commentators generally question the Isaianic authorship of 9:1aa. The line is usually taken as either a gloss on verse 22b or an editor's bridge between the dark picture in verses 21-22 and the hopeful pronouncements in 9:1ab-7. While the line does function as a transition, there is no reason to assign it to a later editor. It forms, instead, a decisive turning point in Isaiah's presentation; having related the coup of Pekah and the resulting fallout in the Northern Kingdom (vv. 21-22), the prophet now shifts his focus to the Southern Kingdom of Ahaz (9:1-7). The comparison between their fates is expressed by the adversative *ki*, which opens the line: "but" or "on the other hand."

Verse 1aa summarizes the bright future of Ahaz's realm: "But there will not be gloom for her who has been oppressed" (*le'asher muṣaq lah*). Neither here nor in the verses that follow does Isaiah clearly identify the referent of "her." If, however, the whole of 8:21-9:7 addresses a southern audience, the referent is probably Jerusalem, or possibly Judah as a whole. The latter would assume, however, that the capital city and the larger country were not yet so thoroughly polarized at the time of this speech (see 8:6-8a).

The above interpretation rests on a particular handling of the text's difficult syntax: *muṣaq* is a noun, "oppression," related to "her" by the preposition *1*, "to" or "for." (The Hebrew appears to read literally: "But there will not be gloom to the one that there was oppression to her.") We might also construe *muṣaq* as a hophal participle, "oppressed" (from the root *m'q*), and the preposition *1* as expressing agency. The line would then read: "But there will not be gloom for the one who has been oppressed by her." The meaning remains essentially the same: "the one who has been oppressed" is Jerusalem or Judah. "Her" refers to either Israel or Samaria, whose rulers had dominated the Davidic Kingdom up to the moment of Pekah's coup and Ahaz's assertion of independence.

The political developments behind 9:1*aa* are difficult to determine with absolute certainty. It is possible that Ahaz's break with Israel gave rise to Isaiah's hopeful declaration. Prior to Pekah's takeover, the Davidides had been more or less vassals of the northern kings for several generations. The foreign policies of the two countries thus coincided. As Menahem and Pekahiah refused to join Rezin in revolt against Assyria, so also Jotham and Ahaz withstood Syrian pressure. In the same way, though, when Israel finally joined Rezin in 736/5, its southern vassal should have followed suit. It did not. Ahaz asserted his independence by persisting in a neutralist foreign policy. To be sure, the Davidic king was to continue vacillating on the issue up to the Syro-Ephraimitic invasion (see 7:1-17). Isaiah 8:21-9:7 might give us reason to think, however, that Ahaz first declared his break with Israel only weeks or even days after Pekah's coup. The prophet applauded the move and proclaimed a new era of prosperity.

Isaiah 9:1ab-7

Verses 1*ab*-7 celebrate at length the independence of Ahaz and promise Yahweh's continued support for the Davidic regime. They are thus an elaboration of the previous declaration. The verses divide roughly into three parts. Verses 1*ab*-3 describe the people's good fortune and their rejoicing. The reasons for celebration follow in verses 4-6, climaxing in a review of the king's exalted status. Verse 7 predicts the eternal rule of the Davidic house, concluding with a pledge of divine support.

Isaiah prefaces his description of the people's new situation (v. 2) with a reflection on earlier events. Interpreting the allusions is difficult, however, for the Hebrew syntax and the meaning of the verbs and their tenses are open to question. We propose the following reading:

(1) Like the time [when] the former one brought the land of Zebulun and the land of Naphtali into contempt and [when] the latter one made harsh the Way of the Sea, Beyond the Jordan, and Galilee of

the Nations, (2) [so now] the people who were walking in darkness have seen a great light, upon those who were living in a land of deep darkness a light has shined.

The translation rests on four decisions. First, the perfect verbal forms should be rendered in the past tense. Second, the two verbs of verse 1—*heqal* and *hikbid*—are parallel in sense, both having negative meanings. Third, "the former one" (*hari'shon*) and "the latter one" (*ha'aharon*) are subjects and refer to specific persons. Finally, verses 1 and 2 belong together as parts of a single sentence. The extended prepositional phrase, "like the time (*ka`et*)" sets forth a previous history against which the new situation of the people (v. 2) is understood.

Scholars generally argue that 9:1 relates how Israel lost significant territory to the Assyrians in the course and aftermath of the Syro-Ephraimitic crisis (734–732). It thus seems to provide a parallel to II Kings 15:29, which reports Tiglath-pileser's seizure of Gilead and Galilee. The Kings text, however, does not actually state from whom the Assyrian king captured the regions, only that he did so during the reign of Pekah. We have argued (see above, chap. 1, sect. 3B and C) that Israel had probably lost the territory in question long before 734–732 and, indeed, had lost it not to Assyria but to Syria and/or its allies. If this reconstruction is correct, Isaiah 9:1 may be taken as a reflection of this earlier period during which "Greater Israel" was gradually reduced to a rump state in Ephraim.

The "former one" who "brought the land of Zebulun and the land of Naphtali into contempt" is probably Jeroboam II. During the early and middle years of his reign, Israel had managed to expand its borders, taking control of Transjordan, Galilee, and the coast. However during the later years of Jeroboam, when Assyrian presence in the west was greatly reduced, the Syrians and others began to encroach on these same areas. The oracles of Amos attest to Jeroboam's troubles in Gilead: Syrians, Ammonites, and Israelites all struggled to control the region (Amos 1:3-5, 13-15, and 6:13). Presumably Pekah's revolt also began during this same time. Amos himself anticipated that Israel would eventually lose the entire Transjordan (6:14).

A few texts may testify to Jeroboam's difficulties in the coastal and Galilean regions. Amos 1:6-8 and 9-10 probably allude to Philistine and Phoenician actions against Israelite and Judean holdings along the coast. Both peoples, moreover, seem to have been working in close cooperation with Syria (reading Aram for Edom in vv. 6 and 9). Hosea 1:5 may reflect consequent troubles in Galilee. In a pronouncement of judgment against the Jehu dynasty, the prophet predicts on Yahweh's behalf: "And on that day I will break the bow of Israel in the valley of Jezreel." The saying appears to anticipate or even assume Israel's loss of the Jezreel Valley and with it, by implication, the Galilean territory to the north. Behind the prophet's words is probably a situation in which Syria had challenged Israel's control of the region. While Hosea 1:5 still looks forward to Israel's complete loss of the area, Isaiah 9:1 reflects on it as a past event. The "former one," Jeroboam, had brought Zebulun and Naphtali "into contempt."

The "latter one" who "made harsh the way of the Sea [the coast], beyond the Jordan [Gilead] and Galilee of the nations" is probably Menahem. He ascended the throne in Samaria after months of civil war in the north, but was able to secure his rule only after great struggle and with Assyrian assistance (see II Kings 15:19-20 and chap. 1, sect. 3C, above). The period then was one of extreme internal weakness for Israel. Consequently, it was also an opportune time for Syria and its allies to capitalize on earlier made inroads into Israelite territory. Isaiah 9:12 probably relates to this period: "Syrians on the east and Philistines on the west devoured Israel with open mouth." If the last part of 9:1 also reports on Menahem's years, the coast, Galilee, and Gilead all seem to have been lost by Israel before the end of his reign.

Isaiah's word choice in verse 1 merits further comment. One may reasonably question whether the two verbs, "bring into contempt" (*heqal*) and "make harsh" (*hikbid*), suitably describe territorial losses by Israelite kings. It is important to note that the selection of verbs is partly determined by Isaiah's interest in word play. The two verbs literally mean "to make light" and "to make heavy." The prophet's remark thus has a certain ironic twist: "Light" treatment and "heavy" treatment amount to the same thing—the loss of

Israelite territory. This word play explains what otherwise seems a strange choice of verbs.

Against the background of Israel's earlier territorial losses, verse 2 describes the recent break of the Davidic kingdom with its northern suzerain—"the people who were walking in darkness have seen a great light." How broadly "people" here should be understood is difficult to say. Certainly, the reference includes the Davidic court and Jerusalem, but possibly larger Judah as well, at least insofar as the Davidic family claims were concerned. Either way, Isaiah's main point is the same. Ahaz's move toward independence is the last phase of a twenty-year history in which Israel gradually lost all holdings beyond the hill country of Ephraim.

In a style reminiscent of thanksgiving psalms, the prophet celebrates this turn of events for the Davidic realm. (Compare the language of v. 2 with Pss. 107:10, 14; 138:7; 23:4; and 18:4-5, 28). This is particularly clear in verse 3. Here Isaiah turns to address the deity directly, crediting Yahweh for the people's new found hope:

You have made rejoicing great [reading *haggilah* for *haggoy lo'*], you have increased gladness. They have rejoiced before you as with the joy of harvest time, just as they rejoice when dividing up spoil.

The words of the prophet reflect the strong backing Ahaz enjoyed among his Jerusalemite supporters. We can easily imagine cultic celebrations within the capital city, thanking Yahweh for the liberation of the Davidic Kingdom from Israelite domination.

Verses 4-6 list specific reasons for rejoicing, each beginning with the conjunction "for" (*ki*). The first of these alludes most clearly to the people's new independence: "For the yoke of his burden and the staff against his shoulder, the rod of the one who was oppressing him, you [Yahweh] have broken just as [on] the day of Midian." The terms here have obvious political meanings (compare, for example, Isa. 10:5, 24-27; 14:2-5, 25; 47:6; Jer. 28:2; 30:8) and make sense as references to the long-standing domination of the Davidic Kingdom by Israel. Isaiah describes the end of this domination as Yahweh's doing and compares it to a traditional example of the people's liberation—the defeat of the Midianites in pre-monarchical times (10:27a-c; see Judg. 6-8).

A second reason for celebration follows in verse 5: "For every boot of the trampling soldier in battle tumult and [every] mantle rolled in blood will be burned [*wehayetah lisrepah*] as fuel for a fire." Here the prophet shifts to the future tense. Having described in verse 4 the breaking of Israel's political strength, Isaiah now predicts an end to the nation's military power. As in 8:1-4, Isaiah is probably anticipating an Assyrian response to the Syrian and Israelite revolt. The rhetorical aim of the prediction is easy to see: to assure the Davidides and the residents of Jerusalem that their new independence from the Northern Kingdom is not a short-term affair but will continue into the distant future.

✓ Verse 6 presents a final reason for rejoicing—the "birth" of a royal "child." Here the prophet drops the style of the thanksgiving psalm and addresses his Jerusalemite audience directly.

For a child [*yeled*] has been born [*yulad*] for us, a son has been appointed [literally, "given"; *nitten*] for us. And authority has fallen [*wattehi*] upon his shoulder and he has been named [*weyyiqra'*] Wonderful Counselor, Mighty God, Everlasting Father, Prince of Peace.

This translation highlights Isaiah's conspicuous return to the past tense. The Hebrew verbs are either perfect forms or imperfect consecutives. The verse then does not predict a future "child" but reflects on a past event and its significance for the present: A child *has been born*; authority *has fallen* upon his shoulders; he *has been named* Wonderful Counselor and so on.

The identity of the royal "child" is a much debated issue. A future messianic interpretation must be ruled out, if we are correct in rendering the verse in the past tense. Two major alternatives then remain. First, the child is a recently born heir of the Davidic house. (The language of the verse is to be taken literally.) Second, "child" is a metaphorical designation for a contemporary Davidic king who, having gone through the coronation-enthronement ritual, now has the status of Yahweh's adopted "son" (compare Pss. 2 and 110 and II Sam. 7:14). This second interpretation, we believe, is the more likely. Verse 6 is not a royal birth announcement to the public (of which, we might add, there are few, if any, Near Eastern examples), but a prophetic statement about the exalted standing of the actual Davidic ruler.

The names ascribed to the king are traditional throne names which the monarch received at his enthronement. The immediate background of this Judean royal protocol is probably Egyptian. In the course of the enthronement ceremony, the new pharaoh received five throne names describing his exalted nature, his special relationship to the gods, and his glorious destiny. In the Judean ritual, the royal titles may have been included in the "testimony" given to the new king (see II Kings 11:12 and compare the "decree" in Ps. 2:7).

The throne names in Isaiah 9:6 reflect the Judean understanding of kingship. The first title, "Wonderful Counselor" (*pele' yo`es*), probably describes the king's extraordinary prudence and judgment in matters of state. (See 11:2, where Isaiah speaks of a "spirit of council" resting on the Davidic ruler. Note also the synonymous uses of "king" and "counselor" in Micah 4:9.) The Hebrew name might be rendered, "He Who Plans Wondrous Things." In this case, the title would emphasize the magnificence of the king's deeds.

The second name, "Mighty God" or "Divine Hero" (*'el gibbor*), suggests the military prowess of the king. The idea is not unique to Israel but characteristic of royal ideology throughout the ancient Near East. The theme of the king's might appears elsewhere in the Hebrew Bible, particularly in the royal psalms. There, the king is portrayed repeatedly as the invincible warrior (2:7-9; 45:3-5; 89:20-23; and 110:1-6). Isaiah alludes to the king's military power also in 11:2. He speaks there of a "spirit of might" resting on the Davidic monarch.

What is striking about the name, "Mighty God" or "Divine Hero," is its apparent attribution of divinity to the king. This characterization is not unique to our passage. In Psalm 45, an ode composed for a royal wedding, the king is addressed: "Your throne, O God (*'elohim*), endures forever and ever" (v. 6). The continuation of the psalm, however, clearly subordinates the monarch to Yahweh: "Therefore God, your God, has anointed you" (v. 7). The text then does not assume the full deification of the king but suggests only his exalted status above normal human beings. Similarly in Isaiah 9:6, the title "Mighty God" does not intend to set the Davidic ruler on a par with Yahweh. It emphasizes his superhuman skill and leadership in military matters. (So the NEB translation, "in battle God-like," correctly expresses the sense of the name. Note also that in Mesopotamia the king is generally understood as a subordinate to the gods; yet, the determinative *ilu*, or "god," is occasionally set before the king's name.)

The third throne name, "Everlasting Father" (*'abi`ad*), alludes to the longevity of the ideal king and to his role *vis-à-vis* his subjects. The first theme appears also in the royal psalms: Yahweh gives to the king "length of days forever and ever" (21:4; compare 72:5). The titles of the pharaoh, "Prince of Eternity" and "Lord of Infinity," attest to the same belief in Egypt.

The characterization of the king as "father" is unusual in the Hebrew Bible (see I Sam. 24:11). The biblical texts ordinarily focus on the monarch's sonship to Yahweh. The epithet "father" does, however, form a regular part of the Accadian royal titulary. There and in Isaiah 9:6, "father" describes the king's care for the well-being of his people.

The fourth throne name, "Prince of Peace" (*śar shalom*), has several meanings. The title describes the king's role as protector of his people against foreign aggression. It also describes his responsibility for the preservation of internal order. The Hebrew word *shalom* suggests abundance and prosperity in all aspects of life. As the "Prince of Shalom," the king is the source of his people's economic, social, and political well-being (see Ps. 72:5-7, 15-16).

The meanings of the throne-names are clear; it remains to be seen which actual Davidic ruler v. 6 describes.

The identification most often proposed for this Davidic king is Hezekiah. In the light of the above analysis of this section, however, Ahaz, his father, is the more probable candidate. Contrary to the assumption of most scholars, Isaiah did not reject this king but supported him, applauding particularly his break with the Northern Kingdom in 736/5. In

9:6, the prophet cites Ahaz's exalted royal status as reason for celebration. Whether the verse reflects directly a recent renewal of his kingship (the ritual enthronement of the Davidic king may have been celebrated annually) or simply reviews the king's standing as proclaimed at the beginning of his reign is difficult to say. In either case, the implication of the prophet's statement would have been clear to his Jerusalemite audience, given current political developments. Ahaz no longer ruled as a vassal of Israel but as a fully independent king with divine legitimation. "Authority has fallen upon his shoulder" and will remain. (Note the play on the word *shoulder* in verses 4 and 6.)

The speech concludes in verse 7 with a promise of continued well-being for the Davidic house. While the general meaning of the prophet seems clear enough, translating the verse is nonetheless difficult. We render the Hebrew as follows:

Of the greatness [*lemarbeh*] of authority and of security [*ulshalom*] there will be no end for the throne of David and for its sovereignty, establishing [*lehahin*] it and sustaining it [*ulsa`adah*] with justice and righteousness, from this time forth and forevermore. The zeal of Yahweh Sebaoth will do this!

This translation rests on three decisions. (1) Contrary to the efforts of many scholars, an additional throne-name is not to be sought at the beginning of the verse. We cannot assume an exact correspondence between the Judean royal protocol and Egyptian practice where five throne names were the norm. (2) The opening Hebrew word, *lamarbeh*, is orthographically impossible because the *m* here is in the form the letter takes only at the end of a word. We emend the *m* to its medial form, following the marginal qere, and translate, "of greatness." The term stands parallel to "security," both being governed by the statement, "there will be no end." (3) The hiphil infinitives, *lehahin* and *ulsa`adah*, express neither purpose nor result but simply accompanying circumstances. The subject of the action is not clearly indicated, but in view of the final sentence, there can be no doubt that Yahweh is intended. He establishes and upholds the Davidic throne.

Isaiah's aim is to assure his audience that their recent independence from Israel is not temporary but will last into the future "from this time forth and forevermore." Significantly, the promise picks up the traditional language and thought of the royal theology. Yahweh "establishes" (*hun*) the "throne" (*kise*) of each Davidic king and sustains his "reign" or "sovereignty" (*mamlakah*; compare II Sam. 7:12-16 and Ps. 89:28-37). Isaiah holds up this traditional belief to the Davidic court and the residents of Jerusalem and urges them to take it seriously. "From this time forth and forevermore," the Davidic regime will stand firmly with divine support. "The zeal of Yahweh will do this!"

12. A WORD AGAINST JACOB (9:8–10:4)

J. L. **Crenshaw**, "A Liturgy of Wasted Opportunity (Am 4, 6-12; Isa 9:7–10:4; 5:25-29)," *Semitics* 1(1970)27-37; A. M. **Honeyman**, "An Unnoticed Euphemism in Isaiah IX 19-20?" *VT* 1(1951)221-23; C. J. **Labuschagne**, "Ugaritic *blt* and *biltî* in Is. X 4," *VT* 14(1964)97-99; C. E. **L'Heureux**, "The Redactional History of Isaiah 5:1–10:4," *In the Shelter of Elyon: Essays on Ancient Palestinian Life and Literature in Honor of G. W. Ahlström* (ed. W. B. Barrick and J. R. Spencer; Sheffield: JSOT Press, 1984)99-119; D. W. **Thomas**, "A Note on the Meaning of *yd`* in Hosea 9:9 and Isaiah 9:8," *JTS* 41(1940)43-44; M. **Wallenstein**, "An Unnoticed Euphemism in Isaiah IX 19-20?" *VT* 2(1952)179-80.

In this speech, Isaiah rehearses a series of events that have befallen Israel (9:8-21) before turning to the current situation (10:1-4). These past events are depicted as acts in which God stretched out his hand to express anger against Israel (see Amos 4:6-12). Even though these events are all past, the punishment of Israel is depicted as not yet complete, since God's anger has not yet abated (see 5:25). Like a parent posed to strike a blow while whipping a wayward child (see 1:5), his hand is stretched out still.

The events alluded to by the prophet were episodes of the recent past that had severely damaged Israelite society. Only

10:3-4*a* concerns future actions—namely, the forthcoming attack of the Assyrians against the anti-Assyrian coalition. The episodes referred to by Isaiah include the earthquake during the reign of Uzziah (9:8-10); the encroachment of Syrians and Philistines on Israelite territory beginning during the reign of Jeroboam II (v. 11-12*a*); the destruction of the house of Jehu, attendant upon Shallum's assassination of Zechariah (vv. 13-17*a*); the civil war and internal strife in the Shallum–Menahem–Pekah conflicts (vv. 18-21*a*); and perhaps the activity of Pekah in the anti-Assyrian rebellion (10:1-2).

The refrain in 9:12*b*, 17*b*, 21*b*, and 10:4*b* divides this speech into four subunits.

(1) Earthquake and enemies (8-12)
(2) Internal turmoil and strife (13-19)
(3) Civil hostilities and warfare (18-21)
(4) The coming judgment (10:1-4)

Isaiah 9:8-12

Verses 8-10 would appear to refer back to the earthquake that devastated Palestine in the reign of Uzziah (see Amos 1:1; Zech. 14:5) and that Isaiah had used as the subject of addresses in 1:2-20 and 2:6-22. (Josephus associated this earthquake with Uzziah's outbreak of leprosy and, apparently like many of the rabbis, with Isaiah's temple vision; see *Ant* IX 225-26.) The earthquake is spoken of as a word of Yahweh sent against Jacob and alighting on Israel. (The sequence of terminology in Isaiah's references—Jacob-Israel-Ephraim-Samaria—could point to either the inclusiveness of the earthquake's disaster [both north and south were included] or the progressive diminution of northern territory.) It could be that Isaiah's references to a word from Yahweh and the identification of this word with the earthquake alluded to Amos's preaching. In Amos 9:1, the prophet seems to have proclaimed a vision about Yahweh's standing on the altar calling for an earthquake.

Verses 8-10 may be translated as follows:

8. A word Yahweh sent against Jacob,
   and it fell upon Israel.

185

9. But the people reasoned, all of them,
       Ephraim and the ruler of Samaria,
       in pride and arrogance of heart, saying,
10. "Bricks have fallen;
       We'll build with dressed stones;
    sycamore timbers have collapsed;
       we'll replace them with cedar."

In Isaiah's description of the earthquake's destruction and the Ephraimites' reaction, he makes no reference to their association of the calamity with Yahweh. Similarly, the disaster evoked no sense of repentance but instead was met with obstinate defiance.

If our earlier assignment of these prophetic allusions to historical events is correct, then two significant factors are noteworthy in verses 8-9. First, the earthquake that tradition recalled in relationship to the reign of Uzziah struck Palestine while Jeroboam II was still on the throne (assuming that vv. 13-17a speak about the end of the Jehu dynasty). Second, the territory under Jeroboam's control was probably already reduced to the point that it could be described simply as "Ephraim."

In spite of this natural calamity, the northerners continued to assume an optimistic and arrogant attitude. Isaiah's quotation of the Ephraimite response in verse 10—"Bricks have fallen; we'll build with dressed stones; sycamore timbers have collapsed; we'll replace them with cedar"—sounds very much like a proverbial saying, expressing the feeling of "better next time."

Instead of rebuilding, Ephraim was in fact confronted with further trouble:

11. Yahweh let the oppressors of Rezin triumph over it,
       and stirred up its enemies;
12a. Syria from the east, and Philistines from the west,
       devoured Israel by the mouthful.

The references here are to the encroachment of Israel's neighbors onto Israelite territory (see the discussion of 9:1 above). Transjordan and the Galilee were overrun by Syria, and Syria and Philistia together may have overrun the Sharon Plain. Although modern translators and commentators are practically unamimous in deleting part or all of the reference to Rezin's oppressors, there is neither textual warrant nor historical justification for such excision. With the encouragement of Urartu, Syria and other western powers had formed one anti-Assyrian coalition after another throughout the first half of the eighth century, as they would continue to do until the turn of the century. The "henchmen" of Rezin set against pro-Assyrian Israel were those in southern Palestine cooperating with the Damascus leadership (see Amos 1-2).

Isaiah 9:13-17

Since the previous events did not bring the nation to its senses and a return to Yahweh (v. 13), God took further action to increase the traumas in the north.

14. Yahweh cut off from Israel head and tail,
     palm branch and reed, in one day!
15. Elder and honored one, that is the head,
     and prophet teaching falsehood, that is the tail.
16. And the leaders of this people became wanderers,
     and the followers became the misguided;
17. thus the Lord does not rejoice over its youngsters,
     and shows no mercy to its fatherless and widows;
   because everyone is defiled and an evildoer,
     and every mouth speaks foolishness.

The generalities of the prophet's descriptions in this section make it impossible to determine his referents with any precision. The overall picture of anarchy and revolution suggests the scenario of the overthrow of the house of Jehu (probably in 745). After a reign of six months, Zechariah, the son of Jeroboam, was assassinated, the victim of a conspiracy led by Shallum (II Kings 15:8-10). The latter reigned for only one month before being struck down in a countercoup led by Menahem, son of Gadi (II Kings 15:13-14). Menahem carried out brutal actions to stabilize his power (II Kings 15:15) and eventually secured his rule through the assistance of

Tiglath-pileser (II Kings 15:19-20; probably shortly after the Assyrian monarch arrived in the west in 743).

The expressions describing opposite ends of a spectrum—head and tail (see Deut. 28:13, 44; Isa. 19:15), branch and reed, honored elder and prophet, leaders and led—indicate the extent of the anarchy and, perhaps, of the polarization of northern society. Things became so bad that Yahweh forsook even the task of caring for the underprivileged (see 1:17) since the whole society was contaminated and wicked. Civil strife cut across all segments of the culture. Any attempt to identify particular individuals behind the prophet's allusions (for example, the "elder and honored one" [Zechariah] and the "prophet teaching falsehood" [Amos or Hosea] is purely speculative since the allusions are so general. (Verse 15 may even be a later interpretive gloss.) According to Isaiah, everyone was given to speaking foolish nonsense (see 32:5). Nonetheless, head and tail (palm branch and reed) may well be allusions to King Zechariah and his assassin, Shallum.

Isaiah 9:18-21

The civil strife preceding Pekah's takeover in Samaria (in 736 or 735) is the topic of this subunit (vv. 18-21). According to verse 21, the strife involved Manasseh against Ephraim, Ephraim against Manasseh, and both together against Judah. Such a situation was produced by the following elements. Menahem, apparently from Tirzah in the tribal territory of Manasseh (II Kings 15:14), had put down opposition to his rule, which was probably centered in Tappuah and its vicinity in northern Ephraim (see Josh. 16:8; 17:8). Further, Pekah, probably a rival monarch already during the last years of Jeroboam's reign, was apparently from northern Gilead (II Kings 15:25), which was Manassite territory (Num. 32:40-42; Josh. 13:29-31). If Pekah was assassinated in 732 (II Kings 15:30) and ruled twenty years (II Kings 15:27), then he must have begun to rule over a portion of Israelite territory, probably supported by Syria, while Jeroboam II was still king. The conflict of Manasseh and Ephraim noted in Isaiah 9:21 thus refers to the strife between these regions in the civil struggles that extended from the latter years of Jeroboam's reign and throughout the rule of Zechariah, Shallum, Menahem, and Pekahiah.

Verse 21 notes that Manasseh and Ephraim were both against Judah. How is this to be understood? The actions of Ephraim against Judah would refer to activity taken by the government in Samaria, while the actions of Manasseh would refer to activity taken by Pekah. In the former case, we have had several occasions to note that in the eighth century Judah was a subordinate state to Israel until Ahaz broke with Pekah (see the discussion of Isa. 9:2). Isaiah could have had this general subordination in mind in his reference to Ephraimite activity against Judah. In all probability, however, he had a much more specific case in mind. According to II Kings 15:19-20, Menahem had to pay Tiglath-pileser one thousand talents of silver "for his [Tiglath-pileser's] hand to be with him to secure the reign of his [Menahem's] hand." The price of one thousand talents was collected by assessing all the wealthy citizens in his kingdom fifty shekels each. If one calculates a talent as three thousand shekels, then about sixty thousand wealthy persons would have been required to pay the special Assyrian tribute. It is highly unlikely that the northern kingdom, given its shrunken borders and the troubles noted in Isaiah 9:8-17a, would have possessed sixty thousand potential "contributors." Judeans, as members of a vassal state, were probably forced to share in the assessment (see Isa. 3:18-26). The wealthy in both Israel and Judah probably passed along part of the burden to the poor. The Israelite burden on Judah, which may normally have included such obligations as supplying troop contingents, thus reached new levels of demand under Menahem.

Manasseh's or Pekah's hostility toward Judah during the reign of Menahem is noted in II Kings 15:37. In this text, associated with Jotham's reign in Judah, we are told that "in those days, Yahweh began to send Rezin the king of Syria and Pekah the son of Remaliah against Judah." At this point, the text gives no indication of what it meant to be "against Judah." Two incidents may be relevant. First, I Chronicles 5:17 speaks of a time when Jeroboam II and Jotham cooperated in activities in the Transjordan. Pekah and Rezin could have taken over territory in this area from the Israelite and Judean kings and thus reduced Judah's possessions.

Second, II Kings 16:6 reports that Rezin recovered the port of Elath on the Red Sea from Judean control. The text associates this episode with the Syro-Ephraimitic siege of Jerusalem, but it seems highly unlikely that the forces of Rezin and Pekah would have been operating against Jerusalem and Elath simultaneously. Perhaps the forces of Rezin and Pekah had cooperatively carried out the capture of Elath earlier than the blitzkrieg against Jerusalem (see discussion of Isa. 7:6).

The internal strife and civil dissent in the north are depicted in several ways in verses 18-20. On the one hand, wickedness rages like a wildfire through the land, consuming the briers and thorns (see 5:6; 7:23-25). Here the destruction of the society is ascribed to human behavior. On the other hand, in verse 19, it is the rage of Yahweh that has burned or blackened the land. In the former, the people are the cause of the calamity, kindling the northern forest fires and producing the socially devastating flames that consume the land. In the latter, the people themselves are the fuel being consumed.

In the internecine struggles, the people seem to have been set on self-destruction. Treatment of fellow citizens is described in terms of eating and consumption. Verse 20*b* says, "Each the flesh of his arm they devour." By dropping one consonant and repointing the text, "his arm" can be read "his neighbor" (so the RSV) or merely by repointing, "his seed" may be read "his offspring." The latter reading would suggest that the prophet described the northern strife in terms of cannibalism and fratricide (see the last part of v. 19).

Isaiah 10:1-4

In Isaiah's recitation of the north's calamitous recent history, he comes, in 10:1-4, to the present. That these verses concern the present situation is indicated by the "woe" introduction, by the use of present participles indicating present conditions and second person address, and by the fact that the calamity in verses 3-4*a* is still future (whereas in the previous verses, the calamities had already struck).

Two different contexts may be proposed as the setting for the actions condemned in verses 1-2. (1) The almost universal consensus is that these verses were concerned with domestic judicial administration within Judah itself. Either new, unjust social laws were promulgated to the benefit of the wealthy and/or ruling classes or existing laws were interpreted so as to deprive the powerless of their goods and property. This approach tends to see the actions condemned as reflective of general conditions, rather than of some specific set of circumstances. Many commentators thus associate 10:1-4 with 5:8-24 and argue for an original connection between these two texts. In this case, 10:1-4 received its present placement through textual dislocation or redactional rearrangement. (2) A context reflecting the international situation of the Syro-Ephraimitic crisis provides a second possibility. The decrees promulgated would thus emanate from the Israelite court in Samaria and be concerned with Israelite-Judean relationships. Such an approach seems to make better sense of the text than the alternatives and at the same time interprets the passage within its literary context, as the conclusion to the speech begun in 9:8, and within a firm historical context.

The woe opening in verse 1 identifies those being denounced as those decreeing iniquitous decrees and promulgating oppressive promulgations. Isaiah's repetitious play on words in this verse makes understanding somewhat difficult. He employs two forms of the verb *ḥqq* meaning "to decree" and two forms of the verb *ktb* meaning "to write." In the latter case, he uses otherwise unattested piel forms of the word. The verb *ḥqq* and the noun *ḥoq* frequently carry the idea of an official edict or decree (see Gen. 47:26; I Sam. 30:25). The nuance of the piel (intensive) of *ktb* is unknown; it may have implied not just "constant writing" but something comparable to our "publishing"—that is, putting something into public circulation.

What are the decrees and promulgations to which Isaiah alludes? One can imagine that in Israel's turbulent history between the years 750 and 735 there may have been numerous royal decrees from Samaria. The several changes in dynasty and the conflicts between Pekah and Menahem (Manasseh and Ephraim) provided occasions for decrees affirming or changing policies. The focus, however, can be narrowed somewhat, since verse 2, especially in the light of the remarks in 9:21, suggests that the edict or edicts had negative consequences. Five possibilities suggest themselves: (1) Menahem's decree, requiring contributions for the special payment to Tiglath-pileser; (2) Menahem's rulings regarding raising annual tribute payments for the Assyrians; (3) the proclamation of Judah's normal (or a special) taxation to be paid to the northern king; (4) an edict by Pekah, declaring Israel's (and Judah's) support for the anti-Assyrian coalition and attendant demands; and (5) Pekah's proclamation of Ahaz and Judah as traitorous in the light of the southern monarch's declaration of independence from Israel (see 8:11-12; 9:2-5).

The consequences of the decrees are spoken of as falling upon those whom Isaiah describes as "needy," "poor," "widows," and "fatherless." How are such terms to be taken? Is Isaiah speaking of actual classes in society, as appears to be the case in other of his texts (1:17, 23; 9:17; 14:30; 25:7; 32:7)? Is the terminology of the oppressed and powerless used here in a metaphorical sense (as may be the case in 25:7)? If metaphorical, then the referents could be the Judeans in general. Are the terms chosen to imply the extent of the royal proclamations—that they touch even the lowest rungs of society's ladder (see 9:16)? Is Isaiah saying that in trying to force Judah's involvement in the anti-Assyrian operation Pekah is threatening the whole of Judean society? Or is the society that is threatened, according to Isaiah (the "my people" of v. 2*a*), actually the Northern Kingdom, itself, or Israel as a totality? In 32:13, the prophet clearly speaks of the people of the north as his people. So here, "my people" may be the total of Yahweh's people, north and south, Israel in the inclusive sense.

In verse 3, Isaiah addresses leading questions to those who have written decrees injurious to the needy, poor, widows, and fatherless: "What will you do? To whom will you flee? Where will you hide?" The day of punishment or visitation refers to a time of reckoning. The expression was ambiguous enough to encompass both the coming day of Yahweh's judgment and the arrival of the Assyrian troops to suppress revolt. The storm from afar could denote either Yahweh from heaven or Tiglath-pileser from Mesopotamia. The final word in verse 3, denoting whatever is to be left, is the Hebrew word *kabod*, normally meaning "glory." Since such a meaning does not seem appropriate in this context, various translations have been proposed: "wealth" (RSV), "riches" (JB), "carcasses" (NJPSV), and "children" (NEB). Such translations assume one of the following as Isaiah's question: "Where will you leave your ill-gotten wealth?" "How will you save yourself when judgment comes?" "What will happen to your offspring when destruction hits?"

One would normally have expected Isaiah's question—"To whom will you flee for help?"—to be answered: "To Yahweh." However, if Isaiah and his audience had in mind the position advocated in Exodus 22:22-24, there was no way that appeal to Yahweh was possible. This text stipulates:

You shall not afflict any widow or orphan. If you do afflict them, and they cry out to me, I will surely hear their cry; and my wrath will burn, and I will kill [from the verb *hrg*] you with the sword, and your wives shall become widows and your children fatherless.

According to this law, those guilty of what Isaiah had accused the leaders of in verses 1-2 would have to flee from Yahweh rather than run to Yahweh. Perhaps this attitude toward the abusers of widows and the fatherless was part of the reason for Isaiah's choice of the social classes mentioned in verse 2.

Verse 4a consists of the prophet's verdict or pronouncement of judgment. However, questions cloud the interpretation of this line. The function of the negative particle *bilty* is uncertain. Is it the decree makers or their *kabod* who are to suffer? One way of reading the text is to take *blty kr`* as *blty ykr`* and translate this and the rest of the sentence as: "Nowhere! It [your offspring] will crouch beneath the captor, and they will fall beneath the slain" [from the verb *hrg*]. The reference to crouching may refer to being sexually assaulted (see Job. 31:10b), and the verb *hrg* is shared by the law of Exodus 22:22-24.

In 9:8–10:4, we possess a scathing denunciation of Israel that sketches the progressive internal disintegration and disarray of the north in a series of historical vignettes. At the end of each depiction, Isaiah proclaims that in spite of the preceding judgmental calamity, Yahweh's anger is still unabated and the divine hand is lifted to strike again. The focus of the speech is not on Israel's wasted opportunities but on the continuity of divine judgment, a judgment not yet finished, waiting to strike again. As Syro-Ephraimitic troops assembled in the north, the prophet rehearsed northern history of the last decade or so and declared that the miserable past was only a prologue. A greater judgment was on its way.

13. ASSYRIA, THE ROD OF YAHWEH'S ANGER
(10:5-27c)

H. **Barth**, *Die Jesaja-Worte in der Josiazeit: Israel und Assur als Thema einer producktiven Neuinterpretation der Jesajaüberlieferung* (Neukirchen-Vluyn: Neukirchener Verlag, 1977); R. P. **Carroll**, "Inner Tradition Shifts in Meaning in Isaiah 1-11," *ET* 89(1977/78)301-4; B. S. **Childs**, *Isaiah and the Assyrian Crisis* (London: SCM Press, 1967); K. **Fullerton**, "The Problem of Isaiah, Chapter 10" *AJSL* 34(1917/18)170-84; G. F. **Hasel**, *The Remnant: The History and Theology of the Remnant Idea from Genesis to Isaiah* (Berrien Springs; Andrews University Press, 1972); F. **Huber**, "Die Worte Jesajas gegen Assur," in his *Jahwe, Juda und die anderen Völker beim Propheten Jesaja* (Berlin/New York: Walter de Gruyter, 1976)35-76; R. **Kilian**, "Jesaja und Assur," in his *Jesaja 1-39* (Darmstadt: Wissenschaftliche Buchgesellschaft, 1983)98-111; P. **Machinist**, "Assyria and Its Image in the First Isaiah," *JAOS* 103(1983)719-37; F. **Wilke**, *Jesaja und Assur. Eine exegetisch-historische Untersuchung zur Politik des Propheten Jesaja* (Leipzig: Dieterich'sche Verlagsbuchhandlung Theodor Weicher, 1905).

In 735, it must have been obvious that a major military confrontation between Assyria and the western coalition was inevitable. Only the exact time and the possible outcome remained at issue. Isaiah had not yet addressed the Israelite-Assyrian problem directly. In earlier addresses, he had spoken of an unidentified enemy who would march into the land and devastate it (5:26-30). In 7:18, 20 and 8:7-8*a*, he had spoken of the Assyrians as a divinely summoned threat against Judah and in 8:4 as the destroyer of Damascus and Samaria. None of these speeches elaborate the details of Isaiah's views on Assyria *vis à vis* Israel, although 7:16 would have made it clear that Isaiah never doubted Assyria's ability to suppress the western coalition. In 10:5-27c, he now offers a comprehensive exposition of his understanding of the relationship of Yahweh and Assyria and the future course of events he envisions. The general views concerning Assyria in this speech are those expounded by Isaiah throughout his career. Only in his ecumenical euphoria, following Sargon's western campaign in 720, would Isaiah temporarily take a more positive attitude toward Assyria.

The text in 10:5-27c is fairly complex, consisting of a Yahweh statement interpreting Assyria's role (vv. 5-7), the prophet's own interpretation of matters (vv. 15-23, 26-27c), a hypothetical speech attributed to Assyria (or the Assyrian monarch; vv. 8-11, 13-14), and a Yahweh oracle of encouragement, addressed to the people of Zion (vv. 24-25). All or part of verse 12 appears to be a gloss for the following reasons. (1) It speaks of Yahweh's work on Mt. Zion and Jerusalem, which was not a concern in 735 since Jerusalem stood under no immediate threat of Assyrian attack. (2) The punishment of Assyria is already announced in the verse but is also described later in the speech in verses 16-19. (3) The passage intrudes into the context, disrupting the speech ascribed to Assyria in vv. 8-11 and 13-14.

The following is an outline of the speech:

(1) A Yahweh statement on Assyria's function (5-7)
(2) A hypothetical speech attributed to Assyria (8-11, 13-14)
(3) Prophetic promise of Assyria's eventual destruction (15-19)
(4) Prophetic prediction of the survival of an Israelite remnant (20-23)
(5) A Yahweh oracle of encouragement addressed to Zion (24-25)
(6) Prophetic assurance of redemption from Assyria (26-27c)

Isaiah 10:5-7

Isaiah's assessment of Assyria is initially presented in terms of parental discipline of a child. Yahweh is the parent, Israel is the child, and Assyria is the rod (or stick) that God will use. The image of a parent whipping a disobedient child is the initial metaphor in the book (see 1:2b-3, 5-6). Isaiah's recurring statement "his hand is stretched out still" (5:25b; 9:12b, 17b, 21b; 10:4b) carries the same imagery—namely, the parent with raised arm poised to strike the wayward child. Of the two terms used in verse 5, "rod" is the more frequent in reference to corporal punishment (see Prov. 10:13; 13:24; 22:15; 23:13-14; 26:3; 29:15); the "staff" was presumably heavier than the rod. Although "rod and staff" could be thought of and used as supports or defensive weapons (see Ps. 23:4), in verse 5 they are associated with fury and thus are negative symbols.

The descriptions of Israel as a "godless nation" and the "people of my wrath" (v. 6 RSV) give Yahweh's reason for using Assyria against his people. The term translated "godless" (RSV, JB) or "ungodly" (NJPSV) really has more to do with pollution or contamination than with irreligion or being non-religious (see Jer. 3:1; Num. 35:33). Israel has contaminated itself, deliberately doing what it knew was wrong (probably by going against the conditions of the Assyrian vassal treaty). The "people of Israel provoke Yahweh" is the sense of the expression "people of my wrath."

The verbs in verse 6a—"send" and "command" or "commission" with their quasi-official meaning—indicate clearly that the forthcoming Assyrian retaliation for Israel's participation in the anti-Assyrian coalition was not an accident of history or even primarily the action of a foreign power. The invasion is ascribed to the work and activity of Yahweh.

The task Yahweh has planned for Assyria is twofold: to loot and plunder the country and to trample it underfoot like mud in the streets (v. 6b). The divine intent is, however, only punishment, not the eradication and destruction of the people and state. In speaking of the Assyrian function—"taking spoil and seizing plunder" (literally "to spoil spoil and to plunder plunder")—Isaiah plays on the name of one of his children, Maher-shalal-hash-baz, using and repeating the words *shalal* and *baz* in their infinitive and nominal forms. Later in the speech, he picks up on the names Shear-jashub and El-gibbor (vv. 20-21).

Assyria will not understand its task as chastisement only, as does Yahweh (v. 7). Instead, Assyria or the Assyrian king will "not so intend, and his mind does not so think (RSV)", but his resolve will be to destroy and to cut off many nations. (Note that the verbs describing the intentions of the Assyrian are future tense.) The Assyrians will not just loot and trample and leave; they will conquer and provincialize. The major difference, therefore, between the divine and Assyrian plans for Israel is their intent and ultimate outcome.

Isaiah 10:8-11, 13-14

In verses 8-11 and 13-14, we possess a hypothetical speech that the prophet has placed in the mouth of the Assyrian ruler. The prophet envisions the monarch, after having captured a series of Syro-Palestinian cities, including Samaria, posing the question: "Shall I not do to Jerusalem as I have done to other cities?" The hypothetical future nature of this speech is indicated by the future/imperfect verbal forms in verses 6 and 7 and the opening in verse 8—"he will say." That is, Isaiah predicts that some time in the future the Assyrian king will make such a speech.

The futuristic and hypothetical character of this speech means that the list of cities whose capture is implied in verses 9-11 cannot be used to date this material. The six major cities noted in addition to Jerusalem came under Assyrian control (sometimes temporarily) or were captured by Assyria at various times: Calno or Calneh (Kullani in Akkadian texts) in 738; Carchemish in 717; Hamath in 738 and 720; Arpad in 740, 738, and 720; Damascus in 732 and 720; Samaria in 722 and 720. Since the time frame for the speech is an imaginary future after these cities have been taken, the time of their actual capture is irrelevant to the question of the date of the material. Speaking in 735, Isaiah probably anticipated that all of these cities associated in one way or another with contemporary anti-Assyrian activity would be taken by Tiglath-pileser when he next moved west. The cities noted—Carchemish, Calno, Arpad, Hamath, Damascus, Samaria, and Jerusalem—represent the main centers of power an Assyrian army would encounter in marching from Mesopotamia to southern Palestine. Carchemish lay on the west bank of the Euphrates River and the other cities are enumerated in a north to south direction.

The Assyrian king is made to brag about his power and status throughout verses 8-11, 13-14. The words of braggadocio ascribed to Tiglath-pileser by the prophet are actually subdued compared to inscriptions of the kings themselves (see below on Isa. 14, chap. 4, sect. 16). The king first of all is made to declare that all his commanders are monarchs; a way of asserting that even the monarch's subordinates were on an equal footing with other rulers. If so, certainly, no rival ruler was the Assyrian's equal. (In v. 8, Isaiah puns on the fact that the Hebrew word for commander was a homophone of the Assyrian word for king.) Frequently, Assyrian rulers described themselves in terms comparable to those used by Ashur-nasir-pal II (883–859).

I, great king, strong king, king of the universe, king of Assyria, king of all the four quarters, sun (god) of all people, prince, vice-regent of Ashur, valiant man, who acts with the support of Ashur and the god Shamash and has no rival among the princes of the four quarters . . . " (*ARI* II § 712).

Second, the king places all the cites of his opponents on the same level: Calno is like Carchemish, Hamath like Arpad, Samaria is like Damascus, and Jerusalem like Samaria. In fact, Samaria and Jerusalem would be expected to be less formidable since they had fewer divine images. (Isaiah's references to images and idols in Samaria and Jerusalem should not be understood as the prophet's denunciation of cultic representations; he is simply wording matters as might the Assyrian monarch whom he is imitating.) The national deities associated with an opponent make no difference in the outcome when confronted by the splendour of the divinely empowered Assyrian monarch.

Third, Isaiah has the Assyrian raise his eyes arrogantly against Jerusalem (v. 11). Earlier, Isaiah had proclaimed the safety of Zion, although Judah would be threatened by the Assyrians (7:18-25; 8:6-8*a*; in fact, Judah seems not to have been threatened by Assyria in the Syro-Ephraimitic crisis). He addresses this issue again at the close of the speech (vv. 24-27*c*).

Fourth, the Assyrian brags about how, through his own strength and wisdom, he has annihilated sovereign states, incorporating them into the Assyrian empire, plundered the wealth of foreign people as one takes eggs when the bird is away from the nest, and overthrown rulers as a raging bull forces everyone in its path to abandon decorum and flee. Again, a quotation from an inscription of Ashur-nasir-pal illustrates some of the sentiments expressed in this text:

I, Ashur-nasir-pal . . . holy creature, martial sovereign, trampler of criminals, shepherd of the four quarters, who has brought all peoples under one authority, avenger of Assyria, who extends the borders of his land, whose heart's desire [the god] Ashur has caused him to achieve so that his just hand has conquered all his enemies . . . Valiant man, foremost of all rulers, who treads upon the neck of rulers, magnificent, lord of lords, tempestuous deluge, who receives tribute and tax from all lands, at the attack of his angry weapons all lands convulse, writhe, and melt as though in a furnace, opener of paths in mountains which rise perpendicularly to the sky like the edge of a dagger. . . . (*ARI* II §§ 712, 714)

The Assyrian monarch's claim to superior wisdom is illustrated in Sargon's letter to the god Ashur, concerning the execution of a campaign against Urartu.

Mount Simirria, a large mountain peak, which stands out like the blade of a lance, raising its head above the mountains where the goddess Belit-ilani resides, whose summit reaches to the heavens above, whose root strikes downward into the midst of Arallu (the lower world;) where, as on the back of a fish, there is no going side by side, and where the ascent is difficult (whether one goes) forward or backward; on whose sides gorges and precipices yawn, to look at which with the eyes, inspires fear;—its road was too rough for chariots to mount, bad for horses, and too steep to march foot soldiers (over it). With the quick and keen understanding with which Ea and Belit-ilani have endowed me,—(the same are the gods) who have freed my limbs (i.e., given me strength) to cast down the enemy's land,—I had (my men) carry mighty bronze pickaxes in my equipment, and they shattered the side of the high mountain as (one does in breaking) blocks of building stone, making a good road (*ARAB* II § 142).

In Isaiah's version of the royal self-praise, everything is stated in terms of the isolated "I" without reference to any deity. As the above quotation illustrates, however, Assyrian monarchs ascribed their conquests and dominance to the deities. Isaiah's omission of divine references is deliberate. It creates a stronger sense of hubris on the part of the Assyrian ruler, refuses to postulate the existence of the Assyrian deities, and leaves unchallenged the assertion that Yahweh was the one who fashioned Assyrian power. (Verse 12*b* correctly senses that one of the issues at stake in vv. 5-27*c* is the pride and arrogance of the Assyrian ruler.)

Isaiah 10:15-19

In verses 15-19, the prophet moves to promise his hearers that eventually Assyria would be destroyed by Yahweh. In verse 15, two questions are asked to which the obvious answer is "No!" The prophet, however, provides elaborated "no" responses. Both questions and answers reflect the simplest sort of deductions based on the common-sense assumption that the user is superior to the instrument employed. (For the argument that the artisan is superior to the product, see 29:16.) Isaiah's point is that Yahweh is the user of Assyria, and, therefore, Assyria, the instrument, should not claim special status over against the user. (Isaiah never claims that Assyria was Yahweh's creation, only the divine instrument; but see 19:25.) The rod and staff terminology with which the speech opened is picked up again in this verse by the prophet.

Verses 16-19 contain the proclamation of divine action against Assyria. Although some of the particulars in these verses remain uncertain and the rare terminology may contain sexual innuendos, the overall sense of the material is perfectly clear. The prophet declares that Yahweh will decimate the forces of the Assyrians with some plague and

Yahweh himself will become a devouring flame. Only a small remnant will be left of the Assyrian forces.

Although it goes unsaid in verses 15-19, the context makes clear that the destruction of the Assyrian forces is envisioned as taking place after Assyria has served as the instrument of Yahweh's judgment. The scenario envisioned in verses 15-19 is as follows: (1) Assyria will attack the Syro-Ephraimitic forces (and the western anti-Assyrian powers) as the instrument of Yahweh's judgment. (2) The Assyrians will not only punish Israel and others by plundering and trampling (thus carrying out the will of Yahweh), but also will overextend their divinely ordained function by annexing territory and eradicating native monarchies. (3) The Assyrian monarch will brag about his achievements and engage in self-glorification as if his accomplishments were his own self-inspired achievements. (4) The Assyrian monarch will even set his eyes on Jerusalem as if it, too, were his for the taking. (5) Because the instrument (Assyria) moves to challenge the user (Yahweh) and vaunts itself against the user (has thoughts about taking Jerusalem), Yahweh will take action against the Assyrians and leave them only an impotent remnant.

Isaiah 10:20-23

In verses 20-23, Isaiah turns his attention to the fate of Israel in view of the predicted Assyrian victory as Yahweh's judgment. He assumes that some of the Israelites will survive. These are referred to in verse 20 as the "remnant of Israel" and "fugitives" ("survivors" RSV) of the house of Jacob." (Similar terms had been used of fugitives fleeing the northern civil strife in 4:2-3.) These two expressions may not refer to the same groups, since "the remnant" could be a reference to those who will survive the war and "the fugitives" may denote those who flee south before hostilities with Assyria erupt. At any rate, Isaiah anticipates survivors.

Two actions of these survivors, one negative and another positive, are described in verse 20. The remnant will not again depend or lean on the one who previously smote them. Here the prophet is referring to Israel's role as a puppet to Syria, which prior to Pekah's takeover had harrassed Israel, confiscated its territory, and encouraged nations in the region to encroach upon its land (see 9:11-12*a*). With Pekah's takeover, Israel switched policy to one of cooperation with Syria, or actually, to a policy involving dependence on and subordination to Syria. The positive action will be that the remnant will lean on Yahweh. Here Isaiah simply assumes that reliance on Syria had been a lack of faith in Yahweh and a failure to rely on him. The "in truth" at the end of verse 20 suggests that Israel viewed its present policy of anti-Assyrian revolt as the will of Yahweh. The prophet disagreed totally and thus spoke of the future, when Israel would "truly" lean on Yahweh, not merely appeal to the deity secondarily.

In verse 21, the prophet plays on the name of his son, Shear-jashub. According to 7:3, Isaiah had named a son Shear-jashub and had taken him to a meeting with Ahaz. No explanation of this name is offered in the text in which the child appears (see the discussion of 7:3-9, above, pp. 122-23). Presumably, Isaiah must have offered some explanation of the name that has not been recorded. Earlier, we assumed that the remnant referred to in the name was the house of David and its supporters and that the name was to be understood as encouragement to Ahaz.

Verse 21 thus declares: "A remnant shall return [*shear yashub*], a remnant of Jacob [*shear ja'akob*] to *'el gibbor*." *'El gibbor* can be translated "the mighty God" (so RSV) and the statement can be understood with reference to a return to Yahweh and thus as a synonymously parallel statement to verse 20*b*. On the other hand, *'el gibbor* in verse 21 can be identified with the *'el gibbor* ("Mighty God") of 9:6, where the expression is used as a title of the Davidic king, in this case, Ahaz. If one understands the text this way, then Isaiah declares that the remnant of Israel that survives the Assyrian onslaught will return to the Davidic monarch. The Israel that survives will again become part of the Davidic state. This, of course, is what Isaiah had implied in his earlier exhortations to the Davidic house (see 7:17).

In verse 22, the prophet addresses Israel directly: "Even if your people, O Israel, were as the sand of the sea, only a remnant would survive in it. Destruction has been inscribed; flooding is righteousness." Here the prophet declares that even if the hypothetical ideal—an Israel innumerable (Hos.

1:10; Gen. 22:17; 32:12; Josh. 11:4)—should exist, still when the Assyrians attack only a faction will be left. God has already decreed and Isaiah has inscribed (see 8:1) destruction (or "wasting away," "loss"; see the use of the word *klyn* in Deut. 28:65 and as the name of a son of Elimelech in Ruth 1:2, 5). The last part of the verse, "flooding is righteousness" appears to be rather cryptic. The term *shtp*, "to overflow, flood," is used in 8:8 to speak of Assyria's movement into Judah like the flooding Euphrates River and in 28:17 to refer to waters washing away a shelter. (Raging waters is a frequent metaphor for destruction in Assyrian royal inscriptions.) In 10:22, however, it is "righteousness" that is overflooding. In such a context, what could "righteousness" (*ṣedaqah*) mean? If related to the Assyrian invasions, as clearly is the case, then righteousness appears to be the action of Yahweh through the Assyrians to reestablish proper order or to restore order disrupted by the Israelite failure to adhere to its treaty obligations with Assyria.

Verse 23 reinforces verse 22: "Surely it is a destructive and decreed thing that the Lord Yahweh Sebaoth is doing in the midst of the whole land."

Isaiah 10:24-27c

Verses 24-27c address the people dwelling in Zion, assuring them they have nothing to fear from the Assyrians and that eventually even their political dominance by this foreign imperial power will come to an end. (The notations of the ancient editors of the Hebrew text [the Masoretes] indicate that they understood all of v. 27 to be a sense unit. Here we ignore the punctuation of the verse in the MT and subdivide it into four sections and read the last section with v. 28 and following.)

24. Therefore, thus says the Lord Yahweh Sebaoth,
     "Do not be afraid of Assyria, O my people dwelling in Zion,
       when it smites with a rod,
       and wields its staff against you,
        on the road to Egypt.
25.   For after a little while the indignation will be finished,
       and my anger will be directed toward their destruction."

26. And Yahweh Sebaoth will brandish a whip against him,
    as when he smote Midian at the Rock of Oreb;
  and his staff will extend to the sea,
    when he wields it on the road to Egypt.
27*a* And it will be in that day,
  b   its [Assyria's] burden will be removed from your shoulder;
  c   and its yoke from upon your neck will be broken.

In verse 24, Isaiah moves to offer assurance and encouragement to Zion in view of the forthcoming military invasion of the area. To do so, he couches the word of assurance in the form of an oracle of Yahweh. In content, the divine oracle (vv. 24-25) is similar to 7:4, in which Isaiah offers encouragement to Ahaz with regard to the plotting of the Syrians and Ephraimites. In verse 24, Isaiah seems to assume that in its campaign Assyria will at least make threatening gestures toward Jerusalem. After all, much of Ahaz's kingdom was disposed to support the anti-Assyrian efforts. Isaiah envisions the Assyrians marching down the coastal highway, the road to Egypt (probably the same as the "way of the sea" in 9:1). The expression "road to Egypt" could have denoted the entirety of the main highway between Damascus and Gaza. When Tiglath-pileser took action against the western coalition in 734, he did so by moving down the Mediterranean coast into Philistine territory and to the border of Egypt—that is, along the road to Egypt. There is no evidence that either Judah or Jerusalem was threatened at the time.

The word of encouragement in verse 24 glides into the word of promise in verse 25—after Yahweh has given vent to his anger against Israel, his wrath will be turned against the Assyrians. The word of salvation continues in verses 26-27 but no longer as an oracle of Yahweh. Such a shift from what the prophet designated as divine address to his own address indicates that frequently statements were formulated as divine address for rhetorical purposes. Such a form gave them greater appeal and a higher claim of authority than normal prophetic words. Isaiah promises his audience that after the use of Assyria as the instrument of his judgment, Yahweh will take up the case against Assyria. To illustrate the nature of Assyrian defeat (v. 26*a*), Isaiah alludes to

Israel's victory over Midian (see Judg. 7), a victory gained in spite of great numerical inferiority (see on 9:4). In his rising up against Assyria, Yahweh's staff will reach to the sea—that is, to the Mediterranean Sea (v. 26b). It is uncertain whether Isaiah's statement of Yahweh's action extending to the sea represents some sort of territorial expectations about political dominance over the area (see 11:14; 27:12-13) or was employed merely because of the reference to the road to Egypt, which paralleled the Mediterranean coast.

The consequence of Yahweh's eventual action against Assyria will be the people's redemption from Assyrian dominance. The burden and yoke of service will be removed and broken. In 735, the Judeans had not been directly related to Assyria in a state of vassalage. Judah's relationship to Assyria had been through Israel. Nevertheless, the Judeans and the Jerusalemites, as subordinate entities within the greater Israel, had felt the burden of Assyrian policies for years and had endured the hardship of tribute payments.

Two specifics about verse 27b-c are worth noting. First, the term translated "burden" could refer to the specific obligations of a vassal state to the overlord (see I Kings 11:28, where a variant of the term refers to forced labor). As such, the "burden" could have involved not only the payment of tribute, an economic burden, but also the requirement to supply contingents of troops or other special forces, a manpower burden. Second, the image of a "yoke" is frequent in Assyrian royal inscriptions where it is used with reference to subjecting another state/ruler or to rebellion against Assyria ("throwing off the yoke").

Verse 27a-c may not be as optimistic as a first reading would indicate. In 8:21–9:7, Isaiah had celebrated Judean assertion of independence from Israel. One might have thought that the removal of Israel's yoke would have freed them from all subservience to a foreign power. In 10:24-27c, Isaiah makes it clear that complete freedom from foreign dominance is yet to be realized, although freedom will certainly come. But in the time immediately ahead, the Assyrian burden must still be borne and its yoke carried.

14. AN ENSIGN FOR THE NATIONS (10:27*d*–12:6)

W. F. **Albright**, "The Assyrian March on Jerusalem, Isa. X 28-32," *AASOR* 4(1924)134-40; P. M. **Arnold**, *Gibeah in Israelite History and Tradition* (dissertation, Emory University, 1986)237-59; H. **Barth**, *Die Jesaja-Worte in der Josiazeit: Israel und Assur als Thema einer produktiven Neuinterpretation der Jesajaüberlieferung* (Neukirchen-Vluyn: Neukirchener Verlag, 1977)54-76; D. L. **Christensen**, "The March of Conquest in Isaiah X 27c-34," *VT* 26(1966)395-99; H. **Donner**, "Der Feind aus dem Norden: Topographische und archäologische Erwägungen zu Jes. 10:27b-34," *ZPDV* 84(1968)46-54; H. L. **Ginsberg**, "Reflexes of Sargon in Isaiah after 715 B.C.E.," *JAOS* 88(1968)47-53; H. **Gottlieb**, "Jesaja, kapitel 12," *DTT* 37(1974)29-32; H. **Gross**, *Die Idee des ewigen und allgemeinen Weltfriendens im Alten Orient und im Alten Testament* (Trier: Paulinus-Verlag, 1967); F. **Lange**, "Exegetische Problems zu Jes. 11," *LR* 23(1975)115-27; J. J. M. **Roberts**, "The Davidic Origin of the Zion Tradition," *JBL* 92(1973)329-44; H. H. **Schmid**, *Shalom: Frieden im Alten Orient und im Alten Testament* (Stuttgart: Katholisches Bibelwerk, 1971); G. **Widengren**, "Yahweh's Gathering of the Dispersed," *In the Shelter of Elyon: Essays on Ancient Palestinian Life and Literature in Honor of G. W. Ahlström* (ed. W. B. Barrick and J. R. Spencer; Sheffield, England: JSOT Press, 1984)227-45.

Isaiah 10:27*d*-12:6 concludes the material in the book relating to the Syro-Ephraimitic crisis (chaps. 7–12). This section constitutes a single speech delivered on the very eve of Jerusalem's siege by Rezin and Pekah. In it, Isaiah predicts the failure of the forthcoming attack and looks forward to the magnificient prosperity lying beyond it for the Davidic house. Yahweh will defend Zion against the arrogant onslaught of the enemy kings; afterward, Davidic sovereignty will eventually extend over a united Israel and Judah and over the surrounding nations. The rhetorical aim of the promise is clear. The prophet is encouraging Ahaz and the residents of Jerusalem to hold out against the coalition forces, standing "firm" in their international neutralist policy (see 7:9*b*), trusting in the age-old claims of the Zion and Davidic traditions.

Scholars generally see in 10:27d–12:6 several small, originally independent units and assign many of the verses to post-exilic editors. (11:10 and vv. 11-16 are rarely, if ever, attributed to Isaiah, while the Isaianic authorship of 10:27d-32, 33-34, and 11:1-19 is more widely debated.) We believe, however, that the allegedly separate units and presumed editorial additions are parts of one speech by the eighth-century prophet. These include the following:

(1) The description of the Syro-Ephraimitic march against Jerusalem (10:27d-32)
(2) A prediction that the attack will fail (10:33-34)
(3) The promise of future prosperity for the Davidic regime and kingdom (11:1–12:6)

The last section, in turn divides into several sub-parts. (a) Verse 1 states generally that the Davidic house will survive and thrive. (b) Verses 2-9 describe the Davidic king—his charismatic endowment, his function as righteous judge, and the paradisiacal peace of his reign. (c) Verse 10 predicts the future prestige of the Davidic regime and the greatness of Zion among the nations. (d) Verses 11-16 look forward to the reconstitution of a great Davidic kingdom. This will include both Israel and Judah, now reconciled, as well as the subjugated peoples of Philistia, "the children of the east," Edom, Moab, and Ammon. (e) 12:1-6 anticipates the future thanksgiving of Isaiah's Jerusalemite audience after their deliverance from the present crisis.

Isaiah 10:27d-32

This section describes a military invasion of Judah and the panic of towns lying in its path.

27d. He came up from Samaria;
28.   he arrived at Aiath.
       He passed through Migron;
          at Michmash he stowed his gear.
29.   He crossed the [Geba] pass;
          at Geba he bivouacked.
       Ramah trembled!
          Gibeah of Saul fled!

30. Raise your voice, O daughter of Gallim!
     Watch out, O Laishah!
   Sound a warning, O Anathoth!
31.   Madmenah is in flight!
   The inhabitants of Gebim flee for safety.
32. Standing at Nob this very day,
       he will shake his fist
         at the mountain of the daughter of Zion,
       the hill of Jerusalem.

Most of the place-names mentioned by the prophet are identifiable: Aiath (*et-Tell*), Migron (*tell-Maryam*?), Michmash (*Mukhmas*), the Geba "pass" (crossing over the Wadi es-Suweinit en route to *Jeba`*), Ramah (*er-Ram*), Geba/Gibeah of Saul (*Jeba`*), Anathoth (*ras el-Harrube*?), and Nob (probably located on Mt. Scopus, just opposite Jerusalem). The locations of Gallim, Laishah, Madmenah, and Gebim are unknown.

The route described here is unusual. North–south travel in the area normally followed the main watershed highway linking Shechem, Bethel, Mizpah, Ramah, and Jerusalem. The army of our text, however, seems to have branched off southeastward at Bethel, taking the more difficult road through Michmash and Geba before picking up the main highway again just north of Jerusalem. While we can only guess at the reasons behind this detour, it seems reasonable to assume that the invading force sought to by-pass the Judean fortress at Mizpah (*tell en-Nesbah*).

Although the route of the army from Aiath to Jerusalem is clear, the starting point of the campaign is uncertain, because of the apparent textual corruption of verse 27*d*. The Masoretic Text reads: "and a yoke will be destroyed because of fatness." As it stands, the line makes poor sense and demands emendation. We follow the majority of scholars in assigning the verb, "will be broken" (*wehubbal*), to verse 27*c* and in changing "yoke" (*`ol*) to the verb, "came up" (*`ala*). Verse 27*d* then reports the outset of the enemy invasion: "he came up from. . . ." The place-name at the end of the line is still uncertain. Several readings have been proposed in place of "fatness" (*shemen*): "wilderness" (*yeshimon*), the "north" (*ṣapon*), Bethel, Rimmon, and Samaria (*shameron*). The last proposal is the most likely, but the decision depends in part on the identification of the enemy.

Nowhere in 10:27d-32 is the invader explicitly named. This has led many to suspect that antecedent material once identifying the enemy has been lost. It is possible however that verse 27d marks an absolute beginning. If the speech were given just prior to the army's arrival at Jerusalem, as verse 32 indicates, Isaiah certainly did not need to name the invader for his audience. If the siege were to begin "this very day," they could hardly have been in doubt as to the referent of the anonymous "he" of these verses.

The location of the verses after a speech about the Assyrians (10:5-27c) leads one to assume that the Assyrians are the subject here also. Thus, three interpretations of the passage follow this line of thought. First, 10:27d-32 describes Sennacherib's campaign against Jerusalem in 701. Second, the verses chart the advance of Assyrian troops, possibly dispatched by Sargon II from Samaria in 715–711. The march presumably aimed at discouraging Hezekiah and other Judean leaders from further involvement in the current Ashdod revolt. Third, the passage is purely visionary—that is, it does not describe an actual campaign but only the imagined route of an Assyrian invasion yet to take place.

Each of these proposals is problematic. Second Kings 18–19 indicates that the troops of Sennacherib approached Jerusalem from the southwest—that is, from the direction of Lachish in the Shephelah (18:14, 17; 19:9). The route described in Isaiah 10:27d-32 can hardly be correlated with the campaign of this king. That the verses describe troops dispatched by Sargon II from Samaria during the Ashdod revolt is possible, but remains highly conjectural. There is no evidence, besides this text, for an Assyrian invasion of Judah from the north and a siege of Jerusalem by Sargon. Finally, interpreting the verses as a visionary account does not square with the detail of the description (for example, "at Michmash he stowed his gear . . . at Geba he bivouacked") nor with the unusual route of the campaign. Furthermore, the perfect verb forms that predominate in this passage probably refer to past action and so reflect an actual march.

These difficulties justify our questioning the original assumption—namely, that verses 27d-32 describe an Assyrian campaign. Only the location of the speech after 10:5-27c points toward this identification. If we examine the material in isolation and ask again which known military campaigns did approach Jerusalem from the north during Isaiah's times, an answer comes easily to mind: the Syro-Ephraimitic invasion of Judah in 735/4. Second Kings 16:5 and Isaiah 7:6 firmly document the campaign, and 10:27d-32 contain nothing that seriously challenges this identification. Although these verses do not describe the invading army as a combination of separate forces, Syrian and Israelite, but refer to the enemy continually in the singular, this may reflect the status of Rezin as the superior member of the alliance. Isaiah 7:1 and 5 similiarly testify to the dominant role of the Syrian king (see above, pp. 118-19 and 126-27).

If 10:27d-32 refer to the Syro-Ephraimitic invasion of Judah, it is reasonable to restore Samaria at the opening of the speech. From the capital city of the Northern Kingdom, the forces of Rezin and Pekah set out southward along the main watershed highway. At Bethel, the coalition army picked up the less traveled road leading through Michmash in order to avoid possible fighting at Mizpah, a Judean fortress (v. 28). The invading troops spent the night at Geba, leaving for the next day an easy seven mile march to Jerusalem (v. 29a). Isaiah's speech seems to have been delivered at this point of the campaign. The prophet comments on the panic of towns still lying more or less in the invader's path (vv. 29b-31) and anticipates his imminent arrival at Nob opposite Jerusalem (v. 32).

Verse 32 is clearly the climax of the entire description: "Standing at Nob this very day he will shake his fist at the mountain of the daughter of Zion, the hill of Jerusalem." The vivid image serves to underscore the pride of the enemy. It is Zion, itself, Yahweh's own place of residence, that the Syro-Ephraimitic forces arrogantly attack.

Isaiah 10:33-34

In these verses, Isaiah predicts Yahweh's imminent action against the "exalted." The announcement of judgment proceeds in metaphorical terms.

33. Behold the Lord Yahweh Sebaoth
    is about to lop off the boughs with a crash!
    And the great in height is about to be cut down
    and the exalted will be brought low.
34. And the thickets of the forest will be cut down with iron
    and the Lebanon with its majesty will fall.

Despite the tendency of most scholars to assign these verses to a late editor, they probably derive from Isaiah. The divine title, "the Lord Yahweh Sebaoth," is employed elsewhere by the prophet (see 1:24; 10:16, 23), and the vocabulary of the verses is generally in keeping with Isaiah's language (compare 2:9-17). The forest/tree metaphor appears in other speeches by the prophet (for example, in 10:18-19), and the basic theme of the passage, Yahweh's humbling of the proud, figures prominently in Isaiah's preaching. Most important, verses 33-34 provide the necessary continuation of verses 27d-32, which alone would have little significance. To the arrogant onslaught of the Syro-Ephraimitic enemy, Yahweh will respond with awesome power, bringing "the exalted low."

The prediction is rooted in the ancient Zion tradition. Celebrated in the cult, it rehearsed Yahweh's defeat of the nations who assemble against the holy city (Pss. 46, 48, and 76). In 10:33-34, Isaiah applies the tradition to actual circumstances: Yahweh will protect Zion against the attack of Rezin and Pekah.

The metaphor, however, derives from a different source. Cutting down the forest of Lebanon is a frequent boast of Assyrian kings in the royal inscriptions (see *ANET* 275 and 276), one with which Isaiah was certainly familiar (see Isa. 14:8 and 37:24). The prophet picks up the language and applies it to Yahweh in 10:33-34. The appropriation is apt, for the actual destruction of the Syro-Ephraimitic forces will come at the hands of the Assyrians, Yahweh's instrument of wrath (see 8:4-7 and 10:5).

Isaiah 11:1–12:6

The prophet moves to predict a bright future for the Davidic regime and kingdom. The promise logically follows the preceding material. The glorious future of the attacked contrasts with the dismal fate of the attackers. (The conjunction that begins 11:1 is to be taken as an adversative, to be translated as "but" or "on the other hand.") Isaiah achieves the transition by continuing the tree metaphor. "The Lebanon with its majesty will fall" (v. 34) while "the stock/stump of Jesse" will grow (11:1).

Verse 1 summarizes the prophet's principal claim, that the Davidic house will not only survive, but also will flourish. Interpreting the verse precisely is difficult, for the translation is not altogether certain. The RSV renders the Hebrew:

> There shall come forth a shoot
> from the stump of Jesse [*miggeza`yisay*]
> and a branch will grow out of his
> roots

If the translation, "stump of Jesse," is correct, the text seems to reflect the territorial reduction of the Davidic Kingdom during Isaiah's early years. This reduction, we have seen, occurred in the years preceding, but especially during, the Syro-Ephraimitic crisis, when much of Judah sided with Rezin and Pekah, thus leaving Ahaz in absolute control of only Jerusalem. The prophet thus claims that this "stump" of a kingdom will not only survive but also will revive and prosper.

The translation "stump," however, is not the only possibility. The Hebrew term *geza`* occurs only three times in the Hebrew Bible: Job 14:7, Isaiah 40:24, and our text. In the first passage, the term clearly refers to the stump of a cut tree. In Isaiah 40:24, however, *geza`* refers to the stalk of a recently planted tree before branches have sprouted. It is possible, then, to translate the phrase in 11:1, "the stock of Jesse," and to understand it as a simple reference to the Davidic house. (The Targum translates *geza`* as "sons.") The text then does not emphasize the reduced state of the Davidic kingdom, only that the regime will prosper.

A third interpretation of verse 1 depends again on a distinct translation. Reading against the late Masoretic accentuation, we might render the Hebrew: "But the shoot from the stock of Jesse will grow forth and the sapling from its roots will sprout" (emending *yipre* to *yiprah*). In this case, the subjects of the sentence, "the shoot from the stock of Jesse" and "the sapling from its roots," may reflect a traditional honorific title of the Davidic king. A close parallel appears in an Assyrian inscription in which Esarhaddon is called "precious branch of Baltil, an enduring shoot"(*IA* § 20). Isaiah's point in 11:1 would again be that the Davidic kingship will flourish.

The differences among these interpretations are slight. Whichever one chooses, two points should be stressed. First, the text does not assume the fall of the Davidic house and thus the events of 586, as many scholars have argued. At most, 11:1 might reflect the reduced state of the kingdom in 735/4. Second, this section did not originally look forward to a future messiah, as the traditional interpretation has argued, but referred to the contemporary Davidic monarch, Ahaz. Other speeches of Isaiah reflect the same support and great expectations for Ahaz (see especially 9:6-7). Furthermore, the context of 11:1 points in the same direction. If 10:27d-34 predict Yahweh's destruction of the Syro-Ephraimitic forces attacking Ahaz in Jerusalem, it is natural to see in the speech's continuation a promise of revival for this king.

Verses 2-9 describe the Davidic king in detail. The portrait begins by reviewing his charismatic endowment: "And upon him will rest the spirit of Yahweh, a spirit of wisdom and understanding, a spirit of counsel and might, a spirit of knowledge and reverence for Yahweh" (v. 2).

The attributes listed derive largely from traditional royal ideology. First Samuel 16:13, for example, narrates how the spirit of Yahweh attached to David after his anointment and remained upon him "from that day forward" (compare II Sam. 23:2 and Isa. 61:1). Extraordinary wisdom and understanding are attributed to David in II Samuel 14:7, but especially to Solomon in I Kings 3 and 10:1-10 (compare Prov. 8:14-16). The royal titles in Isaiah 9:6 include "Wonderful Counselor" and "Almighty God," indicating that counsel and might were also traditional qualities of the Davidic king. Finally, "fear" or reverence before Yahweh is mentioned as an essential characteristic of the Davidic ruler in II Samuel 23:3b (compare Deut. 17:19 and also Isaiah's exhortation to the royal court in 8:13).

Verses 3b-4 describe the king's function as righteous judge, protector of the poor and weak, over against the "violent" (emending *'ereṣ* to *'ariṣ* in v. 4b) and wicked. The picture is again thoroughly traditional. Psalm 72, for example, petitions God to grant the king "justice" and "righteousness" that he may "judge thy people with righteousness and thy poor with justice . . . defend the cause of the poor of the people, give deliverance to the needy, and crush the oppressor" (Ps. 72:1-4; see 72:12-14 and Jer. 22:15-17). Similarly, Psalm 101, a composition possibly written for the coronation ceremony, presents the king's pledge to govern justly (compare II Sam. 23:3b). The theme is not uniquely Israelite, but characteristic of the royal ideology in Mesopotamia and Syria as well (see *ANET* 149, 151, 164-65, and 178).

These examples show that in 11:3b-4 Isaiah is applying to Ahaz the kind of high-flung court language that the Davidides themselves typically used to describe their rule. It is part of the royal ideal rehearsed not only in the enthronement ceremony, but also no doubt on other occasions as well. Behind this stock language in Isaiah 11, however, there may also lie special edicts issued by Ahaz in 735/4, favoring the lower classes in order to gain their support at a time when the king's popularity outside the capital city was low. The strategy of such edicts would correspond to the *misharum* of Mesopotamian kings who, upon ascending the throne or on other special occasions, granted concessions and favors to various constituencies (see the edict of Ammisaduqa; *ANET* 526-28).

VERGIL

The portrait of the Davidic king concludes by describing the paradisaical peace that will accompany his reign (vv. 6-9). Animosity and conflict between weak and strong members of the animal kingdom and between the animal world and the human realm will end. "They shall not hurt or destroy on all my holy mountain [Zion], for the land will be full of the knowledge of Yahweh, as the waters cover the sea" (v. 9).

Two ancient traditions underlie verses 6-9—namely, the Zion traditon and the royal ideology. The first typically depicts Jerusalem in ideal, even mythological, terms. Out of Yahweh's holy city, Psalm 46 states, the river of paradise flows (v. 4). Divine blessing rests on Zion, according to Psalm 132—provisions for her are abundant, even for the city's poor

(v. 13). Fraternal peace prevails in Zion, Psalm 133 states, and there Yahweh has "commanded the blessing, life for evermore."

The royal ideology claims that peace, good fortune, and fertility accompany the reign of the righteous king. Thus Psalm 72 prays for divine blessing on the king: "In his days may righteousness flourish and peace abound. . . . May there be abundance of grain in the land . . . may its fruit be like Lebanon and may people blossom forth from the cities like the grass of the field" (vv. 7 and 16). This claim is also typical of royal ideology in the wider ancient Near East (see *ANET* 159, 164-65, 606, and 626-27).

These examples demonstrate again how seriously Isaiah takes the Zion and Davidic traditions. The prophet picks up their language and applies it to the era he believes will soon dawn: The reign of Ahaz after his deliverance from the Syro-Ephraimitic attack.

Verse 10 describes the future prestige of the Davidic regime among the nations: "And in that day the root of Jesse that endures will become a signal for peoples; nations will seek him and his dwelling place will be glorious" (compare the NJPSV). The exalted standing of Zion is also stressed here. While "dwelling place" refers to the whole of Palestine in Psalm 95:11 and Deuteronomy 12:9, it refers specifically to Jerusalem in Psalm 132:8, part of the liturgy commemorating God's election of Zion and the Davidic dynasty. The same interpretation makes sense in Isaiah 11:10; the text looks forward to the pilgrimage of nations to Zion, there to "seek" the Davidic king.

Most scholars question the Isaianic authorship of 11:10. The arguments marshalled against it are: (a) "In that day" is a redactional formula, setting verse 10 apart as an addition; (b) verse 10 presupposes verses 11-16, which allegedly derive from the post-exilic period, predicting the ingathering of dispersed Israelites and Judeans; (c) while Isaiah speaks of "the branch of his [Jesse's] roots" in 11:1, verse 10 refers simply to "the root of Jesse"—the discrepancy allegedly reflects the carelessness with which a late writer imitated the prophet's phrasing; and (d) in 11:1-9 the Davidic king is important for the salvation of Judah/Israel only, while in verse 10 he has universal significance—he is a "signal" or rallying point for the peoples and nations of the world. This second view of the king's role supposedly derives from a late editor, intent on expanding the prophet's meaning.

The arguments are not convincing. The phrase "in that day" may introduce secondary additions to a prophetic speech, but it can also belong to the original words of the prophet (see Isa. 3:18; 4:2; 7:18-25; and 10:20-27c). "Root of Jesse" varies only slightly from the phrasing in 11:1. The small difference would hardly justify seeing the hand of a late writer. Verse 10 is, indeed, linked to verses 11-16, but the latter may also be attributed to Isaiah, as we will see below. Most important, the exalted status of the king and of Jerusalem among the nations is part and parcel of the royal Zion tradition, upon which Isaiah relies so heavily. It is not in the least surprising that the prophet, after describing the reign of the king in verses 2-9 and alluding to Zion specifically in verse 9, should in verse 10 elaborate on the Zion tradition, predicting the pilgrimage of the nations to the holy city (see Isa. 2:1-5, Pss. 2:11; 18:44-45; 72:8-11; compare Zech. 8:22-23). There they will "seek the root of Jesse."

The precise meaning of the verb here merits further comment. The Hebrew term is *darash*, which generally means "consult" or "inquire of." The term can also have a technical meaning, "to ask for an oracle or ruling." In 11:10, Isaiah probably envisions the Davidic adjudication of international disputes. The picture is similar to the pilgrimage of nations described in 2:1-5. In that text, however, it is Yahweh who judges between the nations; in 11:10 it is his anointed king whom the nations "consult" for legal decisions.

Verses 11-16 anticipate the reunion of Judah and Israel and their domination over the surrounding nations. The material divides roughly into four parts: the ingathering of dispersed Judeans and Israelites by Yahweh (vv. 11-12); the reconciliation between Judah and Israel (v. 13); the defeat and/or subjugation of the Philistines, "children of the east," Edomites, Moabites, and Ammonites (v. 14); and Yahweh's guiding of the "remnant of his people" out of Assyria (vv. 15-16). The first and last parts correspond in theme, forming an inclusio.

Despite the unwillingness of most scholars to assign this material to Isaiah, only two lines should be ascribed to a later writer: verse 11*b* (from "Egypt" onward) and verse 15*aa* ("And Yahweh will destroy the tongue of the sea of Egypt"). The first addition presumably arose under the influence of verse 12*b*, which speaks of "the four corners of the earth" from which the dispersed will return. The second expansion was probably prompted by the allusion in verse 16*b* (here in the form of a comparison) to the exodus from Egypt and also by the exodus imagery applied to Assyria in verse 15*ab-b*. (The "River" refers to the Euphrates; compare 8:7.) The remainder of the verses speak only of a return from Assyria and from the "four corners of the earth" over which Assyrian kings typically claimed to rule (see *ANET* 274, 276, 281, and 289). This theme and others in the material can be best understood as part of Isaiah's message during the Syro-Ephraimitic crisis.

The gathering of the dispersed is a thoroughly traditional theme. In ancient Mesopotamia, it became an essential element of royal ideology. As the righteous ruler commissioned by the gods for the protection of the people, the king is to restore his scattered and exiled subjects to their native land. The motif came to figure prominently also in prophecies of salvation in Israel and Judah. This was true not only of the exilic and post-exilic periods (see for example Ezek. 3:27 and Isa. 56:8), but also possibly of the pre-exilic era—that is, if one is willing to entertain the authenticity of texts such as Micah 2:12, 4:6, and Jeremiah 30:11.

In Isaiah 11:11-16, however, the theme is more than stock prophetic rhetoric. At an earlier point in the Syro-Ephraimitic crisis, Isaiah had denounced both the Israelites and the Judeans and had predicted for them harsh treatment by the Assyrians (see 7:18-20; 8:4 and 7). He may have expected at least limited deportations in accordance with the general Assyrian policy toward rebellious peoples (the theme of exile already appears in 5:13). In Isaiah 11, the prophet assumes this exile proleptically and proceeds to look beyond it to a brighter future. He announces that Yahweh will return the "remnant of his people" to their place (for the role of the remnant concept in Isaiah's preaching, see also 7:3 and 10:20-23) and seems to imply (if vv. 11-16 continue his words in vv. 1-10) that they will prosper under the rule of the Davidic king. He describes this return from exile by the analogy of the exodus. Through the midst of the River (Euphrates), they will cross dryshod and will return on a broad secure highway. (For the later development of this theme by Deutero-Isaiah, see 40:3-5.)

Associated with Yahweh's gathering of the dispersed are the reconciliation between Judah and Israel (v. 13) and their joint domination of the surrounding nations (v. 14). These predictions are in keeping with what we expect from Isaiah. The prophet had witnessed rising tensions between the two countries since the days of Menahem and open conflict during the Syro-Ephraimitic crisis. Isaiah was thoroughly familiar with the "jealously of Israel" and the "hostility of Judah." Furthermore, Isaiah had expressed during the crisis the hope for the reunion of the Northern and Southern Kingdoms under Davidic rule (7:17). The same expectation appears in chapter 11. Relying on traditional ideas about the extent of the Davidic state, Isaiah suggests that the revived kingdom will also include dominance over Edom, Moab, Ammon, Philistia, and "the children of the east" (probably desert tribes). He thus holds out to Ahaz the hope for a return of the monarchy's greatest glory.

The multiple themes that interplay throughout chapter 11 are not distinctive to this section of the book. They find expression in varying forms throughout the material. As a proud citizen of Jerusalem and an uncompromising loyalist to the house of David, the prophet accepted the tenets of the Davidic and Zion theologies as realities undergirded by the promises of Yahweh. Without hesitancy and in rhetorical situations of gravest danger, he challenged his audience to risk its future on the reliability of Yahweh's fidelity.

The speech concludes with 12:1-6. In this section, Isaiah anticipates the future celebration by the king and the people. As in 2:1-5, the prophet is probably quoting traditional material from hymnic and/or thanksgiving psalms in these verses. His special contribution lies in the way he presents the psalm excerpts as prophecy. He sets them forth as a song to be sung "in that day" after Yahweh, "the Holy One of Israel" dwelling in Zion (v. 6), has defeated the Syro-Ephrai-mitic enemy and all other hostile forces. (See 25:9 and 26:1, where Isaiah similarly presents songs and confessions to be recited "in that day.") This future orientation is reinforced by the prophet's promise in verse 3. The line, as we will see below, likely refers to part of the traditional New Year Festival, which Isaiah's audience was to celebrate in the near future.

Verses 1-6 abound with stylistic variations and present a mixture of formal elements. Particularly conspicuous is the change from singular address in verse 1— "and you (sing.) will say"—to plural address in verses 3 and 4—"and you (pl.) will draw . . . and you (pl.) will say." This shift and other apparent inconsistencies may be adequately explained by assuming a change in the addressee. In verses 1-2 the prophet addresses the king specifically, quoting to him part of a psalm that he will sing "in that day." In verses 3-6, Isaiah turns to his Jerusalemite audience at large. The address here begins with a promise (v. 3) and then quotes a traditional hymn that the audience will recite "in that day" (vv. 4-6).

The psalm fragment quoted to the king in verses 1-2 seems to derive from a traditional song of individual thanksgiving. In the introduction, the psalmist speaks directly to Yahweh: "I will give thanks to you, O Yahweh." The reason for thanksgiving then follows: "For you had been angry with me but your anger turned away and you comforted me" (emending *yashab* and *utnaḥameni* to *wayyashab* and *wattena-ḥameni*, respectively). In verse 2, the psalmist turns to the larger congregation and declares his trust in Yahweh as the God of his salvation. (Such confessions typically appear in psalms of lament but are not out of place in songs of thanksgiving. The experience of deliverance naturally gives rise to expressions of confidence.)

A closer look at the psalm fragment reveals a possible connection with royal and/or enthronement psalms. The psalmist declares in verse 2*b*: "For Yahweh is my strength and my song and he has become my salvation." The line has a close parallel in Psalm 118:14 (compare 118:21). This text appears at first glance to be part of a royal thanksgiving for deliverance in battle (see vv. 10-12). The Mishnah, however, relates Psalm 118 to the autumnal Feast of Tabernacles (*Sukkah* 4:5) and thus to the festival of Yahweh's enthronement. (Note the allusion to a temple procession in vv. 19-20 and the reference to a special ritual at the altar in v. 27.) That Isaiah would quote, in 12:1-2, part of a similar liturgy accords well with verse 3, in which the prophet refers explicitly to part of the New Year's ritual. (Note also that v. 2*b* appears in Exod. 15:23, part of the so-called Song of the Sea, which also shows some similarities to enthronement psalms, especially in v. 18.) Whatever the precise genre of Psalm 118 may be, the "I" in verse 14, as well as in Isaiah 12:1-2, is likely the king.

In verse 3, the prophet turns from the king and addresses the larger Jerusalemite audience: "And you will draw water with rejoicing from wells of salvation." According to the Mishnah, the rite alluded to here was performed on the night between the sixth and seventh day of the Feast of Tabernacles. Water from Siloam was carried in stately procession to the temple courtyard, where the high priest poured it on the altar, thereby ensuring the coming of rain in the upcoming year (*Sukkah* 4:9-10). In 12:3, the prophet promises the residents of Jerusalem that they will perform this ritual in the future, just as they have in past years. The implication of the prediction is clear: The prophet's audience will survive the present crisis and be able to celebrate the New Year Festival again and to enjoy the blessings it brings upon themselves and their king.

Isaiah proceeds in verses 4-6 to quote to his audience a song that they will all sing "in that day." The style of the verses is that of the "imperative" hymn, and the content is thoroughly traditional. While the original setting of the psalm cannot be determined with certainty, its connection with the New Year Festival is a plausible assumption, given the apparent relation of verses 1-3 to this same occasion. (Compare vv. 4-6 with Ps. 118:23-26.) The concluding reference in verse 6 to God's dwelling in Zion serves as a fitting end to the prophet's entire speech. The inhabitants of Jerusalem will survive the Syro-Ephraimitic attack and so will be able to declare "in that day" that the protecting divine presence is in their midst.

15. JUDGMENT ON BABYLON (13:1-22)

L. **Alonso-Schökel**, "Traducción de textos poéticos hebreos I (Isa 13)," *CB* 17(1960)170-76; P. A. H. **de Boer**, "An Inquiry into the Meaning of the Term *mś*́," *OTS* 5(1948)197-214;

C. **Boutflower**, *The Book of Isaiah Chapters [I-XXXIX] in the Light of the Assyrian Monuments* (London/New York: Society for Promoting Christian Knowledge, 1930)69-92; K. **Budde**, "Jesaja 13," *Abhandlungen zur semitischen Religionskunde und Sprachwissenschaft* (Festschrift W. W. von Baudissin; Giessen: Alfred Töpelmann, 1918)55-70; S. **Erlandsson**, *The Burden of Babylon: A Study of Isaiah 13:2–14:23* (Lund: CWK Gleerup, 1970); H. S. **Gehman**, "The 'Burden' of the Prophets," *JQR* 31(1940/41)107-21; D. R. **Hillers**, *Treaty-Curses and the Old Testament Prophets* (Rome: Pontifical Biblical Institute, 1964); **Hillers**, "Convention in Hebrew Literature: The Reaction to Bad News," *ZAW* 77(1965)86-90; H. W. F. **Saggs**, "The Nimrud Letters, 1952—Part I: The Ukin-zer Rebellion and Related Texts," *Iraq* 17(1955)21-56; R. D. **Weis**, *A Definition of the Genre Maśśā´ in the Hebrew Bible* (dissertation, Claremont Graduate School, 1985).

Almost without exception, scholars assume that the oracle on Babylon in Isaiah 13 initiates a special section of the book, namely, a collection of oracles against non-Israelite kingdoms. Supposedly, this collection was editorially produced by bringing together material characterized by a focus on foreign nations. Such assumptions would mean that Isaiah 13–23 has been topically, rather than chronologically, arranged. This hypothesis is unacceptable for three reasons. (1) Much of the material in chapters 13–23 is related to Israel and Judah and, therefore, is not speeches on foreign nations. This is the case with 14:1-4*a*, 17:3-14, and 22:1-25. Thus to designate 13–23 as oracles on foreign nations is a misnomer. (2) No clear pattern or rationale for the order of the nations concerned is clear. If the oracles were deliberately arranged, then some criterion should be ascertainable. Isaiah 14:28-32, for example, seems peculiarly located according to any subject or geographical ordering. (3) All the material in Isaiah 13–23, both the foreign nations speeches and those on Israel and Judah, make perfectly good sense, as we shall see, if understood as having a chronological ordering.

When Tiglath-pileser ascended the Assyrian throne in the late spring of 745, Nabu-nasir (747–734) was ruling as king in Babylon, the old cultural capital of Mesopotamia. Throughout Nabu-nasir's rule, the city of Babylon remained loyal to

Assyria in spite of the problems Tiglath-pileser had in southern Mesopotamia. In 734, when Tiglath-pileser was engaged in the west, Nabu-nadin-zeri succeeded his father, Nabu-nasir, to the throne of Babylon. In his second year, the new king was killed in a rebellion that extended far beyond the city. Nabu-shuma-ukin, a district official and leader of the rebellion, ascended the throne in Babylon but was removed from the kingship after a reign of one month and two days. The countercoup was led by an Aramean, Nabu-mukin-zeri, who seized the throne for himself. (Note the parallels of these events to those reported in II Kings 15:8-16, 23-26.) Shortly after his defeat of Damascus in 732, Tiglath-pileser moved to put down the rebellion of Aramean/Chaldean groups in southern Mesopotamia, including Babylon. In 729, Tiglath-pileser captured Nabu-mukin-zeri and took the radical step of becoming himself king of Babylon (*ABC* 71-72). Over four centuries had passed since an Assyrian monarch had laid claim to the Babylonian throne.

Isaiah's oracle in 13:1-22 belongs to the period of Tiglath-pileser's efforts to subdue the rebellion in the city of Babylon. An Assyrian eponym list reports that the Assyrian king fought in Babylonia in 731, remained at home in Assyria in 730, and become king in Babylon in 729. Isaiah's speech against Babylon could date, therefore, within the period of 731 to 729. This fits with the assumption that Isaiah's oracles are arranged chronologically. The preceding oracle, 10:27*d*–12:6, was delivered in the context of the Syro-Ephraimitic siege of Jerusalem in 735/4. Assuming we have no speeches of Isaiah for the years 734 to 731, Isaiah 13 belongs to the prophet's activity immediately following Tiglath-pileser's wars in the west in the years 734–732.

The reference to the Medes in 13:17 does not mean that they were the main force attacking Babylon. During Tiglath-pileser's reign, the Medes, or at least some of them, were subordinate to the Assyrians. In the so-called Nimrud Slab Inscription, Tiglath-pileser describes a campaign to the borders of Median territory: "as far as the city of Zakruti of the mighty Medes, I brought under my sway. My two officials I set over them as governors. The gifts (tribute) of the chieftains of the Medes,—as far as Mount Bikni, I received" (*ARAB* I § 784). Elsewhere (in the so-called Nimrud Tablet;

ARAB I § 795) he describes not only military actions against the Medes, but also the submission of Median regions and chieftains. In the eighth century, the Medes were still living under semi-nomadic conditions, although they possessed cities in the western Iranian plateau. Tiglath-pileser refers to them as the "mighty Medes," and they may have had a reputation as excellent warriors, like the Aramean Itu'a tribe, which the Assyrians used as shock troops in Phoenicia and other places in the empire (see *Iraq* 17 [1955] 127-28). Some of the tribal Medes were probably incorporated into the Assyrian military, and it is this element of the Assyrian forces that Isaiah refers to in 13:17 rather than an attack on Babylon conducted by the Medes.

Isaiah's speech predicting (or announcing) the fall of Babylon indicates that prophets were not only concerned with matters bearing directly on the life of their people, but also functioned as interpreters and commentators on the significant international events of their day. After Assyria's movement into southern Syria-Palestine, some Judean troops may even have been incorporated into the Assyrian army. As the revered religious and cultural center of Mesopotamia, Babylon held a special place in the ancient world. To attack Babylon was comparable to a contemporary assault on the Vatican or Mecca.

In this speech, Isaiah claims that Yahweh was the power behind Assyria's invasion of Babylon. Such a claim meant that Assyria was acting as Yahweh's instrument and thus the Israelite Deity was in control of international affairs. For his Jerusalemite/Judean audience, this would have served as insightful interpretation aiding in understanding international events and also would have offered consolation and assurance that events were not occurring in an undirected, haphazard manner. To emphasize the war as an act of God, the prophet never once mentions the Assyrians and Tiglath-pileser.

The following elements make up the speech:

(1) Editorial superscription (1)
(2) Divine command to summon the warriors (2-3)
(3) Yahweh and his troops (4-5)
(4) Call to wail for the approaching day of Yahweh (6-8)
(5) Description of the day and Babylon's destruction (9-22)

Isaiah 13:1

The editorial superscription, like 2:1, affirms that the following words derive from Isaiah. The word *oracle,* used here and elsewhere in Isaiah, has the idea of something "lifted up," and thus can mean "load, burden." Perhaps an English equivalent would be something like "pronouncement" (so the NJPSV).

The superscription is, of course, not part of the speech itself. It may have been added when the book of Isaiah was being compiled or, more likely, was the heading added to a copy of the speech for identification purposes after the speech was delivered. Such a copy may have been made by the prophet or a court official and preserved in some state or personal archive.

Isaiah 13:2-3

The opening of the speech contains words attributed to Yahweh as if he were a military commander giving orders to subordinate officers preparatory to battle. Three imperatives describe the action to be taken on a bare hill where the signals can be seen and heard: "raise a banner (or ensign), shout out to them, lift the hand." These were all means of giving orders under battle conditions. The goal of the signalling is that the attackers will enter "the noble gates," probably the gates of Babylon. The opening verse, therefore, already anticipates the outcome of the battle.

In verse 3, Yahweh speaks of himself as the commander who has called his consecrated ones (those purified and prepared for warfare; see I Sam. 21:1-6), his mighty men, and his proudly exultant ones, all synonyms for the mobilized warriors, ready for battle. In their military actions, the troops execute Yahweh's wrath.

Isaiah 13:4-5

In verses 4-5, the prophet describes the great host of troops Yahweh is collecting from many nations and kingdoms to carry out his orders. They come from distant lands and from the end of the heavens. Such a depiction reflects the multi-national forces that went to make up the Assyrian militia. The gathering armies are described as the weapons of Yahweh's indignation to destroy the whole of Babylonia.

Isaiah 13:6-8

In verses 6-8, Isaiah addresses the people of Babylon, calling on them to wail for the fate that awaits them—namely, the day of Yahweh, which will come upon them as destruction. Just as Isaiah earlier described the day of the earthquake under Uzziah as the day of Yahweh (2:12), so here the day of Babylon's fall is a day of Yahweh. Employing assonance, Isaiah describes the calamity as "destruction from the Almighty" (as "*shod* from Shaddai").

The description of the Babylonians' reaction to the horror that is coming draws on a typical biblical depiction of how people react to bad news—the hands go limp, the heart melts, terror seizes them, pangs of agony overcome them, pains like those of childbirth overcome them, they gaze at one another in horror, and their faces become livid in fright.

Isaiah 13:9-22

In his description of the day of Yahweh and the destruction of Babylon (vv. 9-22), Isaiah interweaves divine speech (vv. 1-13a, 17-18) with his own depictions (vv. 8-10, 13b-16, 19-22) and speaks of the day as both a cosmic event (vv. 9-12, 13a) and a national human calamity (vv. 14-22). Such features emphasize the fact that the destruction is to be no normal occurrence but an act of God.

The cosmic, transhuman aspects of the episode are spoken of in terms of the malfunction of the heavenly luminaries— the stars, the constellations, the sun, and the moon will be darkened; the heavens will tremble and the earth will shake (vv. 10, 13a). The entire cosmos will run amuck and every source of human pride will be threatened (compare 11b with 2:11, 17). Humans will virtually disappear from the face of the earth (v. 12) and the universe will be brought to the brink of chaos (v. 13a).

On the human level, fright will overtake the people, who will flee to escape (v. 14); those caught will be thrust through with swords (v. 15); infants will be slaughtered, women raped, and homes plundered (v. 16); and the terror-inspiring Medes will go on a rampage (vv. 17-18). Babylon, itself, will look like the ruins of Sodom and Gomorrah (v. 19; compare 1:9) and will lie uninhabited except for the wild beasts that will haunt the halls where princes once strolled (vv. 20-22a).

From the last line of the speech (v. 22b), it is clear that Isaiah anticipated the destruction of Babylon in the very near future "Its time is close at hand and its days will not be prolonged" (RSV).

In actuality, Babylon did not fall, and the city was not destroyed as Isaiah had predicted. Severe fighting did occur, but Tiglath-pileser entered the city peacefully and became its reigning monarch. He describes the course of events as follows:

The lands of Bit-Silani and Bit-Sa'alli I trampled down like a threshing-sledge. Their people my hand captured. Sarrabanu and Dur-Illatai, their great cities, I destroyed so that they were like mounds. Their people I carried off to Assyria. I entered Babylon, holy sacrifices I offered before Marduk, my lord. Babylonia I brought under my sway. (*ARAB* I § 810)

16. YAHWEH'S PURPOSE AND THE DEATH OF A KING (14:1-27)

L. **Alonso-Schökel**, "Traducción de textos poéticos hebreos II (Isa 14)," *CB* 17(1960)257-65; W. H. **Cobb**, "The Ode in Isaiah XIV," *JBL* 15(1896)18-35; P. C. **Craigie**, "Helel, Athtar and Phaethon (Jes 14:12-15)," *ZAW* 85(1973)223-25; A. **Dupont-Sommer**, "Note exégitique sur Isaïe 14:16-21," *RHR* 134(1948)72-80; D. V. **Etz**, "Is Isaiah XIV 12-15 a Reference to Comet Halley?" *VT* 36(1986)289-301; J. **Fichtner**, "Jahwes Plan in der Botschaft des Jesaja," *ZAW* 63(1951)16-33 = his *Gottes Weisheit: Gesammelte Studien zum Alten Testament* (Stuttgart: Calwer Verlag, 1965)27-43; H. L. **Ginsberg**, "Reflexes of Sargon in Isaiah after 715 B.C.E.," *JAOS* 88(1968)47-53; H. **Jahnow**, *Das hebräische Leichenlied im Rahmen der Völkerdictung* (Giessen: Alfred Töpelmann, 1923); G. **Keown**, *A History of the Interpretation of Isaiah 14:12-15*

(dissertation, Southern Baptist Theological Seminary, 1979);
P. **Machinist**, "Assyria and Its Image in the First Isaiah,"
JAOS 103(1983)719-37; J. W. **McKay**, "Helel and the Dawn-
Goddess: A Re-examination of the Myth of Isaiah XIV 12-15,"
VT 20(1970)451-64; W. S. **Prinsloo**, "Isaiah 14:12-15: Humilia-
tion, Hubris, Humiliation," *ZAW* 93(1981)432-38; G. **Quell**,
"Jesaja 14:1-23," *Festschrift für Friedrich Baumgartel* (Erlangen:
Universitatsbund, 1959)131-57; F. **Stolz**, "Die Baüme des
Gottesgartens auf dem Libanon," *ZAW* 84(1972)141-56; F. A.
Vandenburgh, "The Ode on the King of Babylon, Isaiah XIV
4*b*-21," *AJSL* 29(1912/13)111-21.

Isaiah 14:1-27 is a complex text. It opens with an optimistic
prediction about the future of Israel (vv. 1-2). Then follows a
taunt (*mashal*) against the king of Babylon, which takes the
form of a satirical funeral eulogy (vv. 3-20*b*). This ends with a
prayerful wish for the extermination of the king's royal
descendants (v. 20*c*) and an admonition to slaughter the
monarch's sons (v. 21). Two divine oracles announce the
destruction of Babylon and the royal family (vv. 22-23). The
speech concludes with a divine oath (vv. 24-25), in which
Yahweh swears that Assyria will be broken "in my land,"
and the prophet then interprets this divine word as the
purpose that Yahweh has decreed (vv. 26-27).

A central issue in interpreting this speech concerns the
identity of the king of Babylon. Contextually, the oracle
should date from a time following 731–729, the date of Isaiah
13, but prior to the death of Ahaz in 727, the topic of the
following speech in Isaiah 14:28-32. The speech in 14:1-27
becomes clear when interpreted against the international
situation of the years 729 to 727. The king of Babylon, whose
death is announced in the form of a celebrative eulogy, is
Tiglath-pileser.

The Babylonian Chronicles report the following about
Tiglath-pileser's relationship to Babylon in the years 729–727.

The third year of (Nabu)-mukin-zeri: When Tiglath-pileser had
gone down to Akkad he ravaged Bit-Amukkanu and captured
(Nabu)-mukin-zeri. For three years (Nabu)-mukin-zeri ruled Babylon. Tiglath-pileser ascended the throne in Babylon. The second
year: Tiglath-pileser died in the month Tebet. For *eighteen* years

Tiglath-pileser ruled Akkad and Assyria. For two of these years he ruled in Akkad. (*ABC* 72-73)

In his own inscriptions, Tiglath-pileser reports on his capture of the Babylonian region and his assumption of direct authority over the city. He reports that he entered the city, offered sacrifices to the gods, and "they [the gods] loved my priesthood" (*ARAB* I §§ 788, 805, 810). From 729, he described himself as "the great king, the mighty king, king of the Universe, king of Assyria, king of Babylon, king of Sumer and Akkad . . . " (*ARAB* I § 787). For an Assyrian king to assume the throne of Babylon and to live in this old and venerated center of Mesopotamian culture and religion were radical acts with international significance. In the Assyrian eponym lists, the significant events noted for the years 729 and 728 are that "the king took the hand of Bel"—that is, Tiglath-pileser participated as the principle figure, the reigning monarch, in the Babylonian New Year festival.

If Tiglath-pileser was the king of Babylon spoken of in Isaiah 14, then what about the depiction of his death? Unfortunately, we have no account of Tiglath-pileser's death. The final entry on him in an eponym list simply notes that he went on a campaign against some enemy and was succeeded on the throne by Shalmaneser. In the list for the preceding year (728), a portion of the name *Damascus* occurs, which would indicate, along with the evidence from Isaiah and Josephus, that the province of Damascus was his destination. As we noted in the introductory historical essay, the scenario that best explains this situation and takes into consideration all the known facts is as follows. When Tiglath-pileser invaded lower Mesopotamia in 731, the anti-Assyrian forces in the west regrouped. This developing trouble in the west is hinted at in Tiglath-pileser's Nimrud Tablet from 729. In this text, he reports on what appear to be budding revolts in eastern Anatolia and Phoenicia:

Uassurme of Tabal was indifferent toward Assyria's achievements and did not come into my presence. My official, the Rabshakeh. . . . Hulli, son of a nobody, I set upon his royal throne. . . .
My official, the Rabshakeh, I sent to Tyre. From Metenna of Tyre I received 150 talents of gold. (*ARAB* I §§ 802-3)

This text indicates that the Assyrians were forced to remove one monarch from power and assert pressure on Tyre to secure tribute payments. By 728/7, matters had reached a crisis. The province of Damascus and other states, including Israel, must have been in open revolt. Tiglath-pileser set out for Damascus, but the fate of the campaign and the monarch are unknown. He may have died in battle. At any rate, Shalmaneser V, who inherited the throne, was left with the task of putting down the uprising, a feat decisively achieved only by his successor, Sargon. (This turmoil under Shalmaneser forms the larger historical context for Isaiah 15–18 and 28–33.)

The overall thrust of Isaiah's speech in 14:1-27 indicates that it was delivered prior to the death of Tiglath-pileser. This would suggest a date after spring 729, when Tiglath-pileser assumed the throne in Babylon, but before 727, when he died.

The speech contains the following elements:

(1) An introductory word of hope about Israel (1-2)
(2) An address of hope to Israel (3-23), including a taunt against the king of Babylon (4b-20b) and a petition against his house (20c-21) as well as two oracles of Yahweh (22-23).
(3) An oath of Yahweh on the destruction of the Assyrian (24-25)
(4) Prophetic interpretation of the divine oath (26-27)

Isaiah 14:1-2

The prophet opens this speech with an asseverative particle, "Surely," for the sake of emphasis. The subject of the prose introduction is the revitalization of Israel and a reversal of the people's status.

The terms *Jacob* and *Israel* are probably used synonymously in verse 1. Both terms could refer to the whole of Yahweh's people. This understanding is supported by the use of the singulars "house of Jacob" (v. 1) and "house of Israel" (v. 2). The prophet probably deliberately chose the more inclusive and positive terms *Israel* and *Jacob*. At the time of this speech, in 729/8, the old state of Israel, in an inclusive sense, no longer existed. Syria and other states in the area had eaten away its territory (see Isa. 7:2; 9:1) and with the provincialization of Syrian-held territory in 732, only the central hill country of the north was left under Israelite control. When Isaiah spoke judgmentally and negatively about the northern kingdom, he frequently used the term *Ephraim* (7:5-9, 17; 9:9, 21; 11:13; 17:3; 28:1, 3). The names *Israel* and *Jacob*, perhaps even understood to indicate Judah, would call to mind brighter days and stronger political realities than characterized the dismal days of the present. Perhaps Isaiah left the exact referent of his designations deliberately ambiguous. At least, he certainly never affirms a bright future for Ephraim as such.

Yahweh, it is promised, will again have compassion on the people (see 9:17) and again show them favor (v. 1)—that is, Yahweh will take a new attitude toward his people. Note that the prophet here nowhere has the Deity lay down any conditions for this reversal of the people's status. There are no demands for repentance, faith, and so forth. He simply announces and describes future conditions.

The consequences of God's manifestation of compassion and favor are noted (vv. 1*b*-2). (a) God will cause them to rest, be at ease (not "set them" as in RSV) in their own land. Since the days of Jeroboam II, Israel had known little but trouble and turmoil, not because it had been defeated on foreign fields, but because of external pressure on its territory and civil strife within its own land. The place of the people's agony and pain—the land—would be the place of their new status. (b) The alien (the *ger*) will join with the children of Israel and adhere to the house of Jacob. In recent years, the reverse had been the case—Yahweh's people had been forced to choose sides and adhere to the cause of others. (3) Other peoples, who for years had deported and carried away Yahweh's people, will return them to their place—Yahweh's land. (4) Israel will possess the peoples of the nations and use them as male and female slaves. (5) The people will take captive their captors and rule over those who oppressed them.

In this depiction of the changed status to come, the present conditions are replaced by their opposites. The reversal of status is a common biblical motif. Earlier, Isaiah had used the theme to depict the coming judgment of the women of Jerusalem, declaring that their present luxurious conditions would be replaced by their opposite (see 3:16–4:1).

Isaiah 14:3-23

Verses 3-4a introduce the taunt against the king of Babylon, which the people will sing when Yahweh has fulfilled the promise of verses 1 and 2 and has given the people rest. With this verse, the prophet shifts from the use of third person plurals (vv. 1-2) to the use of second person singulars. This represents a move from impersonal to more personal address, from detached to more intimate description.

The king of Babylon, whose "funeral oration" follows, goes unnamed—to be unmentioned is to be unremembered; silence damns, and to neglect is to deemphasize. The funeral oration here has parallels to ancient Near Eastern memorial inscriptions, in which the ruler was praised or engaged in self-praise. The praise in such texts spoke of the character and achievements of the ruler, and ended with some form of request or appeal for continued rule and/or blessing on self and/or posterity. Isaiah has here adopted this form but uses it in a negative and ironic fashion. He turns the genre into a song of mockery. In other words, he is satirizing the type of material one would have found on ancient Assyrian inscriptions. The following, from a text of Tiglath-pileser, gives something of the flavor of the royal braggadocio:

Palace of Tiglath-pileser, the great king, the mighty king, king of the universe, king of Assyria, king of Babylon, king of Sumer and Akkad, king of the four regions of the world; the brave hero, who, with the help of Assur, his lord, smashed all who did not obey him, like pots, and laid them low, like a hurricane, scattering them to the winds; the king, who, advancing in the name of Assur, Shamash and Marduk, the great gods, brought under his sway the lands from the Bitter Sea of Bit-Iakin to Mount Bikni, of the rising sun, and to the sea of the setting sun, as far as Egypt,—from the horizon to the zenith, and exercised kingship over them. (*ARAB* I § 787)

Verses 4b-7 describe the fall of the tyrant who has oppressed peoples and ruled over nations, subjecting them to suffering, persecution, and turmoil. In speaking of the rod (which is to be broken), Isaiah uses some of the same terminology he employed earlier in describing Assyria as the rod of Yahweh's anger (see 10:5). Here, it is Yahweh who will destroy the rod that has lashed the backs of subject nations with unceasing blows. With the breaking of the oppressor, rest and quiet, those commodities so rare under the oppressor's yoke, will be enjoyed by the world. Singing will replace wailing.

In verses 8-20a, the ruler, himself, is mockingly addressed in second person speech. Following verse 8, which has the cypresses and cedars of Lebanon rejoicing over their respite from the Assyrian woodcutters who labored to satisfy the insatiable Assyrian appetite for timber, Isaiah depicts the tyrant's fate by playing on a variety of motifs and using themes drawn from mythology.

Verses 9-11 portray Sheol's welcome of the fallen tyrannical monarch. Sheol, the underground realm where the shades (or shadows) of the deceased go, is pictured as stirring to greet the new arrival. Only kings and leaders are mentioned as being in Sheol in this text, but that may be purely coincidental (see 5:14). The point is that even the great Assyrian monarch will take his place in Sheol like every other earthly monarch. In Sheol, the king suffers the ultimate humiliation—the one who ruled on earth as king of kings is, in Sheol, like every other monarch, weak and worm-coated.

In verses 12-15, Isaiah contrasts the goal and ambition of the monarch with his final destiny. It is widely, and perhaps correctly, assumed that the imagery in this passage is based on a myth about the banishment of a divine being from the heavenly world (see Ezek. 28 for a similar usage). The emperor is described as having fallen from the heavens, but as the text makes clear, it was only in the arrogant ambition of the ruler's own heart that he scaled the heavenly heights. The title assigned the king, "Day Star (or "moon crescent"), son of Dawn," when combined with the idea of falling from the skies, points to the rapid fading of the morning star (Venus) or the crescent of the moon with the coming of dawn. In ancient mythology, Venus, the moon, and other luminaries were considered deities, and mythological tales were told of their struggles and fate.

The king is pictured as arrogantly thinking himself more than human, one who can sit in the divine assembly where the gods hold council. A Jerusalem audience could have heard verses 13-14 as being the Assyrian's claim to sit enthroned in Zion. The old mythological ideas of the god dwelling or of the gods meeting in assembly in the recesses of (Mount) Zaphon (RSV = "the far north") had been transferred to Zion and were used to express Jerusalem's claims about Zion as the divine, holy mountain (see Ps. 48:1-2 and Isa. 2:1-4). Yahweh, too, had assumed the old divine title "Most High" (Elyon). For the loyal Yahwist in Jerusalem, the ultimate arrogance would have been for the Assyrian ruler to claim the right to sit (like the Davidic king?) in the council of God, in the recesses of Zaphon (Mt. Zion).

Isaiah draws the logical conclusion: The ambition to exercise absolute power must be rewarded with absolute humiliation. Instead of the recesses of Zaphon, the Assyrian king is to be brought down to the recesses of the pit, the depths of Sheol (v. 15).

The topics of human arrogance, human pride, and divine judgment are found not just in this text; they pervade many of Isaiah's speeches. He uses them not only in condemnation of foreign powers, but also against his own people (see 2:6-22; 5:13-17).

In verses 16-20, Isaiah employs a different image, that of the unburied corpse. To die and lie unburied was to suffer extreme humiliation. On numerous occasions in the Bible, a prophet is pictured as pronouncing the ultimate judgment on monarchs, not just to lie unburied but to have one's flesh eaten by beasts and one's bones picked cleaned by birds (I Kings 14:10-11; 16:4; 21:23-24; II Kings 9:25-26, 30-37). Isaiah here describes the fate of the fallen monarch—to lie unburied, never to be at rest with the other deceased, to be gazed upon by humans, who will wonder how one who is now such a stinking corpse once engaged in such human atrocities and made the earth tremble.

Just as many ancient inscriptions, after describing the great exploits and high status of the honoree, moved to ask a blessing or called upon future generations to remember the honored one, so Isaiah presents his request: "May the descendant (the deceased king) of evildoers nevermore be named" (v. 20c). Such a petition requests that the one eulogized be lost from human memory. (Isaiah contributed his share to the appeal's fulfillment by never informing us explicitly who this king of Babylon was!)

Monumental and memorial, and especially funerary, inscriptions pronounced a curse or wished ill fate upon any who would damage the inscription (see the inscriptions in *ANET* 499-503; especially that of Yehawmilk of Byblos, p. 502). Isaiah completes his statement on the king of Babylon with an ironic call to destroy his descendants. Who is being ordered to do this (the imperative is a plural form) is not made clear. Perhaps as in inscriptional material, the reference is to an undefined "whoever." (The last word in v. 21, "cities" (`arim) should probably be read "evils" (ra`im).

The two short divine oracles in verses 22-23 are the prophet's affirmation that Yahweh was the one who would take the responsibility for destroying the Assyrian ruling family and for turning Babylon, now the royal residence, into a wasteland. These and the following verses are integral to the speech that began with 14:1. The removal of the tyrant and his oppression will be the work of Yahweh.

Isaiah 14:24-25

The divine oracles quoted in verses 24-25, rather than being a redactional addition or a theological insertion, are part of Isaiah's conclusion to the speech in 14:1-27. They are an integral element of his speech, in fact, the culmination of the speech.

The manner in which Isaiah has cast this material in verses 24-25, and especially the introduction, is significant. The terminology is not that of a normal saying or a normal quotation. It is oath and swearing terminology (see 5:9) and, therefore, far stronger than an expression like "Yahweh says" or "thus says Yahweh." The Deity, Isaiah here declares, has sworn, and thus irrevocably committed himself. What God has sworn is (1) that he will carry out what he has thought and planned already; namely, (2) that he, Yahweh, and not some human power, will break and destroy the Assyrian; (3) that he will do this in his own land (note the reference to Yahweh's land in 14:2); and will (4) thus remove the Assyrian burden and yoke from off his people (see 14:1-3; as Isaiah had already promised in 10:27). What God here swears to do is what Isaiah had proclaimed as a promise in the opening of the speech. Thus the introduction and conclusion of the speech cohere and develop similar thoughts in different genres of speech.

Verses 24-25 make clear that the Assyrian and the king of Babylon are identical. Isaiah's speech in 14:1-27 seems to have been delivered prior to the death of Tiglath-pileser in 727, since the death of the monarch remains in the future. By 727, Israel was in revolt against Assyria (see below, chap. 4, sect. 19). Isaiah would hardly have delivered this speech in chapter 14 under such conditions.

Isaiah 14:26-27

Isaiah ends his speech with his own clarification of matters in verses 26-27. In these verses, he picks up on his image of the outstrectched hand. In 5:25, the prophet had described the destruction of the earthquake during Uzziah's day as Yahweh's action: "He stretched out his hand against them and smote them." There he also argued that God was not finished with the punishment of his people: "In all this, his anger is not abated and his hand is stretched out still." In describing the earlier sufferings of Israel in 9:8–10:4, Isaiah spoke of these actions as God's punishment but warned that more was to come: "In all this, his anger is not abated and his hand is stretched out still" (9:12b, 17c, 21b; 10:4b). Now in 14:26-27, Isaiah clearly identifies God's outstretched hand with the Assyrian power: "This is the hand that is stretched out over all the nations." But that is not the end of the matter, says the prophet, because what Yahweh has purposed —namely the punishment of his people by Assyria and then his destruction of Assyria (see 10:12)—no one can annul. Yahweh's hand is stretched out, and no one can stop it, but it is now stretched out against Assyria, too.

17. REJOICE NOT, O PHILISTIA (14:28-32)

J. **Begrich**, "Jesaja 14, 28-32: Ein Beitrag zur Chronologie der israelitisch-judäischen Königszeit," *ZDMG* 86(1932)66-79 =

his *GS* (1964)121-31; K. **Fullerton**, "Isaiah 14: 28-32," *AJSL* 42(1925-26)86-109; W. A. **Irwin**, "The Exposition of Isaiah 14:28-32," *AJSL* 44(1927–28)73-87; A. K. **Jenkins**, "Isaiah 14, 28-32—An Issue of Life and Death," *Folia Orientalia* 21(1980)47-63; H. **Tadmor**, "Philistia under Assyrian Rule," *BA* 29(1966)86-102; D. J. **Wiseman**, "Flying Serpents?" *TB* 23(1972)108-10.

King Ahaz of Judah and Tiglath-pileser of Assyria died in the same year (728–27). The demise of the Assyrian monarch was probably widely greeted with rejoicing and rebellion. Isaiah, too, celebrated his death, either in actuality or, more likely, in anticipation, as Isaiah 14 makes clear. Nonetheless, for Isaiah the work of the Assyrians in the plan of God was not finished with Tiglath-pileser's death. When Philistia moved to join the rebellion and apparently sought to entice Judah and Jerusalem to participate, Isaiah issued a stark warning, a warning intended for his own people as much as for Philistia. Philistia seems to have revolted against Assyrian hegemony just before or at the time of Tiglath-pileser's death. This revolt was not suppressed until years later, when Sargon marched against Hanuna, king of Gaza in 720.

The heading to this Philistine speech was probably added in the editorial process, since it is not an integral part of the address itself, and, in fact, does not mention Philistia. Such a heading, giving the speech a chronological frame of reference, bears the appearance of dating for official purposes. It is possible that such a notation was added to a copy of the speech when it was officially set aside as archival data.

The speech is properly located chronologically. The preceding address (14:1-27) anticipated Tiglath-pileser's death and eulogized the monarch in a sarcastic funeral oration. The actual death of the Assyrian ruler is presupposed by verse 29. Thus this oracle is exactly where one would expect it to appear in an arrangement based on chronological considerations.

The opening line of the address proper contains a second person warning to Philistia, advising that celebration/revolt is not an appropriate posture, even though Tiglath-pileser has died. The reference to "all of you," which reappears in verse 31a, was perhaps used by the prophet to indicate that all the Philistine cities—Ashdod, Ashkelon, Ekron, Gath, and Gaza—are being addressed, although Gaza, the city nearest Egyptian territory, was the ringleader in the Philistine anti-Assyrian movement at the time.

The warning in verse 29a is followed by evidence offered to substantiate the warning. The rod that smote Philistia (Tiglath-pileser) may have been broken, but Isaiah, mixing metaphors, promises that from the root stock, used as a metaphor for the royal house (see 11:1), would come a serpent/adder/flying serpent. The snake terminology may play on the fact that rods/walking sticks were carved and shaped to produce a snake appearance.

Verse 30 continues to give reasons why Philistia should not be celebrating: "the first-born of the poor will feed, and the needy lie down in safety" (RSV). Although Isaiah's point is not entirely clear, such a statement implies two things: (1) the upper, landowning classes, the most susceptible to military service and looting and exile after defeat, would suffer if rebellion occurred, thus (2) allowing the poor, landless classes, the least harmed and threatened by foreign attacks, to occupy property and live in some security (see II Kings 25:8-12).

In verse 30b, different words are used to say the same thing expressed in verse 30a. Some uncertainty exists about how to translate this half verse because of the Hebrew use of both first and third person verbs. But since the prophet often moves back and forth between divine/non-divine and first person/third person address, perhaps this should not bother us. The terms *root* ("root stock") and *remnant* (survivors of battle) probably would have been understood as referring to the royal house and upper classes respectively.

In verse 31, Isaiah calls upon the Philistines to engage in activity exactly opposite to that presently underway. Instead of rejoicing, there should be wailing. The gates are ordered to wail and cry out as if already in a state of distress and need; the people are told to dissolve in fear, for the enemy is coming from the north, leaving behind the smoke of burning towns and marching in unassailable, discipline order.

Verse 32 no longer addresses the Philistines directly but is the prophet's response to the Philistine emissaries who have come or might come to Jerusalem seeking cooperation and support for the rebellion. Isaiah's advice is a reaffirmation of Yahweh's protection of Jerusalem: "Yahweh has founded Zion, and in her the afflicted of his people find refuge." Yahweh's protection, not some anti-Assyrian coalition, is what offers solace to his people.

18. AN ORACLE ON MOAB (15:1–16:14)

L. **Alonso-Schokel**, "Traducción de textos poéticos III. Isa. 15-16," *CB* 18(1961)336-46; S. **Mittmann**, "Das südliche Ostjordanland im Lichte eines neuassyrischen Keilschriftbriefes aus Nimrud," *ZDPV* 89(1973)15-25; W. **Rudolph**, "Jesaja XV-XVI," *Hebrew and Semitic Studies Presented to G. R. Driver* (London: Oxford University Press, 1963)130-43; H. W. F. **Saggs**, "The Nimrud Letters, 1952—Part II: Relations with the West," *Iraq* 17(1955) 126-60; W. **Schottroff**, "Horonaim, Nimrim, Luhith und der Westrand des 'Landes Ataroth': Ein Beitrag zur historischen Topographie des Landes," *ZDPV* 82(1966)163-208; A. H. **van Zyl**, *The Moabites* (Leiden: E. J. Brill, 1960).

When Tiglath-pileser was in the eastern Mediterranean seaboard in 734–732, one of the kings who offered him tribute was Salamanu of Moab (*ANET* 282). Whether Moab was a participating member of the anti-Assyrian coalition at the time or was merely to pay tribute is not known. No biblical text explicitly accuses the Moabites of harassment against Judah during this period, and no Assyrian text implicates Moab in the conspiracy. A few years earlier, when Amos condemned Moab, he did so by denouncing the Moabite king for burning to lime the bones of the king of Edom (Amos 2:1-3) but does not accuse Moab of actions against Israel or Judah. In Isaiah 11:14, Isaiah describes a future time when Ephraim and Judah would take action against Philistia, Edom, Moab, and Ammon, which clearly reflects animosity against Moab.

First Chronicles 5 supplies information that, when compared with Isaiah 15–16, could indicate that tensions existed between Judah and Moab in the days of Ahaz and Hezekiah.

According to this Chronicles text, the tribes of Reuben and Gad were important in Transjordan during the days of Jotham and Jeroboam II (5:1-17). These two tribes appear to have been semi-sedentary groups who, like Aramean and Arabic tribes at the time, doubled as special military forces (5:18-22). Some of these tribes, especially the Reubenites, spread out widely in Gilead and Bashan (see 5:3-10). Isaiah 15–16 indicates that prior to Shalmaneser's invasion, the Moabites had expanded considerably in Transjordan, probably in competition with or at the expense of these Israelite tribes.

One piece of evidence could support the view that Moab was in alliance with Syria at the time of the Syro-Ephraimitic crisis. When Rezin attacked the port city of Elath, on the Gulf of Aqaba (II Kings 16:6), he would have passed through Moabite territory. Moab, however, may have simply passively acquiesced to such troop movements rather than having given active support.

The state of vassalage accepted by Moab in 734/2 is illustrated by a letter from an Assyrian official to the reigning monarch (probably Tiglath-pileser), which reports

I have inspected forty-five horses from. . . .officials of the Egyptians, the people of Gaza, of Judah, of Moab, of the sons of Ammon, when they entered Calah on the twelfth, delivered them at their hands (ND 2765; Saggs, 135)

Isaiah 15–16 indicates that Moab was part of the renewed anti-Assyrian coalition in the west in 728/7. Probably Shalmaneser V, rather than Tiglath-pileser, took action against Moab. That Shalmaneser was active in the Transjordan area is noted by the prophet Hosea, who warned Ephraim that "as Shalman destroyed Beth-arbel [a city in Transjordan] on the day of battle; mothers were slashed in pieces with their children. Thus it shall be done to you, O Bethel" (Hos. 10:14b-15a). We have no Assyrian texts concerning Shalmaneser's wars in the west. From Josephus (*Ant* IX 283-87), we learn that the Assyrians were engaged in Phoenicia and Syria throughout much of Shalmaneser's reign. Probably the Assyrian king was forced to fight on several fronts in Syria-Palestine. One contingent of his troops may have taken action against Moabite territory, while other units fought elsewhere. In his oracle on Damascus, Isaiah indicates that not only was Ephraim involved in rebellion (17:3), but also Moab seems to have suffered before the other two. Isaiah 17:2 declares "the cities [or citadels] of Aroer [in Moab] are deserted" but implies that Damascus and Ephraim are yet to be attacked. If Moab was attacked first, this would explain the appearance of the oracle on Moab in Isaiah 15–16 before the speech on Damascus/Israel in chapter 17.

A few general comments on Isaiah 15–16 are in order before proceeding to more specific discussion. The two chapters form a unit. This is already indicated by the (probably editorial) single heading—the "oracle (or "burden, pronouncement") on Moab." The chapters, especially 15, are full of place names, some identifiable, others not. At times, it is difficult to know if a word indicates a place name or not. For example, the last word in chapter 15 may be read as a place name, Adamah (or Admah), or as the word for "land," "ground." The language in the speech is very terse, at times almost cryptic. Difficulties in understanding many of the particulars of the text are already indicated in the ancient versions. There is at least one quotation within the speech, although its beginning and end are not clearly indicated.

We assume that the speech reflects an Assyrian assault on Moab, presumably from the north, devastation in the Moabite tableland, the flight of the people, an embassy to Jerusalem requesting that Moabite fugitives be allowed to take asylum in Judah, and a prophetic response, recommending denying the Moabites their request. Whether the speech is based on an actual appeal and response involving negotiations between the two states or is reflective of only a hypothetical situation which could have occurred during the crisis is unknown. At the time, Hezekiah had just inherited the throne in Jerusalem and Isaiah's speech could be seen as the prophet's recommendation of policy in the situation.

The following appears to be the contents of the speech:

(1) A description of the plight of the Moabites (15:1-9)
(2) Introduction to the Moabite petition for asylum (16:1-2)
(3) The petition (16:3-5)
(4) The response (16:6-14).

Isaiah 15:1-9

In 15:1-9, the prophet describes the calamity that has struck the Moabite countryside, the people's reactions and the efforts of the general population to flee, and his own "empathetic" identity with their plight.

The description of the destruction of Moabite cities does not follow a clear geographical pattern—that is, the places mentioned do not indicate a clear line of march and assault by the Assyrian army. One would have assumed that in an attack by Assyria, the troops would have marched southward down the main trunk road through Transjordan and would have attacked towns along this route in a north to south direction. There is, however, no such pattern reflected in Isaiah's speech. This could be explained in one of two ways. First, the prophet could be simply picking and choosing place names at will without any effort to do so in any structured form. Second, the Assyrian forces that moved into southern Transjordan may not have been a large united front that operated by taking one town and then moving systematically to the next. The troops may have been a number of smaller units that spread out through the region and attacked various cities simultaneously. Earlier, we noted that Shalmaneser seems to have been fighting on several fronts in the west, and this dispersion of his troops may explain why he apparently never enjoyed the decisive victories of either his predecessor or his successor.

The cities mentioned in 15:1-9, whose locations can be identified, range throughout the Moabite plateau. Some, like Az, Kir (Kir-hareseth), and others, lay south of the River Arnon (Wadi Mujib) in the more traditional land of Moab. Others, like Dibon, Nebo, Medeba, Heshbon, and so forth, lay to the north of the Arnon.

Although the opening verse would seem to indicate that Moab was practically ready to collapse, the rest of the text, and especially 16:14, suggests otherwise—namely, that the people had time to flee, carrying along their moveable property, and to make contact with Judah and to negotiate asylum. Verse 9 also implies that more trouble lies ahead. This verse is difficult to interpret. The Hebrew refers to Dimon, but ancient versions read Dibon as the city talked about. The verse also seems to contain a divine oracle that threatens more disaster, but such a divine threat is not found elsewhere in chapters 15-16, except for the prophet's concluding statement. Possibly a textual error has occurred in the transmission of verse 9b (*'aryeh* ["lion"] for *'ereh* ["I see"]). Such an assumption allows the NEB to translate

> The waters of Dimon already run with blood;
> yet I have more troubles in store for Dimon,
> for I have a vision of the survivors of Moab,
> of the remnant of Admah.
>
> Isaiah 15:9

The prophet presents the Moabite people, giving expression to their fears and anxieties. Wailing, wearing sackcloth, shaving the head and beard, leaving the fields unattended, weeping, fright, and other typical responses to distressful situations are noted. The royal house (see RSV margin on 15:2) and the capital city Dibon are depicted as going to places of worship (to the *bamahs*) to weep and lament.

The prophet, in verse 5, speaks of his "empathy" with the people. His expressions of sympathy, however, may have been only diplomatic language and expressions of "politeness" or, even more likely, pure sarcasm since, in the last analysis, Isaiah recommends that Judah close the border to any migration of Moabites into the country.

Isaiah 16:1-2

In 16:1, Isaiah speaks of an official embassy sent to Jerusalem requesting help and the right of asylum. The general sense of this verse is clear, although it contains several textual problems. Perhaps it should be translated as follows:

> The rulers of the country have sent [a present of] lambs,
> from Sela by way of the desert,
> to the mountain of the daughter of Zion.

Such a translation would imply that Moabite leaders had sent a gift to the Judean king (see II Kings 3:4) via the Edomite city of Sela (in the vicinity of Bozrah) and across the Judean wilderness to Jerusalem. They hoped by such a present to secure the aid of Judah.

Verse 16:2, describing Moabite women trying to flee across the Arnon rift, might fit better with the unit in 15:1-9 since it appears to form part of the description of the people's plight. Grammatically, it does not appear to be a part of the following appeal addressed to the Judean leaders. Nonetheless, it may once have been stated so as to constitute the opening of the Moabite appeal: "Like fluttering birds and scattered nestlings are the daughters of Moab at the fords of the Arnon, so. . . . " After this emotion laden statement of the distressful situation, the actual appeal would have followed.

Isaiah 16:3-5

The petition of the Moabite emissaries is given in verses (2)3-5 and should be read as a direct quotation. The petition requests the king (Hezekiah) to give the people of Moab a hearing and to grant the homeless refugees the privilege of finding solace and safety in the shade of Judah's protection. (The entire speech is filled with diplomatic compliments and niceties!) The NEB expresses the sense of verses 3-4*a*:

> "Take up our cause with all your might;
>   let your shadow shield us at high noon, dark as night.
> Shelter the homeless, do not betray the fugitive;
>   let the homeless people of Moab find refuge with you;
>   hide them from the despoiler."

The quotation continues. Verse 4*b* should be interpreted as a clause stipulating the time limit of the refugees' recourse to Judean protection:

> "Until the oppressor is no more,
>   and destruction has ceased;
> and he who tramples under foot,
>   has vanished from the land."

Verse 5 continues the request, making the appeal in a flattering manner by complimenting the Judean king.

"Established in mercy is a throne,
and one sits upon it in truthfulness,
in the tent of David;
one who judges and seeks justice,
and is swift to do the right thing."

Such a king, the emissaries imply, would surely do the right, proper, and merciful thing and aid the homeless of Moab.

If verses (2)3-5 are a quotation of the Moabites' request for refuge, how is the presence of such a quotation in a prophetic speech to be explained? Is the Moabite request purely a creation of the prophet, who uses it to offer his response and thus his opinion about what should be done in such a situation? Is this an actual request of the Moabites, which Isaiah took up and incorporated into his speech? Are chapters 15–16 something like a royal court stenographer's record of words spoken in an actual historical situation? Which of these conditions stands behind chapters 15–16 cannot be determined, but none should be ruled out as a possibility.

Isaiah 16:6-14

In verses 6-11, Isaiah responds to the Moabite request. In verses 6-7, his attitude is very openly harsh and condemnatory. In verses 8-11, especially verses 9-11, his tone seems to change drastically, and he appears to empathize intensely with the Moabites. In reality, his statements in verses 9-11 are rife with cutting sarcasm. In order to understand the prophet's sarcastic attitude, it is necessary to understand the history of the Moabite-Israelite struggles over territory in Transjordan.

Four towns are mentioned in verses 8-11: Elealeh, Heshbon, Jazer, and Sibmah. All of these were towns which at one time or another in earlier days had been Israelite cities. Elealeh, Heshbon, and Sibmah were towns in close proximity to one another, which the Israelites had once occupied and rebuilt (see Num. 21; 32:3, 37-38; Josh. 13:17-19). Jazer, which lay at the border of Ammonite territory north of the Heshbon region (Num. 21:24), was settled by Levites from Hebron at the time of David (I Chron. 26:31) and was claimed as Israelite territory

(Num. 21:32; 32:35). Both Heshbon and Jazer had once been Levitical cities (Josh. 21:39).

Three times during its history, Israel/Judah controlled large portions of Transjordan. In the tenth century, David conquered much of the land north of the Arnon River and Solomon presumably continued to rule over some or all of this area. For about half a century after the death of Solomon, the Israelites probably controlled little, if any, of Transjordan. During the reign of the Omride family in Israel (885–843), much of Transjordan again came under Israelite control. Following the death of Ahab (see II Kings 1:1), Moab, under King Mesha, regained its independence (see the so-called Moabite stone of King Mesha; *ANET* 320-21). Again in the eighth century, Jeroboam II and Jotham resecured territory in Transjordan, probably including the plateau just east of the northern end of the Dead Sea (II Kings 14:25; I Chron. 5:1-22). This Israelite expansion into Transjordan had been especially sanctioned as an act of holy war (see the reference to the sanction of the prophet Jonah in II Kings 14:25 and note I Chron. 5:22). The towns of Elealeh, Heshbon, Jazer, and Sibmah were all in this area. Toward the end of Jeroboam's reign, this region was retaken by the Moabites, and the Israelites/Judeans were driven out or massacred. Thus when Isaiah refers to weeping over the fall of these towns, his audience, whether Moabite or Judean, would have caught the glitter of his verbal sword.

The pride of Moab is ridiculed in verse 6 as having turned out to be nothing but empty talk. Those who once bragged are told in verse 7 to change their tune and wail. The viticultural excellence of the Heshbon and Jazer regions and the importance of the wine trade from their vineyards dominate verses 8-10. In these verses, the prophet plays on the weeping theme. He will weep over the fall of these (Israelite) cities in Moab and the loss of their good wine, but his weeping will not be for Moabite cities.

Isaiah concludes his sarcastic remarks with a double entendre that borders on the vulgar: "Therefore my bowels for Moab like a lyre will make music, and my innards for Kir-heresh"(="city of silence," a play on name of the Moabite city Kir-hareseth, mentioned in v. 7).

Verse 12 is offered as an aside to the main part of the speech and probably was addressed fundamentally to the Judean audience or to Hezekiah. If we transpose the collective singulars in the verse into plurals, an expansive translation would look like this:

And should it happen [should Moabites be admitted temporarily into Judah], when the Moabites wanted to worship, when they wearied themselves over the *bamah* [a place of worship], and when they came to his [Yahweh's] sanctuary to pray, they would not be allowed.

Verse 13 explains that this has been the verdict of Yahweh from of old. Here Isaiah is alluding to the type of opinion concerning the Moabites that became enshrined in Deuteronomy 23:3—"No Ammonite or Moabite shall enter the assembly of Yahweh; even to the tenth generation, none belonging to them shall enter the assembly of Yahweh."

To this old word of Yahweh, Isaiah now adds a further divine word. In three years, in spite of Moab's vast numbers, the country will be decimated and its survivors few and inconsequential. Isaiah's use of the expression "three years, like the years of a hireling" could refer to the exactness of the count (three years, no more, no less) or to the burdensome length the time will appear to be (three years counted off one long day at a time). If the latter, Isaiah has Yahweh announce a long, slow death for Moab.

19. OLD COALITIONS NEVER DIE (17:1-14)

J. **Day**, "Asherah in the Hebrew Bible and Northwest Semitic Literature," *JBL* 105(1986)385-408; M. **Delcor**, "Le probème des jardins d'Adonis dans Isaïe 17, 9-11," *Syria* 54(1977)371-94; H. **Donner**, *Israel unter den Völkern* (Leiden: E. J. Brill, 1964)38-42; H. J. **Katzenstein**, *The History of Tyre: From the Beginning of the Second Millennium B.C.E. until the Fall of the Neo-Babylonian in 538 B.C.E.* (Jerusalem: Schocken Institute for Jewish Research of the Jewish Theological Seminary of America, 1973)220-58; G. **Smith**, "On a New Fragment of the Assyrian Canon Belonging to the Reigns of Tiglath-pileser and Shalmaneser," *TSBA* 2(1873)321-32.

Assyrian troubles in the west in the early 720s must have been widespread. Assyrian records hint at budding trouble in Tabal and Tyre sometime before the death of Tiglath-pileser (*ARAB* I §§ 802-3). Isaiah 15–17 indicates that the provinces of Damascus and the kingdoms of Israel and Moab were part of the anti-Assyrian front. Philistia, also, may have been involved (see Isa. 14:28-32).

Josephus contains a report of some of this opposition to Assyria, which is based, so he claims, on Tyrian archives and attested by the Greek author Menander (*Ant* IX 283-87). Josephus states that "the king of Assyria came with an army and invaded Syria and all of Phoenicia." He proceeds to quote Menander's description:

And Elulaios [Luli in Assyrian texts], to whom they gave the name of Pyas, reigned thirty-six years. This king, upon the revolt of the Kities [Cyprians], put out to sea and again reduced them to submission. During his reign Selampsas [Shalmaneser], the king of Assyria, came with an army and invaded all Phoenicia and, after making a treaty of peace with all [its cities, except Tyre], withdrew from the land. And Sidon and Arke [Acco] and Old Tyre [Ushu in Assyrian texts; the mainland city of Tyre] and many other cities also revolted from Tyre and surrendered to the king of Assyria. But, as the Tyrians for that reason did not submit to him, the king turned back again and attacked them after the [other] Phoenicians had furnished him with sixty ships and eight hundred oarsmen. Against these the Tyrians sailed with twelve ships and, after dispersing the ships of their adversaries, took five hundred of their men prisoners. On that account, in fact, the price of everything went up in Tyre. But the king of Assyria, on retiring, placed guards at the river and the aqueducts to prevent the Tyrians from drawing water, and this they endured for five years, and drank from wells which they had dug.

Several conclusions may be drawn from this text. (1) The revolt against Assyria in 728/27 was widespread. (2) Much Phoenician territory was taken by or capitulated to the Assyrians. (3) Luli continued to hold out against Assyria throughout the reign of Shalmaneser, since the attempted Assyrian blockade of Tyre, the island city, did not succeed in achieving its objectives.

Ephraim and Damascus, along with Moab and perhaps other south Syro-Palestinian kingdoms, were involved.

Apparently, in the province of Damascus, Assyrian authority had been overthrown and a monarchical state reconstituted (see Isa. 17:3). King Hoshea of Israel apparently capitulated to the Assyrians early on in Shalmaneser's campaign. "Against him came up Shalmaneser king of Assyria; and Hoshea became his vassal, and paid him tribute" (II Kings 17:3). As we know, Hoshea's capitulation was only temporary; he soon rebelled again, apparently under strong popular pressure, and appealed to Egypt for military aid (see Isa. 28–31 and II Kings 17:4). Isaiah's proclamation on Israel in chapter 17 belongs to the earliest phase of the conflict.

The following is the outline of the speech's content:

(1) Introduction: a divine oracle announces the devastation of Damascus and Ephraim (1-3)
(2) The first description of the day of coming judgment (4-6)
(3) A second description of the day (7-8)
(4) A third description of the day (9-11)
(5) Conclusion: assurance that Yahweh will protect and save (12-14)

Isaiah 17:1-3

The heading of this speech—"the oracle on Damascus"—is actually a misnomer since the majority of the speech concerns Ephraim. The heading here, as in most, if not all, cases in Isaiah 13–23, is secondary and represents a heading placed at the top of a copy of the speech when put away for official purposes. The jotted down title for identification purposes was arrived at by taking the first place name to appear in the text.

Verses 1-3, like 4-6, are presented as a divine word/oracle. The oracle has a stark announcement quality about it without much elaboration or elucidation.

1. "Behold, Damascus will cease to be a city,
    and will become a heap of ruins.
2. Deserted are the cities [or citadels] of Aroer;
    they shall be for flocks
      who shall rest there undisturbed.

3. The fortress will disappear from Ephraim,
   and the monarchy from Damascus;
and the remnant of Syria will be
   like the glory of the children of Israel,"
      says Yahweh of Hosts.

Although Damascus and Ephraim had only recently (in 733–32) been the objects of an Assyrian campaign, they were now again (in 728–27) vying for freedom from Assyrian overlordship. (Did Isaiah's speech in chapter 14 contribute to the optimism about revolt?)

The pattern reflected in the case of Damascus was rather typical in the ancient world. A city would rebel, the rebellion would be suppressed, certain political-economic measures would be taken by the foreign monarch, a short period of submission would follow, then further rebellion would take place. Obviously, when ancient cities were taken, in spite of the string of synonymous verbs the Assyrians used to describe their attacks and conquests, they were generally not obliterated. (Isaiah, in chapter 13 and elsewhere, of course, uses similarly exaggerated terminology.)

The speed with which the anti-Assyrian coalition revived in the west, between the years 732–729/8, indicates two things. First, political scheming and covert negotiations among states in the area must have been a constant in the life of the region. Second, the decisive question was not whether an anti-Assyrian coalition would form or should be formed but rather over the most opportune time, or for Isaiah, the divinely ordained time.

The opening of verse 2, which practically all modern translations emend from the original, makes good sense in its context in spite of some ambiguity about its particular content. One way to read the text is to see only one city involved, namely the Aroer on the northern edge of the Arnon gorge (Deut. 2:36; II Sam. 24:5). A translation reflecting this understanding would be, "the citadels of Aroer are deserted." (A feature of the remains at the ruins of Aroer is two large structures with heavy wall fortifications.) Such an interpretation would have Isaiah warning Damascus and Ephraim that a key Moabite fortress city had fallen. (Aroer is not mentioned in Isa. 15–16.) Moabite resistance had now collapsed. Another way of reading the text is to assume that it refers to two Aroers: "The cities of Aroer are forsaken." In addition to the Aroer on the Arnon, there was another more northern Aroer in the vicinity of Rabbah-Ammon, the Ammonite capital (Josh. 13:25; Judg. 11:33). If the two cities are referred to, then Isaiah is denoting southern and northern points of the land overrun by Assyria.

Verse 3 contains two pairs of parallel terms: of Damascus, kingdom/remnant, and of Ephraim, fortress/glory. It was probably the surviving remnant of the old city (or royal family) that had sought to revive the monarchy in Damascus. The glory of Ephraim is clearly Samaria, and presumably the fortress was the royal quarter in the capital.

Isaiah 17:4-6

The divine oracle on the day of Yahweh (vv. 4-6) explains the nature of the coming judgment on Ephraim. Damascus drops out of the picture. The description is straightforward. After using the imagery of weight loss, Isaiah employs comparisons drawn from crop harvesting. The judgment will be a time of reaping and beating, but a little will remain left over.

Israel is compared to a field of grain in the Valley of Rephaim, part of the upper branches of the Sorek Valley near Jerusalem, where the farmland was probably so carefully gleaned that little was left after harvest. In verse 4, the expression usually translated "the glory of Israel" should probably be read as "the weight of Jacob" to parallel "the fat of his flesh."

Isaiah 17:7-8

The second description of that day in the speech (vv. 7-8) is not given as a divine oracle but merely as Isaiah's word. The parallelism of his text is better if the words *altars, asherim,* and *incense burners* are omitted as glosses.

In that day,
> humanity will give attention to its maker,
>> and its eyes will look to the holy one of Israel;
> and it will not give attention to the works of its hands,
>> and will not look to that which its fingers have made.

Isaiah 17:7-8

Altars, asherim, and *incense burners* might thus be later glosses intent on making clear or more specific to what the prophet had alluded, although we cannot be certain. At any rate, 17:8 is closely parallel to 2:8, 20 (see 27:9). The original point is that, in the day of trouble, nothing humanly produced, not even the accoutrements of worship, will make any difference. People will stand before their maker and not rely on what they have made; only Yahweh, the holy one of Israel, will matter (compare 2:17). As in 2:6-22, Isaiah does not here condemn cultic accoutrements *per se* and certainly not the cult itself.

Isaiah 17:9-11

The third in-that-day saying in the speech (vv. 9-11) is again not given as a Yahweh oracle. The section teems with translation difficulties. Verse 9 declares that the strong cities will be abandoned, apparently as cities in Canaan were deserted when the Hebrews invaded. Verse 10a accuses the people of having forgotten God and not remembered "the Rock of your refuge." Verses 10b-11a seem to spell out how this failure to remember God manifests itself. The text is problematic. Most scholars see in the section references to Israel's religious apostasy and worship of other gods (particularly the Adonis cult). Another way of viewing Isaiah's charge is to see it in a political perspective, which fits the context better than a charge of religious illegalities. The references to plants and plantings should be seen, as in so many cases in Isaiah (see 1:29; 4:2; 5:1-2; 6:13, and so on), as denoting political realities and situations. The following is a hypothetical translation:

10b. Therefore, though you set out attractive plants,
    and plant foreign slips;
11. on the day of your setting out you make it grow,
    and in the morning of your planting you make it sprout;
  the harvest will vanish on the day of gathering, a
    day of calamitous pain.

The planting, or seedling, that is set out and expected so quickly to grow refers to the plans for revolt against Assyria (similar plant imagery is used in denouncing the plans involving the Ethiopians in 18:4-6). Only two or three years earlier, Hoshea had himself been "planted" on the throne in Samaria, and now he is already cultivating rebellion. That the rooted cutting is foreign indicates that the plot to revolt was not Ephraimite or home grown but a plan Ephraim bought into through outside influence, probably that of Damascus, which again later revolted in the time of Sargon (see *ANET* 285). The unusual word translated as "attractive" is the Hebrew *na`amanim*, and one is tempted to translate it "Na`aman plants" and see in Isaiah's remark a sarcastic reference to the general Na`aman, who commandered the Syrian army at a time when Israel suffered severely at the hands of Syria a century earlier (II Kings 5).

Isaiah 17:12-14

Isaiah concludes this speech with a woe section that picks up on on the old cultic themes of the onslaught of the nations (see Pss. 46; 48; 76), the intervention of Yahweh, and the rescue of the threatened. Given the international situation— the Assyrian army composed of units of many nations campaigning in the west—the unit seems right at home. Isaiah used the material in this context to assure his Judean audience that "the nations might rage, kingdoms totter, and the earth melt" (Ps. 46:6) but Yahweh's people could rest secure.

Apparently in Judah, the new king, Hezekiah, took no active part whatever in the revolt of Tiglath-pileser's last year and Shalmaneser's first. Refusing Moabite refugees (Isa. 15–16) fleeing from Assyrian forces must have been viewed by Assyria as neutrality in the conflict, even though Judah had other reasons for its animosity toward Moab. In Isaiah 17, the prophet gives no hint that Judah is threatened.

20. AMBASSADORS IN PAPYRUS BOATS (18:1-7)

M. **Elat**, "The Economic Relations of the Neo-Assyrian Empire with Egypt," *JAOS* 98(1978)20-34; S. **Frankenstein**, "The Phoenicians in the Far West: A Function of Neo-

Assyrian Imperialism," *Power and Propaganda: A Symposium on Ancient Empires* (ed. M. T. Larsen; Copenhagen: Akademisk Forlag, 1979)263-94; M. **Lichtheim**, *Ancient Egyptian Literature: Volume III: The Late Period* (Berkeley/London: University of California Press, 1980)66-84; N. **Na'aman**, "The Brook of Egypt and Assyrian Policy on the Border of Egypt," *TA* 6(1979)68-90; B. **Oded**, "The Phoenician Cities and the Assyrian Empire in the Time of Tiglath-pileser III," *ZDPV* 90(1974)38-49; H. W. F. **Saggs**, "The Nimrud Letters, 1952—Part II: Relations with the West," *Iraq* 17(1955)126-60.

During the second half of the eighth century, the XXVth Ethiopian dynasty exerted increasing pressure on and control over the Delta region of Egypt (see above, chap. 1, sect. 2). Three phases in their efforts can be discerned. The Ethiopian pharaoh, Piye, whose dates are probably 753–713, initially sought to control the region with limited military presence and reliance on friendly local leaders. When this failed and struggle for power among various important families in the Delta threatened to turn the area into a zone of civil strife, and with Assyrian influence now extending to Egypt's northern border, Piye invaded the Delta. This was in his twenty-first year, or about 732. Piye forced the Delta leaders to submit to his authority, at least temporarily, but then returned upstream to his capital city. Finally, in the third phase, Shabako, upon succeeding Piye, moved into the Delta permanently and asserted his authority as sole ruler.

Isaiah 18 belongs, as its present literary context indicates, to the second phase of Ethiopian activity—that is, after Piye's invasion and the increase of Ethiopian influence in the Delta. The text, therefore, probably belongs to the early period of Shalmaneser's efforts to suppress the anti-Assyrian revolt in Syria-Palestine. The Ethiopians apparently sent special ambassadors along the Mediterranean seaboard—in seagoing papyrus ships—to explore local conditions and sentiments concerning the indecisive conflict with Assyria. The long-standing commercial relationships between the Phoenician cities and Egypt would certainly have been threatened by Shalmaneser's attempt to blockade Tyre. A letter from an Assyrian official written to the royal court, probably during the reign of Tiglath-pileser (ND 2715), demonstrates that the

Assyrians were trying at that time to regulate trade with Egypt: "I [the Assyrian official] spoke to them in this manner: 'Henceforth have timber brought down here [to Tyre], do your work upon it, but do not sell it to the Egyptians or to the Palestinians [the Philistines]'"(Saggs, 127-28). The Ethiopians were thus attempting to preserve and secure friendly relations along the coast. However, their actions could only be understood as having anti-Assyrian objectives. Kingdoms struggling against the Assyrians no doubt looked on the Ethiopian initiatives as signals that they could expect military assistance in the future.

The following outlines the content of this speech:

(1) Introduction: woe statement on the Ethiopians (1-2*a*)
(2) Order for messengers to go to Assyria and to make a proclamation to the nations (2*b*-3)
(3) The reasons for Isaiah's position (4-6)
(4) Conclusion: Zion to receive gifts from Assyria (7)

Isaiah 18:1-2a

The introduction to this speech calls attention to the Ethiopian ambassadors who, sailing along the Mediterranean coast, would have put in at various ports. Perhaps some Ethiopians had now arrived at Jerusalem or were on their way to confer with King Hezekiah. Isaiah greeted the embassy with harsh denunciation and proposed drastic measures to call attention to their presence.

The title assigned to Ethiopia—land of *ṣilṣal kenapayim*—probably means something like "land of sailing ships" (or "sail boats"), rather than "land of whirring wings" (the latter translation referring to Ethiopia as a land of flying insects).

Isaiah 18:2b-3

In verse 2*b*, Isaiah "orders" swift messengers to go to Mesopotamia ("the land the rivers divide") to the Assyrians. The messengers are not the Ethiopian ambassadors or some heavenly beings. What Isaiah does in verse 2*b* is to offer his proposal of what to do in the light of Ethiopian movement and influence in southern Syria-Palestine. His recommendation is that swift messengers hasten to Assyria to make known that the Ethiopians are up to no good in Syria-Palestine. Some of the terms used in the description of the Assyrians apparently speak of them as a nation "tall and smooth, a people feared near and far," although the meaning of the Hebrew is uncertain. This description has generally led scholars wrongly to assume that verse 2*b* refers to the Ethiopians (see the NJPSV). Other words used are even more uncertain. The penultimate phrase in the verse seems to refer to the Assyrians' unintelligible speech: "gibber and chatter" (so NJPSV; see Isa. 28:10; 33:19; Deut. 28:49; Jer. 5:15).

Verse 3 may be taken either as Isaiah's warning to the nations of the world or as the word the messengers should proclaim on their way to Assyria.

All inhabitants of the world and dwellers on earth:
[Hear this] "When an ensign is raised on the mountains, watch out;
and when the ram's horn is sounded, take heed!"

This message, cast as a warning to the nations, was especially for Judah's and Hezekiah's hearing. What it recommended was that when war plans are made (at the instigation and cooperation of the Ethiopians) and the calls to battle sounded, don't be among the number opposing Assyria!

Isaiah 18:4-6

In verses 4-6, Isaiah gives the two-fold rationale for his position. The first is stated as a word of Yahweh to him: Yahweh will offer no support for the budding rebellion. Also, before the harvest season (before plans can reach fruition), this new growth (the rebellion) will be pruned away and its supporters left like unburied corpses on the field of battle for the beasts and birds to feed on.

4. Because thus Yahweh said to me:
    "I will set back quietly and in my abode watch it—
    like scorching heat in the time of light,
    like a cloud of dew in the heat of harvest time."

5. Because before the time of harvest, when blossom season is over,
   when the berry becomes a ripening grape;
  he will cut off the shoots with pruning hooks,
   and lop off the spreading branches.
6. They shall all be abandoned to the birds of the mountains,
   and to the beasts of the earth;
  and the birds will pick them apart,
   and all the beasts of the earth will tear away at them.

Several facts about this text should be noted. (a) It is uncertain where the divine oracle ends. We have limited it to verse 4. This verse opens with the particle *ki*, and what follows is assumed to represent one of Isaiah's reasons offered for his position. Verse 5 also begins with *ki*, which would indicate that a new thought is begun. (b) The identity of the "he" (or "one") in verse 5*b* is left unclarified. Is it Yahweh? The Assyrian ruler? Perhaps Isaiah deliberately left the matter ambiguous. (c) Just as in chapter 17, Isaiah uses agricultural imagery to make his point. In 17:10*b*-11, he accused Ephraim of setting out an imported plant (adopting plans for rebellion sprouted in Damascus and elsewhere) and of expecting it to grow immediately (hoping for good results from premature preparations). Here he argues that the plans for revolt, even with Ethiopian aid, will be cut off like new and unwanted growth on grape vines. (d) Yahweh, he declares, will not commit himself to support this new rebellion; he will keep hands off and function as an observer. Yahweh will take the same posture in this situation that Isaiah recommended to Ahaz in the days of the earlier coalition—unsupportive of the revolt (see Isa. 7:3-9). (e) The present plan for revolt is to Yahweh only a flash in the pan, insubstantial and soon passing, like blazing heat in the light of day and dew in the summertime. Given a little time, they both disappear, the heat with the coming of evening and the dew in the light of the sun. (f) The supporters of the present revolt will end up scattered on the battlefield, before the harvest is past, their corpses to be picked and gnawed clean by birds of prey and wild beasts. (g) As so frequently, Isaiah engages in wordplay. Ethiopia is described as the land of *ṣilṣal* wings (= sail boats) and the unwanted growth on the grape vines, which will be pruned away, is the *zalzallim*.

256

Isaiah 18:7

Isaiah concludes his speech by picking up on his recommendation in verse 2*b*. In the latter passage, Isaiah had recommended that swift messengers be sent to the Assyrians, alerting them of Ethiopian intervention in the area. Now he says, "in that time"—that is, after the half-baked plans for revolt have failed—the Assyrians will show their gratitude by sending gifts to Mt. Zion, the place of the name of Yahweh Sebaoth. (Until Judah's participation in the Ashdod-led revolt of 713–712, Assyria seems to have treated the country with leniency.) Isaiah's reference to the sacred city or the temple mount as the place of the name of Yahweh shows his familiarity with a central concept of Deuteronomic theology: Mt. Zion is the place that Yahweh has chosen to make his name dwell (see Deut. 12:11).

21. ASSYRIAN, EGYPTIAN, AND ISRAELITE ECUMENISM (19:1-25)

A. **Causse**, "Les origines de la diaspora juive," *RHPR* 7(1927)97-128; M. **Elat**, "The Economic Relations of the Neo-Assyrian Empire with Egypt," *JAOS* 98(1978)20-34; A. **Feuillet**, "Un sommet religieux de l'Ancien Testament: L'oracle d'Isa 19:19-25 sur la conversion de l'Egypte," *RSR* 39(1951)65-87; C. J. **Gadd**, "Inscribed Prisms of Sargon II from Nimrud," *Iraq* 16(1954)173-201; N. **Na'aman**, "The Brook of Egypt and Assyrian Policy on the Border of Egypt," *TA* 6(1979)68-90; B. **Porten**, "The Diaspora: The Jews in Egypt," *CHJ* I(1984)372-400; J. F. A. **Sawyer**, " 'Blessed be My People Egypt' (Isaiah 19:25): The Context and Meaning of a Remarkable Passage," *A Word in Season: Essays in Honour of William McKane* (ed. J. D. Martin and P. R. Davies; Sheffield: JSOT Press, 1986)57-71; H. **Tadmor**, "The Campaigns of Sargon II of Assur: A Chronological–Historical Study," *JCS* 12(1958)22-40, 77-100; W. **Vogels**, "L'Egypte mon peuple— L'Universalisme d'Is 19, 16-25," *Bib* 57(1976)494-514 (see further bibliography under chap. 1, sect. 2).

The events associated with Sargon's suppression of the Syro-Palestinian anti-Assyrian coalition and his actions with regard to the Egyptians in 720 constitute the historical background for Isaiah 19. (The absence of speeches in this context from the year 728/7 [the date of Isaiah 17 and 18] to sometime just after 720 [the date of Isaiah 19] is explained by the fact that the collection in Isaiah 28–33 belongs to this period but was given its present location in the book by the editors to prepare for the account of Sennacherib's threat to Jerusalem in Isaiah 36–37.)

In the Nimrud Prism (see Gadd, 179-82; *TUAT* I 382), Sargon reports on his defeat of the Samarians who had stubbornly continued their revolt against the Assyrians, even after Shalmaneser's arrest of King Hoshea and after the city fell in 722. The text then gives an account of Sargon's disposition of Samaria and reports on actions taken by him with regard to Egyptian-Assyrian relations.

27,280 people [of Samaria] with their chariots and the gods they trust, I counted as spoil. 200 chariots as my muster I mustered from among them. The rest of them I caused to take their dwelling in the midst of Assyria [incorporated them into the provincial system]. I restored the city of Samaria, and greater than before I made it. I settled within it people of the lands my own two hands had conquered. My officer I placed as prefect over them and together with the people of Assyria I counted them. I made the splendor of Ashur my lord overwhelm the Egyptians and Arabians. At the mention of my name their hearts palpitated and their arms fell. The closed commercial center [or perhaps "borders"] of Egypt I opened. The people of Assyria and Egypt I made mingle together and had them trade.

Prior to his innovative moves with regard to Egyptian-Assyrian relations, Sargon had defeated the Philistine leader, Hanunu of Gaza, destroyed the town of Raphia, and repelled a token Egyptian force dispatched by one of the Delta princes (*ARAB* II § 55; *ANET* 284-85). Thus his actions in the area cannot be seen as an expression of Assyrian weakness. Sargon, as the head of a new ruling family in Assyria, was obviously inaugurating a new policy with regard to Egypt, one that led Isaiah to declare him the savior of Egypt (Isa. 19:20). Sargon's attitude was clearly directed against the Ethiopians and their control of Egypt. His vision of a cooperative alliance between the Assyrians and the Egyptians continued to influence Assyrian policy until the end of the empire. Relations between the two soured only when the Ethiopians controlled the Delta and Delta chieftains "supported" the pharaohs of the XXVth dynasty. Later kings of the Sargonid dynasty were to invade Egypt but only in an effort to force the withdrawal of the Ethiopians. After his victory over the XXVth dynasty at Memphis (in 671), the Assyrian king Esarhaddon bragged: "All Ethiopians I deported from Egypt—leaving not even one to do homage" (*ANET* 293).

Under the new arrangements, Sargon no doubt saw Assyria and the Delta Egyptians trading and together controlling not only the naval commerce along the coast, but also the overland Arabian trade route that terminated in the Gaza area. Along the eastern Mediterranean seaboard, only Tyre remained outside Assyrian control. Tyre, however, was a major maritime power with various trading colonies throughout the Mediterranean world. Highly important was the fact that Tyre dominated the island of Cyprus. Sargon's friendly overtures toward the Egyptians may also have been partially motivated by a desire to disrupt the longstanding commercial association between Egypt and Tyre.

The Assyrian policies must have created the sense of a new age dawning for the Palestinian area. Isaiah certainly became caught up in the euphoria of ecumenism.

The following is an outline of Isaiah's speech on Egypt:

(1) Introduction: Yahweh comes to Egypt (1)
(2) Divine oracle: chaos in Egypt (2-10)
(3) Prophetic denunciation of the wisdom of Egypt (11-15)
(4) Five prophetic predictions (16-25)

Isaiah 19:1

This speech opens with Isaiah's depiction of Yahweh's coming to Egypt. "Riding on a cloud," as the means of divine movement from one place to another, was a widespread image in the ancient Near East, although even the ancients would probably have acknowledged a metaphorical dimension to such talk. Most ancient high gods were associated with the heavens, the sky, storms, clouds, and so forth (see

Pss. 18:10-12; 29; 68:33; Deut. 33:26). The gods of Egypt, represented by the idols, are clearly declared inferior to Yahweh; at his presence, they will tremble, and the hearts of their supporters and worshipers will melt before true divinity. For any ancient person visiting Egypt, the number and variety of iconographic representations of the gods and the numbers of temples and priests must have been startling.

Isaiah 19:2-10

The divine oracle in the speech occurs without introduction. The notation at the end of verse 4—"says the Lord, Yahweh of hosts"—could serve as a subscription, indicating that verses 2-4 are a divine oracle. The quotation attributed to the Deity, however, appears to continue at least through verse 10. The attribution of material to Yahweh at the end of verse 4 seems to close out one topic, and the following verse introduces a new subject but continues the quotation of the divine oracle.

In verses 2-4, Yahweh predicts a period of internal strife and civil war in Egypt, culminating in the oppressive rule of a strong king. Isaiah is doing two things here. First, he is predicting the course of historical events after they have happened. As we noted above in the introduction to this speech (see further, above, chap. 1, sect. 2), Egyptian history in the 740s and 730s was a time of multiple competing dynasties and chieftains, civil war, and the increasing dominance of Pharaoh Piye over the whole of the Nile Valley. Piye, the Ethiopian ruler who invaded the Delta late in the 730s, is the hard master and fierce king mentioned in verse 4. Second, Isaiah has Yahweh claim that the course of Egyptian events has been his work.

The second part of the divine oracle (vv. 5-10) shifts the focus from historical events to natural phenomena. The central calamity predicted to befall the Egyptians is the drying up of the Nile, the river on which the valley civilization depended. The Nile, independent of local rainfall in Egypt, was generally rhythmic in its rise and fall. Fed by rains falling deep in equatorial Africa, the river began its rise in about mid-June and reached its maximum flood stage by mid-October. The annual inundation provided not only water, but also nutrient rich alluvial deposits for the land. Fascination with the rhythm of the Nile finds expression in several biblical texts, including the book of Isaiah's earlier contemporary, Amos (8:8; 9:5). Several Egyptian texts refer to the failure of the Nile to rise sufficiently to water the land (see the late Ptolemaic text in *AEL* III 94-103). Whether some recent abnormality in the Nile flood lies behind Isaiah's prediction cannot be determined.

The consequences of the failure of the Nile are spelled out in verses 6-10. Canals will dry up and water plants will wither away (v. 6), crops will fail (v. 7), fish and fishing industries will disappear (v. 8), combers and weavers in flax will despair (v. 9), and spinners will be downcast: "all wage earners will be grieved" (v. 10).

Isaiah 19:11-15

In verses 11-15, Isaiah moves to condemn the Egyptian leadership in Zoan (Tanis) and the governmental counselors to the pharaoh. The prophet here apparently has in mind a specific political situation. Enough has been said about the overall political situation during this period (see above, chap. 1, sect. 2). The content of verses 11-15 becomes clearer when analyzed in the light of the particular politics of the Delta pharaohs. In 720, the last pharaoh of the XXIInd dynasty, Osorkon IV, was ruling in the eastern Delta, but the dynasty was only a shadow of its former greatness. The XXIInd dynasty, founded in the middle of the tenth century by Shoshenq I, the biblical Shishak (I Kings 14:25-26), had ruled in Egypt for over two centuries. The dynasty had supported the anti-Assyrian coalition organized to halt the westward movement of Shalmaneser III and had a token force at the battle of Qarqar in 853 (*ANET* 278-79; *TUAT* I 360-62). Presumably, this anti-Assyrian policy was continued by the dynasty. Similarly, the family of Tefnakht in Sais seems to have gone along with an anti-Assyrian attitude prior to 720 (see below, chap. 4, sect. 30). It was, therefore, probably Osorkon IV or Tefnakht to whom Hoshea appealed for help in 726. In 720, when Sargon arrived in the Gaza region, he was met by an Egyptian force (*ANET* 285; *TUAT* I 383), probably sent to the defense of Philistia by either Osorkon IV or Tefnakht. Thus as late as Sargon's invasion, Delta princes were continuing to support anti-Assyrian movements in Syria-Palestine. This international position, this anti-Assyrian posture, was obviously one of the examples of bad policy for which Isaiah criticized the Delta leaders. (Osorkon IV and Tefnakht were apparently won over to a pro-Assyrian attitude in 720. When Sargon was again in southern Syria-Palestine, in 716, he received a gift of horses from an Egyptian pharaoh, probably one of these two [*ANET* 286].)

A further factor in the policies of the Delta princes prior to 720 was their attitude toward the Ethiopians. Isaiah probably has this in mind also in his critique. When Piye invaded the north, in about 732, Osorkon IV capitulated rather quickly, much more quickly than Tefnakht in Sais, who finally, however, did submit (see *AEL* III 78-79). Thus in the intervening years, 732 to 720, the Delta leaders had gone along nominally with Ethiopian policies in the Delta. (When some of the Delta leaders moved to cooperate with Assyria after 720, this brought upon them the ire of the Ethiopians. When Shabako invaded the Delta in 713, Osorkon had already died, but Bocchoris, the successor to Tefnakht, was captured and burned alive [Manetho, fragments 66-68].)

Isaiah's denunciation of the Egyptian leaders chides them and their advisors for their lack of wisdom (vv. 11-13). Interestingly, the pharaohs of this period were recalled in later tradition as the wisest of Egyptian rulers. Bocchoris, apparently the son of Tefnakht, who ruled over Memphis (see v. 13) as well as a large portion of the rest of the Delta, was referred to by the later Greeks as Bocchoris the Wise (Diodorus I, 45.2). Reporting on the reputation of Bocchoris, Diodorus notes that he "in sagacity far surpassed all former kings" (I, 65.1) and that as a lawgiver "so wise was he in his judicial decisions as well [as in his general wisdom], that many of his judgments are remembered for their excellence even to our day" (I, 94.5). Isaiah, of course, held a contrary opinion.

A number of specific facts should be noted about verses 11-15. (a) The advice offered by court advisors is declared stupid and foolish, and the advisors should cease claiming a reputation based on appeals to the past (v. 11). (b) The wise men of Egypt cannot fathom "what Yahweh of hosts has planned for Egypt" (v. 12; see vv. 16-25). Here Isaiah indicates that he sees Sargon's new policies in the region as part of the purposes of Yahweh. (c) The leaders of Zoan and Memphis (which was probably under the authority of the family of Tefnakht at the time) are accused of leading Egypt astray—that is, of following bad policies (v. 13). (d) The cause of Egypt's confusion is said to be Yahweh, who "has infused into them a spirit that warps their judgment" (v. 14, NEB). This picks up on a theme of the Yahweh oracle in verses 2-4 and repeats the imagery of drunken leadership found in Isaiah's earlier condemnation of Ephraim (see 28:1-4). (e) The course of Egypt's future is said to be determined by Yahweh, not by the Egyptians (v. 15).

Isaiah 19:16-25

In verses 16-25, Isaiah offers five predictions about future conditions that will result from Yahweh's (and Sargon's) plans for the region. To what extent Isaiah may have made such predictions in hopes of recommending them as components of Assyrian policy in the area cannot be determined, but certainly should not be discounted—that is, he may have hoped that the Assyrians would transform his predictions into political realities.

First of all, in verses 16-17, Isaiah predicts that Egypt will cease being a dominant force in the area. In fact, the Egyptians will lose their macho attitude and become "like women," trembling with fear before Yahweh. Even the little land of Judah will be a terror to Egypt, and merely the mention of the name will bring fear. These new conditions would be the consequence of Yahweh's plan, which he had purposed concerning the Egyptians. One wonders if there was not some particular event that lay behind Isaiah's reference to the Egyptian fear of Judah in this text. One episode suggests itself as a possibility. As we have noted, after Sargon, in 720, subdued the rebel areas in the north (Hamath, Arvad, Simirra, Damascus, and Samaria), he moved south and was met by an Egyptian force in the Gaza area (*ANET* 285). In his account of this episode, Sargon puns on the nature of the affair and the Egyptian attitude. The Egyptian commander whose name or title is treated as meaning "shepherd" acted like one "whose flock had been stolen, he fled alone and disappeared." Judah, as a loyal vassal of Assyria at the time, may have supplied troops for this engagement of Sargon. If so, one can understand Isaiah's reference to the Egyptians' becoming like women before the hand of Yahweh and his statements that Judah would be a terror to the Egyptians and that the mere mention of Judah would bring fear to their hearts. Hezekiah's expansion in the southwest into territory formerly held by Egypt probably occurred at this time, and with Assyrian consent (see I Chron. 4:34-43).

Isaiah's second prediction (v. 18) is that there will be five cities in Egypt speaking the language of Canaan (Hebrew?) and swearing allegiance to Yahweh of hosts. (The final words in this text—"one of these will be called the City of the sun"—is probably a later gloss.) The reference to the cities in Egypt is probably to the existence of Judean trading colonies in the country. Part of Sargon's plan to make the Egyptians and Assyrians intermingle and trade may have involved a program of encouraging the establishment of such trading colonies. Judah, with its history of neutrality *vis à vis* Assyria, may have been given a special role in the new conditions in the area, or at least Isaiah hoped for or recommended such a Judean advantage. Under Hezekiah, a vigorous trade program was probably initiated with Egypt. In Sennacherib's list of the tribute received from Hezekiah, many items appear to have been of Egyptian origin—couches and chairs inlaid with ivory, elephant hides, ebony wood, and so on (see *ANET* 288).

Isaiah's third prediction (vv. 19-22) is the most complex in this unit. Five elements figure in the conditions of "that day." (a) There will be an altar to Yahweh in the midst of the land of Egypt that will serve as a sign and witness to Yahweh (vv. 19*a*, 20*a*). (b) There will be a pillar to Yahweh at the border of Egypt (v. 19*b*). (c) When the Egyptians cry out to Yahweh, he will send them a savior and defend and deliver them (v. 20*b*). (d) Yahweh will be acknowledged by the Egyptians, who will offer sacrifice and vows to him (v. 21). (e) Yahweh will both smite and heal Egypt when they turn to him (v. 22). All these factors are to be understood in the light of events associated with Sargon's actions following his 720 triumph.

(a) The Yahwistic altar in the land of Egypt, which will serve as a sign and witness—that is, as testimony—to Yahweh is probably to be associated with the trading colonies noted in verse 18. If Judeans were settled in Egypt, as verse 18 implies, the establishment of a cultic site there would certainly not be out of the question. Just as the Judean military colony at Elephantine, in a later period, had its temple (see *ANET* 491-92), so also would Judeans in Egypt at this time have possessed a cultic place. Even if the Deuteronomic law of a single cultic place in the land (Deut. 12) had been promulgated by the time of Isaiah, the existence of an altar in Egypt—that is, outside the land—would not have been considered heretical.

(b) The reference to a pillar (*maṣṣebah*) to Yahweh on the border of Egypt probably has the following circumstances as its background: The traditional northern border of Egypt had been the Wadi Besor, the Brook of Egypt, which flowed into the Mediterranean Sea just south of Gaza. Here Tiglath-pileser had set up a stela in 734, claiming that Assyrian dominance extended to that area. In Sargon's clarification of matters in the region after his defeat of Hanunu of Gaza and his destruction of the city of Raphia in 720, Hezekiah's territory was extended to include some of the area between Wadi Besor (just south of Gaza) and Wadi el-Arish (about forty-five miles south of Gaza). First Chronicles 4:34-43 reports Hezekiah's occupation of this area and his suppression of the Meunites and Amalekites in the region, probably with Sargon's permission, if not with Assyrian help. The *maṣṣebah* referred to would have been an inscribed stela set up as evidence of Hezekiah's claim to this region (see the reference to Saul's setting up a similar marker in Carmel; I Sam. 15:12).

(c) The savior whom Yahweh "will send" to redeem the Egyptians (from the Ethiopians) is, of course, Sargon. What Isaiah here alludes to is the Sargonid policy of cooperation with the Delta princes and the "new age" envisioned as a consequence of the new conditions. Just as Adad-nirari III had been hailed as a "savior of Israel" following his attack on the Syrian oppressor of Israel (see II Kings 13:5), so also Isaiah hailed Sargon as Egypt's redeemer. For Isaiah, the work of Sargon was the work of Yahweh.

(d) The references to the Egyptians' knowing Yahweh and participating in Yahwistic sacrifice may simply be a prophetic prediction or expectation influenced by the new Sargonid policies. On the other hand, it may reflect some specific occurrence that took place in working out new relationships in the area. If the Egyptians and Judeans entered into trade agreements and some form of political alliance, then the ceremonies involved may have included mutual oath rituals and the offering of sacrifices (see Isa. 30:1).

(e) The final element in this section is more general than the other predictions. What Isaiah had in mind in the smiting and healing of Egypt is not spelled out and could simply be a prophetic way of declaring that Egypt is under Yahweh's sway. "Smiting" and "healing" may employ a set of opposites to indicate inclusiveness, namely that Yahweh will take action against Egypt.

The fourth section in this unit of predictions is verse 23. In this verse, the prophet moves beyond the present to an idealized future, although the imagery builds on the new state of affairs under Sargonid policy. The vision conceives of a future characterized by intense commerce and communication between Egypt and Assyria. In this new arrangement, the Egyptians will work with (not "worship with" as in the RSV) the Assyrians.

In the final prediction, Isaiah sees Israel as the third power in the world, along with Egypt and Assyria. As such, Israel will be a blessing in the midst of the earth. Israel, along with Assyria and Egypt, will be the blessed of Yahweh. In this text, Isaiah obviously has been caught up in the ecumenical euphoria of his day and is dreaming big dreams for Israel. The Israel he is talking about was no doubt conceived as an Israel encompassing north and south, something comparable to the idealized version of the age of David and Solomon, a united land under Davidic rule. The ambitions and expansive national policies of Hezekiah (see above, chap. 1, sect. 3E) no doubt drew on such dreams of the future. This expectation of Isaiah, however, does not differ greatly from Isaiah's earlier promise to Ahaz, which foresaw a return to Davidic-Solomonic conditions (see 7:17). As we shall see later, Isaiah clung to these expectations (see 27:12-13), and Hezekiah hoped to achieve them in his own day.

22. A PROPHETIC DEMONSTRATION (20:1-6)

L. **Bonner**, "Rethinking Isaiah 20," *OTWSA* 22-23(1979-80)32-52; G. **Fohrer**, *Die symbolischen Handlungen der Propheten* (Zurich: Zwingli-Verlag, 1953); P. **Kleinert**, "Bemerkungen zu Jes. 20-22 und 2 Kön. 18-20," *TSK* 50(1877)167-80; B. **Lang**, "Prophecy, Symbolic Acts, and Politics: A Review of Recent Studies," in his *Monotheism and the Prophetic Minority: An Essay in Biblical History and Sociology* (Sheffield: Almond Press, 1983)83-91; G. L. **Mattingly**, "An Archaeological Analysis of Sargon's 712 Campaign Against Ashdod," *NEASB* 17(1981)47-64; A. **Spalinger**, "The Year 712 B. C. and its Implications for Egyptian History," *JARCE* 10(1973)95-101; H. **Tadmor**, "The Campaigns of Sargon II of Assur: A Chronological Historical Study," *JCS* 12(1958)22-40, 77-100; **Tadmor**, "Philistia Under Assyrian Rule," *BA* 29(1966)86-102; E. M. **Wright**, "The Eighth Campaign of Sargon II of Assyria (714 B.C.)," *JNES* 2(1943)173-86.

The ideal conditions that Isaiah had anticipated and advocated as a consequence of the new Assyrian-Egyptian relations did not materialize. That Israel/Judah should be the third great power in the world, along with Assyria and Egypt, had not come about. When anti-Assyrian fervor, led by Ashdod, later resurfaced in the area, Judah, in spite of Isaiah's protests, became involved. Chapter 20 is a prophetic narrative that reports the radical steps Isaiah took to get across his position.

In order to appreciate the historical context of Isaiah's public demonstration against Judah's participation in anti-Assyrian activity, we need to note Sargon's statements in regard to the course of events. Over a period of time, Ashdod displayed opposition to Assyria and sought to gain support for a major move against Sargon. No doubt Ashdod had suffered economically from Assyria's dominance over commerce in the area. Prior to taking overt military action against the budding rebellion, Sargon sought to defuse matters by changing the leadership in Ashdod. The following is his account.

Azuri, king of Ashdod, planned in his heart not to pay tribute, and sent messages to the kings round about him, filled with hatred of Assyria. Because of the evil which he had done, I did away with his rule over the people of his land; Ahimiti, his full brother, I set up as king over them. The Hittites, plotters of iniquity, hated his rule and elevated to reign over them Yamani without claim to the throne, who like themselves did not know fear of my sovereignty. (*ARAB* II § 62)

Several factors in Sargon's activity should be noted. (a) The opposition to Assyrian rule was a popular movement among the Philistines. (b) Since the king of Ashdod, Azuri, had gone along with popular sentiment and had sought to enlist other states in the move, he was deposed. (c) The new king, Ahimiti, obviously in favor of a policy of continued submission to Assyria, was unable to hold the throne. (d) Ahimiti was deposed by his own people, and Yamani was placed on the throne to carry through a policy of opposition to Assyria. (e) The entire sequence of events, beginning with the initial stages under Azuri and ending with the capture of Ashdod, must have stretched over several months or even a few years. The revolt may have been inaugurated as early as 715/14. Sargon put down the revolt in 712/11.

Ashdod's movement against the Assyrians must have been following a policy encouraged by other states. Sargon does not tell us who these states were. Tyre, who had retained its independence and influence, seems a likely candidate. Anatolian kingdoms, Midas of Phrygia, and even the Greeks, who were becoming more dominant in the Mediterranean at the time, were probably involved. The Chaldean ruler, Merodach-baladan (see Isa. 39), who had seized the throne of Babylon in 722, was moving to take the offensive against Sargon. Probably the visit of his ambassadors to Jerusalem to encourage revolt was part of the background to the Ashdod-led rebellion (see below, chap. 4, sects. 23 and 36). When the revolt was being planned, Sargon, himself, was leading a major campaign against King Rusa (about 734–714) of Urartu in the mountainous regions around Lake Urmia. The time seemed opportune.

Eventually, several powers in southern Syria-Palestine became involved in the anti-Assyrian movement. The damaged Nineveh Prism A of Sargon mentions the lands of Philistia, Judah, Edom, Moab, and those who dwell on the islands as participants (*ANET* 287; *ARAB* II §§ 193-95; *TUAT* I 381-82). This group then appealed to an Egyptian pharaoh for help. In 713/12, Egypt was undergoing radical political changes. The Ethiopian pharaoh, Piye, had died and was succeeded by his brother, Shabako, who quickly invaded the Delta and brought to heel the Egyptian princes. By 712, Shabako seems to have been thoroughly in command of Lower Egypt.

When Assyrian troops finally campaigned against Ashdod, they encountered little resistance in the area. Yamani fled to Egypt but was afforded no refuge. Even the Ethiopians, at this time, were unwilling to aid the anti-Assyrian monarch:

The king of Ethiopia . . . whose fathers since the far-off days of the moon-god's time, had not sent messengers to the kings my fathers, to bring their greetings,—(that Ethiopian king) heard from afar of the might of Assur, Nabu, and Marduk and the terrifying splendor of my royalty overpowered him and fright overcame him, in fetters, shackles and bonds of iron, he cast him [Yamani] and they brought him before me into Assyria, after a most difficult journey. (*ARAB* II § 63; see *ANET* 286)

The Assyrian troops captured the Philistine cities of Ashdod, Ashdod-by-the-sea, and Gath and perhaps Judean towns in the Shephelah. Sargon claims to have annexed the Ashdod region. He describes the action taken as: "I reorganized their cities and placed an officer of mine as governor over them and declared them Assyrian citizens and they bore my yoke" (*ANET* 286; *ARAB* II § 62). Since a later king of Ashdod appears in Assyrian texts, Sargon seems not to have provincialized the area but to have placed special forces in the region and garrisons in some of the cities and to have appointed a high-level official over southern Palestine.

While in the Palestinian region, Assyrian forces certainly took action against Judah, as we shall see in discussing Isaiah 22:1-14. At the time, a special set of circumstances seems to have existed in Judah. Hezekiah's life-threatening sickness, associated with his fourteenth year (see Isa. 36:1; 38:1 and, below, chap. 4, sect. 34), rendered the king incapable of fully administering his kingdom. His fourteenth year was probably 713/12 and thus he was perhaps ill throughout much of the crisis. Several factors in this situation should be noted and will be discussed more fully in relation to chapter 22. (1) Shebna probably functioned, in his capacity as "over the household," as acting monarch during the period. (2) He and other leaders, along with widespread popular support, pulled Judah into limited cooperation in the revolt. Thus as at Ashdod a popular movement over against the reigning monarch fostered the rebellion. (3) Shebna carried out the project of constructing the Siloam tunnel. (4) Isaiah's drastic demonstrations, described in this chapter, were probably conditioned by the circumstances of the time. With a king temporarily out of power, possibly even quarantined, a popular movement underway, and governmental officials unsympathetic to his cause, Isaiah took to the streets.

Isaiah 20 is a prophetic narrative, telling how Isaiah had opposed the rebellion and had demonstrated against it and the participants' expectation that Egypt and the Ethiopians would aid them in their cause. The narrative contains no direct address by Isaiah. It does report, in the form of two divine oracles, that Isaiah's actions were carried out at Yahweh's command and that these actions symbolized the fate of the Egyptians and the Ethiopians.

This prophetic narrative was formulated by circles sympathetic to Isaiah and thus presumably opposed to the 713–711 revolt. The story was told to demonstrate that Isaiah had been right in his assessment of the situation. It is surprising that the narrative, unlike Isaiah 7, has not preserved any direct statements of the prophet, himself. The first divine oracle (v. 2) is presented as an explanation of why Isaiah did what he did and the second (vv. 3-6) as a summary of what he declared to be the import of his walking around Jerusalem naked or only partially clothed.

If verse 2 were omitted from the text, the passage would be grammatically smoother. This verse has been introduced into the text as confirmation that Isaiah's actions were divinely motivated. The divine oracle in verses 3-6 grammatically continues the chronological note in verse 1. This oracle, however, may have been given its final formulation under the influence of Sennacherib's campaign in 701, when Ethiopian and Egyptian troops were captured and exiled by the Assyrians. Therefore, we may have in chapter 20 a narrative like those in Isaiah 38–39, which has been shaped by the events of 701. In the case of chapter 20, however, the events were so anchored to a particular historical context that the story retained its original setting.

One can imagine that behind this narrative about Isaiah lie the following circumstances. In order to oppose Judean participation in the Ashdod affair, Isaiah publicly demonstrated by removing his sackcloth dress and walking around Jerusalem only partially clothed or naked—that is, he dressed as one might be when carried away captive. (That Isaiah removed the sackcloth he is wearing could suggest that sackcloth was the typical attire of a prophet or, more likely, that Isaiah was already publicly mourning the turn of events before he resorted to a more drastic display of opposition.) Isaiah justified his actions by appealing to divine sanction—he was ordered by Yahweh to perform his deeds. Isaiah's dress, or lack thereof, was to illustrate the coming deportation. In its present form, the oracle in verses 3-6 uses Isaiah's "dress" to illustrate the deportation of Ethiopians and Egyptians. This may have been how Isaiah originally interpreted his behavior. It would make more sense, however, if Isaiah were acting out how his own people and the other local supporters of the revolt would be carried into exile, rather than those whom they hoped might assist them. No Ethiopian/Egyptian force seems to have been involved in the 713–711 rebellion, although some Ethiopians and Egyptians may have been in the area as special emissaries. In 701, the situation was quite different.

23. THE ORACLE ON THE SEALAND (21:1-17)

W. E. **Barnes**, "A Fresh Interpretation of Isaiah XXI 1-10," *JTS* 1(1900)583-92; C. **Boutflower**, "Isaiah XXI in the Light of Assyrian History," *JTS* 14(1913)501-15; J. A. **Brinkman**, "Merodach-Baladan II," *Studies Presented to A. Leo Oppenheim* (ed. R. D. Biggs and J. A. Brinkman; Chicago: Oriental Institute, 1964)6-53; **Brinkman**, "Elamite Military Aid to

Merodach-baladan II," *JNES* 24(1965)161-66; F. **Buhl**, "Jesaja 21:6-10," *ZAW* 8(1888)157-64; W. H. **Cobb**, "Isaiah XXI 1-10 Reëxamined," *JBL* 17(1898)40-61; P. **Dhorme**, "Le desert de la mer (Isaïe, XXI)," *RB* 31(1922)403-6; I. **Eph`al**, *The Ancient Arabs: Nomads on the Borders of the Fertile Crescent 9th-5th Centuries* B.C. (Jerusalem/Leiden: Magnes Press/E. J. Brill, 1982); K. **Galling**, "Jes. 21 im Lichte der neuen Nabonid-texte," *Tradition und Situation* (Festschrift A. Weiser; ed. E. Würthwein and O. Kaiser; Göttingen: Vandenhoeck & Ruprecht, 1963)49-62; P. **Lohmann**, "Das Wächterlied Jes 21, 11-12," *ZAW* 33(1913)20-29; **Lohmann**, "Zur strophischen Gliederung von Jes 21, 1-10," *ZAW* 33(1913)262-64; A. A. **Macintosh**, *Isaiah XXI: A Palimpsest* (Cambridge: Cambridge University Press, 1980); E. **Sievers**, "Zum Jesaja 21:1-10," *Vom Alten Testament* (Festschrift K. Marti; Giessen: Alfred Töpelmann, 1925)262-65.

The years 714 and following saw Sargon and the Assyrian forces battling on several fronts. (In *ARAB* II §§ 42 and 71, Sargon mentions conducting simultaneous campaigns in various areas.) One area of conflict was eastern Anatolia, the northwestern frontier of the empire. In this region, the legendary King Midas of Phrygia had organized opposition for some time. The Phrygian king had gained allies as far south as Carchemish, which Sargon had moved to subdue and provincialize in 717 (*ARAB* II § 8). Beginning in 715, Sargon took the offensive against rebellious states in eastern Anatolia, recapturing several towns in Que, which had been taken by Midas. In 713, a major campaign was conducted against Tabal and, in 711, against towns on the borders of Phrygia and Urartu.

A second front was against persistent Urartu to the north of Assyria proper. Eventually, in 714, Sargon led a major and dangerous campaign against the Urartians, who had plagued Assyria for over a century. Several Urartian strongholds were levelled, and the countryside was looted and burned (*ARAB* II §§ 19-22; 140-78). A third front was created by the anti-Assyrian coalition in southern Syria-Palestine, which we noted in discussing Isaiah 20.

The fourth front was against Aramean and Chaldean tribes in southern Mesopotamia and adjacent areas. In his annals,

Sargon moves, as does Isaiah 20–21, from speaking of the battle against Ashdod (*ARAB* II § 30) to describing his struggles against the Aramean and Chaldean tribes in general and against Marduk-apal-iddina (Merodach-baladan) in particular (*ARAB* II §§ 31 following). The Babylonian Chronicles inform us that the Chaldean chieftain, Merodach-baladan, had seized the throne of Babylon shortly after the death of Shalmaneser V (*ABC* 73). He became king in Babylon almost simultaneous to Sargon's accession to the throne in Assyria. The Babylonian Chronicles report that "from the accession year of Merodach-baladan until the tenth year, [Assyria or Sargon] was belligerent towards Merodach-baladan" (*ABC* 75).

In about 713/12, Merodach-baladan went on the offensive against Assyria. (The visit of his ambassadors to Jerusalem, reported in Isaiah 39/II Kings 20:12-19, probably preceded this action.) The Babylonian Chronicles note this offensive; unfortunately, the text is broken: "The tenth year [712]: Merodach-baladan ravaged . . . and plundered it" (*ABC* 75). Sargon describes matters from the Assyrian point of view:

Merodach-baladan, son of Iakin, king of Chaldea, seed of a murderer, prop of a wicked devil, who did not fear the lord of lords, put his trust in the Bitter Sea, with its tossing waves, violated the oath of the great gods and withheld his gifts. Humbanigash, the Elamite [here Sargon errs since this ruler had died in 717; see *ABC* 74], he brought to his aid and all of the Sutu, desert folk, he caused to revolt against me; he prepared for battle and made straight for Sumer and Akkad. Twelve years [here Sargon jumps ahead to the outcome of the struggle] he ruled and governed Babylon, the city of the lord of the gods, against the will of the gods. (*ARAB* II § 66)

Sargon details his attack against Merodach-baladan and his allies, the flight of Merodach-baladan, and the Assyrian capture of Babylon and other cities (*ARAB* II §§ 31-41, 66-69). Eventually, in 709, Sargon assumed the throne in Babylon.

Into Babylon, the city of the lord of the gods, joyfully I entered, in gladness of heart, and with a beaming countenance. I grasped the hands of the great lord Marduk, and make the pilgrimage to the "house of the New Year's Feast" (*ARAB* II § 70).

Even after the takeover of Babylon, efforts to subdue the Aramean tribes continued for some time.

Isaiah's speeches, or pronouncements, on "the wilderness of the sea" (probably a reference to what the Assyrians called *mat tam-tim*, "the Sealand" or Lower Mesopotamia) and Dumah and Arabia have Sargon's attack on southern Mesopotamia and Merodach-baladan and his allies as their background. The interest in Babylon by the prophet was based on the fact that Babylon (Merodach-baladan) had enticed Judah to participate in anti-Assyrian action over Isaiah's protests only shortly before. The announced fall of Babylon was confirmation of Isaiah's position.

The following is an outline of the chapter's contents:

(1) A description of the attack on the south (1*b*)
(2) The prophet's vision of the affair (2-5)
(3) A Yahweh oracle (6-7)
(4) The watchman's report (8-9)
(5) Conclusion (10)
(6) Oracles on Dumah, Arabia, and Kedar (11-17)

Isaiah 21:1b

The prophet opens with a comparison of the viciousness of the attack on the Sealand to a whirlwind from the desert. Sargon describes this move, perhaps long prepared for, in the following fashion: "At the command of Assur, father of the gods, and the great lord Marduk I made ready my chariot, set my camp in order and gave the word to advance against the Chaldean, the treachous enemy" (*ARAB* II § 66).

Isaiah 21:2-5

In verses 2-5, Isaiah describes the vision he has seen (v. 2), his reaction to the scene (vv. 3-4), and the fate of those attacked (v. 5). The vision takes the form of a divine oracle, consisting of three lines. The first portrays the plunderer/destroyer (Sargon) at work. The second calls upon Elam and Media to join the attack—probably a reference to troops from regions dominated by the Assyrians who had been commandeered into the Assyrian army. The third has Yahweh announce that he has brought an end to the sighing in the southland. Interestingly, Sargon also described his campaign as relieving the suffering and injustice of Chaldean and Aramean oppression: "The people of Sippar, Nippur, Babylon, Borsippa, who were imprisoned therein through no fault of theirs,—I broke their bonds and caused them to behold the light. Their fields, which since days of old, during the anarchy in the land, the Sutu had seized, I returned to them" (*ARAB* II § 40).

Isaiah describes his reaction in the typical terms used to speak of one's response to bad news or a dreadful situation (vv. 3-4). Whether the prophet here speaks in empathetic or sarcastic tones is not completely clear. Given his opposition to the anti-Assyrian movements of the time and Merodach-baladan's role, the latter was probably the case.

The people being attacked are described as going on about their normal routines until the enemy is upon them (v. 5). Here Isaiah, perhaps, draws on a widespread pattern of speaking about the overthrow of the enemy: They feast before they fall (see Dan. 5). The celebration is shattered by the call to arms.

Isaiah 21:6-7

The oracle of Yahweh (vv. 6-7) orders that a watchman be posted to pick up some word of the progress and outcome of the battle from travelers from the region. Isaiah here depicts himself as either the watchman or the one to whom the sentry reports.

Isaiah 21:8-9

Isaiah has his imaginary sentry (or himself as sentry) express his faithfulness at the task (v. 8) and ultimately report the word that arrives: "Fallen, fallen is Babylon, and all the images of her gods are shattered to the ground."

Isaiah 21:10

Isaiah closes his prophetic presentation on the Assyrian attack by declaring to his audience that his message is from

God; he has announced only what he has heard (v. 10). The Judean population, recently threshed and winnowed by Sargon's troops (see below, chap. 4, sect. 24) and hoping against hope that Sargon would fail and Merodach-baladan be victorious, is told what will happen. The watchman can only bear the news of what he sees and hears, disappointing as it may be.

Isaiah 21:11-17

The oracles on Dumah (vv. 11-12), Arabia (vv. 13-15), and Kedar (16) all refer to regions and groups in the Arabian Desert, stretching from Sinai to Babylonia. At the time of Merodach-baladan's aggressive expansion, numerous Chaldean tribes in Lower Mesopotamia, south of Babylon, and Aramean tribes in the desert south and west of Mesopotamia were in league with him. Sargon refers to many of these tribal groups in describing his southern campaign, but none of the names in Isaiah 21:11-17 appears in his inscriptions. In the next century, references to Arabia and Kedar become common in Assyrian inscriptions.

In the oracle on Dumah, a desert oasis (see Gen. 25:14), the question and answer seem to imply that no clear perception of events can be expected for a while. Or perhaps the sense is that Dumah should not expect good times ("morning") to come, since bad times ("night") are not yet past.

The oracle on Arabia plays on the theme of military danger and flight from battle. Caravans must guard their whereabouts, and fugitives, overcome with hunger and thirst, must be cared for as they make their way to the oases, fleeing the weapons of battle.

Finally, Isaiah issues a prediction over Kedar, which, like Arabia, may have been an inclusive term for much of the Arabian desert. The prediction, formulated as a divine oracle, declares that Kedar, after a long, burdensome year, will lose its glory, and its warriors will practically cease to exist—that is, within a year, Sargon and the Assyrians will have completed their job of suppressing revolt in the Sealand and the adjacent desert regions.

24. HE TOOK AWAY THE COVERING OF JUDAH
(22:1-14)

R. **Amiran**, "The Water Supply of Israelite Jerusalem," *Jerusalem Revealed: Archaeology in the Holy City 1968-1974* (ed. Y. Yadin: Jerusalem/New Haven: Israel Exploration Society/ Yale University Press, 1976)75-78; M. **Broshi**, "The Expansion of Jerusalem in the Reigns of Hezekiah and Manasseh," *IEJ* 24(1974)21-26; G. R. **Driver**, "Isaiah I-XXXIX: Textual and Linguistic Problems," *JSS* 13(1968)36-57; J. A. **Emerton**, "Notes on the Text and Translation of Isaiah xxii 8-11 and lxv 5," *VT* 30(1980)437-51; A. J. **Everson**, "The Days of Yahweh," *JBL* 93(1974)329-37; A. D. **Tushingham**, "The Western Hill under the Monarchy," *ZDPV* 95(1979)39-55; J. **Wilkinson**, "Ancient Jerusalem: Its Water Supply and Population," *PEQ* 106(1974)33-51.

This speech belongs to the occasion of celebration in Jerusalem, following the departure of the Assyrian Army from southern Palestine in 711, after Sargon's forces had captured Ashdod and Gath and dissipated the anti-Assyrian coalition. The speech indicates that some Assyrian action was taken against Judah but that the country escaped without major damage. Since Isaiah had opposed any participation in this revolt against Assyria (see chapter 20), he now castigates the people for their involvement.

The oracles against Shebna and Eliakim (22:15-25), although separate speeches and probably dating from a slightly later time, belong to the same general historical context as 22:1-14. The following circumstances seem indicated by these speeches when viewed in the light of their larger chronological and historical setting.

First, Hezekiah's sickness, which tradition associates with his fourteenth year (Isa. 36:1; 38), would have plagued him about the time of the planning and execution of this anti-Assyrian movement—that is, about 713–712. Hezekiah's illness must have been extremely severe, since there was concern for his life, and may have involved isolation, as in the case of Uzziah. Second, during the king's illness, Shebna seems to have assumed control over the administration of the state. In 22:15, Shebna is referred to as "the one over the household" (Lord Chamberlain), the same position held by Jotham during the illness of his father, King Uzziah (II Kings 15:5). Hezekiah apparently had no son to whom he could turn over the reins of government as had Uzziah. Hezekiah's son and successor, Manasseh, became king in 697 at the age of twelve; therefore, he was born in about 709. Third, it was Shebna and his associates, rather than Hezekiah, who ventured to participate in the revolt in spite of Isaiah's drastic warning (see Isa. 20). Fourth, the Siloam tunnel was apparently excavated during Shebna's leadership. If 22:11*b* refers to Hezekiah, then the tunnel whose construction he had planned was built without his consultation. (It is interesting to note that in Sargon's description of Ashdod's actions at the time, reference is also made to the construction of a moat or tunnel so that "20 cubits down they reached the nether waters"; *ARAB* II § 195, *ANET* 287.) The inscription carved in the wall of the Siloam tunnel makes no reference to the king, which would be surprising if Hezekiah oversaw its construction but not if Shebna supervised the work. (The inscription, however, is fragmentary and, therefore, its full text is unknown.) Fifth, after the debacle of the revolution and Hezeiah's recovery, Shebna was demoted from his post as chamberlain, although he remained a high official (Isa. 36:3). In his speech denouncing Shebna, Isaiah seems to have recommended far more drastic measures.

The absence of any reference in Assyrian texts to military action against Judah in 712/11 is a bit surprising. Sargon clearly mentions Judah's association with the rebel city Ashdod (*ARAB II* § 195; *ANET* 287) but says nothing about Judah in describing the suppression of the revolt. In his inscription set up to commemorate the restoration of Ashur-nasir-pal's palace, Sargon does refer to himself as "subduer of the land of Judah, which lies far away" (*ARAB* II § 137; *ANET* 287). It is doubtful that this refers to any action against Judah taken in 712/11, since this inscription mentions Judah just before noting the capture of Hamath in 720. The text also treats the capture of Carchemish (717) as if it were Sargon's latest triumph, thus indicating a pre-712 date for the text. At any rate, to speak of himself as "subduer of Judah" may mean nothing more than that Judah was his vassal. (In fact, "Judah" here may be the north Syrian region of Yaudi.)

Sargon may have failed to mention action against Judah in 712/11, since what occurred was only a minor skirmish and Judah was a secondary participant, rather than a ringleader in the revolt. (No mention is made of action against Moab, Edom, or other participants either.)

The title for this speech, traditionally translated "Valley of Vision," is derived from verse 5 and represents the annotation made on a copy of the speech for identification purposes. "Valley of Vision" is a rather peculiar expression with regard to the content of this speech. The address is, first of all, almost entirely concerned with past events. Second, the events described recall Judah's defeat at the hands of the Assyrians in 712/11 as a consequence of their participation in the Ashdod-led revolt. Two other options instead of "vision" could make sense in this context. First, Isaiah may have been referring here to an actual geographical site, an actual valley in which a military encounter occurred. Unfortunately, we know of no valley bearing such a name. Second, the Hebrew noun *ḥizzayon* may be better translated here as "calamity" rather than "vision." An Arabic cognate has this same meaning, and the Hebrew verb *ḥeza* may have a similar sense in Job 34:32. The heading in 29:1 might then read, "the oracle on the valley of calamity."

If Isaiah does here use the term *vision*, then he may have employed the term sarcastically. The leadership of Jerusalem had dreamed their great "vision" of freeing themselves from Assyrian domination. In rallying their support, and in countering Isaiah's position against the revolt, they may have spoken of this "vision." After their calamitous debacle, Isaiah chides the leadership, mocking their great expectations, which now lie in ruins around them.

The address may be divided into the following sections:

(1) A denunciation of the city's celebration of its survival (1b-4)
(2) A description of the past day of Yahweh (5-8a)
(3) A second description of the past day (8b-11)
(4) A third description of the past day (12–13)
(5) The verdict of Yahweh (14)

Isaiah 22:1b-4

Isaiah opens his address with a denunciation of the behavior of the people (1b-2a). Jerusalem's population had been celebrating and shouting, no doubt as the main Assyrian force withdrew from the area to join Sargon's attack on the Sealand. The recent events, Isaiah says, certainly did not warrant celebration, but the opposite (see vv. 12-13). The prophet's description of what happened, in verses 2b-3, has been translated in various ways, but all the translations agree that whatever happened, the episode was a shameful affair. If one assumes that the verb '*sr* in this text means "to huddle together," one gets the following translation:

2b. Your slaughtered ones were not slaughtered by the sword,
     they were not war casualties.
3. All your leaders fled together,
     out of bow-shot they huddled;
   all of your captured ones had huddled together,
     they had fled far away [from the field of battle].

This passage suggests the following about the Assyrian encounter with the Judeans: (1) The Judean military commanders abandoned the field of battle when the Assyrians attacked. (2) They fled together, huddling out of danger, to save their lives. (3) When the "battle" was over, some of those Judean leaders were captured and executed.

Without the leadership of their king and with opinions divided over the feasibility of revolt, Judean society seems to have been torn into factions. The army that had taken the field had little heart for battle, and its commanders had even less courage.

Isaiah declares that this explains his attitude after the calamity (v. 4). He had wanted, as he told the people, only to be left alone to weep and mourn over the absurd disaster that had befallen the people and the city of Jerusalem.

Isaiah 22:5-8a

In verses 5-8a, Isaiah describes the past day of Yahweh, the day when the Assyrians moved against Judah. It was a day of

"tumult and trampling and trauma in the valley of calamity."
The air was filled with the cries of battle. Troops from Elam
and Kir in the army of Sargon led the assault. Chariots spread
out through the valleys, and horsemen moved into the gates
of Judean cities.

For Isaiah, the saddest and most devastating blow of all
was not the humiliation in battle. It was the consequence of
the people's participation in revolt: "He has taken away the
covering of Judah" (v. 8a). Judah had never before been
treated by the Assyrians as a hostile power (see 18:7). In the
734–32 wars, Judah had remained loyal to Assyria. In
728–722, Judean leaders had given only token aid at the most
to Ephraim's cause, but either it was not sufficient to warrant
Assyrian reprisal or else Shalmaneser had been unable to
move against Judah because of his involvement on so many
fronts. Under Sargon, Judah had received preferential
treatment (see above, chap. 4, sect. 21). Now that was all over
and Judah's special status was gone. Sargon took away
Judah's covering, its exemption from normal treatment.
Although Isaiah does not spell out the full details of Judah's
new status, it undoubtedly involved a new phase of close
supervision and the establishment of an Assyrian citadel and
force in Jerusalem (see 28:19 and, below, chap. 4, sect. 27).

Isaiah 22:8b-11

In verses 8b-11, Isaiah provides another review of past
events. This time he summarizes the efforts carried out in
Jerusalem in preparation for the revolt against Assyria. A
number of the leaders' activities are noted. (a) They "trusted"
(nbṭ) in the weapons of the House of the Forest (v. 8b).
Isaiah's charge here is probably two-pronged. First of all, the
leaders did not trust in Yahweh, whom Isaiah had said all
along had his plans and purposes for Assyria. Second, the
leaders had apparently taken over the royal arsenal and its
military supplies. The House of the Forest had been
constructed by Solomon (I Kings 7:2-5; 10:17), and, during
the illness of Hezekiah, the rebels in Jerusalem had used its
armaments without royal sanction. (b) Weak places and
breaches in the city of David, the royal palace complex, had
been repaired (v. 9a), probably with the idea that it could

serve as a last bastion of defense if needed. Such encroachments on royal terrain no doubt infuriated Isaiah, being the loyal royalist he was. (c) Some type of work was done on the lower pool, probably to be identified with the modern *birket el-hamra*, which lies just over two hundred yards below the modern pool of Siloam. The reference to "collecting the waters" of this pool may mean either that it was dammed up to increase the available water supply for the city and the increase of soldiers and horses in the vicinity or that it was obstructed as a result of the construction noted in verse 11 (v. 9*b*). (d) Houses in Jerusalem were demolished to provide an immediate supply of stones for strengthening the city walls (v. 10). Again, Isaiah's condemnation was probably based not only on his opposition to the rebellion, but also on other factors. The demolition of houses would have left some citizens of Jerusalem homeless, forcing them to abandon the sacred city. For the prophet, the right to reside in Jerusalem was a unique honor and having the opportunity to live within its walls was almost a religious privilege (see 4:2). In addition to his opposition to the displacement of Jerusalemites, Isaiah would have opposed the leaders' usurpation of royal prerogatives with regard to the holy city. The reigning Davidic monarch was responsible for the welfare of the town's citizens. If the entire city of Jerusalem was crown property, the demolition of houses without royal sanction would have been a serious matter. (e) The construction of a resevoir between the two walls for the waters of the old pool (v. 11*a*) probably refers to the construction of the Siloam tunnel, which brought water from the Spring of Gihon under the city of Jerusalem to the pool of Siloam. The two walls noted in verse 11*a* refer to the old wall of the city and a secondary city wall built to enclose the expansion of the city to the west.

Isaiah concludes his enumeration of the misdeeds of the Judean leaders with the comment that they "did not look to (*nbṭ*) him who had planned it; or have regard for the one who had purposed it long ago" (v. 11*b*). Two main options for interpreting this passage are possible. First, the leaders are condemned for prematurely carrying out a rebellion against Assyria, which Yahweh had planned all along. Second, the leaders are condemned for having constructed the tunnel under the city without consulting Hezekiah, who had planned the project earlier. Given the literary context (all the actions condemned by Isaiah in 8b-11a represent the leaders' presumptive encroachment on royal prerogatives) and the historical conditions (Hezekiah's incapacity), the latter alternative is preferable.

Isaiah 22:12-13

In verses 12-13, Isaiah returns to the issue of the celebration of the city noted in verses 1b-2. When the main Assyrian force withdrew, Jerusalem rejoiced. Isaiah declares that what "that day" needed and what Yahweh had called for was not celebration but exactly the opposite. The people should have lamented with weeping and mourning and by shaving their heads and wearing sackcloth. Instead there was a festival atmosphere, an "eat, drink, and be merry for tomorrow you die" attitude. Oxen and sheep were slaughtered; feasting and drinking were the orders of the day.

Isaiah 22:14

Isaiah concludes his caustic address with a divine oracle, which he claims Yahweh revealed to him in his ear (v. 14). The divine word is given in oath form: "This iniquity of yours will not be purged until you are dead" (see below, on 27:8-9, pp. 317-18).

25. TWO OFFICIALS CONDEMNED (22:15-25)

N. **Avigad**, "The Epitaph of a Royal Steward from Siloam Village," *IEJ* 3(1953)137-52; K. **Fullerton**, "A New Chapter out of the Life of Isaiah," *AJT* 9(1905)621-42; A. **Kamphausen**, "Isaiah's Prophecy Concerning the Major-Domo of King Hezekiah," *AJT* 5(1901)43-74; H. J. **Katzenstein**, "The Royal Steward (Asher `al ha-Bayith)," *IEJ* 10(1960)149-54, E. **König**, "Shebna and Eliakim," *AJT* 10(1906)675-86; R. **Martin-Achard**, "L'oracle contre Shebna et le pouvoir des clefs, Es. 22, 15-25" *TZ* 24(1968)241-54; T. N. D. **Mettinger**, *Solomonic State Officials: A Study of the Civil Government Officials of the Israelite Monarchy* (Lund: CWK Gleerup, 1971)70-110.

Isaiah 22:15-25 has its setting in the aftermath of the events denounced in 22:1-14. The movement to participate in the revolt, without the support or leadership of King Hezekiah, had seriously divided Judean society. Isaiah had opposed this turn of events and engaged in public demonstration on behalf of his position. The Judean army, and especially its commanders, had only half-heartedly fought against the Assyrians, and, in fact, many had fled the field of battle (22:3). The revolt, of little military consequence for Judah and Assyria, had nonetheless ended Judah's special treatment at the hands of the Assyrians (22:8*a*).

With the "war" over, Isaiah turned on the Judean leaders, especially Shebna, one of the revolt's ringleaders and the "acting monarch" during Hezekiah's incapacitation. After the conflict, Shebna had been removed fron his old office and replaced as "the one over the household" by Eliakim. Shebna retained the position of secretary (see Isa. 36:3). For Isaiah, Eliakim was no improvement over Shebna.

The following elements make up this speech:

(1) The prophet's report of his commissioning (15)
(2) The condemnation of Shebna (16-19)
(3) The condemnation of Eliakim (20-25)

Isaiah 22:15

Isaiah claims that he was directly commissioned by Yahweh to carry out his attack on Shebna. His direct attribution to Yahweh of his action and at least part of his condemnation (v. 16) was no doubt partially due to the fact that he was challenging an established official duly placed in office and thus not to be treated lightly.

Isaiah 22:16-19

The first part of Isaiah's speech denouncing Shebna (v. 16) is presented as a direct word of God, which the prophet has reported he was commissioned to give. The divine word is a caustic and sarcastic condemnation for his failure as a leader. The digging of the Siloam tunnel is metaphorically used both to speak to Shebna's abuse of authority (his leading of the revolt) and to describe the punishment he deserves (what he dug was his own tomb). The divine oracle, to highlight the sarcasm, both addresses and speaks about Shebna, moving back and forth between second and third person references. The entire address is deeply passionate and was probably spoken in animated fashion accompanied by gestures.

"What right did you think you had here, and who did you think you were here,
  that you quarried out here for yourself a tomb?
O my quarrier, an exalted position was his tomb,
  O my carver, in the rock is a habitation for him!"

                                                    Isaiah 22:16

In mocking Shebna, Isaiah refers to the tunnel running under the city as Shebna's tomb. If it were his "tomb," then Shebna would be "buried in the city" (note the repetition of "here") but to be buried in the city was a prerogative reserved for Judean kings. Thus Isaiah accuses Shebna of acting as though he were a Davidic monarch!

The condemnation is continued by the prophet's own denunciation.

17 Behold, Yahweh will shake you like something shaken out,
    you mighty hero, and delouse you like something deloused!
18. Wrapping up, he will wrap you up like a turban,
    like a ball of cloth, [he will throw you] into a wide-open land!
  There you will die, and there your glorious chariots,
    you shame of your master's house!
19. I will push you out of your office,
    and from your post, he [King Hezekiah] will remove you!

In this section, Isaiah first of all compares Shebna to a garment or a piece of cloth. Garments and cloth were given vigorous shaking in order to free them from body parasites, especially lice. Yahweh's treatment of Shebna is compared to such action. Then his action is compared to wrapping up cloth, so as to produce a turban or a ball, which will then be thrown into "a country wide of hands." The latter expression may mean nothing more than open terrain or a wide-open space. Maybe children played "ball" or "keep away" in such settings. At any rate, Shebna is condemned to a place "beyond the city" where he can die with all his glorious chariots, whose destroyed remains probably dotted the terrain as monuments to a foolish, lost cause.

Finally, Isaiah promises to do everything he can to have Shebna removed from office and assures him that the king, who probably resumed his functions shortly after the crisis was over, will eventually kick him out of office.

Isaiah 22:20-25

In verses 20-25, Isaiah moves to condemn Eliakim, whom Hezekiah had placed in Shebna's old post in the reordering of his cabinet. The speech is apparently delivered as a Yahweh oracle or in imitation of a speech of the king, so the "I" would denote either the Deity or the king. Although the text probably imitates or even repeats some of the spoken elements of an installation ritual, Isaiah uses these in a mocking, sarcastic manner. The climax of the speech is Isaiah's pronouncement of disaster for Eliakim in verse 25.

In verses 20-21, Isaiah describes what happened on the day of Eliakim's elevation. The new Lord Chamberlain, described sarcastically as "my servant," is properly clothed and invested with authority. The garments and authority are specified as those of Shebna—"your robe, your girdle, your authority." Isaiah had no higher expectations for Eliakim than he had had for Shebna. The status of being "over the household" carried with it the roles of being "father to the one ruling in Jerusalem (that is, the Davidic monarch) and the house of Judah" (v. 21*b*) and of being the superior custodian of royal affairs (v. 22). If such expressions reflect the actual wording of a ritual, Isaiah no doubt gave them a snarl as he said them—a father whose earlier actions had created turmoil and dissension among his "family" and a custodian of Davidic affairs who had treated royal prerogatives with irresponsible disregard (see 8*b*-11).

In verses 23-24, Isaiah is apparently no longer playing on the words of the ceremonial investiture. Nonetheless he is still chiding Eliakim and continues the disdaining third person references. Two images are used to describe Eliakim in these verses: a peg nailed in a fixed place and a seat (or throne) of honor to the house of his father. Again Isaiah may be engaging in ironic sarcasm. Jerusalem had moved, in the recent revolt, from its firmly fixed policy. Whether nepotism is to be inferred from the second image is uncertain, but the official's position ("over the house") was to look after the honor of his "master's house" (see v. 18*b*) and the "house of Judah" (see v. 21*b*) and not the "house of his father."

One wonders if "seat" or "throne" were not used euphemistically with regard to the toilet, as in modern times, since Isaiah moves to employ scatological terms in verse 24: "They will hang on him the whole weight of his father's house—the emissions and the excrements—every little pot, from the bowls to the jars." The firm, or fixed, place may have been where vessels used for toiletry were specially stored or hung to prevent their accidental employment for any other purpose.

Isaiah concludes his denunciation of Eliakim with a prediction in the form of a Yahweh oracle (v. 25). The time will come when the peg nailed in a fixed place will give way and the burden that hung upon it will be broken and fall and the peg cut off because this is what Yahweh has decreed.

26. THE DEMISE OF TYRE (23:1-18)

P. R. **Ackroyd**, "Two Old Testament Historical Problems of the Early Persian Period," *JNES* 17(1958)23-27; T. **Fischer** and U. **Rüthersworden**, "Aufruf zur Volkslage in Kanaan (Jesaja 23)," *WO* 13(1982)36-49; H. J. **Katzenstein**, *The History of Tyre from the Beginning of the Second Millenium* B.C.E. *until the Fall of the Neo-Babylonian Empire in 538* B.C.E. (Jerusalem: Schocken Institute for Jewish Research of the Jewish Theological Seminary of America, 1973); J. **Lindblom**, "Der Ausspruch über Tyrus in Jes. 23," *ASTI* 4(1965)56-73; J. **Linder**, "Weissagung über Tyrus: Isaias Kap. 23," *ZKT* 65(1941)217-21; E. **Lipiński**, "The Elegy on the Fall of Sidon in Isaiah 23," *EI* 14(1978)79*-88*; N. **Na'aman**. "The Shihor of Egypt and Shur that is before Egypt," *TA* 7(1980)95-109; J. N. **Postgate**, "Assyrian Texts and Fragments: 5. Sargon's Letter Referring to Midas," *Iraq* 35(1973)21-34; W. **Rudolph**, "Jesaja 23:1-14," *Festschrift für F. Baumgärtel* (Erlangen: Universitätsbund, 1959)166-74; W. G. E. **Watson**, "Tribute to Tyre (IS. XXIII 7),"

VT 26(1976)371-74; C. F. **Whitley**, "The Term Seventy Years Captivity," *VT* 4(1954)60-72.

Two factors lie behind Isaiah's speech on Tyre: (a) the city's important role in Mediterranean maritime commerce and (b) international political developments involving Assyrian relationships with Anatolian and Cypriote kingdoms in about 709. Over the years, Tyre had retained its independence from Assyria despite its participation in the 734-732 and 728-727 revolts in the west against Tiglath-pileser. The city had paid tribute to Tiglath-pileser over the years. In spite of being under siege throughout Shalmaneser V's reign, the city never surrendered. During this time, a Phoenician fleet in the service of Shalmaneser was decimated by the Tyrian navy (see Josephus, *Ant* IX 283-87). During most of the second half of the eighth century, Tyre thus remained a major sea power serving as an international commerce carrier throughout the Mediterranean world and exercising dominance over numerous far-flung trading colonies and control over the kingdom states on the island of Cyprus.

Throughout the years, Tyre and other Phoenician, as well as the Philistine, states had had strong commercial relationships with Egypt. Sargon's cooperative trade program between the Assyrians and the Delta Egyptians must have been a serious blow to Tyre. When the Ethiopians came to dominate the Egyptian Delta in about 713, the period of cooperation between Egypt and Assyria momentarily drew to a halt. Tyre no doubt was the beneficiary of this new set of circumstances, again becoming Egypt's dominant trading partner.

In 709, two events occurred that shifted power and influence away from Tyre and greatly reduced the city's importance for the time being. First of all, leaders on Cyprus capitulated to Assyria and sent tribute to Sargon in Babylon (see *ARAB* II § 70; 180-89; *ANET* 284).

Seven kings of Ia', a district of Cyprus whose distant abodes are situated a seven days' journey in the sea of the setting sun, and the name of whose land, since the far-off days of the moon-god's time, not one of the kings, my fathers who ruled Assyria, and Babylonia, had heard, these kings heard from afar, in the midst of the sea, of the deeds which I was performing in Chaldea and the Hittite-land, their hearts were rent, fear fell upon them, gold, silver, furniture of maple and boxwood, of the workmanship of their land they brought before me in Babylon, and they kissed my feet. (*ARAB* II § 70)

Almost simultaneously with the submission of the Cypriote kings, Midas of Phrygia sent word to Sargon wishing to enter into an alliance with Assyria.

While I was engaged in the subjugation of Bit-Iakin and the overthrow of the Aramean tribes and while I was waging bitter warfare against the land of Iatburu, which is on the border of Elam, my official, the governor of Kue (Cilicia) made a raid against Mita of the land of Muski [Midas of Phrygia] and three of his provinces. His cities he destroyed, devastated and burned with fire. Their heavy spoil he carried off. And that Muskean Mita, who had not made his submission to the kings who went before me, without changing his mind (*i.e.*, he had consistently refused submission), sent his messenger to me, to the sea of the rising sun (where I was) (offering) to do (feudal) service and to bring tribute and gifts. (*ARAB* II § 71)

A letter from Sargon to an Assyrian governor in eastern Anatolia (ND 2759; see Postgate) and dating from the earliest phase of the cooperative alliance between Assyria and Midas discusses the consequences of this new relationship. In speaking of the unsubmissive states in eastern Anatolia, Sargon tells his governor: "You, from this side [from the east], and the Phrygian [Midas], from that side [from the west], will squeeze them, so that soon you will tie your rope with them."

With Cyprus and Phrygia on Assyria's side, Tyre stood to lose its commercial power in the eastern Mediterranean. In one text, a cylinder inscription made at the dedication of his new capital at Dur-Sharrukin late in his reign, Sargon seems to associate the surrender of the Cypriote kings with the fate of Tyre. "[Sargon] the mighty in battle, who caught the Iameaneans [Cyprians] out of the midst of the sea in shoals, like fish, and subdued (or quieted) Cilicia (Que) and Tyre" (*ARAB* II § 118). In addition to Tyre, Egypt would also have been greatly affected by the Assyrian control of Cyprus.

Isaiah's speech celebrates Tyre's loss of importance in Mediterranean sea trade and attributes this new state of affairs to Yahweh. The appearance of Tyre in some of the verses and Sidon in others has led some scholars to assume that the chapter is a combination of a Sidon speech and a Tyre speech. Such a division of the text is uncalled for once it is realized that, at this time, Sidon and Tyre were part of a single kingdom. None of the Near Eastern texts from Tiglath-pileser to Sargon refer to Sidon, which indicates that it was either of no importance or else was considered part of the Tyrian kingdom. Sennacherib's later inscriptions refer to Luli, king of Tyre, as the king of Sidon, suggesting that the names could be used interchangeably in the eighth century.

Verse 13 is probably a gloss or has undergone extensive glossing. Although the Hebrew is not completely clear, this verse in its present form seems to claim that it was not the Assyrians but the Chaldeans (Babylonians) who placed Tyre under siege. The person who added this gloss was aware that Tyre's fate was not sealed by the Assyrians and that the Babylonians had placed the city under siege. In fact, Nebuchadrezzar kept the city under siege for years (from about 585 to 573; see Ezek. 26-28; Josephus, *Ant* X 228).

Like many of Isaiah's speeches, this one is mostly concerned with present conditions and recent events. Only verses 15-18 are genuine predictions about the future.

The following is an outline of the text's contents:

(1) A taunting song over the end of Tyrian sea power (1-6)
(2) Yahweh has purposed it (7-12, 14)
(3) Predictions of Tyre's recovery (15-18).

Isaiah 23:1-6

The opening verses in this speech were delivered as taunting calls for ports and ships to lament over the new commercial conditions, which Isaiah understood, perhaps overly optimistically, as the end of Tyrian power in the Mediterranean.

Verse 1b calls for the ships of Tarshish to wail because Tyre is devastated. Whether "ships of Tarshish" refers to a type of ship (see 2:16) or to ships from the port of Tarshish, generally assumed to have been located in Spain (see Herodotus, *Histories* I 163; IV 152; *ANET* 290), remains uncertain. In verse

6, Tarshish seems to be a place name. Whether ships or site, the time for wailing, the prophet declares, is at hand. The last line of verse 1 indicates that the report of changed conditions came to Tyre from Cyprus. This clearly indicates that the speech is not describing an actual destruction of the city of Tyre but is concerned with the altered international economic situation produced by the capitulation to Assyria by Cypriote kingdoms.

The inhabitants of the Mediterranean coast, and especially Sidon, are exhorted to silence in verse 2. Sidon is here to be understood as equivalent to Tyre, since Sidon at the time was apparently under Tyrian authority. The description of Tyre-Sidon in this verse notes the kingdom's commercial clout—its ships sailed the sea and it served as merchant for the nations. Tyre's close ties to Egypt are also noted—the grain of Shihor (to be located in the region between Philistia and the eastern Delta) and the produce of the Nile would refer to Egyptian commodities transported in Tyrian vessels.

Verse 4 calls on Sidon to be ashamed or to blush—that is, to show her embarrassment now that her sea trade, and especially the Cypriote arrangement, has turned sour. The "fortress of the sea" is Cyprus, now forced to admit that, in submitting to Sargon, she has become an unproductive trade partner. Her fate is described metaphorically as a woman's infertility:

> I no longer travail in labor pains,
> I no longer give birth;
> and I no longer rear young boys,
> nor raise up young girls.

The terms used to denote young males and young girls refer to prepubescent youths. The *bethulah* was not a "virgin" but a pre- or non-menstrual female (see *Mishnah Niddah* 1:4).

Verse 5 notes that the news of the changed conditions in the eastern Mediterranean will produce anguish in Egypt. After the Ethiopian takeover in the Nile Delta, just after 713, the Sargonid plan of cooperation between Egypt and Assyria was temporarily placed in abeyance. The Ethiopians no doubt were allied with Tyre and used Tyrian merchants as middlemen in Egyptian trade. After 709, the Ethiopians seemed to have pursued a strong and aggressive anti-

Assyrian policy in the region. Isaiah thus recognized the impact the submission of Cyprus and Phrygia to Assyria would have on Ethiopian/Egyptian commerce, both imports and exports.

A final port noted by Isaiah is Tarshish (v. 6), probably Tartessus in southern Spain, or maybe Sardinia. The reference here is to the fact that Tyre carried on commerce with and had trade colonies in the western Mediterranean world. Perhaps the meaning of the verse is that if one passed over (took ship) to Tarshish, there too the inhabitants would or should be wailing.

Isaiah 23:7-12, 14

The second section of the speech turns to the question of why conditions have developed as they have and who is to take the blame or credit for such developments. Isaiah begins with two questions. The first chides Tyre, comparing its present (and presumed future) status with past conditions. The second asks who has caused this loss of status and humiliated this ancient and powerful kingdom. For the prophet, it was all the work of Yahweh, who acted to defile all glory and to humiliate all the honored (v. 9).

The Hebrew of verse 10 is obscure. Perhaps the first word should be emended to read "work" in the sense of "till." The verse could then be translated: "Till your land, O daughter of Tarshish [Tyre], like the Nile Valley [is tilled]; there is no girdle [nothing holding you back] anymore." At least, the verse chides Tyre and suggests that the city make its living by hard agricultural work rather than by more glamorous mercantile pursuits.

In verse 11, Isaiah employs one of his favorite expressions used to describe calamities—"He [Yahweh] stretched out his hand" (see 5:25; 9:12b, 17b, 21b; 10:4b; 31:3). The shakeup of the nations and kingdoms is here attributed to Yahweh. God has commanded that the strongholds of Canaan—that is, Phoenicia or the eastern Mediterranean—be destroyed. (Although Isaiah does not mention it here, he clearly envisioned the time when Israel would rule the whole of Palestine, including the Phoenician coastlands; see Isa. 19:24-25; 27:12.)

Verse 12 contains the only Yahweh oracle in the speech. It, too, chides Tyre-Sidon, promising the city that it would exult no longer nor find rest, even if it should pass over to Cyprus. The last line of this verse might be an allusion to Assyria's prohibition of Cypriote trade with Tyre-Sidon. Tyrian ships were no longer even to be allowed to dock in Cypriote harbors (see *ANET* 533-34 for such Assyrian restrictions imposed on Tyre by Esarhaddon).

Isaiah 23:15-18

In verses 15-18, Isaiah turns his attention to the future of Tyre. Three elements in his predictions are noteworthy. (a) He predicts that Tyre will be forgotten for seventy years or for the lifetime of a monarch (v. 15*a*). Seventy years as a period of destruction for a city or region was a way of saying that no one now alive would see its transformation. This figure, as the time something would stay in ruins after being destroyed on divine command, is found in several Near Eastern texts (see *ARAB* II § 650; Jer. 25:11-12, 29:10; see also Ps. 90:10). (b) The prophet predicts that after seventy years, Tyre can make a comeback (vv. 15*b*-16). The prophet suggests that after seventy years, the city, like an aged, forgotten whore with no clientele, can make her circuits, trying to renew relationships on the basis of past memories. (c) The prophet promises that after seventy years, Yahweh will visit and restore Tyre so that the city again will be a mistress to the nations, but under Israelite control, offering her services wherever they are needed (vv. 17-18). Then her wages and her profits shall be holy (or dedicated) to Yahweh and for the use of those who abide (or function) in his presence. The income will be used to purchase food and fine clothing. Normally, anything holy to Yahweh could only be used or consumed by the priests. If this is what Isaiah refers to, then he is saying that Tyre's income will be used by the priests and in the service of Yahweh in the temple. However, since the prophet, in 4:2, says that everyone living in Jerusalem shall be called holy, he may here refer to the use of Tyre's income by Jerusalemites as a whole. At any rate, he predicts a future with an ironic twist: The income of Tyre the whore would support the people (or priests) of Jerusalem the holy.

293

27. A CANTATA OF SALVATION (24–27)

G. W. **Anderson**, "Isaiah XXIV–XXVII Reconsidered," *SVT* 9(1963)118-26; R. J. **Coggins**, "The Problem of Isaiah 24–27," *ET* 90(1979)328-33; J. **Day**, "A Case of Inner Scriptural Interpretation: The Dependence of Isaiah xxvi. 13-xxvii.11 on Hosea xiii 4-xiv. 10 (Eng. 9) and Its Relevance to Some Theories of the Redaction of the 'Isaiah Apocalypse,'" *JTS* 31(1980)309-19; J. A. **Emerton**, "A Textual Problem in Isaiah 25:2," *ZAW* 89(1977)64-73; **Emerton**, "Notes on Two Verses in Isaiah (26:16 and 66:17)," *BZAW* 150(1980)12-25; G. **Fohrer**, "Der Aufbau der Apokalypse des Jesajabuches (Is. 24–27)," *CBQ* 25(1963)34-45 = *BZAW* 99(1967)170-81; C. H. **Gordon**, "Leviathan, Symbol of Evil," *Biblical Motifs* (ed. A. Altmann; Cambridge: Harvard University Press, 1966)1-9; M. L. **Henry**, *Glaubenskrise und Glaubensbewährung in den Dictungen der Jesajaapokalypse* (Stuttgart: Kohlhammer Verlag, 1967); W. H. **Irvin**, "Syntax and Style in Isaiah 26," *CBQ* 41(1979) 240-61; D. G. **Johnson**, *Devastation and Restoration: A Compositional Study of Isaiah 24-27* (dissertation, Princeton Theological Seminary, 1985); M. J. **Lagrange**, "L'apocalypse d'Isaie (24–27)," *RB* 3(1894)200-231; L. D. **Levine**, "Sennacherib's Southern Front: 704-689," *JCS* 34(1982)28-58; E. **Liebmann**, "Der Text zu Jesaia 24-27," *ZAW* 22(1902)285-304; 23(1903)209-86; J. **Lindblom**, *Die Jesaja-Apokalypse: Jes. 24-27* (Lund: CWK Gleerup, 1938); P. **Lohmann**, "Die selbständigen lyrischen Abschnitte in Jes 24–27," *ZAW* 37(1917/18)1-58; W. R. **Millar**, *Isaiah 24–27 and the Origin of Apocalyptic* (Missoula: Scholars Press, 1976); E. S. **Mulder**, *Die teologie van die Jesaja-apokalipse* (Groningen/Djarkarta: J. B. Wolters, 1954); B. **Oded**, *Mass Deportations and Deportees in the Neo-Assyrian Empire* (Wiesbaden: Dr. Ludwig Reichert Verlag, 1979); B. **Otzen**, "Traditions and Structures of Isaiah XXIV–XXVII," *VT* 24(1974)196-206; H. **Ringgren**, "Some Observations on Style and Structure in the Isaiah Apocalypse," *ASTI* 9(1973)107-15; W. **Rudolph**, *Jesaja 24-27* (Stuttgart: Kohlhammer Verlag, 1933); J. M. **Sasson**, "The Worship of the Golden Calf," *Orient and Occident* (Festschrift C. H. Gordon; ed. H. A. Hoffner, Jr.; Kevelaer/Neukirchen-Vluyn: Butzon & Bercker/Neukirchener Verlag, 1973)151-59; H. **Tadmor**, "The Campaigns of Sargon II of Assur: A

Chronological-Historical Study," *JCS* 12(1958)22-40, 77-100; J. **Vermeylen**, "La composition littéraire de l'apocalypse d'Isaie (Is. XXIV–XXVII)," *ETL* 50(1974)5-38; A. H. **van Zyl**, "Isaiah 24–27; Their Date of Origin," *OTWSA* 5(1962)44-57.

If the speeches of Isaiah are arranged chronologically, then chapters 24–27 should belong to a period following 709, the date of the speech on Tyre. The content, as well as the literary-chronological context of Isaiah 24–27, suggests that these chapters belong to the period of Judah's revolt against the Assyrians in 705 and following—that is, to the period of general revolt throughout the empire at the time of Sargon's death.

In 707–706, Sargon celebrated the inauguration of his new capital city at Dur-Sharrukin (Khorsabad). In the following year, he was forced to move swiftly to the northwestern frontier of the empire, to Tabal, being summoned either by his governor in the region or by his new ally, King Midas. His enemy, an otherwise unknown Eshpai the Kulummean, was probably a Cimmerian tribal chieftain. The Cimmerians, a nomadic group from the north, had moved into the region following Sargon's decimation of the Urartian kingdom in 714. The Assyrian monarch was apparently killed on the battlefield. The final entry in the eponym lists for the reign of Sargon reports: "King killed, camp of the king [taken]." (The Cimmerians eventually overran the kingdom of Midas, as well, in 696–695).

Rebellion broke out in various regions of the empire. In the east, the Aramean and Chaldean tribes, the Arabs, the Elamites, and the indefatigable Merodach-baladan asserted their independence. In Anatolia, in the west, numerous provinces and kingdoms rebelled, and, according to classical sources, Greeks moved into Cilicia (see *AS* 162). In the southwest, a coalition of Phoenician and Philistine cities and King Hezekiah rebelled, no doubt with the blessing and support of the XXVth Ethiopian dynasty in Egypt. Whether the kingdoms on Cyprus gave up their allegiance to Assyria is unknown. They are not mentioned again in Assyrian texts until the time of Esarhaddon (680–669), who reports that their kings bowed at his feet and paid tribute (*ARAB* II § 710; *ANET* 290).

Isaiah was a strong supporter of this revolt, seeing it as part of a great action of God in history. He had earlier opposed Judean revolts against Assyria, but that opposition was based on the inopportuneness of those earlier occasions. Isaiah had proclaimed that the Assyrians would be destroyed (10:16-27; 14:24-27; 33:1), but he had warned against impatience (5:19; 28:16), arguing that the Assyrians must first carry out their task as an instrument of Yahweh (10:5-6; 29). But in 705, Isaiah saw the inauguration of "plans formed long ago, plans faithful and sure" (25:1).

In chapters 24–27, constant reference is made to the destruction of a city or a fortified area or quarter of a city. The following descriptions of this "place" that had been destroyed appear: "city of chaos" (*qiryath tohu*; 24:10); "city" (*`ir*), "fortified city" (*qiryath beṣurah*), "palace of strangers" (*'armon zarim*) in 25:2; "city of terrifying nations" (*qiryath goyim `ariṣim*; 25:3); "lofty city" (*qiryath nisgabah*; 26:5); and "fortified city" (*`r beṣurah*; 27:10). What is being referred to in these descriptions is not a specific city but a particular part of a city, namely, the fortified Assyrian citadel in Jerusalem garrisoned with troops, probably from various countries, charged with the military supervision of Jerusalem and Judah. Such a citadel, comparable to the Seleucid stronghold in Jerusalem at the time of the Maccabean wars (see I Macc. 1:33-35; 6:18-27; 11:20-23; 13:49-52), was located in some elevated portion of the town. The terms `ir and qiryath are used elsewhere in Hebrew to denote not just walled towns but walled enclosures or quarters in a town. Isaiah 17:2, which speaks of the "cities" or "fortified quarters" in the Moabite town of Aroer, may be an example. The "city of David" in Jerusalem was the enclosed palace complex, rather than the entire city of Jerusalem (see II Sam. 6:16; I Kings 2:10; 8:1; and elsewhere).

The Assyrian citadel was probably constructed in Jerusalem following Judah's participation and defeat in the Ashdod-led revolt of 712/11. Isaiah's sharp critique of the Judean leaders at the time of that revolt, especially Shebna and Eliakim (see 22:15-25 and above, chap. 4, sect. 25), was very harsh. His statement that "he [Sargon] has taken away the covering of Judah" (22:8a) meant that Judah had lost its favored status as a consequence of its participation in the revolt (see chap. 4, sect. 24). The changes made in Assyrian policy with regard to Judah would have included increased surveillance in the state and the construction of quarters for Assyrian forces in Jerusalem. Only limited, if any, direct Assyrian supervision over Judah would already have existed prior to the revolt (see 33:18-19; see below, chap. 4, sect. 33), but a new state of affairs was put into place following Judah's participation in the rebellion. The nature of this new policy was probably comparable to what Sargon reports with regard to Ashdod: "I reorganized (the administration of) these cities [Ashdod, Gath, and Ashdod-by-the-Sea] (and) settled therein people from the [regions] of the East which I had conquered personally. I installed an officer of mine over them and declared them Assyrian citizens and they pulled (as such) the straps (of my yoke)" (*ANET* 286; see p. 269).

Isaiah 24–27 was probably composed by the prophet for use on some festive occasion that celebrated Judah's assertion of freedom from Assyrian domination and the destruction of the Assyrian citadel in Jerusalem. (As Jerusalem had earlier celebrated its independence from Israel; see above, chap. 4, sect. 11.). Such a festive occasion may have been either some specially called celebration or, more likely, one of the autumn new year festivals following the outbreak of revolt in 705. Therefore, either 705 or 704 appears a likely date.

Internal evidence in chapters 24–27 indicates that some of the events had already taken place or were in progress or were planned in conjunction with the revolt. (1) As we noted in the preceding paragraphs, the Assyrian citadel in Jerusalem had been destroyed. (2) Revolt seems widespread throughout the Assyrian empire. This is indicated by the references to the far-flung celebrations in 24:14-16. (3) The move to expand the territory held by Hezekiah seems already to be underway (see 26:15). All along, Isaiah had held out hope for an expanded state under Davidic governance. In 735 he had offered such expectations to Ahaz (see 7:17; 9:7; 11:13-14). Following the western campaign of Sargon, he had expressed these nationalistic interests in terms of a strong Israel, comprising the major power between Egypt and Assyria (19:24-25). In the days to come, he predicted in 709, Tyre would be subordinate to Jerusalem (23:17-18). The nationalistic hopes of a state extending from the Euphrates to the Brook of Egypt are reaffirmed as the conclusion to chapter 27 (see vv. 12-13). Hezekiah shared these nationalistic expectations. Hezekiah had extended his territory in the southwest shortly after Sargon's movement into the area (see I Chron. 4:39-43 and, above, chap. 4, sect. 21). Second Kings 18:8 notes Hezekiah's war against the Philistines, which may have been carried out in conjunction with or prior to the 705 revolt. Hezekiah certainly had his sights on taking the north (see above, chap. 1, sect. 3E). It is entirely possible that Hezekiah's forces moved into the old northern territory of Israel and possibly even into Transjordan once the revolt was underway. (4) The religious reforms of Hezekiah, including the closing of non-Jerusalemite shrines, is alluded to in 27:9, but it is uncertain whether the reforms were past or in progress (see II Kings 18:4*a*). It is possible, although admittedly highly speculative, that 27:1 alludes to the destruction of the Nehustan, the bronze serpent in the temple (see II Kings 18:4b), since Leviathan is referred to as *nahash*. (5) The death of Sargon may be alluded to in 26:14.

Scholars have long noted the liturgical character of Isaiah 24–27. These liturgical features, which we will note in more detail below, lend support to the view that Isaiah 24–27 was composed for use in a festival celebration. At this point, we must comment on the nature of festival celebrations but can do so only briefly. Two biblical texts, Exodus 32:1-20 and II Samuel 6, give some indications of the activities associated with major festivals.

The first of these texts is the story of the making of the golden calf in the wilderness. Here we are concerned, however, only with noting some of the features of the celebration. Among the ritual elements mentioned are the offering of burnt offerings, the presentation of sacrifices of well-being ("peace offerings" in the RSV), eating and drinking, game playing or sporting ("to play" in RSV) in 32:6, antiphonal singing (probably the meaning of the piel of `anah`), and dancing in 32:17-19.

Second Samuel 6 describes David's bringing of the ark to Jerusalem. In the narrative, the following ritual actions are noted: making merry with various musical instruments (v. 5), rejoicing (v. 12), sacrifices (v. 13), dancing (or whirling,

v. 14), shouting, blowing of the ram's horn (v. 15), leaping and dancing (or whirling, v. 16), further sacrifices (v. 17), blessings (v. 18), and the distribution of gifts (v. 19).

All of this suggests that festival celebrations incorporated a broad and diverse number of activities. This diversity of actions in cultic celebrations was probably matched by a similar diversity in the oral presentations. Such a diversity of forms and genres is contained in Isaiah 24–27. It is interesting to note in this regard what I Maccabees 13:51-52a tells us about the events associated with the Maccabean capture of the Seleucid citadel in Jerusalem in 141:

> On the twenty-third day of the second month, in the one hundred and seventy-first year, the Jews entered it with praise and palm branches, and with harps and cymbals and stringed instruments, and with hymns and songs, because a great enemy had been crushed and removed from Israel. And Simon decreed that every year they should celebrate this day with rejoicing. (RSV)

Isaiah had himself earlier spoken of the great celebration to come when Assyrian power was broken (30:29-33).

The following is an outline of the contents of chapters 24–27:

(1) Yahweh lays waste the present orders of the world (24:1-13)
(2) Shouting from the ends of the earth (24:14-16)
(3) Proclamation of judgment (24:17-23)
(4) A psalm of thanksgiving (25:1-5)
(5) Affirmation of the good time coming (25:6-12)
(6) A song of triumph (26:1-6)
(7) A prayer of trust (26:7-19)
(8) An oracle of assurance (26:20–27:1)
(9) A new song of the vineyard (27:2-6)
(10) The time of guilt is past (27:7-11)
(11) The Great Israel to come (27:12-13)

Isaiah 24:1-13

Isaiah's proclamation that Yahweh is now moving to refashion and reorder the world opens with what appears as almost a thesis sentence: "Behold, Yahweh is demolishing the earth and laying it waste; he will twist its surface and scatter its inhabitants" (24:1). This depiction by the prophet envisions Yahweh's present action as if God were leveling or tearing down earth's orders and structures in order to redo creation. Thus there are numerous analogies and allusions in this material to the traditions and views now embodied in Genesis 1–11.

In verses 2-13, Isaiah describes the work of Yahweh's demolition of the present structures of life and the consequences of this action. The normal relationships and distinctions in society—priest-people, slave-master, maid-mistress, buyer-seller, lender-borrower, creditor-debtor—will no longer hold (v. 2). The world will lose its normal structures because God has decreed that this should happen and has spoken his word to bring it about (v. 3).

Verses 4-13 spell out in more detail what has been declared in verses 1 and 3 and partially illustrated in verse 3. Verse 4a speaks of the earth as already undergoing change. Here and throughout much of chapters 24–27, the prophet engages in wordplay, employing terms that sound alike. If this material was recited or sung responsively or antiphonally, such wordplay may have been used as a device to involve the participants more fully in the performance and to give a rhythmic quality to the recitation.

Verse 4b introduces a new element in the portrayal: "The exalted of the people of the world languish." For an audience in Isaiah's time, this could only denote the Assyrians. In fact, the destruction of Assyrian power was understood as the dominant feature in Yahweh's reordering of the world.

In verse 5, the prophet offers a theological rationale for Yahweh's action. The earth has been polluted by its inhabitants (or rulers). The source of this pollution is the people's transgressions. The idea that the land and the earth could be polluted by human sin, and especially violence and the shedding of blood, is widespread in the scriptures (see Lev. 18:24-30; Num. 35:33; Deut. 21:1-9). The laws and the statutes and the eternal covenant that people have violated would here refer to the laws of creation or the universal principles assumed to be binding on all people. In the biblical tradition, these would refer to the Noachic regulations (see

Gen. 9:16; where the expression "everlasting covenant" occurs).

The consequence of human transgression is described in verse 6*a* as a curse that devours the earth. This is simply an impersonal, equivalent way of saying God's anger is working itself out upon the human family. Human sin, in other words, is seen as setting into operation a process that, if unrectified, produces ill consequences. The earth's inhabitants must pay the penalty for their behavior. They who sow must also reap. Isaiah argues that harvest time has come. The destruction of humans and the reduction of population through warfare are seen in verse 6*b* as some of the consequences of the curse's operation, as part of the inevitable result of transgressing the moral order.

Manifestations of the operation of the curse or of God's demolition of the present orders are further expounded in the verses that follow. The images and examples that Isaiah uses to illustrate his case are interesting and diverse. Three primary examples are used: wine and strong drink, merriment and mirth, and the destruction of the citadel. Wine (and strong drink), one of the primordial blessings gracing human life (see Gen. 5:29; 9:20-21), is personified as mourning and languishing; it is no longer consumed or is lacking (vv. 7*a*, 9, 11*a*). Merriment and good times have disappeared, and celebration is at a low ebb (vv. 7*b*, 8, 11*b*): "All joy reached its eventide." The city of chaos has been broken down, its houses barred, and the gate to the citadel demolished (vv. 10, 12). The citadel is described, in verse 10, as "the city of chaos" or "*tohu*-town." Whether Isaiah coined this nickname for the Assyrian fortress or whether it was so named by the Jerusalem population is unknown. Nonetheless, its name fits the imagery being employed by Isaiah, recalling as it does the imagery reflected in Genesis 1:2, in which the earth is *tohu* before God's creation. The destruction of the citadel is thus viewed by Isaiah as part of the reversion to disorder and chaos out of which new order can arise.

The conclusion to this section affirms that the divine transformation of the present orders will occur everywhere. God's action will shake the nations and the whole of the world like the beating of olive trees when they are gleaned at the end of the harvest season (v. 13).

Isaiah 24:14-16

In verses 14-16, the prophet celebrates the widespread outbreak of revolt by referring to the shouts to be heard from east to west. The material in these verses, and especially in verse 16, has the character of a chant, and we should probably think of its being recited antiphonally.

14. They lift up their voices,
> they sing for joy,
>> over the majesty of Yahweh!
> They shout from the sea (the west);
15. therefore in the lands of daybreak (the east),
> they glorify Yahweh!
> On the coastlands of the sea,
>> "The name of Yahweh,
>> the God of Israel!"
16. From the end of the earth,
> the sound of praise we hear,
>> "Glory to the Righteous One!"
> And, one says,
>> "wasted am I, wasted am I, woe am I."
>> "The deceitful ones, they have deceived,
>>> and the deceit of the deceitful ones, they have deceived!"

Several points should be made about the interpretation of this text. (a) The shouting that is depicted as coming from east and west refers to the outbreak of rebellion that ranged from Media and Babylon in the east to the shores of Cilicia in the west and probably to Cyprus in the Mediterranean. (b) Since the prophet attributes all activity to the work of Yahweh, it is Yahweh whom he has the revolting peoples praise and honor. (c) The chanting quality of verse 16*b* can be seen in its alliterative character:

razi-li razi-li 'oy li bogedim bagadu ubeged bogedim bagadu

(d) The first quotation, "Wasted am I, wasted am I, woe am I," is to be taken as the shout mocking those being overwhelmed in the rebellion, that is, the Assyrians and their supporters. (Earlier, Isaiah had used the term *razah* to describe what would happen to Ephraim; see 17:4). (e) The interpretation of the last part of verse 16 is problematic but plays on terminology used earlier by the prophet (see 33:1). It could be taken as a chanting imitation of a battle cry and could be understood as: "The deceitful ones [the Assyrians and their allies], they [the rebels] have deceived." Or it could be understood, like the preceding line, as the hypothesized cry of the Assyrians: "The deceiving one [the rebels] have deceived; with the deceit of deceivers, they [the rebels] have deceived." (f) The verb in verse 17*b*, which we have revocalized and read as "one says," actually is "I say." It is possible that "I say" is correct and that the prophet made such a declaration in leading the celebrative chant.

Isaiah 24:17-23

Verses 17-23 logically carry on the thought of the preceding sections. Verses 1-13 have described Yahweh's action to produce disorder and disarray in the orders of the world. Verses 14-16 depict the outbreak of revolt throughout the empire. Such rebellion was part of the ordained plan of Yahweh, part of the creation of chaos out of which a new world situation would arise. Verses 17-23 declare that there is no escape from the actions of Yahweh, which will extend even into the heavenly realm. In a world turned upside down, one thing remains certain: "Yahweh reigns as king on Mt. Zion and in Jerusalem and before its elders he is honored."

Verses 17-18*a*, like verse 17, is an elaborate play on words. The terms for terror (*pahad*), pit or trench (*pahat*), and snare or trap (*pah*) were used because of their similar sounds and because the prophet could use the three to illustrate the inescapability of Yahweh's actions. After a rather straight-forward statement in verse 18*b*, the material returns to alliterative wordplay in 19-20*a*. The NJPSV preserves something of the repetitive quality of the language:

> The earth is breaking, breaking;
> The earth is crumbling, crumbling;
> The earth is tottering, tottering;
> The earth is swaying like a drunkard;
> It is rocking to and fro like a hut.

Such rhythmic language would lend itself to chanting, and the recitation of the text may have been accompanied by dancing and dramatic enactment.

The universality of Yahweh's actions is demonstrated by the prophet when he declares that the windows of heaven are opened and the foundations of the earth tremble (v. 18b; see Gen. 7:11; 8:2). As at the time of the flood, the earth is undergoing radical change.

Part of the earth's problem is its evil: "Its (the world's) transgression lies heavy upon it and it [the old world order] will collapse [under the weight of its transgression] and will not rise up again" (v. 20b). This text parallels verses 5-6, in which the world is described as polluted from the human violation of divine order.

In verses 21-23, the prophet proclaims that Yahweh's day of judgment is coming. Both heavenly powers—"the host of heaven, in heaven"—and human rulers—"the kings of the earth, on earth"—will be punished. The host of heaven is to be identified with the angelic beings or deities associated with the various nations (see Deut. 32:8). The kings on earth are the earthly parallels to the heavenly powers. The powers, presumably heavenly and earthly, are to be imprisoned together and after some time will undergo punishment (v. 22). In metaphorical and mythological terms, Isaiah has here proclaimed that part of Yahweh's action against the present orders will be the binding and eventual punishment of evil powers. The universality of the work of Yahweh is said to involve even the moon and the sun (see Amos 8:9).

This depiction of universal turmoil, rebellion, and world disorder, which runs throughout chapter 24, is brought to a conclusion in verse 23b with an affirmation that Yahweh, the God who lays waste the world (v. 1), reigns as king in Zion/Jerusalem and is there held in honor.

Isaiah 25:1-5

Chapter 25 opens with a thanksgiving psalm formulated in the first person, that is, as an individual psalm. This psalm fits nicely into its context. The preceding chapter ended on a note of confidence and confession, namely that Yahweh reigns in Zion. The psalm in verses 1-5 can thus be seen as a response to the whole of chapter 24 and especially 24:23b. The close connection with the preceding material is indicated by the fact that the psalm picks up on the theme of the destroyed citadel, a theme that helps tie together all of 24–27 (see 24:10, 12; 25:2, 5; 26:5-6; 27:10-11).

The psalm opens with a statement of intention, namely, to exalt Yahweh and praise his name (v. 1a). The first reason given for offering praise is that God "has carried out a marvelous thing, [namely], plans made long ago, [plans] certain and sure" (v. 1b). That Yahweh had laid plans for Israel/Judah/Jerusalem is a frequent theme in Isaiah's preaching. How clearly Isaiah understood and proclaimed these purposes or plans of God remains uncertain. He had chided his contemporaries, as early as the reign of Uzziah, for wanting a hasty revelation of God's purpose (see 5:18-19). As early as 735, he had related the Assyrians to the work and purpose of Yahweh (see 10:5-19) and made clear that these plans included not only using the Assyrians to punish his own people, but also the eventual destruction of the Assyrians. This position was reiterated in 728/7 when the prophet proclaimed that the Assyrian would be destroyed in Yahweh's land (see 14:24-27). In chapter 28 the prophet warned that the time had not come (in 727/6) for revolt and apparently gave Hezekiah the nickname, "the one who stands firm (or is faithful) will not be in haste" (28:16b). In 28:21, Isaiah spoke of the strangeness of Yahweh's work, namely, the use of Assyria to punish his own people. In 31:8-9 and 33:17-19, Isaiah spoke of the time coming, when the land would be free from Assyrian domination.

All of these texts come from the time prior to the Assyrian capture of Samaria in 722. Therefore, Isaiah very early on had proclaimed the eventual overthrow of Assyria. Such proclamation would clearly have stimulated the formation of plans for revolt and the coordination of Judah's plans with those of other countries. Quite early in his reign, Hezekiah must have become party to such plans for revolt, and his economical, political, and religious programs were geared to this end and to the conquest of the whole of the area from the Brook of Egypt to the Euphrates River. At the time of the 728/7 revolt (see Isa. 17) and again in the revolt of 727 and following (see Isa. 28-33), Isaiah opposed rebellion against Assyria, no doubt believing that divine plans had not yet reached that stage. In 712/11, he strongly opposed Judah's participation in the revolt spurred on by Ashdod in the west (see Isa. 20).

In 705, matters were different. Now human plans for revolt and Yahweh's plan to destroy Assyria coalesced. Isaiah was undoubtedly a catalytic agent for revolt, as the whole of 24–27 indicates. Assyria had been used by Yahweh to punish the Northern Kingdom in 734–32, 728/7, and 725–20. Judah and Jerusalem had felt the onslaught of Assyria as a consequence of the 712/11 rebellion and the subsequent direct Assyrian dominance in Judah. Thus Yahweh seemed to have carried out his purposes with Assyria.

Monarchs throughout the empire probably carried on negotiations for years over plans for rebellion. The economic pressure put on Tyre and therefore on Egypt, with the submission to Sargon of Cypriote leaders and Midas of Phrygia in 709, must have brought the Ethiopians fully into the formation of plans for revolt.

Presumably, the "plans made long ago," which Isaiah mentions in the psalm (v. 1*b*), involved not only Yahweh's purpose, but also human plans for coordinated revolt at the time of Sargon's death. When he died in battle in a strange land at the hands of barbarians, this was perceived as Yahweh's blessing, as a marvelous thing, as the beginning of Yahweh's transformation of the world.

The second motivation for thanksgiving given in the psalm is the destruction of the Assyrian citadel (v. 2).

> You have turned a city into a stone heap,
> a fortified quarter into a ruin,
> a citadel of strangers into a city no more;
> it will never be rebuilt.

Here the action of destroying the Assyrian fortress in Jerusalem is attributed directly to Yahweh and is viewed as part of the marvelous things undertaken by him.

The result of Yahweh's destruction of the citadel is spelled out in the couplet of verse 3.

Therefore a strong people [Judah], they glorify thee; the citadel of tyrannous nations [the garrisoned Assyrians and attached national forces], they fear thee.

The verbs in the text are imperfect forms that express the ongoing consequences of past events. The people of Yahweh are described as a strong people, no doubt, having rallied completely behind the cause. The multi-national force stationed to oversee Jerusalem and Judah had been taught the fear of Yahweh.

The third motivation for praise is given in verse 4*a*-*c*.

> You have been a stronghold to the poor,
>> a stronghold to the needy in its distress,
>> a shelter from the storm and a shade from the heat.

Here the psalm alludes to the protective care Yahweh had given his people in preserving them through times that saw much more turmoil and devastation in other countries. In this verse, Isaiah plays on the idea of Yahweh as a stronghold over against the Assyrian citadel, which ultimately did not protect its occupants. In addition, he draws on terminology used earlier in describing Jerusalem (see 4:6).

The fourth motivation for praise occurs in verses 4*d*-5.

> The fury of the tyrants, like a storm against a wall—
>> like a burning heat in Zion,
>>> the voice of strangers you have quieted;
>> like a burning heat in the shade of a cloud,
>>> the song of the tyrants you have silenced.

The translation given here assumes that *ṣayon* (dry place) should be revocalized to read Zion. It may, however, only be a pun on Zion. Isaiah draws frequently on the imagery of fire to depict Yahweh and his judgment (for example, see 10:16-17) and here applies it to the destruction of the citadel.

Isaiah 25:6-12

In verses 6-12, the material turns to aspects of the good times coming. Five factors are noted. (1) Yahweh will make a feast for the nations of the world on Mt. Zion, a feast with fine wine and fat animals. The universality of the envisioned banquet corresponds to what one finds elsewhere in Isaiah, namely, an emphasis on Mt. Zion as a religious center for the nations (see 2:2-4) and on Yahweh as the instigator of revolt and the object of the rebels' praise (24:14-16). The festival celebration that served as the occasion for the writing and use of 24–27 would certainly have involved feasting and drinking and, therefore, what is announced as future is already anticipated in the present. Representatives of other nations participating in the revolt may have been present in Jerusalem for this festive occasion, since Hezekiah was an important figure, a ringleader, in the movement in the Palestinian area.

(2) Yahweh will destroy on Mt. Zion the covering and veil that lie spread over all peoples (v. 7). The covering and veil, signifying mourning, encompass all nations and denote Assyrian dominance over the world. In other texts, Isaiah speaks of political and religious conditions in terms of a covering or shade or special enclosure (see 4:5; 22:8*a*) The place where Yahweh will destroy this covering—that is, the Assyrian dominance—is to be Mt. Zion. Again, this is a consistent feature of Isaiah's preaching, namely, that Assyrian power would be finally broken in Jerusalem or in Yahweh's land (see, for example, 14:24-25; 30:33). Behind such a view lies the Zion theology celebrated in the Jerusalem cult, which depicted the nations and powers of the world attacking the holy city, only to be put to flight (see Pss. 46; 48; 76). The destruction of the Assyrian citadel in Jerusalem would have served as a sign and foretaste of things to come.

(3) With the third factor, Isaiah moves somewhat into the more ethereal realm: Yahweh will swallow up death forever (v. 8*a*). The prophet's proclamation on this issue was no doubt a reaction to the enormous slaughter of people that had occurred in the series of anti-Assyrian revolts in the west. In 24:6, the description of the curse that devours the earth involved the reduction of population. Certainly this text should not be read as if the prophet were proclaiming the inauguration of a new age in which people would never die.

(4) Verse 8*b*, "the Lord Yahweh will wipe away tears from all faces," may be seen as continuing the thought of verse 8*a* or even as a synonymous assertion. Warfare and exile must have touched almost every family in antiquity. In presently known texts, Tiglath-pileser III claims to have deported over 350,000 people in his program of transplanting and mixing

populations. Over 200,000 are noted in Sargon's inscriptions. There must have been many tears that sorrow-grooved the faces of Assyrian subjects.

(5) Finally, Isaiah asserts that Yahweh's actions will result in the removal of the reproach of Yahweh's people (v. 8b). Why Judah should have been viewed negatively by other nations is not spelled out, but the reason is not difficult to discern. For years Judah had talked about but not joined in anti-Assyrian revolts. The pattern of non-participation had been broken only once, in 712/11, and then the support was only half-hearted and not led by the king. Judah stood by as an observer, or according to many as a disloyal subordinate, when the northern kingdom went under. Now the scene was different; Judah, Hezekiah, Isaiah, and Yahweh were on the side of the rebels. No longer would Judah be the object of international scorn.

Verses 9-12 appear to form a subunit within the speech. Two issues are the focus of attention. First, in verse 9, Isaiah asserts that the people can confess "on that day" that to have waited on Yahweh—that is, to have waited for the opportune time—was, after all, the best policy. Isaiah had argued this position all along, namely, that revolt must wait until the time was ripe and until Yahweh inaugurated the uprising. Now that that day had arrived, people could proclaim that God was their salvation and could be glad and rejoice in that fact. One could hardly avoid noting that, in this affirmation, the prophet played on his own name, Isaiah, (*yesh`eyahu*) meaning "Yahweh has saved" or "Yahweh is salvation" (see 8:18).

Second, in verses 10-12, Isaiah affirms that Yahweh's hand will rest on Mt. Zion, and as a consequence Moab will be trodden down and its fortifications laid low. Three possibilities exist for explaining why reference might be made to Moab at this time in a genuine saying of Isaiah. (a) Moab may have been chosen as the embodiment of anti-Judean sentiments. As chapters 15–16 demonstrate, Isaiah had no sympathy for Moab and Moabite causes. (b) The Assyrians may have utilized Moabite troops as one of their contingents garrisoned in the citadel in Jerusalem. If this was the case, the annihilation of the Assyrian forces in storming the citadel would have involved the killing of Moabites. Isaiah and the Judeans may have seen this as the beginning of Judah's dominance over Moab. (c) As we noticed earlier, part of Hezekiah's expansionist program, sanctioned by Isaiah, included Judean dominance over the Transjordan, including Moab (see 11:14). Isaiah may here be alluding to plans for a Judean invasion of Transjordan, or the invasion may already have begun. At any rate, and in spite of some difficulties in translating verses 10b-12, Isaiah here proclaims Judah's dominance over the region and does so in rather scatological terms (compare 16:11).

Isaiah 26:1-6

The song in 26:1-6 picks up again the themes of the destruction of the citadel and of Judah as a strong people. Although the song is presented as one to be sung in "that day," it is clear that "that day" is the occasion of the present celebration. Verses 1b-2 speak of the strength of Jerusalem over against the destruction of the citadel in verses 5-6. In between are two sayings, one addressed to the Deity as an affirmation (v. 3) and another addressed to the people as an admonition (v. 4).

The content of the song alludes to pilgrims entering the city of Jerusalem (v. 2) and probably to a celebrative trampling through the ruins of the destroyed citadel (vv. 5-6).

Numerous structural parallels exist between this song and such entry liturgies as those reflected in Psalms 15, 24, and 118. Verse 1b celebrates the greatness of Zion and reflects the type of proclamation that would greet pilgrims arriving at the city or temple enclosure walls: "A strong city is ours, [where] he has set up salvation, walls and a rampart." To this acclamation (compare Ps. 24:1-2), the pilgrims respond: "Open the gates that the righteous nation may enter, the one having remained steadfast" (v. 2). The speaker(s) of verse 2 continue(s) by addressing God with a saying that sounds proverbial (v. 3). The speaker(s) of verse 4, in an actual liturgy, would perhaps have been the same as that of verse 1b. With verses 5-6, there is united acclamation and celebration of the destruction of the citadel. The elevated fortress and its inhabitants have been laid low in the dust. The fate of the mighty has been reversed. Now the poor and the oppressed—that is, the former subjects—trample and dance in the ruins of the oppressor's habitation.

Isaiah 26:7-19

With verse 7, a section begins that is constructed as a communal prayer to God. The section ends with verse 19. In form and content, the prayer shares many features with psalms of lament.

The prayer opens with a statement of confidence: "The path for the righteous is level, O upright one, the way of the righteous you make smooth" (v. 7). The way and path of Yahweh denote Yahweh's way of handling the Assyrians. "Level" and "smooth" could be taken as referring to either the easy and unobstructed nature of Yahweh's actions or the obvious and self-evident manner of his work. The statement of confidence, in communal address, continues in verse 8: "Indeed, for the path of your judgments, O Yahweh, we have waited; for your name and your renown is the soul's desire." Here the prophet affirms that what the people have waited for was some decisive indication of Yahweh about his course of action, the course of action, on which Yahweh would place his name and stake his reputation. Throughout his career, the prophet had proclaimed that when the hour came and the time was ready, Yahweh would act and make known his directions (see 30:19-22). Now the course of Yahweh's action was clear, and his sanction and imprimatur had been placed on the development of events.

In verses 9-10, the material shifts to first person address: "My soul, I have longed for thee in the night; indeed, my spirit, in my waking, I have yearned for thee; because when your judgments are manifest to the world, the inhabitants (or rulers) of the earth learn righteousness; when the wicked is favored, he does not learn righteousness, the proper things he perverts in the world and pays no respect to the majesty of Yahweh." Isaiah, in this text, says that he has longed in the past for Yahweh to make known his course of action for the world and has yearned for Yahweh to establish righteousness in the world. If this prayer was used in communal worship, then the people would themselves, and the king especially, have confessed their yearnings and longings in the midst of celebrating the new conditions that had now dawned.

In verses 11-12, the prayer moves to petition, but it is petition partially expressed in the form of affirmation:

11. O Yahweh, your hand is raised high,
     but they do not see it;
  May they see [your zeal for your people] and be ashamed;
     indeed, may the fire for your adversaries consume them!
12. O Yahweh, you will appoint peace for us;
     surely all our doings you have worked on our behalf!

In its context, this request asks that God bring to completion the work already begun, that the adversaries of Judah be destroyed and its people know peace. The activity of the people—their rebellion, their destruction of the Assyrian citadel, and their expansion of territory—is declared to be the work of God, the manifestation of his zeal on behalf of his people (see 9:7*d*).

Verses 13-18 are presented as a confession to Yahweh, explaining and offering an apology for the past acts of his people. In verse 13, Isaiah reminds Yahweh that the people have been ruled over by other lords than Yahweh but that in the last analysis they have remained faithful to Yahweh, acknowledging only his name. These overlords are now dead because Yahweh has destroyed them, and all remembrance of them will be lost (v. 14). In verse 15, the prophet reminds Yahweh that he has increased Judah's territory and extended its borders, thus bringing glory to himself. Here the prophet at least alludes to the expansion of Judean territory in the southwest following the 720 invasion of Sargon (see I Chron. 4:34-43; and, above, chap. 4, sect. 21). Further expansion of Judean territory may have occurred in conjunction with the outbreak of the revolt in 705.

In verse 16, Isaiah offers an apology and explanation to Yahweh for the abortive revolt of 712/11, which the prophet had condemned in the name of Yahweh (see 22:14). His explanation is that the people had acted, thinking their participation in the revolt was divinely sanctioned, but they had been wrong: "O Yahweh, in the time of distress they had sought thee; they were overcome by enchantment; your chastisement was upon them." Isaiah's explanation is that the people had acted in good faith but had been deceived by wrong advice and by misunderstood sanctions. At the time, in 711, Isaiah had declared that the people's wrong would never be purged until after the death of the leaders of the revolt. Now, however, with the leaders still alive, Yahweh seemed to be bringing salvation. This situation Isaiah had to explain. In verse 16, he does so by suggesting that the 712/11 revolt had been (mis)understood as divinely sanctioned, though Isaiah, himself, had proclaimed Yahweh's word against it. In 27:9, he returns to this issue and expounds on how this wrong can be expiated.

In verses 17-18, Isaiah, no longer talking about "they" but now about "we," places himself among the people and continues the apologetic explanation.

17. Like a pregnant woman when she draws near to giving birth,
     she writhes and cries out in her pains;
          so we became in your presence, O Yahweh.
18. We were with child, we writhed, we yearned [reading *kamu* for
     kemo]
          we gave birth, but it was only wind!
     We did not work salvation in the land,
          the ones ruling the world [the Assyrians] did not collapse!

Here, Isaiah compares the Judean efforts of 712/11 to the pains of childbirth, to yearning that the fetus would pass; but the consequence, he says, was no more than passing gas. Salvation did not come; the enemy did not fall. The people's hope that the time had come, that they could give birth to a new period of freedom, had been only false labor.

In verse 19, Isaiah concludes the prayer and closes out the address to God. Both the translation and the interpretation of this text have been widely discussed, with diverse conclusions drawn. Two matters seem certain. First of all, Isaiah is not here engaging in a theological discourse on life after death or resurrection from the dead. Second, the context would relate the passage to Isaiah's intercessory apology on behalf of the instigators and participants in the abortive rebellion of 712/11.

Two possible interpretations suggest themselves. First, Isaiah could here be interceding, in metaphorical terms, on behalf of those who died in that struggle. In that case, he would be asking that their deaths not be in vain—that is, that the cause for which they died, Judean independence from Assyrian domination, would now be realized and thus "they would live" through the eventual triumph of the cause they espoused. Unlike the cause of the oppressors who were dead and would not rise again (see v. 14), those who died for Yahweh would "see" triumph. Second, Isaiah may not be talking about those who have actually died but those upon whom he had already pronounced God's verdict of death. After the 712 revolt, Isaiah had proclaimed the oath of Yahweh: "This iniquity of yours will not be purged until you are dead" (22:14). Now, in the dawning of the new age, Yahweh's salvation was being experienced, the iniquity of the previous rebellion had apparently been purged. Many of the leaders and participants in the 712/11 revolt, however, were still living and presumably participating in the present, divinely sanctioned revolt. These were the "dead" on whose behalf Isaiah now interceded. In this light, the following expanded translation would be the sense of verse 19:

May the ones you have declared dead live, O Yahweh.—"My deceased will rise," says Yahweh. "Awake and shout for joy you sleepers in the dust!"—Surely a dew of the daybreaks is your dew, O Yahweh, and on the land of the shades it will fall.

Isaiah 26:20–27:1

In 26:20–27:1, we have a word of assurance that may be taken as a response to the lamenting that has preceded in verses 7-19. Throughout chapters 24–27, such assurances and prophecies of the coming glorious times of redemption appear following material on other or related topics (see 24:21-23; 25:6-12; 27:12-13).

In 26:20-21, Isaiah proclaims that it is only a matter of a little time before the curse will be past because Yahweh is coming forth from his place to execute judgment on the ruler of the world. In imagery analogous to the description of the final plague in Egypt (see Exod. 12:21-36), Isaiah advises his audience to enter their bed chambers, to shut their doors behind them, and to await the outpouring of Yahweh's wrath. The punishment of Yahweh on the Assyrians who "inhabit the earth" will be swift. The execution of the judgment of Yahweh will involve the earth's giving an account of the blood shed upon it. The idea behind such a statement is the assumption that all blood shed through violence produces iniquity, which must be punished or cultically neutralized (see Gen. 4:10; Deut. 21:1-9). Thus Isaiah proclaims that God will hold the Assyrians accountable for the violence they have carried out across the face of the earth.

In 27:1, Isaiah describes the coming action of Yahweh as his slaughter of the primordial beast Leviathan. In many ancient mythologies, creation involved the slaughter of a primordial dragon or beast, which represented the chaotic elements in the world. Fragments of this myth, in which the dragon embodies evil, are found in the Hebrew Bible (see Pss. 74:12-17; 89:9-11). Here Isaiah identifies Assyria with Leviathan, the chaos dragon.

One of the adjectives used to describe Leviathan is *nahash*. According to II Kings 18:4, Hezekiah "broke in pieces the bronze serpent that Moses had made, for until those days the people of Israel had burned incense to it; it was called Nehushtan." One wonders whether this old relic was destroyed in the cultic celebration of the outbreak of revolt, with the bronze serpent being identified with Leviathan/Assyria.

Isaiah 27:2-6

In 27:2-6 Isaiah offers a new song of the vineyard as a counterpart to his earlier condemnatory song of the vineyard (see 5:1-2). This song, like much in chapters 24–27, was probably sung and chanted by the prophet and the audience in some antiphonal fashion. This explains the directive "sing it" or "sing of it," in verse 2 as well as the rhythmic, jumpy quality of the material.

The description of the vineyard as "pleasant" or "pleasing" indicates that the prophet is now speaking of the people in terms of God's favor. Unlike the earlier song, this one celebrates rather than condemns. From the beginning of the song, Yahweh is clearly the lord of the vineyard. In looking after the vineyard as its keeper, Yahweh is said to water it routinely (compare 5:6b) and to guard it day and night lest any harm befall it (compare 5:2b). There are no longer any hard feelings toward the vineyard; in fact, Yahweh fights the thorns and briers like any good gardener would (compare 5:6; 7:23-25). The briers and thorns, as in 10:17, are to be understood as the Assyrian oppressors.

In verse 5, the topic seems to change, for the prophet has Yahweh speak of how the vineyard cares for its owner. (A comparison of translations demonstrates that seldom has this shift been noticed.) Verses 3-4 describe Yahweh's care for his vineyard; verse 5 should then be translated:

Rather, it [the vineyard] has strengthened my fortress [or refuge];
  it makes [has] peace with me,
  peace it makes [has] with me.

Three further points should be noted about this verse. (a) The prophet plays on the name of Hezekiah (in Hebrew *yehizqiyahu* or *hizqiyyah*) by using the verb *hzq*, which forms the main element in the king's name. (b) What Isaiah refers to here is work carried out on the temple during Hezekiah's reign: "He [Hezekiah] opened the doors of the house of Yahweh, and repaired [or strengthened; the verb is *hzq*] them" (II Chron. 29:3). The vineyard thus looks out for the owner. (c) That the vineyard now has peace with Yahweh indicates that the hostility between owner and vineyard, reflected in the original song of the vineyard, is over.

In verse 6, the prophet declares that in the coming days Jacob will either take root or will give root to the coming generations. At any rate, the prophet is probably alluding to the house of David in his use of term *root* (see 11:1, 10). The future for Jacob is promising: "Israel shall sprout and blossom, and they [the Israelites] will fill the face of the earth with produce."

Isaiah 27:7-11

Isaiah opens the next section (vv. 7-11) with a chant-like, assonance-filled line:
hakkemakkath makkehu hikkahu 'im kehereg harugayu horag

The following is a possible translation and the sense of the text:

Like the smiting of the one [Assyria] who smote him [Israel] has he [Yahweh] smote him [Assyria] or like the slaughter with which they [the Assyrians] slaughtered him [Israel] has he [Assyria] been slaughtered?

The answer to these questions is presumably affirmative—namely, Assyria, whom God used to smite Israel, has now been smitten by Yahweh. This would indicate that Israel's days of suffering are over; the vineyard has been trampled, and now the trampler is the trampled (see 5:5).

In the verses following Isaiah clarifies his thoughts on how the people now stand before Yahweh. That the people, both Israel and Judah, had committed iniquity was a basic element in Isaiah's preaching. If Yahweh was now destroying the instrument of his punishment (v. 7), this would indicate that the people had been forgiven, the iniquity purged. In verses 8-9, Isaiah explains how he understands the purgation of the people's iniquity and the fact that they were now at peace with God (see v. 5; compare 6:6-7).

Verse 8 describes actions that functioned to purge the iniquity:

In trampling, in sending her away, you contend with her.
He drove away with his fierce blast in the day of the east wind.

The trampling (the Hebrew word appears to be a by-form of *sa'an*; see 9:5) was the Assyrian oppression and occupation of Israel/Judah. The sending away was Yahweh's refusal to aid his people. With these acts he contended with his people. Then he drove away with his fierce blast—that is, in the Assyrian attacks on Israel and Judah, Yahweh drove away or removed his people.

In verse 9a, Isaiah makes his theological point. In Yahweh's driving away of his people, or in his removal of them, the iniquity of Jacob is purged. The slaughter/exile of the people is viewed as the means of purging the iniquity of the people. Earlier, Isaiah had declared that the iniquity of the Judean leaders in the 712/11 revolt would not be purged until after they had died (see 22:14). But Shebna and Eliakim and others were still alive (see 36:3), and Yahweh's action in saving the people from the Assyrians was indicative of the fact that the iniquity had been purged. Verse 8 is Isaiah's explanation of the purgation. Perhaps verse 8a is formulated as direct address to God because it was originally Yahweh's oath that declared that purgation was not possible for the Judean leaders.

In the remainder of verse 9, Isaiah relates the purgation of the people to the centralizing cultic reforms of Hezekiah.

And this is the full fruit [or the final fruition] of the removal of his sin:
when he makes all the altar stones like crushed chalkstones;
Asherim and incense altars will stand no more.

The final step in the people's forgiveness and in their reacceptance by Yahweh is declared to be the destruction of the cult places outside Jerusalem. Isaiah here urges the people to participate in the cultic reforms of Hezekiah. The activity indicated in verse 9 clearly must be related to the actions of King Hezekiah, reported in Deuteronomistic terminology in II Kings 18:4a: "He removed the high places, and broke the pillars, and cut down the Asherah." In associating the purgation of the people's iniquity with this cultic reform, Isaiah was acting as either an advocate to help initiate reform or a supporter of a reform already underway; probably the latter was the case.

Verses 10-11 return to a celebration of the destruction of the Assyrian citadel. Here, as throughout chapters 24–27, its demise is seen as the dawn of a new age, as evidence of the renewed good favor between Yahweh and his people.

10. Indeed, the fortified city is deserted,
    an abandoned encampment, neglected like the wilderness.
    There calves will graze, and there take their rest,
    and forage its growth.
11. Women will break up its dry remains
    and build fires out of it.

Surely, that was not a people with understanding;
therefore the one who made it [the Assyrian king] will show
them [its occupants] no mercy,
and he who planned it will show them no favor.

Isaiah 27:10-11

The citadel has been destroyed, and Isaiah again proclaims that it will not be rebuilt (see 25:2).

Isaiah 27:12-13

With verses 12-13, Isaiah closes out his composition produced for the great celebration of Judah's assertion of independence from Assyria. These verses speak of a great Israel that lies ahead, the culmination of Yahweh's action on behalf of his people.

And it will happen, in that day, Yahweh will thresh from the channel of the Euphrates to the Brook of Egypt, and you will be gathered together, one children of Israel. And it will happen, in that day, a great ram's horn shall be sounded and they shall come, the ones languishing in the land of Assyria and the ones scattered in the land of Egypt, and they shall worship Yahweh on the holy mountain in Jerusalem.

Four elements in this promissory prediction are especially noteworthy. (a) Yahweh will clear the territory from the Euphrates River to the Brook of Egypt of its peoples in order that the children of Israel may dwell there. This theme of a great state of Israel runs throughout Isaiah's preaching (see 9:7; 19:24; 23:18) and was a national hope of the time of Hezekiah. (b) The territory will comprise one united people. Again, this theme had been sounded over and over by the prophet (see 7:17; 11:13-14; 33:17). (c) The Yahwists in far-flung places would return to the land, from the far reaches of the world, from Assyria in the north to Egypt in the south (see 11:12; 14:1-2). (d) Yahweh would be worshiped on his holy mountain, on Mt. Zion in Jerusalem.

This was a glorious vision. Yahweh would have one people, gathered in a broad land, worshiping in the one holy place, Mt. Zion in Jerusalem. Although it went unspoken, for

Isaiah there would be one ruler, the Davidic king reigning in Jerusalem.

28. THE DRUNKARDS OF EPHRAIM AND THE FOOLISH LEADERS OF JERUSALEM (28:1-29)

S. **Amsler** and O. **Mury**, "Yahweh et la sagesse du paysan. Quelques remarques sur Esaïe 28, 23-29"; *RHPR* 53(1973)1-5; G. R. **Driver**, "'Another Little Drink'—Isaiah 28:1-22," *Words and Meanings: Essays Presented to D. W. Thomas* (ed. P. R. Ackroyd and B. Lindars; London: Cambridge University Press, 1968)47-67; C. **Exum**, "Isaiah 28-32: A Literary Approach," *SBL 1979 Seminar Papers* (ed. P. Achtemeier; Missoula: Scholars Press, 1979), vol. 2, 123-51 = *Art and Meaning: Rhetoric in Biblical Literature* (ed. D. J. A. Clines et al.; Sheffield: JSOT Press, 1982)108-39; K. **Fullerton**, "The Stone of the Foundation," *AJSL* 37(1920)1-50; W. W. **Hallo**, "Isaiah 28:9-13 and the Ugaritic Abecedaries," *JBL* 77(1958)324-38; S. H. **Hooke**, "The Corner-Stone of Scripture," *The Siege Perilous* (London: SCM Press, 1956)235-49; W. H. **Irwin**, *Isaiah 28-33: Translation with Philological Notes* (Rome: Biblical Institute Press, 1977)1-43; L. **Koehler**, "Zwei Fachwörter der Bausprache in Jesaja 28, 16," *TZ* 3(1947)390-93; J. **Lindblom**, "Der Eckstein in Jes. 28:16," *Interpretationes ad Vetus Testamentum Sigmundo Mowinckel* (Oslo: Forlayet Land og Kirke, 1955)123-32; O. **Loretz**, "Das Prophetenwort über das Ende der Königstadt Samaria (Jes. 28:1-4)," *UF* 9(1977)361-63; P. G. **Mosca**, "Isaiah 28:12e: A Response to J. J. M. Roberts," *HTR* 77(1984)113-17; D. L. **Petersen**, "Isaiah 28, a Redaction Critical Study," *SBL 1979 Seminar Papers* (ed. P. Achtemeier; Missoula: Scholars Press, 1979), vol. 2, 101-22; G. **Pfeiffer**, "Entwohnung und Entwohnungsfest im Alten Testament: Der Schlüssel zu Jesaja 28,7-13," *ZAW* 84(1972)341-47; J. J. M. **Roberts**, "A Note on Isaiah 28:12," *HTR* 73(1980)49-51; **Roberts**, "Yahweh's Foundation in Zion (Isa. 28:16)," *JBL* 106(1987) 27-45; A. **van Selms**, "Isaiah 28:9-13: An Attempt to Give a New Interpretation," *ZAW* 85(1973)332-39; S. C. **Thexton**, "A Note on Isaiah XXVIII 25 and 28," *VT* 2(1952)81-83; E. **Vogt**, "Das Prophetenwort Jes 28:1-4 und das Ende der Königsstadt Samaria," *Homenaje a Juan Prado* (ed. L. Alvarez Verdes and E. J. Alonso Hernandez; Madrid: Consejo Superior de Investigaciones Cientificios, 1975)108-30; J. W. **Whedbee**, *Isaiah and Wisdom* (Nashville: Abingdon Press, 1971)51-68.

Chapters 28–33 of Isaiah reflect the period of Ephraim's last years as a state and thus chronologically belong after Isaiah 18. The rebellion that broke out in the west in the last year of Tiglath-pileser (728–727) was not thoroughly suppressed until Sargon's campaign in 720. In the intervening years, Shalmaneser was almost continuously occupied with the revolt in the west, but was not able to deal it a death blow. He continued the campaign begun by his father. As we have noted, this was probably the occasion for Hoshea's initial submission to Shalmaneser (II Kings 17:3).

An Assyrian eponym list reports that Shalmaneser spent 726 "in the land," that is, he did not personally lead his troops in battle but stayed in Assyria. Why the king did not campaign that year is not stated. Josephus, in describing Shalmaneser's actions in the west (*Ant* IX 283-87), reports that several Phoenician cities had quickly submitted to him (probably in 727). He then notes that Shalmaneser "turned back again" after having initially withdrawn and this time placed Tyre under siege and sought through employment of a Phoenician navy to capture the island city of Tyre. When this failed, Shalmaneser continued his land blockade of the city.

This course of events is best explained by assuming a scenario in which Shalmaneser carried through on the campaign against the west begun by Tiglath-pileser. During 727, the Assyrian forces moved against Damascus, Moab, Phoenicia, and Ephraim. Shalmaneser was certainly not as successful as he had hoped and the revolt had not been squelched as quickly as Isaiah had imagined (see Isa. 18:5-6). The following year, 726, Shalmaneser stayed in Assyria, probably mustering additional forces in hopes of more successfully facing the broad rebellious front in the west. During this year of the Assyrian king's absence from the front, the leaders in Samaria, believing that Assyrian power was weakening, thought the time opportune to appeal to Egypt for assistance (II Kings 17:4; Isa. 30–31). Since the Ethiopians had sent ambassadors to nations along the

Mediterranean seaboard only shortly before (see above on Isa. 18; chap. 4, sect. 20), the Ephraimites probably had reason to believe Egyptian aid would be forthcoming. Apparently, at the time, there was also growing sympathy in Judah and Jerusalem, where Hezekiah had only recently ascended the throne, to support Ephraim's cause (Isa. 28:14-22). This support, which Isaiah opposed, led the prophet to assume that Jerusalem might also be laid under siege (Isa. 29). Judeans supported the Ephraimite cause at least to the extent of allowing Ephraim's ambassadors to move through the country on their way to Egypt (Isa. 30:6-7). Isaiah consistently denounced Ephraim's gamble and predicted that the Egyptian appeal would prove useless (Isa. 30-31).

When Shalmaneser returned to the west in 725, Hoshea was subsequently taken captive (by Assyrian troops stationed in Samaria?), and Samaria was later placed under siege (II Kings 17:4). The length of the siege, three years (II Kings 17:5), was probably the consequence of Shalmaneser's being simultaneously engaged in efforts against Tyre and possibly elsewhere. Even after Hoshea was arrested (or surrendered?), revolt continued in Samaria and rekindled after the death of Shalmaneser (see above on Isa. 19, chap. 4, sect. 21).

The following is an outline of chapter 28.

(1) Denunciation of the leaders of Samaria (1-13)
(2) Denunciation of the leaders in Jerusalem sympathetic to Ephraim's revolt (14-22)
(3) Yahweh will not thresh forever (23-29)

Isaiah 28:1-13

Isaiah's woe denunciation of Ephraimite leadership in the first section of this speech seems to presuppose a situation in which the country is again moving toward rebellion against Assyria. Since there is no reference in this chapter to any appeal to Egypt for help (see chapters 30–31), an early stage in the planning would seem to be the most likely setting. The specific historical situation was probably the months following Hoshea's initial submission to Shalmaneser (probably in 727) but prior to Ephraim's sending of ambassadors to Egypt to secure aid (726). Late in 727 or early in 726 would seem to be the historical horizons.

Isaiah compares the political planning and chicanery going on in Samaria to a drunken brawl and the leaders to a group of inebriates. The politicians and religious leaders offer advice worthy of a bunch of drunks. At the same time, the leaders are spoken of as a floral arrangement or garland. The course of Samaria's revolt indicates that the move to rebel against Assyria was a policy strongly supported, if not originated, by the general population. This popular support is indicated by the fact that even after the king was imprisoned in 725, the rebellion continued, and after Shalmaneser took the city in 722 rebellion again erupted before Sargon reached the area in 720.

The prophet opens with an identification of those he denounces:

> Woe, O majestic garland, drunkards of Ephraim,
>   fading flower of its glorious beauty,
> which is upon the head of a rich valley;
>   O those overcome with wine.

Samaria is here called the glorious beauty that adorns the head of a rich valley, and its leaders are depicted as the wreath or garland that adorns the city. But the wreath is described as drunkards, as those senseless from wine.

In verses 2-4, Isaiah issues an announcement: Yahweh has one strong and mighty—namely, Assyria and Shalmaneser —who is like a mighty storm and a torrential stream and who will cast down to the ground. The leaders of the city will be trodden underfoot and consumed as quickly as one devours the first ripe fig of summer. Thus Isaiah predicts that the leadership of Ephraim will be swiftly dealt with once hostilities begin.

Verses 5-6 describe what conditions will be once the leaders are squelched. "In that day," Yahweh will become a glorious garland and a beautiful wreath to the remnant that is left. The removal of the leaders will allow the true leader (Yahweh) to function. The prophet proceeds to single out two among the remnant for whom Yahweh will be special.

One of these is the person "who sits upon the justice." This is not a reference to a judge or to one who lives a particularly just pattern of life. Here the phrase refers to those who favored adherence to the principle of justice—that is, in this case, adherence to the terms of the vassal treaty instituted earlier between Hoshea and Shalmaneser. The second, "those who turn back the battle in the gate," does not refer to warriors but to those who opposed rebellion in the deliberations about revolt. The gate was a place of popular deliberation and trial. Here the prophet speaks favorably of those who stand up in such deliberations against going to war. The fact that such deliberations among the common people took place—in the gate—would indicate that rebellion was more the result of popular pressure than a state policy initiated by the king.

In verse 7, Isaiah singles out prophet and priest for condemnation. These also are condemned for drunkenness, which is the prophet's metaphorical way of describing the foolishness of their participation in the planning of rebellion. The imagery of inebriation is carried throughout the verse, but the references to staggering in vision and stumbling in judgment make it clear that political matters, not rowdy drunkenness, are the real issue.

Verse 8 functions as a summarizing statement: Samaria is like a place after a drunken brawl—vomit is on every table and filth is everywhere. If we transpose this into political language, Isaiah says that all Samaria supports the ill-conceived plans for revolt and the city staggers toward its destiny like a drunk reeling from too much wine. The city is inebriated with the wine of revolt.

Given the situation in Samaria, where everyone seems drunkenly deluded, the prophet asks, "Who could one teach knowledge and make understand what ought to be heard?" (v. 9a). To his question, he offers a sarcastic, hypothetical answer; "Those newly weaned from milk; youngsters just off the breast" (v. 9b). His explanation of the manner in which they would have to be taught, in verse 10, is generally understood either as gibberish, imitating foreign speech, or as the way young children might be taught, perhaps the rudiments of the alphabet. It may be nothing more than imitation of "baby talk." The text hardly makes sense and probably was not intended to communicate except through imitation:

ṣaw laṣaw ṣaw laṣaw qaw laqaw qaw laqaw.

If this is a play on alphabetic instruction, the only thing proper seems to be the order of the letters, since ṣ comes before *q* in the Hebrew alphabet. Isaiah is probably playing on both infantile instruction or childish gibberish and what appeared to the Israelites as peculiarities in Akkadian speech. In 18:2, he refers to the Assyrians as the *qaw qaw* nation. That Isaiah is referring to Assyrian speech in verses 10 and 13 is suggested by verse 11. Yahweh will have to speak to this people (in Samaria) by means of stammering lips and an alien tongue. God had tried to say to them, "This (non-rebellion) is rest; give rest to the weary; and this is repose," but they would not listen (v. 12). Instead of accepting foreign domination for a time and finding rest after two rebellions and a period of bloody civil war, the people of Samaria were hastening into another frantic revolt. They had learned nothing; they were like newly weaned children fresh from the breast. So Yahweh's word to them will be like childish gibberish but will be taught by the Assyrians: "*ṣaw laṣaw ṣaw laṣaw qaw laqaw qaw laqaw*" (v. 13). In their actions, they will prove to be helpless children: "Thus they will walk, and they will totter backward, and they will hurt themselves, and become entangled, and be caught."

Isaiah 28:14-22

In verses 14-22, Isaiah shifts his focus and denounces ᴛe leaders in Jerusalem, many of whom were apparently in favor of supporting the brewing Ephraimite revolt. Shalmaneser's failure to suppress the rebelling powers in the west during his initial campaign may have encouraged Judean leaders to think of revolt or at least to give support to Ephraim's cause.

The references to a "covenant with death" in this section are to be understood as sarcasm. What Isaiah probably is referring to is the argument of some Jerusalem leaders that the city would escape harm if it offered assistance to Israel or even rebelled. The references to deception and falsehood could imply that the Judean leaders argued that they could operate undercover and not be detected. Some may have even concluded that the Assyrians were now incapable of putting down open rebellion.

Isaiah's talk about a covenant with death or an agreement with Sheol does not necessarily allude to a god of death, or *mot*, although such a figure does appear in mythological texts from thirteenth-century B.C.E. Ugarit in northwestern Syria. The prophet's sarcasm pokes fun at those advocates of rebellion, who, perhaps drawing on the belief in Zion's inviolability, claimed immunity from the normal course of events. Such an appeal at this time in history, Isaiah declared, was based on lies about as realistic as a covenant with death that promised immortality. For Judah and Jerusalem to have aided the rebels while continuing as a vassal state to Assyria would, of course, have constituted deception and disloyalty, lies and falsehood.

In a Yahweh oracle, Isaiah has the Deity point to the true source of confidence (vv. 16-17*a*), and pronounce destruction on the pro-rebellion Judeans and their expectations (vv. 17*b*-20). The opening of the Yahweh oracle in verse 16 is difficult to translate and has engendered a host of interpretations. There are two primary problems.

First, the words of Yahweh, in the Hebrew, open with a first person reference, "Behold me" (or "I"), but immediately shift to a third person singular verb form. One would expect a participial form of the verb if the thought in the text is continuous. (Such forms appear at this point in the Isaiah scrolls from Qumran.) If the third person verb is retained, the following possibilities suggest themselves. (a) The *hinni*— "Behold I"—is an error for *hinneh*—"Behold" without a pronoun reference—or else the pronominal signifier is to be ignored. The third person verb would thus refer to someone other than Yahweh. (b) One can retain the *hinni* and assume that Yahweh is depicted as saying, "Behold I, the one who. . . . " (c) Isaiah may have been deliberately ambiguous, alluding to both Yahweh and the one (Hezekiah) who was carrying out Yahweh's work in Zion.

The second problem is the fact that Isaiah uses various forms of the word *ysd*, meaning "to lay" or "to found" or "to construct." This type of terminological repetition appears in many places in the book (see especially 25:1*b* and 33:1), and such wordplay seems to have been a feature of Isaiah's preaching. In addition, verse 16 contains other terms, relating to architectural construction, whose meanings are not clear.

We assume the following about verse 16. (a) The text has more than one level of allusion referring not only to what Yahweh has done/is doing in Zion but also to what Hezekiah has done/is doing in Zion. (b) The architectural construction, noted above, has reference to construction projects undertaken by Hezekiah in Jerusalem. (c) Hezekiah's new construction work in Jerusalem embodied what Isaiah saw as the proper attitude for the time—namely, not frantic rebellion but attention to the needs of the present with an eye to the future, when Yahweh, himself, would lead the people in a movement of liberation from Assyria. (d) The expression at the end of the verse—"He who stands firm will not be in haste"—was not only a recommendation of policy but was also Isaiah's nickname, or perhaps a throne name, for Hezekiah, who displayed the opposite attitude to the political position of Ephraim's leaders. The use of the term *'mn* here is similar to that in 7:9 (see above, pp. 128-29), denoting standing firm in a policy of non-alignment with anti-Assyrian forces. The following is a tentative translation of verse 16:

> Therefore, thus says the Lord Yahweh,
>   "Behold I, the one who is laying stone in Zion,
>   proven stone, the splendid corner,
>   firmly constructed;
>   'He who stands firm will not be in haste.'"

The figure of Hezekiah and his stance of non-cooperation with the anti-Assyrian forces lie at the background of this oracle. Both the king, himself, and the royal projects undertaken by him, as well as Hezekiah's attitude in this time of crisis and uncertainty, are given Yahweh's seal of approval by the prophet.

Exactly what construction project in Jerusalem is alluded to by Isaiah remains uncertain. Two possibilities from Hezekiah's reign may be indicated. First, according to II

Chronicles 29:3, Hezekiah opened and strengthened the doors of the temple. The chronicler explains this as if it meant that the temple doors had actually been shut previously and, therefore, worship had been cancelled (29:6-7). This seems more like a theological homily than a description of actuality. Probably what Hezekiah did was to widen and rebuild the temple entrances (see II Kings 18:16). This construction, however, hardly seems to be what Isaiah is talking about in this verse. Second, II Chronicles 32:5 notes that Hezekiah rebuilt the collapsed city wall, strengthened the Millo of the city of David, and constructed a second wall. The repair of the collapsed wall (earlier damaged in the siege of the city?) may be related to other information preserved about the walls of Jerusalem. After the northern king, Joash, defeated the Judean king, Amaziah, four hundred cubits of the Jerusalem city walls were said to have been pulled down. Second Kings 14:13 says that the wall was destroyed "from the Ephraim Gate to the Corner Gate." The Hebrew expression for the latter gate is *sha`ar happinnah* (see also II Chron. 26:9). Apparently the *sha`ar happinnah* was a gate near the northwestern corner of the city. If so, the *pinnah* of Isaiah 28:16, translated "corner" above, would have been the northwestern corner of the main Jerusalem/Zion wall, one of the city's most vulnerable spots. Thus in repairing the city walls (II Chron. 32:5), Hezekiah rebuilt, or completed the reconstruction of the northwest corner, the *pinnah* of the city wall. *Pinnah* is also used to refer to a leader, a "corner" of the community (see Isa. 19:13). The precious *pinnah* laid by Yahweh is, therefore, not only the corner of the city wall but also Hezekiah, the firm support, the leader of the city, the one who stands firm. The proven stone mentioned in this verse thus denotes not only good stone for construction but also Hezekiah, who had stood the test and had not joined the earlier rebellion.

The construction imagery is continued in verse 17*a*. In this text, Isaiah picks up the word *qaw*, used earlier in verses 10 and 13 and employs it here in its technical sense of a "measuring line." In addition, he uses the term *plummet*, denoting the weight attached to a cord for measuring the vertical angle of a wall. "Justice" and "righteousness" are said to function as the standards for measurement. Given the circumstances, what would these terms denote? That they refer to certain moral standards or ideals seems too general. The issue at hand was whether to cooperate in an anti-Assyrian revolt. Such a move required vassal states to repudiate unilaterally whatever alliance relationship they had with the reigning Assyrian monarch. Justice and righteousness in this case would denote fidelity to treaty commitments. This is why Isaiah can describe the plans for rebellion as lies and falsehoods.

With verse 17b, Isaiah implies a strong contrast between what Hezekiah and Yahweh are doing—namely, erecting a firmly built construction in Zion—and the proposals of the pro-rebellion leaders. Their plans are only a temporary expedient, only an impermanent refuge or shelter, which the hail and waters of an Assyrian attack will quickly overwhelm and sweep away. Hezekiah's and Yahweh's program and policy, that supported by Isaiah, call for patient waiting and continued submission to Assyria, not some hasty, half-baked plan for asserting independence. When the Assyrians attack like an overwhelming "scourge," like a roaming flood, the anti-Assyrian alliance—the covenant with death—will be annulled and will collapse, and the scourge will beat down its proponents (v. 18). Verse 19 asserts that the scourge of the enemy will not be a momentary phenomenon that quickly passes but a constant feature of life. Once the Assyrians move into Judah—that is, once they have to take action to put down a Judean revolt—their presence will become a constant feature of life, and the message they bring and the lesson they teach will be sheer terror.

In verse 20, which may be a part of the Yahweh oracle, Isaiah quotes a proverbial expression used to describe a person in dire straits: "The couch is too short for stretching out, and the cover too narrow for curling up" (NJPSV). When the scourge hits home, when the Assyrians move in, there will be no way to find comfort.

In verses 21-22, Isaiah turns to his depiction of what will happen if rebellion becomes the policy of state. Yahweh will fight against his own people. As he rose up at Mt. Perazim (presumably an allusion to events now reported in the story in II Sam. 5:17-25) and was wroth in the valley of Gibeon (presumably an allusion to the events now reported in the story in Josh. 10:6-14), so Yahweh would fight against his own people. In an assonance-filled declaration, Isaiah states the peculiarity of such divine behavior: "To do his deed, strange would be his deed; to work his work, alien would be his work!"

With verse 22, Isaiah returns to confront directly the scoffers of verse 14, those Jerusalemite leaders contemptuous of Hezekiah's policies of non-participation in the revolt and of patient submission to Assyria. The leaders are warned not to scoff "lest their bonds be made stronger." What Isaiah means here remains uncertain. Were certain opponents of Hezekiah's position already being restrained, or is this merely some general cliche of warning? More likely, Isaiah here warns the people that if they revolt, the Assyrians will win, and their control over the vassal state of Judah will be intensifed (see above, on 22:8, chap. 4, sect. 24). The prophet tells his audience that he has heard a decree about the calamity and destruction that are to come from Yahweh upon the whole of the land if general rebellion erupts (see 10:23).

Isaiah 28:23-29

In verses 23-29, Isaiah moves to assure the people that judgment and destruction are not Yahweh's last word. In a series of images drawn from agricultural pursuits, the prophet argues that different times and different conditions require different actions. The farmer does not forever plow, for the one plowing also sows; God has taught that this is right and proper (vv. 23-26). After the crops are harvested, they are not all treated the same way. What is proper for the product is what must be applied. This, too, is something God has taught (vv. 27-29). God, who is wonderful in counsel and excellent in wisdom and has instructed people in the propriety and timeliness of agricultural pursuits, should also be trusted in his instructions about the propriety of events in the political sphere. For Isaiah, the times called for one not to be in haste; rebellion was not God's will for the time. Beyond the plowing, the sowing, and the waiting would come the harvest. But not now.

29. ZION TO BE THREATENED BUT SAVED (29:1-24)

W. F. **Albright**, "The Babylonian Temple-Tower and the Altar of Burnt-Offering," *JBL* 39(1920)137-42; S. **Feigin**, "The Meaning of Ariel'.' *JBL* 39(1920)131-37; A. H. **Godbey**, "Ariel, or David Cultus," *AJSL* 41(1924-25)253-66; W. H. **Irwin**, *Isaiah 28-33: Translation with Philological Notes* (Rome: Biblical Institute Press, 1977)44-67; F. **Lindström**, *God and the Origin of Evil: A Contextual Analysis of Alleged Monistic Evidence in the Old Testament* (Lund: CWK Gleerup, 1983) 96-105.

In this chapter, Isaiah continues his attack on those in Jerusalem who advocated revolting against Assyria and cooperating with the Ephraimite rebels. At the same time, the prophet draws on elements of the Zion theology to declare that, although the city might be attacked, it would be defended by Yahweh and not finally be taken. Thus in this speech, as elsewhere in the book, Isaiah proclaims that Zion will not only be attacked and threatened but will also be rescued at the climactic moment.

The material in this chapter does not indicate that Judah and Jerusalem, or even Samaria, were under any immediate threat from Assyria. Ephraim's rebellion, which brought Shalmaneser on the scene in 727, had been momentarily sidetracked by Hoshea's submission. In the days that followed this initial submission, the fires of rebellion were rekindled. Sufficient time passed to allow Jerusalemites to push for joining the movement and to scoff at Hezekiah's and Isaiah's position of non-involvement. That Isaiah's predictions about a speedy decimation of Israel had not materialized (see 17:4-9) probably had put the prophet on the defensive. Some Jerusalemites, similar to the general population in Samaria, hoped to push the royal court into revolt.

The following is an outline of the speech's content.

(1) Jerusalem will be threatened and attacked but saved (1-8)
(2) An address to the equivocating Jerusalemites (9-12)
(3) A condemnation of superficial loyalty (13-14)

(4) Denunciation of political intrigue (15-16)
(5) The future as a reversal of the present (17-24)

Isaiah 29:1-8

The prophet opens this speech with a unit replete with first person references but without the speaker's being identified (vv. 1-5). The ancient audience, like the modern reader, must have wondered: "Who is going to attack the city like David of old?" The audience could have thought it was the prophet speaking as if he were Yahweh, but without the usual indicators of divine address. Was the prophet having Yahweh now describe his strange work and alien deed (28:21)? On the other hand, listeners could easily have assumed that the prophet was speaking as if he were Shalmaneser, the Assyrian monarch. The tension over who is to attack Zion builds and is not resolved until, in verse 6, Yahweh is presented as Zion's defender.

Isaiah begins by referring to Jerusalem as Ariel. The exact meaning of *'ariel* is uncertan, although other texts suggests a meaning like "altar hearth"—that is, the top of the altar where sacrifices were burned (see Ezek. 43:15-16). References to *'ariels* appear in II Samuel 23:20, in which they could refer to either persons or structures, and an *'ariel david* (royal altar?) is mentioned in the Moabite inscription as something dragged away from a site (see *ANET* 320). Isaiah apparently chose this designation for the city for two reasons. First of all, it allowed him to play on the name as he spoke about the enemy's turning the city into an "altar hearth" (v. 2). In the second place, it allowed the prophet to describe the horror of an attack on the city without directly saying the word *Zion* or *Jerusalem* in the same breath with describing an enemy assault. That Ariel refers to Jerusalem is indicated by the phrase "the city where David encamped" (or "against which David encamped").

The time designation in verse 1b—"Add year to year, let the feasts circle round"—goes with verse 2 and the following, rather than with verse 1a, which simply identifies Isaiah's addressees. The time envisioned by the prophet was probably after the lapse of a year or a full cycle of the festival seasons. The withdrawal of Shalmaneser from Syro-

Palestine and his return to Assyria, where he spent 726, probably form the background of Isaiah's speech. The monarch's absence from the scene may have been the occasion for the scoffing by Jerusalem's leadership, their mockery of Isaiah, and an upsurge in pro-rebellion sentiment. Isaiah was thus forced onto the defensive. His argument was that when the year passed and the festivals rolled around, then Ariel would be oppressed. No doubt, the hearers could have initially understood the speaker—the "I" in verses 2-3—as Shalmaneser, promising that he would attack the city as had David long ago. Enough uncertainty about who was to attack Ariel and turn the city into an altar hearth would have remained to have created anxiety in the audience lest it was Yahweh speaking.

The attacker describes the siegework thrown up around the city (v. 3), the humiliation of being beaten into the dust from which appeals will be made (v. 4), and the incalculable number of the forces that will attack the city (v. 5).

After painting a portrait of the humiliating attack on Ariel and leading his listeners to await a description of the city's destruction, Isaiah drastically shifts the tone of the presentation at the end of verse 5: "suddenly, in an instant. . . . " Then follows a description of Yahweh's intervention and the divine rescue of the city. With the ferocity and the forms of a mighty storm, Yahweh will save the city so that the threat will suddenly appear as a dream, like a nightmare from which one awakes with conditions unchanged and with only the memory of things dreamed (vv. 6-8).

Isaiah 29:9-12

With verse 9, Isaiah turns to address his audience, the people of Jerusalem, directly. He opens with rare and reduplicated verb forms that suggest images of equivocation and incomprehension (v. 9a). We might translate verse 9a loosely as "fiddle and faddle, hem and haw." The prophet attacks the Jerusalemite population that has shown uncertainty and has wavered over what course of action to take in the debate over revolt. The change in the Hebrew verbal forms from plural imperatives in verse 9a to plural perfects in verse 9b is to be explained by the fact that in the latter Isaiah is speaking of the proponents of revolt: "*they* (the ones pushing for revolt) *are drunk* but not from wine; *they stagger* but not from strong drink." As in 28:1-8, Isaiah here describes the compulsion to rebellion as drunkenness and inebriated idiocy.

In verse 10, Isaiah declares that the people's inability to understand and their equivocation must be the consequence of Yahweh's having cast on them a deep sleep, closing their eyes and hooding their heads so they become incapable of seeing things aright (see 6:9-10). (The references to prophets and seers in verse 10 are probably editorial glosses.) In verses 11-12, Isaiah compares their perception of the whole matter to that of one who cannot read the words of a sealed document because it is unopened or to that of a person with an open document who has never learned to read.

Isaiah 29:13-14

In verses 13-14, the prophet introduces the first clearly Yahweh oracle in the address. The oracle is composed of two parts, an accusatory denunciation of the population (v. 13) and a statement about divine action (v. 14). In the denunciation, the people are accused of having no real devotion and commitment to Yahweh; their hearts are far from him, and their obedience is superficial. The divine action that is promised in verse 14 is not specified, other than to declare that it would be some marvelous or awesome thing that would baffle or overawe the people—that is, it would make clear the divine intention—and in the process the wisdom of the wise and the learning of the learned ones would fail or no longer be made public. Here Isaiah is referring to those who, in favoring rebellion, saw themselves as the ones who really understood the political and historical realities and could offer their wisdom and understanding, advocating revolt as the wise course of action.

Isaiah 29:15-16

In verses 15-16, Isaiah again denounces the secret plotting going on among the leaders who hoped to bring the south into the ranks of the rebels (see 28:14-15). They are accused of working undercover, of trying to hide their activity from Yahweh, and of assuming that their deeds will not become known (to the Assyrians? to Yahweh?). In verse 16, the prophet compares the actions of those counseling revolt to the defiance of a product against its producer.

Isaiah 29:17-24

The speech closes with a presentation about the future (vv. 17-24), a future that Isaiah describes as near at hand (v. 17a). The central thrust of verses 17-19 is the reversal of status. God will set things as they should be (see v. 16a). What exists now will be transformed into its opposite: the (forest of) Lebanon will become an orchard (Carmel), Carmel (an orchard) will become a forest, the deaf will hear (see vv. 11-12), the blind will see (see v. 10), the humiliated will rejoice in Yahweh, and the land's needy will shout with joy over the Holy One of Israel. This will come about because the ruthless (the Assyrians?) will be no more (see v. 6), the scoffer will vanish (see 28:14), cut off will be all those anxious to accuse, those making others guilty through a word (of slander), those setting traps for the ones who want to settle matters publicly in the gate, and those throwing into confusion the one in the right. Such descriptions indicate the strongly divided opinion and tensions that must have existed in Jerusalem over the issue of revolt (see Mic. 7:5-6, which probably belongs to the same period).

Verses 22-24 conclude with a Yahweh oracle that speaks of the new situation to prevail "in the house of Jacob" (probably to be understood as designating the whole people of Yahweh). No longer will people be ashamed and their faces pale because of humiliation and oppression. Instead, the house of Jacob will behold the offspring Yahweh has given them and the people will hallow their God and stand in awe. Those confused and uncertain will acquire understanding, and those backbiting and complaining will receive instruction. In other words, the troubled, confused, and uncertain state of affairs that had torn apart the people and divided them into factions will disappear, and a new state of national existence will result.

30. WOE TO THOSE WHO GO DOWN TO EGYPT
(30:1-33)

J. A. **Emerton**, "A Textual Problem in Isaiah xxx.5," *JTS*
32(1981)125-28; R. **Gordis**, "Some Hitherto Unrecognized
Meanings of the Verb *shub*," *JBL* 52(1933)153-62; A. H. **Gray**,
"The Beatitude of 'Them that Wait,'" *ET* 48(1936)264-67; A.
Guillaume, "Isaiah's Oracle Against Assyria (Isaiah 30:27-
33) in the Light of Archaeology," *BSOAS* 17(1956)413-15;
G. C. **Heider**, *The Cult of Molek: A Reassessment* (Sheffield:
JSOT Press, 1985)319-32; W. H. **Irwin**, *Isaiah 28-33: Translation
with Philological Notes* (Rome: Biblical Institute Press, 1977)68-
106; K. A. **Kitchen**, *The Third Intermediate Period in Egypt
(1100-650 B.C.)* (Warminister: Aris & Phillips, 1973)372-76; A.
Kuschke, "Zu Jes 30:1-5," *ZAW* 64(1952)194-95; L. **Laberge**,
"Is 30,19-26: A Deuteronomic Text?" *EglT* 2(1971)35-54; R. F.
Melugin, "Isa 30:15-17," *CBQ* 36(1974)303-4; J. J. M. **Roberts**,
"The Teaching Voice in Isaiah 30:20-21," *Christian Teaching:
Studies in Honor of LeMoine G. Lewis* (ed. E. Ferguson; Abilene:
Abilene Christian University, 1981)130-37; L. **Sabottka**, "Is.
30, 27-33: Ein Übersetzungsvorschlag," *BZ* 12(1968)241-45;
K. -D. **Schunck**, "Jes 30,6-8 und die Deutung der Rahab im
Alten Testament," *ZAW* 78(1966)48-56.

In 732, Hoshea led an uprising in Samaria that toppled the
Syrian stooge Pekah from the throne (II Kings 15:30).
Hoshea's conspiracy was probably a last-ditch effort to avoid
an Assyrian siege of the capital city. At the time, Damascus
and Syria had probably already fallen or were in their last
days. II Kings 15:29 reports on Tiglath-pileser's capture of
Ijon, Abel-beth-maacah, Janoah, Kedesh, Hazor, Gilead, and
Galilee and the deportation of people from these places. The
places noted had already been taken over by Syria from Israel
during the reigns of Jeroboam II and Menahem (see Isa. 9:1).
This territory—described in Isaiah 9:1 as the land of Zebulun,
the land of Naphtali, the land beyond the Jordan, and Galilee
of the nations—was absorbed into the Assyrian empire when
Tiglath-pileser made Assyrian provinces of "the widespread
land of Hazael," that is, the regions ruled by Rezin (see *TUAT*
I 376-78, although reading lines 9-11 to refer to Israel is
highly uncertain). Hoshea's uprising saved what remained

of the old state of Israel—namely, the central hill country south of the valley of Jezreel. Hoshea was recognized as king by the Assyrian monarch. Tribute was imposed on Israel, but no clear reference is made in Assyrian texts to the reduction of Israelite territory (*ANET* 284 [the first paragraph of the inscription on p. 283 has been incorrectly restored]; see *TUAT* I 373-74).

By 728, Hoshea and Samaria had again become involved in an anti-Assyrian movement (see Isa. 17, and, above, chap. 4, sect. 19). When the Assyrians moved back into Syria-Palestine, Hoshea capitulated and resumed paying tribute to Assyria, probably in 727 (II Kings 17:3). The new Assyrian monarch, Shalmaneser V, was unable to suppress the widespread revolt immediately and spent 726 back in Assyria. During this interval, Hoshea, apparently under popular pressure, sent messengers and gifts to Egypt hoping to secure Egyptian aid for the rebels.

II Kings 17:4 reports that Hoshea "sent messengers to So, king of Egypt, and offered no tribute to the king of Assyria, as he had done year by year." Since no Egyptian pharaoh named So is attested to in ancient sources, two possible alternatives for interpreting this text have been suggested.

One approach is based on emending the text to read, "He sent messengers to Sais, to the king of Egypt." In this case, the Egyptian ruler would have been Tefnakht, who reigned in Sais in the western Delta. Diodorus (I.45.2) has preserved a story about Tefnakht that, in explaining his devotion to the simple life, reports an incident that occurred while he was "on a campaign in Arabia." This would indicate that he was active in Syria-Palestine at some point during his career.

A second interpretation of this text retains the present reading and takes So as an abbreviation of the name *Osorkon* (IV). This pharaoh ruled in Tanis in the eastern Delta near Palestine. His family, the XXIInd Dynasty, had long followed a policy of encouraging anti-Assyrianism in Syria-Palestine.

At any rate, both Tefnakht and Osorkon IV were, at least nominally, under the authority of the Ethiopian ruler, Piye, who had recently sent ambassadors into Syria-Palestine (see Isa. 18 and, above, chap. 4, sect. 20). On the surface, all evidence thus pointed to a favorable hearing in Egypt for any appeal from anti-Assyrian rebels in Syria-Palestine.

Hoshea's appeal for Egyptian aid forms the immediate background of Isaiah 30. Verses 6-7 would indicate that Judeans were cooperating in a limited way with Israel (see Isa. 28:14-22). The Judeans at least allowed Israelite ambassadors to pass through their territory on the way to Egypt. That the Israelites traveled through Judean territory rather than down the coastal highway would indicate that the Assyrians held the Palestinian coastal region. The area north of Philistia ("the way of the sea" in Isa. 9:1) had most likely been provincialized by the Assyrians in 734 or 732.

The following outline of this speech's contents assumes that the entire chapter is a single address. The break at verse 6 with its reference to "an oracle on the beasts of the Negeb" might appear to indicate a new speech. The thought, however, is continuous, and the "title" referring to the beasts of the Negeb could either be a gloss to clarify who the "they" in verse 6 refers to or an actual catch phrase used by the prophet for dramatic effect.

(1) A woe denunciation of the Israelite appeal to Egypt (1-5).
(2) Oracle on the beasts of the Negeb (6-7)
(3) A prediction of defeat for Israel's plans (8-18).
(4) A prediction of Zion's salvation and Assyria's destruction (19-33)

Isaiah 30:1-5

Isaiah denounces the Israelites as stubborn children who go against God's will (see 1:2-3). According to the regulations laid out in Deuteronomy 21:18-21, such children could be put to death. The two terms used to describe recalcitrant children in the Deuteronomy text are *srr* and *mrh*, both of which are picked up by Isaiah, *srr* in verse 1 and *mrh* in verse 9. The rebellion of the sons is spelled out in a series of expressions:

1. to carry out a plan,
     but not mine;
   to pour out a libation,
     but not of my spirit;
   thereby adding
     rebellion to rebellion;

2. setting out to go down to Egypt,
    without asking me;
  to seek refuge in the protection of pharaoh,
    to seek shelter in the shadow of Egypt.

Throughout his preaching, Isaiah declared that Yahweh had not only a plan for Assyria to serve as his agent of punishment but also a plan to destroy Assyria. But rebellion at this time was not Yahweh's plan (see 30:18*b*). "To pour out a libation" probably refers to rituals involved in sealing an alliance (see 19:21 and the discussion of this text, above, p. 266). The term we have translated "rebellion" is the common Hebrew word *ḥṭ'*, normally translated "sin." In international relations, the Assyrians used the term in both its nominal and verbal forms to denote rebellion against their authority. Later, when Hezekiah rebelled against Sennacherib, for example, the Judean king described his actions with the words, "I have sinned" ["done wrong", the verb is *ḥaṭ'ati*] (II Kings 18:14). Isaiah's use of the word is double pronged. In going against the will of Yahweh, the Israelites sin. In appealing to Egypt, they are rebelling ("sinning") against Assyria. In 735, Israel had rebelled and had done so again in 728. And now, in 726, Isaiah declares, "You are adding rebellion to rebellion."

In verses 3-5, Isaiah predicts that the attempt to secure help from Egypt will only result in Israel's shame and disgrace. Although Israel's leaders have arrived at Zoan (Tanis in the eastern Delta) and its messengers may reach even as far as Hanes (Heracelopolis in Upper Egypt, north of the Fayyum), Egypt's help will prove to be not merely worthless but even harmful. Everything about this people—a people that does not profit—raises a stink (v. 5*a*). All Israel will gain from them is embarrassment and reproach.

Isaiah 30:6-7

The Israelite negotiators probably made their way to Egypt preceded by caravans carrying gifts for the courts. In verse 6 Isaiah describes the transportation of the people's wealth and treasures on the backs of asses and camels through the Negeb desert. The Negeb is spoken of as a land of trouble and anguish, the same terms used to speak of Israel after the takeover by Pekah (see 8:22), and a place of the lion and the lioness, the viper and the flying serpent. It must have struck Isaiah as ironic to watch beasts of burden carrying Israelite wealth into the desert, a symbol of anarchy and disorder, in hopes of finally bringing order to Israelite life. Like the Negeb desert, Egypt offered little and, like the Negeb, the future held only trouble and anguish. At the end of verse 6, Isaiah repeats the epithet that he had applied to Egypt in verse 5: "a people that does not profit."

In verse 7, Isaiah gives Egypt another name: "Rahab, a noisy one, a sitting one." Although various translations of this name are made—"Rahab Quelled" (NEB), "Rahab who sits still" (RSV)—the meaning is rather clear: Egypt, in spite of its big talk and bluster, could not be counted on to act when needed. The translation above assumes that *hem* is from *hmh* meaning "to raise a noise" and that *shabeth* is from *yshb* meaning "to sit." Years later, Jeremiah would hang a similar epithet on the Egyptian pharaoh: "Noisy one who lets the hour go by" (Jer. 46:17). The designation of Egypt as Rahab appeals to the old mythological tale of the chaos dragon (see Isa. 27:1). (For other references to Rahab, see Ps. 89:10; Job 9:13; 26:12; Isa. 51:9.)

Isaiah 30:8-18

In verse 8, either Isaiah orders the recording of his word or Yahweh orders the prophet to write it down. If the latter is the case, there is nothing in the text to indicate that this directive is divine address. The first difficulty in interpreting this verse is, therefore, to determine who is speaking and who is being addressed. A second problem concerns what was to be written down. A third problem concerns what "with them" (not "before them" as in the RSV) denotes. Although it is impossible to decide the issues conclusively, the following appears to be the meaning of the text: Isaiah orders that his name for Egypt—"Rahab, a noisy one, a sitting one," indicating that in spite of its talk, Egypt would not act—be written down, probably in a public place along with his other inscribed slogans and pronouncements that were offered as predictions before the events (see 8:1, 16).

In verses 9-11, Isaiah explains the reason for writing down the pronouncement. The people are rebellious and deceitful children and will not accede to the verdict (*torah*) of Yahweh, as proclaimed by Isaiah. They will even try to influence their own seers and visionaries either not to perform their function or else to proclaim slippery and devious words. In other words, they attempt to secure divine oracles that condone what they already want to do (see on 8:19-20). Thus Isaiah orders that Yahweh's verdict pronounced through him be written down as a reminder and a witness for coming days.

Two oracles of Yahweh are quoted to clinch the argument that appealing to Egypt, like rebellion against Assyria, is a foolish, senseless policy doomed to destroy those who carry it out. The first, in verses 12-14, condemns the people for rejecting Yahweh's word (the torah of v. 9; see 1:10; 5:24b), for trusting in a devious undercover plan (the scheme of rebellion while under the domination of and in a treaty relationship with Assyria), and for relying on it (Egypt). The consequence of this iniquity (the term `*awon* can denote either the act or the consequence of the act) will be like the collapse of a bulging wall (v. 13) or the shattering of a pottery container, leaving no fragment large enough to scoop up firecoals or to dip up water (v. 14).

The second oracle (vv. 15-17) quotes Yahweh's recommendation of the proper action, the people's counter response, and Yahweh's sentence of judgment. What Yahweh had called for was the opposite of what Israel was doing. Yahweh had counseled "sitting still and taking rest," "keeping quiet and showing trust"—that is, in the political context, submission to Assyria and acquiescence to the status quo. Instead of waiting for Yahweh (see v. 18) and enduring Assyrian domination for a time, Israel inaugurated a policy of action, a policy of rebellion.

One of the things the Israelites sought in Egypt was horses (see 31:1). Throughout the period of the XXVth Ethiopian dynasty, frequent references to horses from Egypt appear in ancient Near Eastern texts (see Deut. 17:16). The consequence of the people's action will match their wrongdoing:

"We will take horse and flee";
   therefore you shall be put to flight:
"We will ride apace";
   therefore swift will be the pace of your pursuers.

Isaiah 30:16

The people will be overcome on the battlefield. A thousand will flee from a single attacker; at the sight of five opponents, all will flee (see Lev. 26:8, 17; Deut. 28:25).

Even after pronouncing condemnation and judgment on the people, Isaiah declares that Yahweh is still waiting to show favor and mercy, since he is a God of justice, but the blessing is "for those who wait on him" (see 28:16). Here Isaiah reiterates a pervasive element in his preaching—Yahweh will destroy the Assyrians but in his time and in his way. Blessed are those who wait until the time is ripe, and Yahweh chooses the hour.

Isaiah 30:19-33

Following the condemnation of Israel's appeal to Egypt for support of its rebellion from Assyria, Isaiah moved to assure Zion that matters would go well with the city (vv. 19-33). If the present form of verse 20 is correct, then Isaiah seems to envision some future danger and period of adversity for the city—there will be bread of adversity to eat and water of affliction to drink. This allusion could indicate that Jerusalemites and Judeans had been cooperating with the Israelite rebellion to a degree that led Isaiah to anticipate some form of Assyrian retaliation. This clearly seems to be the case in chapters 28–29, which condemn some Jerusalemite leaders (28:14-22) and anticipate an attack on Jerusalem (29:1-5). These chapters, however, probably come from an earlier period than does Isaiah 30. Since the latter dates from about 726, chapters 28–29 reflect earlier conditions before the second phase of revolt was in full swing and appeal had been made to Egypt.

Another way of reading verse 20 is to assume that the final letter in both *lehem* (bread) and *mayim* (water) should have been duplicated with the following words. This would give a text that reads "bread without adversity and water without affliction." Such an understanding of the text means that throughout verses 19-33 Isaiah is proclaiming a bright future for Zion.

The central thrust of verses 19-22 is to assure Jerusalem that Yahweh will make known his "way," or his course of action, so there will be no uncertainty about what Judah's position ought to be *vis à vis* the Assyrians. Isaiah proclaims that the people need weep no more. His reference to the city's weeping may indicate that Jerusalemite and Judean society, as in the Syro-Ephraimitic crisis, had again been torn and troubled over what stance to take when their "kin" in the north had planned, and were now again carrying out, rebellion against Assyria (see 28:14-22, where support for the revolt is hinted at more strongly). In verse 19, Isaiah promises the people that when they appeal to Yahweh he will answer as soon as he hears, that is, as soon as the words are spoken.

In explaining how Yahweh will make known the "way," Isaiah refers to "your teacher" (v. 20). It is uncertain whether the "teacher" or "the one who teaches you" refers to God, to the king, or to Isaiah, although most translations and interpretations assume that God is the referent. The title *teacher* occurs nowhere else in Isaiah. Two things are said explicitly about the teacher. He will no longer hide himself or be out of sight (the Hebrew verb occurs only here, and thus its meaning is somewhat uncertain), and the people's eyes will behold the teacher. If this text is speaking about God, as the context suggests, then Isaiah is declaring that Yahweh would make himself (his views) clearly obvious. The people would not only see, but they would also hear as if directed from behind whether they should turn to the right or to the left (v. 21). In describing this mode of Yahweh's making known his way, Isaiah may be countering not only those who favored revolt and claimed divine sanction for the rebellion (see 8:19; 30:22), but also his own earlier proclamation, which referred to God's teaching the people (the Israelites) through men of strange lips and gibberish talk (see 28:9-13). Verse 22 declares that the clear directions of Yahweh will make the use and consultation of images superfluous, and the people will treat them as polluted materials. (Here the prophet employs language associated with menstruation; see 4:4.). Isaiah does not condemn the use of images and idols *per se*; he merely declares that the people who apparently were using them to ascertain the divine will would treat them as useless contaminants and dispose of them.

Isaiah promises that in the good time of coming salvation supernormal events will occur. The time of salvation is described first negatively and then positively. Negatively, it will be a day of great slaughter when the towering ones (not "towers" as in RSV)—namely, the Assyrians—will fall (v. 25*b*). Positively, it will be a day when Yahweh binds up the hurt and heals the wounds of his people (v. 26*b*). The "supernormal" events will consist of plenteous rain, marvelous productivity in the fields, extravagance in the care of livestock, and abundance of water (vv. 23-25*a*) as well as the intensification of the light of the sun and the moon (v. 26*a*).

The depiction of the coming of Yahweh's name in verses 27-28 lends dramatic and poetic color to Isaiah's promise that Yahweh will take action against the Assyrians. Multiple metaphors appear in this subunit—a consuming fire, a thunderstorm, a flooding stream, and a restraining bit. The object of Yahweh's coming and the victims of his wrath will be the nations and the peoples, not Israel or Judah.

In verses 29-32, Isaiah describes the good times to come in terms of the jubilant celebrations associated with festivals. Various features of festival celebrations are noted—nocturnal singing, gladness of heart, pilgrimage accompanied by flute music, the sound of timbrels and lyres, and probably war dances (vv. 29, 32; for a description of such nocturnal festivities and dancing, see *Mishnah Sukkah* 5:1-5; see also, above, chap. 4, sect. 27). The occasion for such exuberant celebrations would be the destruction of Assyrian power. Isaiah describes this destruction in terms of Yahweh's making his voice heard so as to strike the Assyrians with terror and in terms of blows landed by his arm to the accompaniment, on the one hand, of cloudburst, tempest, and hailstones and, on the other hand, music making and celebration by the people. The conclusion of this depiction of Assyria's destruction (v. 33) associates the event with a "fireplace" in the Jerusalem area, probably the site referred to in later texts as Topheth, where apparently human sacrifice was occasionally made to Molech but within the bounds of

Yahwistic worship (see Jer. 7:31-32; 19:6-15; II Kings 23:10; Ezek. 20:25-26). Similar imagery is used in 31:9*b*, which speaks of Yahweh as one whose fire is in Zion and whose furnace is in Jerusalem. Isaiah describes this burning place as a site prepared for "the king" (*hammelek*), namely, the king of Assyria, thus punning on the term Molech.

> Surely, Tophteh (or a burning place) has long been prepared,
>   surely for the king it is made ready, deep and wide;
> its pyre is fire and wood in abundance;
>   the breath of Yahweh, like a stream of brimstone, kindles it.

In spite of some difficulties in translating and understanding this final verse, it seems clear that Isaiah proclaimed the destruction of Assyrian power and the Assyrian king in the environs of Jerusalem. The language Isaiah uses here is highly metaphorical and dramatic, drawing on the cultic imagery of the decimation by Yahweh of any enemies attacking Zion (see Pss. 46, 48; Isa. 29:6-8). The belief that Assyrian power would be broken in the land of Yahweh, itself, seems to have been a characteristic feature of Isaiah's preaching (see Isa. 14:24-27).

31. EGYPT IS HUMAN NOT DIVINE (31:1-9)

B. S. **Childs**, *Isaiah and the Assyrian Crisis* (London: SCM Press, 1967)33-35, 57-59; H. **Donner**, *Israel unter den Völkern* (Leiden: E. J. Brill, 1964)135-39; G. R. **Driver**, "Isaiah I–XXXIX: Textual and Linguistic Problems" *JSS* 13(1968)36-57; T. G. **Glasson**, "The 'Passover', a Misnomer: The Meaning of the Verb Pasach," *JTS* 10(1959)79-84; W. H. **Irwin**, *Isaiah 28–33: Translation with Philological Notes* (Rome: Biblical Institute Press, 1977)107-17.

The speech in chapter 31 presupposes the same general historical situation as chapter 30—namely, the appeal by Israel and King Hoshea for Egyptian aid in their budding revolt, renewed against Assyria and Shalmaneser V in 726. In both structure and content, the two speeches are parallel. Both denounce the Israelite appeal to Egypt (30:1-7; 31:1-3*a*), proclaim defeat for the plan (30:8-18; 31:3*b*), offer an alternative to rebellion (30:15; 31:6), declare that Zion will be divinely protected (30:19-29; 31:4-5), and promise that Assyria will be destroyed in an annihilation connected with Yahweh's "furnace" in Jerusalem (30:33; 31:7-9).

The manner in which the prophet addresses those he rebukes in the two chapters indicates that chapter 31 postdates chapter 30. In 30:2, Isaiah speaks of "those setting out to go down to Egypt," but in 31:1 of "those going (or "having gone") down to Egypt." In addition, the infinitive forms in 30:1 suggest the initiation, rather than the execution, of an action. Thus, chronologically, the two chapters are closely related, but priority lies with chapter 30.

The following is an outline of the speech in chapter 31:

(1) A woe denunciation of the Israelite appeal to Egypt (1-3)
(2) An assurance of divine protection for Zion (4-5)
(3) An appeal to the Israelites to give up their plans for revolt (6)
(4) An assurance that Assyria will be destroyed by Yahweh (7-9)

Isaiah 31:1-3

The opening section of this speech rebukes the Israelite embassy for going down to Egypt to secure help in the revolt against Assyria. The passage opens with a woe exclamation, followed by a participial phrase designating the culprits being denounced ("those going down to Egypt for help"). A series of verbal clauses follows, describing the actions constituting the offenders' misdeeds. The appeal to Egypt is seen, on the one hand, as relying on horses and trusting in chariots and their steeds and, on the other hand, as the result of failure to look to Yahweh the Holy One of Israel (see 17:7) and to seek his guidance (v. 1). The clear implication of verse 1 is that had the Israelites looked to Yahweh and consulted him—that is, inquired of him through his spokesman—then God would clearly have advised against placing hope in Egyptian aid against Assyria. Of course, Isaiah condemned not only reliance on Egypt for aid in the revolt but also the revolt itself (see 17:4-6; 28:2-4).

In verse 2, Isaiah makes four declarations with regard to Yahweh, whom the Israelites had not consulted. (1) Yahweh too is wise. Perhaps the advocates of revolt against Assyria were claiming rebellion to be the "wise" choice, the timely step to take, and thus promoting themselves as wise. But for the prophet, the Israelite advisors were not the only ones possessing wisdom, if in fact they did. (2) God is the one who has brought misfortune. The prophet here appears to allude to some earlier calamity or evil state that Yahweh brought upon Israel. No doubt, he is referring to either the calamitous consequences of the Syro-Ephraimitic alliance for Israel or, more likely, the state of affairs (the humiliation of capitulation and the burden of special tribute) resulting from Hoshea's surrender to Shalmaneser only a short time earlier (II Kings 17:3). That revolt too, in spite of Isaiah's judgment (chap. 17), had also been seen by the Israelites as the wise action for the time. (3) God has not cancelled his words. Just as Isaiah had Yahweh earlier denounced Israel's rebellions and announced the failure of their actions, so now he affirms that the words of Yahweh still stand; they have not been cancelled or called back. (4) Yahweh will rise up against the house of evildoers and against the help of the workers of iniquity. From the context, it is clear that "house of evildoers" and "workers of iniquity" refer to Israel, at least to those in its midst who advocate revolt against Assyria and reliance on the Egyptians, and that "the help" (or hoped-for aid) refers to Egyptian assistance.

The evil and the iniquity that Isaiah accuses the Israelites of perpetrating is not specified by the prophet. Given the context and the political dimensions of Israel's action, the prophet probably had in mind more than just the nation's failure to consult Yahweh or to adhere to his will and avoid rebellion (see 30:15-16). Israel's rebellion and appeal to a foreign power represented the transgression and repudiation of the nation's vassal treaty with the Assyrians (see 30:1; II Kings 18:14; Ezek. 17:11-21).

Numerous Assyrian vassal treaties from the ninth century B.C.E. and later are extant (see *ANET* 532-41, 659-61). Significant features of these texts are (a) the complete allegiance and loyalty demanded by the Assyrian overlord, (b) horrible curses and calamities (some acted out symbolically in the ritual of treaty making) pronounced upon the violator, and (c) the invocation of a plethora of divine beings to oversee the treaty arrangements and to punish offenders. Whether Isaiah had this complex of conditions in mind when he declared the rebellious Israelites to be a house of evildoers and workers of iniquity cannot be determined for certain (see the earlier discussion of 30:1). Given the circumstances and historical context, however, the prophet's range of vision is more likely to be political—that is, concerned with Assyrian-Israelite relations—than purely moral or theological.

Just as verse 1 describes the actions of Israel around two polar opposites—going to Egypt and trusting in its armaments over against looking to Yahweh and inquiring of him—so verse 3*a* presents another antithesis. Egypt is only human, not divine; its horses are flesh, not spirit. The contrast between human/divine and flesh/spirit implies the futility of Israel's plans over against the will of God. Egypt is to Yahweh as humans are to God; Egyptian horsepower is mere flesh without spirited power. The objects of Israel's confidence are only human without saving power before Yahweh (see 2:22).

Verse 2*b* describes the consequences of God's coming action: He will stretch out his hand and the helper (Egypt) will stumble and the helped (Israel) will fall and together both of them will perish. Earlier, Isaiah had spoken of a series of calamities as the consequence of God's stretching out his hand (5:25; 9:12, 17, 21; 10:4) and of Assyria as the outstretched hand (14:26). The prophetic verdict is that against Yahweh, and against Assyria as the instrument of the divine, Israel and Egypt are like impotent human flesh.

Isaiah 31:4-5

Verses 4-5 affirm the promise of the divine protection of Zion. The introduction to this section—"Surely, thus Yahweh has spoken to me"—is somewhat unusual but not without parallel in Isaiah (see 5:9; 21:16; 22:14). Isaiah seems, in such cases of appeal to a private, intimate communication, merely to be affirming in a special way the revelatory and certain character of his proclamation.

Two images are used to depict the divine defense of Zion. First, as a lion growls over its prey to ward off any who might attempt to sieze it—even a shouting, noisy band of shepherds—so also Yahweh will protect Mt. Zion and its hill. Although many commentators understand verse 4 as a depiction of Yahweh's coming destruction of Jerusalem, such a reading of the text clashes with both the straightforward sense of the verse and its parallel in verse 5. As the lion growls "over its take" (`al-ṭarpo`), so also Yahweh will descend to fight "upon Mt. Zion and its hill" (`al-har-ṣiyon we`al-gibe`atah). Isaiah engages in a little ironic wordplay in his description of Yahweh's protection of Zion, a wordplay that illustrates the cohesion of verses 4-5 with verses 1-3. Yahweh Sebaoth (note the militant title; see above on 1:24) "will go down" (*yered*) to fight on behalf of Mt. Zion; the Israelites are "the ones going down" (*hayyoredim*) to Egypt. The second image, like the first, is drawn from the world of nature. Like birds on the wing (defending their nest or young) so Yahweh will hover over Jerusalem, encircling and passing back and forth over the city, defending it (v. 5).

Isaiah 31:6

Verses 6 and 7 consist of an appeal to the Israelites to give up their plans for revolt and the reason such action should be taken. The appeal utilizes the word *shub*, which Isaiah frequently used earlier (see the discussion on Shear-jashub, above, pp. 122-23). In 30:15*a*, he had Yahweh call on the Israelites for *shubah*, but instead the people's program was to rely on Egyptian aid (30:15*b*-16). In verse 6, to *shub* would be the opposite of going down to Egypt for help (31:1)—that is, it would mean abandoning the plans for revolt and continuing to submit to Assyrian authority.

Two problems arise in the interpretation of verse 6, and they become obvious in a literal translation: "Return [second person plural] to the one for whom they have [third person plural] so deeply revolted, O children of Israel." First of all, who is the one to whom the Israelites should return and against whom they have deeply revolted? The referent here could be either Yahweh (see 29:15), since reliance on Egypt was tantamount to failure to consult Yahweh (31:1), or

Shalmaneser, the Assyrian king against whom Israel was rebelling. The text does not make it possible to determine which of these Isaiah had in mind; in fact, he may have been deliberately ambiguous, since returning to either would in reality be submission to both. Second, does Isaiah distinguish between those who have deeply revolted (the "they" in the text) and those whom he advises to return? Assuming that the verbal forms, and thus the change in persons, are significant, Isaiah would be appealing to Israel in general to rise up against the pro-Egyptian/pro-revolt party that had gained dominance over Israelite politics and now had negotiators in Egypt. That Israelite society had been strongly divided was indicated in earlier Isaianic texts (see 28:6). That King Hoshea seems to have supported the revolt only half-heartedly is suggested by the fact that he allowed himself to be, or was taken, prisoner early in the revolt (see II Kings 17:4*b*).

The reason offered by Isaiah to support his appeal is stated as a warning in verse 7: "Because in that day everyone will disavow [or reject] the silver and gold images which your hands have made for you." (The word *sin* at the end of the verse, missing from some ancient versions, appears to be a gloss.) Isaiah uses this terminology of "discarding" images elsewhere to speak of the human reaction when confronted with Yahweh's overwhelming action (see 2:20; 17:8; 30:22). His description appears to function as a slogan to describe human reaction when God acts in such a fashion as to render superfluous the use of mediating cultic artifacts. "In that day" would refer to the occasion of Yahweh's judgment of the rebellious Israelites, namely, the Assyrian move to suppress the revolt by Shalmaneser on his return to the west.

Isaiah 31:7-9

The divine oracle in verses 8-9*a*, which concludes this speech, was both a promise and a warning to Isaiah's audience. To the scheming Israelites, bent on rebellion and gambling their wealth and future on Egyptian aid, the prophet warns that Assyria's fall will not be the result of human plotting—"Assyria will fall, by no human sword, and no mortal sword will consume it." Here the prophet alludes to his earlier declaration that Egypt was mortal, not divine, and their horses flesh and not spirit (v. 3). The Israelite goal, the downfall of Assyria, will be achieved but by divine, and not human, power. To those presently opposing revolt, Isaiah's words were ones of promise ("Assyria will fall"); to those pursuing rebellion, they were words of doom ("by no human sword"). The features of Assyria's demise are noted in verses 8b-9a, although the particulars described are somewhat uncertain. The following is a possible, but hypothetical, translation:

> It [Assyria] shall falter from before the sword,
> and its select troops shall melt away;
> and its fortress shall pass from being an alien residence,
> and its officials shall collapse from fear.

This translation is based on the following assumptions. (1) The prophet plays on the terms *mss* ("to melt, waste away"), *nss* ("to falter"), and *nws* ("to flee"). (2) *Baḥurim* ("young men" RSV) refers to specially selected forces that the Assyrians placed in trouble spots throughout the empire, including such groups as the Itu'a Aramean tribe, employed in Phoenicia and elsewhere (see 28:9-13; *Iraq* 17[1955]127-28). (3) The term *sela`*, usually translated "rock," here refers to an Assyrian fortress, probably in Samaria and occupied by Assyrian forces, the *baḥurim*. (4) The noun *magor* is not the word for "terror" but a homonym meaning a "place, residence for aliens" (see Gen. 17:8). (5) The officials would include those charged with supervision of vassal states (see 33:18-19).

Comparison of modern translations of verses 8b-9a illustrates how differently the text can be read. In spite of this diversity, the overall sense of the material is clear: Assyria will totter and fall as a result of Yahweh's action.

In concluding the divine oracle, Isaiah refers to Yahweh as one whose fire is in Zion and whose oven is in Jerusalem. Such terminology and imagery appear also in 10:17 and 30:33. The association of Yahweh, Jerusalem, and "fire-places" emphasizes Jerusalem as the center of significance in the development of events, Yahweh as the destroying, powerful deity, and Jerusalem, the cultic center *par*

351

excellence, as either the place or the origin of the oppressor's downfall.

32. A KING IN RIGHTEOUSNESS SHOULD REIGN
(32:1-20)

W. H. **Irwin**, *Isaiah 28-33: Translation with Philological Notes* (Rome: Biblical Institute Press, 1977)118-34; B. **Stade**, "Jes. 32.33," *ZAW* 4(1884)256-71; G. **Stansell**, "Isaiah 32: Creative Redaction in the Isaian Traditions," *SBL 1983 Seminar Papers* (ed. K. Richards; Chico: Scholars Press, 1983)1-12.

Isaiah's speech in chapter 32 belongs to the period of Israel's revolt against Shalmaneser and thus to the nine year reign assigned King Hoshea (II Kings 17:1). At this point, we need to look again at what the Kings account tells us of Hoshea's rule.

The editorial verdict passed on him in II Kings charges Hoshea with doing evil in the sight of Yahweh, "Yet not as the kings of Israel who were before him" (II Kings 17:2 RSV). This conditional judgment of Hoshea is milder than that usually applied to northern monarchs by the editors of the Kings material. That Hoshea was not as evil "as the kings before him" refers to the fact that Hoshea neither exercised nor asserted Israelite authority over Judah. Ahaz had broken with Israelite policy and asserted Judean independence from the north once Pekah, with Syrian assistance, assumed the throne and adopted an anti-Assyrian posture (see the discussion of 9:2, above p. 179). Hoshea apparently never sought to assert northern dominance over the south; this may have been part of the Assyrian arrangement for the area established by Tiglath-pileser.

From Assyrian records, we know that Hoshea was placed on the throne or was recognized as king in Samaria by Tiglath-pileser (*ANET* 283-84; *ARAB* I §§ 815-19; *TUAT* I 373-74). According to II Kings 17:3, Shalmaneser came up (or marched) against Hoshea, who became his servant (vassal) and paid him tribute. This would have been in 727, when Shalmaneser continued the efforts of his father to suppress the revolt in the west that had begun in 728 (see Isa. 17 and,

above, chap. 4, sect. 19). Hoshea's submission to Shalmaneser did not last very long: "But the king of Assyria caught
Hoshea in an act of treachery: he had sent envoys to King So
of Egypt, and he had not paid the tribute to the king of
Assyria, as in previous years" (II Kings 17:4*a* NJPSV).
Hoshea's treachery, or his appeal to Egypt, was carried out
in 726 while Shalmaneser remained at home in Assyria.
This renewed Israelite move toward rebellion was condemned early on by Isaiah (chaps. 28–29), who also
denounced the embassy to Egypt to acquire armaments
(chaps. 30–31).

Second Kings 17:4*b* notes that the Assyrian king arrested
Hoshea and shut him up in prison. This must have been in
725 or at the time of Shalmaneser's return to the west (see
Josephus, *Ant* IX 283-87) unless Hoshea was earlier arrested
by Assyrian troops stationed in Samaria. The circumstances
of Hoshea's arrest and whether it involved some peace
initiative during which Hoshea was surreptitiously siezed
cannot be determined, although they may be hinted at in
Isaiah 33:7-9.

Sometime after Hoshea's arrest, Shalmaneser invaded or
marched against "all the land" of Israel, placing Samaria
under siege for three years (II Kings 17:5). In Hoshea's ninth
year, probably 723/2, Shalmaneser captured Samaria (see
ABC 73), and exiled Israelites to various places, according to
II Kings 17:6.

Isaiah's speech in chapter 32 belongs to the period after
Hoshea's arrest but before the fall, and probably the siege,
of Samaria. According to 32:14, the palace is deserted and
the noise (or pomp) of the city (or royal quarter) is left
behind (see Hos. 10, which presupposes the same
background). This suggests that Hoshea had already been
taken into custody. Verses 9-11, however, assume that
some features of normal life were still possible in Samaria.
The countryside, on the other hand, seems to be suffering
ravishment from Assyrian forces. This would have been
when Shalmaneser "went up against all the land" (II Kings
17:5*a*) but before he marched against Samaria and placed it
under siege (II Kings 17:5*b*).

Isaiah's speech in this chapter may be divided into the
following outline:

(1) A depiction of the righteous rule of a king (1-8)
(2) A call for the women of Samaria to lament (9-13)
(3) A proclamation of a good time to come (14-20)

Isaiah 32:1-8

This opening section, verses 1-8, which describes the nature and consequences of proper monarchical rule, probably functions as both judgment on the present situation in Samaria and on the conditions producing that situation and as an affirmation of true monarchical rule as embodied in the person of Hezekiah.

Scholars have often commented on two characteristics of the section: its similarity to wisdom teachings and its lack of any real prophetic or promissory quality. The latter has been described in terms of the text's failure to speak clearly about the advent of a future ruler; the text, in other words, seems to be speaking of an actual reigning monarch.

Structurally, the material in verses 1-8 may be divided into three subunits on the basis of content. Verses 1-2 note the nature of a righteous and just government; verses 3-5 comment on the results of such rule; and verses 6-8 describe the fool, the knave, and the noble.

The section opens with what would have been a commonly accepted proposition: "Surely, a king should rule in righteousness [or legitimately] and as for ministers [princes], in justice they should govern." Such an assertion of common sense knowledge may be seen as a harsh judgment on the administration of Hoshea in Israel. Twice in his reign, in 728/7 and again in 727/6, he led his nation, or was pressured, into rebellion against Assyria. On both occasions, important consequences resulted. In 727, Hoshea had been forced to capitulate and pay indemnity, at the moment Israel's ravishment by the Assyrian army was just beginning. On the other hand, the assertion about righteous government may be seen as an affirmation of the Davidic family's ruling in Jerusalem. In spite of pressure and the temptation to join an anti-Assyrian coalition in 735 (Isa. 7–8), 728/7 (Isa. 17), and 727/6 (Isa. 28–29), the house of David had resisted. Ahaz had remained aloof from the coalition, and the prophet had declared him a ruler concerned with justice and righteousness (9:7; 11:3*b*-5). Judah had escaped any devastating onslaught from the Assyrian army, even though Isaiah had expected the countryside to suffer severely (7:18-25; 8:7-8*a*). Hezekiah, too, refused to become involved with anti-Assyrian fronts, even though advocacy of such a policy gained a limited hearing in Jerusalem (28:14-22).

In verses 2-8, Isaiah expounds on the qualities of good government, condemning recent Israelite politics in the process. Isaiah 32:2-8 may be read as a more theoretical presentation of the same issues that the prophet addressed in 28:1-8. The latter text contains harsh condemnations delivered in the heat of passion when Isaiah was attempting to thwart another rebellion; the former text presents more dispassionate articulations after calamity has struck. In 728/7, Isaiah was trying to dissuade his contemporaries from a course of action. Now, sometime about 725, he expounds on the larger picture of what good administration, so lacking in the north, had produced.

Verse 2 describes the protective functions of a good king and good ministers of state. The righteous leader functions as a source of protection against life's storms: "Each will be like a refuge from the wind and a shelter from rainstorms" (v. 2*a*; see 4:6; 28:17*b*). The house of David had steered a cautious course in international politics and thus had sheltered its people from the gales and tempests of military conflict. Positively, righteous leaders are "like brooks of water [an oasis] in a desert place and like the shade of a massive rock in exhausting terrain" (v. 2*b*).

In verses 3-8, Isaiah continues to speak in generalities, but in generalities that allude to the type of behavior that led Israel into its calamitous revolt.

3. Seeing eyes will not be smeared over,
    and the ears of hearing ones will listen.
4. The mind (heart) of impulsive ones will give consideration to knowledge,
    and the tongue of stammerers will be quick to speak eloquent things.
5. The fool will no longer be called "noble,"
    and of the knave, he will not be said to be honorable.

6. For the fool speaks foolishness,
     and his mind (heart) works iniquity;
       to produce impiety,
       and to ascribe confusion to Yahweh;
       to spill the life of the hungry,
       and he deprives the thirsty of drink.
7. And as for the knave, his tools are evil,
     and he plots wicked deeds;
       to enlist the oppressed ones with lying words,
       and the poor ones by talking justice.
8. But the noble one plans noble acts,
     and he stands upon his noble deeds.

Isaiah's referents in this section are not difficult to
determine. The seeing eyes that were smeared over and the
hearing ears that failed to listen are those who saw and
realized that revolt was not a desired or feasible objective at
the time and yet would not or could not change the course of
affairs. The impulsive ones were those rash to act, quick to
move the people into rebellion without thinking matters
through. The stammerers and stutterers (the term is
uncertain and occurs only here in biblical Hebrew) are those
who spoke out against the war so hesitatingly as to mumble
or muffle their opposition. The fools and knaves that came to
be called honorable were the leaders who rallied the
population behind revolt at a time when Hoshea's leadership
was weak and inadequate for the needs of the hour. (That the
war was popularly supported is evidenced by the fact that
rebellion continued after the arrest of Hoshea and reignited
following the death of Shalmaneser.) The noble one who
plans noble deeds and continues to stand on these refers, in
general, to those who opposed revolt but also, of course, to
King Hezekiah, who refused to join the anti-Assyrian revolt
and remained loyal to the Assyrian monarch.

In describing the actors and the actions of those who led
Israel into revolt, the prophet drew on previously employed
imagery. In 28:1-13, Isaiah had chided the leaders in Samaria
as drunken idiots. In 29:9-16, he had condemned the
pro-rebellion Jerusalemites for loss of sight and improper
vision, a failure to understand the times. The disorder
attributed to northern society, in which the rebels assumed

authority, reminds one of the depiction of Jerusalem run by neophytes in 3:1-8. That the war was (wrongly) carried out in the name of Yahweh (32:6*b*) is probably already alluded to in 31:7.

Isaiah 32:9-13

Having indirectly condemned and explained the breakdown in Israelite politics, which led to the revolt against Assyria, Isaiah turns in verses 9-13 to the particularities of the situation in the north and calls on the women of the city to bewail the country's coming condition. The addressees are identified as women and daughters—that is, the females—who are further specified by two adjectives, "unperturbed" *sha'anannoth;* see Jer. 30:10) and "unsuspecting" (*boṭeḥoth;* see Judg. 18:10). Neither of these terms is used here to suggest an overconfident or arrogant attitude. The sense is of people unaware that the normalcy of conditions will suddenly be altered and that a state of crisis and abnormalcy will arise (see Amos 6: 1-3 where a similar situation is assumed). Isaiah, in a warning, calls on the women to "rise up," in the sense of being startled or alerted to attention: "Hear my voice, give ear to my speech." The prophet's words are to alert the hearers to the approach of danger.

The opening of verse 10 stipulates the time within which the initial alarm will be transformed into more panicked and frenzied activity. The expression "days upon [or "on, over, in addition to," and so on] a year" has been variously translated: "next year," "in a little more than a year," or "when the year is out." The expression may be understood as comparable either to "before the year is over," or to "early next year." This is indicated by the references to features of the harvest cycle in verse 10*b*: "[You will be troubled] because ended is the grape harvest; ingathering will not come." Grape harvesting occurred in late summer, and the ingathering from the threshing floor and winepresses occurred before the coming of the fall rains. The festival of ingathering (*'asip*) celebrated the latter occasion and marked the completion of the old and the beginning of the new year (see Exod. 23:16*b*; 34:22*b*). If the references to agricultural activities are taken literally, then Isaiah spoke of the grape harvest that was over and the future ingathering that would not come: "Before the year is over [or "shortly into the next year"], you will be riled up. . . . " Isaiah thus seems to have anticipated that the Assyrian onslaught would quickly descend on the people, so quickly that time would not allow for harvested crops to be safely stored away.

In verses 11-13, Isaiah calls on the women to undergo the rites of mourning for land soon to be decimated. Rituals of mourning included agitated body actions (v. 11*a*), stripping bare the body from the waist up, tying the clothes around the waist (with sack cloth?) to prevent complete exposure (v. 11*b*), and beating on the breasts (v. 12*a*) as well as various sounds of wailing and lamenting (see photograph 459 in *ANEP*). The items to be lamented in this case include pleasant fields, fruitful vines (v. 12), "the land of my people [soon] to produce thorns and briers, all the delightful homes, and the bustling city" (Samaria; v. 13).

Isaiah thus anticipated a great devastation of the north by Shalmaneser's forces. Even after the arrest of Hoshea, the Israelite revolt continued and no pro-Assyrian party was capable of gaining control of the state. The prophet assumed that the Assyrian monarch would move quickly to suppress the continuing uprising. Thus he called upon the Israelite women to begin already the process of lamentation for the destruction that would strike before the fall festival.

Isaiah 32:14-20

In the last section of this speech, Isaiah turns to a description of an idealized future that will be realized when "the spirit is poured out on us from on high."

The stage for the outpouring of the divine spirit is set by verse 14. Most commentators connect this verse with what precedes (vv. 9-13) and see it as descriptive of the future conditions to be produced by Assyrian forces and to be lamented in advance. The text is better understood, however, as descriptive of conditions already existing immediately following the arrest of Hoshea, but prior to Samaria's siege. The passage may be translated:

> Surely, the palace is unattended,
> > the noise of the royal quarter is left
> > behind;
> the citadel and watchtower have become,
> > according to the treaty, denuded spots
> > forever;
> a delightful place for wild asses,
> > pasture for flocks.

This translation is based on the following considerations. (1) The description depicts the conditions of the monarchical complex in Samaria after the incarceration of the Israelite king by Shalmaneser's forces. Thus the palace complex and the royal quarter of the city are unattended and abandoned, and the activity and pomp associated with the royal family have ceased. (2) The citadel (`ophel*) and the watchtower denote the military installations associated with the Israelite royal precincts. (3) The superfluous Hebrew temporal expression *b`d* is a scribal error for *k`d*, in which the term `*d* (Akkadian *adê* or *adû*) denotes the treaty or one of the stipulations of the Assyrian-Israelite agreement concluded between Shalmaneser and Hoshea after the latter's initial surrender to the Assyrians in 727 (II Kings 17:3). (4) The Hebrew term *me`aroth* (dens) should be read *ma`aroth* (denuded spots), from the verb `*rr*, meaning "to strip bare" (see v. 11*b*). (5) Part of the Assyrian treaty threatened that such action would be taken—namely, the royal-military (and religious?) complex would be levelled "forever"—if insurrection occurred. (Isaiah may not be quoting the exact terminology of the agreement since he seems to be playing on the use of the verb `*rr*, used earlier in verse 10b in an imperative command addressed to the Samarian/Israelite women.)

The speech assumes that the conditions proleptically bewailed by the lamenting females in verses 12-13 will last until the intervention of God to produce the transformations in nature and society depicted by the prophet in verses 15-20. God's intervention, spoken of in terms of the outpouring of the spirit, will result in radical changes. The wilderness areas, used only for occasional grazing land, will be transformed into farmland, and the ordinary, but fruitful, farmland will be so productive as to look like a forest (v. 15*b*;

see 29:17). Justice and righteousness (proper social order) will prevail throughout the land, from the wilderness regions to the fruitful farmlands (v. 16; see v. 1). The consequence of righteousness will be peace, with the result that quietness and trust will be everlasting qualities of life (v. 17; see vv. 9-11). People will dwell in peaceful settlements, secure dwellings, and untroubled resting places (v. 18). Even the weather will be cooperative—"It will hail in the depression of the forest" (v. 19a), where no destructive damage will be done. This translation of verse 19a is based on deriving *beredeth* from *yrd*, meaning "to go down" and thus reading the noun as the "going down place" or "depression." Cities will not have to be fortified because of the prevailing peaceful conditions: "And in the Shephelah [the vulnerable foothills between the hill country and the coastal plain] the city will lie low," that is, without high-flung wall fortifications (v. 19b). The ones sowing by water sources, in areas where ordinarily foreign troops, refugees, and marauders would frequent to get water, will be blessed and harvest their own crops. Blessed also will be those who allow their cattle and asses to wander loose, since they need not worry about thievery (v. 20).

Whether Isaiah in some way associated these idyllic conditions to come with the Davidic family in Jerusalem remains uncertain. The speech certainly began, as we have argued, with allusions that could be understood to refer to the Davidic house and Hezekiah (see v. 1). The association of the spirit with the Davidic monarchy is clear in 11:2, and Isaiah may have assumed that the outpouring of the spirit would be channeled through the Davidic monarch. Nothing in verses 15-20, however, indicates explicitly that the particular conditions of the northern monarchy and its royal complex would be altered in the age of salvation to come.

33. YAHWEH FOR US (33:1-24)

B. S. **Childs**, *Isaiah and the Assyrian Crisis* (London: SCM Press, 1967)112-17; H. **Gunkel**, "Jesaia 33, eine prophetische Liturgie: Ein Vortrag," *ZAW* 42(1924)177-208; D. R. **Hillers**, "A Hebrew Cognate of Unussu/Unt in Is. 33:8," *HTR* 64(1971)257-59; S. **Mowinckel**, *Psalmenstudien II. Das Thron-*

besteigunsfest Yahwäs und der Ursprung der Eschatologie (Kristiania: Jacob Dybwad, 1922)235-38; R. **Murray**, "Prophecy and the Cult," *Israel's Prophetic Tradition: Essays in Honour of Peter Ackroyd* (ed. R. Coggins et al.; Cambridge: Cambridge University Press, 1982)200-216; J. J. M. **Roberts**, "Isaiah 33: An Isaianic Elaboration of the Zion Tradition," *The Word of the Lord Shall Go Forth: Essays in Honor of David Noel Freidman* (ed. C. L. Meyers and M. O'Connor; Winona Lake: Eisenbrauns/American Schools of Oriental Research, 1983)15-25; S. **Schwantes**, "A Historical Approach to the *'r'lm* of Isa. 33," *AUSS* 3(1965)158-66; B. **Stade**, "Jes. 32. 33," *ZAW* 4(1884) 256-71.

The liturgical character of Isaiah 33, with its parallels to certain of the psalms in both structure and content, has long been noted. Within it one finds petition, description of distress, confession of faith, divine oracle, and elements of a cultic entrance litany.

We propose that this text is a unity, composed by the prophet as a text for use in some major festival in which Israelites from the north, fleeing the Assyrian devastation of the countryside, were integrated and welcomed into the worshiping community of the Jerusalem temple and into residency in the city. The depiction of devastation in verses 7-9 seems to indicate an early phase in Shalmaneser's second campaign to the west but prior to the actual siege of Samaria. As we have noted before (see above, chap. 4, sects. 19 and 28), Josephus provides excerpts from the Tyrian archives, transmitted by Menander (*Ant* IX 283-87). These excerpts speak of an initial campaign in the region by Shalmaneser, followed by a temporary withdrawal, and then a second invasion in which the region, at least in Phoenicia, was subdued with only Tyre holding out. We have dated Shalmaneser's first campaign, a continuation of that begun by Tiglath-pileser, to 728–727 and have associated Isaiah 15–18 with this background. Shalmaneser's stay in Assyria during the year 727–726 occasioned renewed sentiment for revolt in Samaria, which found some advocacy even in Jerusalem itself (Isa. 28–29). The move to rebellion led to Israelite appeals to Egypt for assistance (Isa. 30–31). On Shalmaneser's return to the west in 725, Pekah was arrested, and Assyria took action against Israel and other powers in the area (Isa. 32). Isaiah seems to have anticipated a rebellion-ending blow to be struck against Samaria in the late summer and early fall of 725, between the completion of the harvest and the fall ingathering of the products celebrated in the autumn festival (Isa. 32:10). Therefore, a possible setting for the liturgy in chapter 33, welcoming Israelite refugees/pilgrims to participation in Jerusalem worship and residence in the city, would have been the fall festival of 725.

The following is a translation of the chapter, dividing the material according to its content and speakers.

(A). Prophetic Denunciation of Assyria (v. 1)
 1. Woe, O destroyer, and you who have not been destroyed,
      O plunderer and they have not plundered you!
    When you have finished, O destroyer, you shall be destroyed,
      and when you have completed your plundering, they shall plunder you!

(B) Petition of the Israelites (v. 2)
 2. O Yahweh, be gracious to us,
      on thee we wait.
    Be thou our morning strength,
      indeed, our salvation in the time of distress.

(C). Confession of Faith by the Israelites (vv. 3-6)
 3. From the sound of your roaring, the peoples fled;
      from your exaltation, the nations scattered.
 4. And spoil was gathered in, like the ingesting of the locust;
       and like the locust swarm leaps, so one leaped on it.
 5. You are exalted, O Yahweh, because you are the one dwelling on high,
      the one who has filled Zion with justice and righteousness.
 6. And the steadfastness of your times has resulted in
      abundance, salvation, wisdom, and knowledge;
    the fear of Yahweh, that has been his treasure.

(D). Description of Distress (vv. 7-9)
 7. Behold, the *'r'lm* cry without;
      peace envoys weep bitterly.
 8. Highways are desolate,
      the wayfarer has vanished.

One breaks treaty,
  rejects obligations,
    and gives no regard to human life.
9. One mourns; the land is miserable;
  one has humiliated Lebanon; it rots away;
  Sharon has become like the Arabah;
  and one is snatching away Bashan and Carmel.

(E) *Divine Oracle (vv. 10-14a)*
10. "Now I arise," Yahweh says,
  "now I exalt myself, now I lift myself up.
11. You conceive chaff; you give birth to stubble;
  your spirit like fire consumes you.
12. The peoples will be burned to ash;
  they are cut down thornbushes, in fire they will be burned.
13. Hear, you distant ones, what I have done,
  and acknowledge, you near ones, my might!
14a. Sinners in Zion were afraid,
  the impious ones were siezed with trembling."

(F) *Inquiry of the Israelites (v. 14b)*
14b. Who among us can sojourn with a consuming fire,
  who among us can sojourn with the ever burning hearths?

(G) *Response to the Inquiry (vv. 15-16)*
15. The one walking righteously and the one speaking honestly,
  the one pushing away gain from extortion,
  the one jerking back his hands from holding bribes,
    the one stopping his ears from listening to violence,
  the one closing his eyes from the sight of evil;
16.   that one shall dwell on the heights;
  the rocky fortress shall be his refuge;
  his food supplied and his drink assured.

(H) *Prophetic Description of the Israelites' New Conditions (vv. 17-20)*
17. A monarch in his splendor your eyes shall behold;
  you shall see a far flung country.
18. Your mind will reminisce over the terror:
  "Where is the one who counted? Where is the one who
    weighed?
  where is the one who numbered the towers?"
19. The barbarous people you will not see,
  the people whose obscure speech defied understanding,
  jabbering in an incomprehensible tongue.

20. Look upon Zion, the city of our festivals!
    Your eyes will behold Jerusalem,
a secure habitation, a tent that is not moved about,
    whose stakes will never be pulled up,
        nor any of its guy lines be broken.

(I) *Oath of the refugees (vv. 21-24)*
21. Surely, there is the Majestic Place, Yahweh-for-us,
    a source of rivers, of broad streams;
no galley ship will enter it,
    and no stately vessel sail past it.
22. Surely, Yahweh is our judge,
    Yahweh our commander,
        Yahweh our king;
            He will save us.
23. Your [Zion's] guy lines are spread wide;
    no—they are firmly set;
thus you [Zion] will rejoice over them;
    no—they will spread wide an ensign,
then prey will be apportioned out, spoil in abundance;
    [even] the lame will pillage booty.
24. And never will the inhabitant [of Zion] say, "I am debilitated";
    the people residing in her will be forgiven iniquity.

Although many uncertainties plague attempts to translate this chapter and enormous differences of opinion exist about both the text's historical setting and its literary genre, we believe that its general content and basic meaning are clear. Difficulties in translation and interpretation will be noted as we progress through the text's subunits.

Refugees seeking asylum and safety in Jerusalem and the southern kingdom have been the topics of previous Isaianic oracles. In 4:2-3, Isaiah advocated the acceptance into Jerusalem of refugees fleeing the civil strife in Israel. There he designated as "holy" those granted the privilege of settling in the holy city and envisioned Jerusalem as a sheltering refuge (4:4-6). In chapters 15–16, Isaiah advocated turning a deaf ear to the appeal of Moabites wishing to take up temporary residence in the kingdom.

The issue of what attitude to take toward political refugees from Assyrian campaigns must have been particularly touchy. Too friendly an attitude toward such groups by a vassal state might have been interpreted by the Assyrians as collusion and cooperation and thus as insubordination. Relations between Israelites and Judeans, however, involved special considerations. Both were members of what had historically been one state, or at least two kingdoms of a cooperative entity. Judeans and Davidides certainly would have claimed kinship with, if not the right of dominance over, Israel and Israelites. In noting the Assyrian onslaught against Israel, for example, Isaiah speaks of "the soil of my people" (32:13). Israelites and Judeans shared in the worship of a common deity and a similar cult. Finally, those seeking refuge in Judah and Jerusalem were most likely to have been persons opposing rebellion against Assyria and thus those sharing the political views of Isaiah, Hezekiah, and the anti-rebellion party in Jerusalem and Judah. Northern opponents of rebellion (see 28:5-6) may have been fleeing the hostility of their own people as much as Assyrian aggression.

In this liturgy, Isaiah stresses the distinctive commitments of the Jerusalem community—opposition to rebellion against Assyria at the moment, fidelity to the Davidic king, and confidence in Zion as Yahweh's especially protected domain. Those seeking refuge within its confines were required to swear allegiance to such theological and political positions. Thus Isaiah 33 is clearly consistent with the prophet's previous proclamation. In fact, it is a document embodying the essence of his preaching.

Prophetic Denunciation of Assyria (v. 1)

The liturgy opens with a woe denunciation of Assyria (v. 1). The terminology used to speak of the oppressor, "destroyer" and "plunderer," occurs elsewhere in Isaiah, always with the same referent (16:4; 21:2; 24:16). The prophet, of course, avoids use of the names "Assyria" or "Shalmaneser," otherwise he would, as a member of a vassal state, have risked the charge of sedition. The pronouncement of woe continues to reflect the view of Assyria expressed earlier (see 10:5-27), namely, that Assyria has a divinely appointed task to destroy and plunder and must execute this as an instrument of Yahweh before being destroyed itself.

Petition of the Israelites (v. 2)

The petition of the Israelites (v. 2) asks merely for Yahweh's mercy and not for any destruction of an enemy. Thus the prayer requests an acceptance of the petitioners and refuge from Yahweh, which will be their salvation in this time of distress. No special motivation or reason is offered in the petition as the basis for their acceptance. Nonetheless, they come as Yahweh's devotees and worshipers.

Confession of Faith by the Israelites (vv. 3-6)

In the refugees' confession of faith (vv. 3-6), they testify, first of all, to the fact that the current devastation of Israel and adjacent areas is the work of Yahweh. Again, this is consistent with Isaiah's preaching throughout the crisis (chapters 28–32)—namely, that at this time rebellion against Assyria, even in the name of Yahweh, would be severely punished by Yahweh, and in fact constituted rebellion against Yahweh. The peoples and nations who scattered before the Assyrian military were Israel and its neighbors. The sound of Yahweh's roaring and his exaltation were manifested in the coming of the Assyrian troops. Yahweh is spoken of as the one who has been or is exalted in the entire episode—not the Assyrians, who loot everywhere. Yahweh is further depicted as the one dwelling on high (as resident in Jerusalem? as the dominant power directing international affairs?) and as the one who has filled Zion with justice and righteousness. It is possible to translate verse 5 as, "Exalted is [or was] Yahweh, because the one dwelling on high [the Davidic monarch] has filled Zion with justice and righteousness." With either interpretation, it is clear that in this context justice and righteousness have to do with a specific political situation—that is, being just and righteous refers to fidelity to the vassal treaty with Assyria.

Verse 6 is difficult to both translate and interpret. First of all, the passage contains a reference to Yahweh in the third person in the context of second person address to the Deity—"the fear of Yahweh, that has been his treasure [or store]." This may be explained as simply a slip in addressee (as often occurs in prayers!), or the expression "fear of

Yahweh" may have been so common that one used it in direct address to Yahweh rather than "fear of you." The pronominal suffix "his," used with treasure, may refer to the Davidic king rather than to Yahweh, especially if the king is the one referred to in verse 5 as the "one dwelling on high." Second, the first part of the verse is even more difficult. The prophet uses the term *'emunah*, based on the word *'mm* ("to be firm, to stay put," and so on), which he has previously employed (see 7:9*b*; 28:16*b*) in reference to political policy. Here, however, *'emunah* is modified by "your times," whose exact meaning remains unclear. The idea seems to be that the Davidic kings' adherence to Yahweh's timetable, *vis à vis* the Assyrians, has resulted in "abundance, salvation (or "abundance of salvation"), wisdom, and knowledge." That is, the unwillingness to participate in untimely anti-Assyrian revolt has produced rewards for Jerusalem (see 18:7) and has been the wisest policy.

Description of Distress (vv. 7-9)

The description of the distress (vv. 7-9) depicts the results of the Assyrian efforts to put down the widespread revolt. Verse 7 appears to describe efforts made to settle the conflict. Uncertainty about the identity of the *'r'lm* (vocalized as *'er'ellam*) renders all interpretation suspect. A similar term occurs in II Samuel 23:20 and Isaiah 29:1, 2, and 7. Suggested meanings include "heroes, valiant ones, leaders, priests, royal guards" and so on. The term appears to parallel "peace envoys" (or "messengers of peace") who may have been negotiators seeking terms with Assyria or the Israelites opposed to rebellion. At any rate, one group cries without— that is, is unsuccessful—and the other weeps bitterly. Both expressions suggest a destitute and desperate situation. General anarchy reigns—highways are deserted, no travelers are on the road, political treaties are broken, law and order have broken down, persons take their lives into their own hands, and existence is miserable everywhere. Lebanon and the Sharon Plain have been subjugated, and Bashan and Carmel are being attacked. Here the description reflects the same situation as chapter 32, namely, Samaria had not yet been attacked in force. Shalmaneser seems to have had troops fighting in various places but on no single united front (as earlier in 727; see chaps. 15–18).

Divine Oracle (vv. 10-14a)

In the divine oracle (vv. 10-14a), Isaiah has Yahweh take credit for the Assyrian devastation. Verse 11 appears to be addressed to the revolting nations, declaring that their plans have been nothing but waste straw and that their spirit (their rebellious actions) has started the fire that is now destroying them. Verse 12 announces their fate. In v. 13, Yahweh calls on nations near and far to acknowledge what he has done. Even the sinners and impious ones in Jerusalem (those initially favoring revolt; see 28:14-22) have seen the futility of their advocating rebellion.

Inquiry of the Israelites (v. 14b)

Beginning with verse 14b, form critically, the material shares many parallels with the question-answer schema of the entry litanies, or liturgies, used when pilgrims ceremoniously entered the sanctuary (see Ps. 15; 24; 118; see also Isa. 26:1-6). The inquiry of the refugees (v. 14b) poses the question: "Given the circumstances, who can sojourn in Jerusalem in the presence of Yahweh?" (see Pss. 15:1; 24:3). The description of Yahweh in terms of a consuming fire occurs frequently in Isaiah (9:19; 10:16-17; 30:33; 31:9) and no doubt draws on the imagery of the sacrificial cult in Jerusalem (4:5) and its environs (30:33).

Response to the Inquiry (vv. 15-16)

The prophetic response to the inquiry (vv. 15-16)—like the priestly responses in Psalms 15:2-5; 24:4-5; and 118:20—is stated fundamentally in moral or ethical terms. Two characteristics of the qualifications in verse 15 are worthy of note. First of all, the prophet seems to have composed the response so that each of the six qualities specified designates a different bodily action: walking, speaking, pushing away, snatching, stopping the ears, and closing the eyes. Second, most of the actions noted probably have a political nuance in the context apropos to loyalty to Judah/Assyria and submission to authority.

The pronouncement of the blessing received (see Pss. 15:5*b*; 24:5) indicates the right of the petitioners to worship, or in this case also to reside, in Jerusalem. (Note the use of *gur* and *shakan* in 33:14*b* and 16*a* and in Ps. 15:1.) The essentials of life, in this case food and drink, are also promised to the refugees (v. 16*b*), indicating perhaps some form of state welfare system (see 14:32).

Prophetic Description of the Israelites' New Conditions
(*vv. 17-20*)

In verses 17-20, the prophet expounds on the distinctive qualifications and conditions of Jerusalem over the status of matters in the north, whence the refugees have come. First of all, in Jerusalem, in the person of Hezekiah of the Davidic line, the refugees will see a real monarch, a king in true splendor (v. 17*a*; the court braggadocio is evident). Truly, here was a monarch who ruled righteously (see 32:1). (Note the description of Samaria in 32:14, where the royal quarters are deserted.) Second, the refugees will also behold a far-flung kingdom (v. 17*b*). In comparison to Israel's ever-dwindling territory, the Davidic state certainly compared favorably; at least Judah was not currently losing territory. Third, Isaiah tells the new arrivals that the constant terror of the past, the constant supervision of Assyrian officials that had been a part of Israelite life probably since the first revolt in 735, will not be found in Jerusalem. (Something of the supervision of vassal states by Assyrian officials is alluded to in 28:9-13, 19-20.) The refugees will possess only a recollection of the Assyrian census takers, tribute collectors, and fortification inspectors since these are not a part of Judean life (v. 19). (They were to become so after the 713–711 revolt in which Judah lost its favored nation status; see 22:8*a*). Fourth, Isaiah points to Jerusalem, a city sitting secure, an unmoving tent (not changing camps every time the winds of rebellion blew), where the national festivals are held (v. 20).

Oath of the Refugees (vv. 21-24)

The refugees respond with an oath of confession that would have served as their statement of allegiance and blessing on the capital city. The opening portion of the oath (introduced with the particle *'im*; see 22:14*b*) is difficult to translate since it is uncertain whether Yahweh or the city is being talked about. We have assumed in the above translation that verse 21 speaks of the city and have taken Yahweh-for-us as a metaphoric name for Jerusalem. Another reading of the text is to translate it as "there the majestic Yahweh is for us." The difference is only slight and the general thrust similar. The description of Zion as a place of broad streams is based on a mythology perhaps associated secondarily with the city (see Pss. 46:4; 48:7; Ezek. 47:1-12). Lying behind the idea of the streams of Zion is the concept of the sacred city as the garden of the Deity (the garden of Eden; see Ezek. 28:11-19) from which flowed the streams of the world (see Gen. 2:10-14). Verse 21*b* indicates the impregnability of the city.

Verse 22 shifts the attention from Zion to Yahweh, whom the refugees describe as judge, commander, king, and savior. Such an affirmation constituted a pledge of fidelity to Jerusalem's deity.

The attention shifts back to Zion in verse 23, which contains something like a blessing of a future hope. The passage is variously translated with most assuming that the verse develops the ships-sailing imagery of verse 21*b*. We assume that the imagery picks up on Jerusalem as a tent (see v. 20*b*). (The term *yeḥazzequ*, "they are firmly set," is a play on the name Hezekiah, both the verb and the noun being built on the root *ḥzq*.) This verse expresses the hope of territorial expansion on behalf of the Davidic house, expansion that will involve the acquisition of so much spoil that even the lame, unable to participate in war, will receive a share.

Finally, the person dwelling in Zion will never have reason for complaining and, above all, will be forgiven iniquity, even the Israelite from a nation that committed iniquity in rebelling against its foreign sovereign, breaking treaty, and disobeying the word of Yahweh (v. 24; see 30:13).

34. AGAIN ZION THREATENED BUT DELIVERED
(36:1–37:38)

P. R. **Ackroyd**, "Isaiah 36-39: Structure and Function," *Von Kanaan bis Kerala* (Festschrift J. P. M. van der Ploeg; ed. W. C. Delsman et al.; Kevelaer/Neukirchen-Vluyn: Butzon und Berker/Neukirchener Verlag, 1981)3-21; B. S. **Childs**, *Isaiah and the Assyrian Crisis* (London: SCM Press, 1967); R. E. **Clements**, *Isaiah and the Deliverance of Jerusalem: A Study of the Interpretation of Prophecy in the Old Testament* (Sheffield: JSOT Press, 1980); R. **Deutsch**, *Die Hiskiaerzählungen. Eine formgeschichtliche Untersuchung der Texte Js. 36-39 und 2 R 18-20* (Basel: Basileia, 1969); D. N. **Fewell**, "Sennacherib's Defeat: Words at War in 2 Kings 18:3-19:37," *JSOT* 34(1986)79-90; K. **Fullerton**, "Isaiah's Attitude in the Sennacherib Campaign," *AJSL* 42(1925/26)1-25; J. B. **Geyer**, "II Kings XVIII 14-16 and the Annals of Sennacherib," *VT* 21(1971)604-6; L. L. **Honor**, *Sennacherib's Invasion of Palestine: A Critical Source Study* (New York: Columbia University Press, 1926); W. A. **Irwin**, "The Attitude of Isaiah in the Crisis of 701," *JR* 16(1936)406-18; A. K. **Jenkins**, "Hezekiah's Fourteenth Year: A New Interpretation of 2 Kings xviii 13–xix 37," *VT* 26(1976)289-94; O. **Kaiser**, "Die Verkündigung des Propheten Jesaja im Jahre 701," *ZAW* 81(1969)304-15; J. A. **M`Clymont**, "Hezekiah," *HDB* 2(1900)376-79; J. **Meinhold,** *Die Jesajaerzählungen Jes 36-39* (Göttingen: Vandenhoeck & Ruprecht, 1898); A. R. **Millard**, "Sennacherib's Attack on Hezekiah," *TB* 36(1985)61-77; H. M. **Orlinsky**, "The Kings-Isaiah Recensions of the Hezekiah Story," *JQR* 30(1939/40) 33-49; H. H. **Rowley**, "Hezekiah's Reform and Rebellion," *BJRL* 44(1961/62)395-461 = his *Men of God: Studies in Old Testament History and Prophecy* (London/New York: Thomas Nelson and Sons, 1963)98-132; H. W. F. **Saggs**, "The Nimrud Letters, 1952—Part I," *Iraq* 17(1955)21-50; N. **Sarna**, "The Abortive Insurrection in Zedekiah's Day (Jer. 27-29)," *EI* 14(1978)89-96; W. H. **Shea**, "Sennacherib's Second Campaign," *JBL* 104(1985)401-18; H. **Spieckermann**, *Juda unter Assur in der Sargonidenzeit* (Göttingen: Vandenhoeck & Ruprecht, 1982); E. **Vogt**, "Sennacherib und die letzte Tätigkeit Jesajas," *Bib* 47(1966)427-37; H. **Wildberger**, "Die Rede des Rabsake vor Jerusalem," *TZ* 35(1979)35-47.

Isaiah 36–39 consists primarily of narratives about Hezekiah and his reign, in which the prophet Isaiah plays a prominent role. Chapters 36–37 center around Sennacherib's campaign to the west in 701 and constitute the only material in Isaiah 1–39 initially related to Sennacherib's invasion. (At the editorial stage, Isaiah 28–33 was used to prepare for the narratives about Sennacherib's invasion, prior to the insertion of Isaiah 34–35 and the addition of Isaiah 38–39.) Chapters 38–39 center on Hezekiah's illness and the visit to Jerusalem of emissaries from the Babylonian king, Merodach-baladan. As we indicated earlier, Hezekiah's sickness and the visit of the Babylonians occurred at a date much earlier than Sennacherib's invasion and, in fact, should be related to the period of the Ashdod-led anti-Assyrian rebellion in the west in 714–711. Thus the events reflected in chapters 38–39 have the same general historical background as Isaiah 20–22.

Some general observations on this material are in order. First, Isaiah 36–39 and II Kings 18:13–20:19 are similar in many ways, including the general sequence of events. However, while parallel, they certainly are not identical. In addition to numerous minor variations between the accounts, two major differences appear. The account of Hezekiah's capitulation to Sennacherib in II Kings 18:14-16 has no parallel in Isaiah. The thanksgiving prayer of Hezekiah in Isaiah 38:9-20 has no parallel in II Kings.

Second, Isaiah 36–37, paralleled in II Kings 18:13 and 18:17–19:37, clearly has Yahweh's protection of Zion in fulfillment of the predictions of Isaiah as its central motif. Isaiah 38, paralleled in II Kings 20:1-11, characterizes Isaiah as a wonder worker. Isaiah 39, paralleled in II Kings 20:12-19, has the Babylonian exile as its primary concern and thus anticipates the preaching of redemption from exile by Deutero-Isaiah in chapters 40 and following. This would indicate that these three units of tradition were initially produced independently of one another. Since all three traditions are reflective of concerns indigenous to the book of Isaiah, they are best seen as having been formulated as part of the Isaianic traditions and subsequently incorporated into the Kings material. The material in II Kings 18:14-16 probably never circulated as part of the Isaianic traditions. (Placing

II Kings 18:14-16 and 18:17–19:37 in sequence certainly created tensions in the Kings material.)

Third, scholars have generally assumed that we have three parallel versions of the Assyrian negotiations with Hezekiah. One, generally designated Account A, is found in II Kings 18:13-16. The other two (Accounts B¹ and B²) are divisions made in the material of II Kings 18:17–19:37. According to this scheme, Account B¹ consists of II Kings 18:17–19:9*a* + 36–37 (Isa. 36:2–37:9*a* + 37–38), and Account B² is composed of II Kings 19:9*b*-35 (Isa. 37:9*b*-36). The argument that the B material actually consists of two parallel accounts of what must have been a single Assyrian emissary to Jerusalem is based on similarities between the episodes within the two accounts (messengers arrive from the Assyrian king; demands for surrender are stated; Hezekiah reacts; and Isaiah speaks) and the fact that two different consequences result (in one, the Assyrian army is miraculously slaughtered, and in the other, Sennacherib withdraws, returns home, and is assassinated).

Fourth, reconstruction of the particular course of events associated with Sennacherib's western campaign is extremely difficult, if not impossible, in spite of extensive biblical and non-biblical texts. The various Akkadian texts of Sennacherib that relate to this campaign (see *AS*; *ARAB* II §§ 239-40, 283-84, 309-12, 347; *ANET* 287-88; *TUAT* I 388-91) in conjunction with the biblical accounts indicate the broad features of the events. (a) Sennacherib defeated several kingdoms along the eastern Mediterranean seaboard and captured several Judean cities in southwestern Palestine, seizing booty and captives. (b) He fought Ethiopian-Egyptian forces that had moved into the area in support of the anti-Assyrian coalition. (c) Negotiations were carried on between Hezekiah and Sennacherib, and at some point the Judean king capitulated. He agreed to pay indemnity, which was sent to Nineveh after Sennacherib had returned home, but he was allowed to retain his throne in Jerusalem.

Matters that remain uncertain include the following. (a) The nature of Hezekiah's contact with the Assyrian king is unclear. According to II Kings 18:14, Hezekiah sent messengers to Sennacherib at Lachish and agreed to accept terms of surrender. According to II Kings 18:17 (Isa. 36:2), the

Assyrians sent emissaries to Hezekiah from Lachish. Second Kings 19:8 (Isa. 37:8) implies that negotiations continued after the Assyrian king had moved his camp from Lachish to Libnah. One could hypothesize that Hezekiah agreed to capitulate when Sennacherib sent delegates from Lachish to Jerusalem (in the so-called Account B[1]) and later received the terms of capitulation from the Assyrian king, sent from Libnah (Account B[2]). Account B[1] thus probably contains a reasonably accurate report of the Assyrian visit and the demands for surrender. B[2], which is based on the receipt of written terms of surrender sent by the Assyrian king, has been recast to conform to the structure of B[1]. (b) Whether Jerusalem was ever placed under siege is a disputed point. Sennacherib claims the following about the Judean capital: "Hezekiah I made a prisoner in Jerusalem, his royal residence, like a bird in a cage. I surrounded him with earthwork in order to molest those who were leaving his city's gate" (*ANET* 288). The metaphor of "shutting up like a bird in a cage" does not itself imply an actual siege (for Tiglath-pileser's use of the expression, see *ARAB* I § 776), neither does the reference to making Hezekiah a prisoner. The earthwork thrown up around Jerusalem would not have constituted a siege of the city, but only work preparatory to such an endeavor. Sennacherib thus never mentions a full siege of and attempt to capture Jerusalem.

Fifth, the western campaign of Sennacherib was the subject of folkloristic legendization in both Egypt and Judah. In his history, the Greek historian Herodotus (II. 141) tells a version that he learned in Egypt. The story reports that when Sennacherib, the "king of the Arabians and Assyrians," marched against Egypt, the Egyptian ruler had no support from his military, since he had recently deprived the soldiers of their traditional land grants. In his predicament, the ruler went to a temple, where he bewailed the potential calamities confronting him. While lamenting, he fell asleep and received a divine vision promising that the god would let the king suffer nothing disagreeable from the attack but would send messengers to aid him. Awaking, he gathered what followers he could and set out for Pelusium on the northern Egyptian border. After the Egyptians arrived at the battle-front, a horde of field mice invaded Sennacherib's camp and devoured the Assyrian forces' quivers and bows and the leather handles of their shields. On the morning of battle, the Assyrians discovered that they were bereft of arms, and many were slain. Herodotus reports that the salvation of the Egyptian ruler was commemorated by a statue of the king with a mouse in his hand and an inscription saying, "Whoever looks on me, let him revere the gods."

The legendary quality of the biblical narrative (in the so-called B Accounts) is obvious from several factors: The story is portrayed as a struggle between Sennacherib, the king of Assyria, and Yahweh, the God of Jerusalem; prayer and prophecy are stressed as the Judean weapons; and the enemy is either destroyed by divine intervention or dies at the hands of his own people, in this case his sons. Some of the features in the biblical narrative, however, are probably based on Isaiah's earlier preaching (compare Isa. 37:36 to 10:16 and 17:14).

Sixth, the diplomatic speech-making and negotiations ascribed to the Assyrian emissaries in Isaiah 36:4-20 are probably reasonably authentic. Akkadian letters (ND 2632 and 2717) written to the Assyrian court report of the employment of such tactics in Assyrian efforts to put down the revolt of Nabu-mukin-zeri in Babylonia in 731 (see *Iraq* 17[1955]23-29).

Seventh, the reference to the fourteenth year of Hezekiah as the date of Sennacherib's invasion has raised numerous chronological problems, since the assignment of his fourteenth year to 701 clashes with other references that have him on the throne before the fall of Samaria in 722 (see II Kings 18:9-10). By the turn of the last century, most major theories offered to explain the fourteenth-year reference had already been formulated. (a) Many scholars assume that Hezekiah became king in 715; therefore, his fourteenth year would have been 701. The references to dates for his reign prior to the fall of Samaria are either in error or refer to the time when he was a co-regent with his father, Ahaz. (b) The number fourteen is a scribal mistake for some other number, either twenty-four, twenty-seven, or some other figure. (c) The reference to his fourteenth year originally concerned an invasion of Sargon in 713 or thereabouts, probably the Assyrian campaign to suppress the Ashdod-led revolt. The mistake is thus not in the number of the year but in the name of the Assyrian ruler. (d) Another explanation argues that Hezekiah proclaimed that a new era had begun during his reign and thus the figure refers to the fourteenth year of that era. (e) Others understand the fourteenth year as the date when Hezekiah became ill and that it was originally the time reference for the events behind chapters 38 and 39. When the traditions of Hezekiah's sickness were edited in terms of the Babylonian exile, so as to anticipate the material in Isaiah 40 and following, they also came to be associated with the last major episode in Isaiah's and Hezekiah's lives, namely, Sennacherib's invasion. The illness and invasion thus came to be assigned to the same period. The last of these theories is the one we have adopted as most likely (see, above, chap. 1, sect. 3A).

Our discussion of the four speeches attributed to Isaiah in these chapters (37:6-7, 21-29, 30-32, 33-35) is based on a number of assumptions. (1) Having been a supporter and initiator of the revolt against Assyria at the time of Sargon's death in 705 (see Isaiah 24–27 and, above, chap. 4, sect. 27), Isaiah continued his support throughout the 701 invasion. (2) A period of warfare in southwestern Palestine preceded any Assyrian emissary to Jerusalem, demanding surrender of the city by Hezekiah (36:4-10), or the surrender of Hezekiah by the citizens of the city (36:11-20). (3) No major Assyrian force ever moved against Jerusalem. Some troops may have been dispatched to the town's environs to set up a temporary blockade, but no sustained assault was undertaken to capture the town. (4) The authentic words of Isaiah during the crisis have been preserved in 37:22b-35. (5) Although presently edited to precede the statements about Sennacherib's defeat and withdrawal, these three speeches may have come from various times in the crisis.

The speech attributed to Isaiah in 37:6-7 seems clearly to have been formulated in the light of the assassination of Sennacherib by his son in 681, as has 37:37-38 (see *ABC* 81-82). Sennacherib was murdered as part of an attempted palace rebellion. Therefore, probably all of the short speech in 37:6-7 was produced in popular tradition, or by the editors who put together the material of chapters 36–37, and is non-Isaianic.

In 37:22b-29, we possess a scathing denunciation of Sennacherib. One striking feature of this passage is its direct address to the Assyrian ruler, who is not present. This second person direct speech is fairly common, however, in the so-called prophetic oracles against the nations. Several texts in Isaiah use this technique where, in at least some of the cases, the addressee is neither present nor necessarily expected to be informed of the speech's content (see 14:8-20; 17:29-32; 21:13-15; 23:1-14; 33:1). In this particular case, Isaiah may have assumed that Sennacherib's messengers (v. 24) would transmit the material. However, frequently the denunciation and pronouncement of judgment on the enemy or other nation are intended to function as words of assurance to the native hearer, in this case, Hezekiah and Jerusalem.

The speech condemns the Assyrian monarch for two wrongs. First of all, the king has mocked and reviled (or "taunted and blasphemed," NEB) Yahweh, the Holy One of Israel (v. 23). The reference here would be to the taunting of Hezekiah by the Assyrian messengers, since to taunt the messiah (the anointed ruler) was to taunt Yahweh (see Ps. 2:1-3). The Assyrians had built a case against Hezekiah, seeking to demoralize him and the city of Jerusalem using the following arguments. (a) Hezekiah was relying on mere confidence and words rather than strategy and power (36:45). (b) The Judean reliance on Egypt was misplaced, since the Egyptian pharaoh could not be relied on without injuring oneself (36:6). (c) Yahweh, himself, must be displeased with Hezekiah, since the king had torn down the Deity's high places and altars and had required Judah and Jerusalem to worship at one altar only (36:7; see II Kings 18:4; Isa. 27:9). (d) Hezekiah was so short of qualified militia that he could not supply the troops if Sennacherib supplied the horses (36:8-9). (e) The Assyrian ruler was attacking Judah at the explicit command of Yahweh (36:10). The reference here may be to the fact that the Assyrians had carried away from Samaria the cultic items (the golden calf? see Hos. 10:5-6) associated with Yahweh (see *Iraq* 16[1954]180) and thus could receive divine responses. Or the Assyrians may be alluding to the stipulations of an Assyrian-Judean treaty between Sargon and Hezekiah, in which the Judean monarch called down on himself the wrath of Yahweh for breaking the treaty. (It is uncertain whether at that time Assyrian vassal treaties bound the successors of the participating monarchs or were limited to the lifetime of the covenanting partners.) (f) Finally, the Assyrians appeal to history—have any national deities saved their countries from Assyrian conquest? (36:18-20).

Second, after condemning Sennacherib for mocking Hezekiah, the speech condemns him for hubris (37:24b-25). Extravagant claims bordering on braggadocio were made by practically every Assyrian ruler and appear on most of their inscriptions (see, above, chap. 4, sect. 16). Knowledge of such claims and probably inscriptional materials were common throughout Assyrian vassal kingdoms. Isaiah here places in the mouth of Sennacherib terminology typical of such texts. Scaling Lebanon's heights, felling its huge trees (perhaps an allusion to various kings; see Ezek. 31:3-14), and drinking the waters of other lands are given as examples of the monarch's greatness and claims to universal lordship over kings and nations. The reference to drying up the streams of Egypt (v. 25b) may simply be a proverbial expression (see 11:15; 19:5-6). On the other hand, it could indicate that Isaiah's oracle against Sennacherib was delivered after the Assyrians had engaged the Ethiopian-Egyptian army at Eltekeh in the coastal plain.

To indicate the ultimate insignificance of Sennacherib over against Yahweh, Isaiah expounds two ideas. First of all, Jerusalem is depicted as a youthful female who not only spurns the advances of the mighty Assyrian, but also makes fun of him and tosses her head in contempt behind his back (v. 22b). By opening his denunciation of Sennacherib with this image, Isaiah was not only putting down the king but also was stressing the sacred character of Zion. Jerusalem was no ordinary female to be claimed at will. Second, Isaiah has Yahweh claim that Assyrian conquests have been merely the execution of his will (vv. 26-28). At this point, the prophet shifts to divine address, thus positing the divine "I" over against the "I" of the Assyrian braggart. In Sennacherib's statements in verses 24-25, eight first person references and pronouns occur.

But who is that "I" in comparison to Yahweh? The one really in command is Yahweh. The idea that the Assyrians were carrying out the will of Yahweh and that their conquests and destructions were the manifestations of divine plans was one Isaiah had proclaimed for decades (see 10:5-19; 8:6-8*a*; 7:18-25, and so on). Yahweh has complete knowledge of the Assyrian monarch (v. 28) and, therefore, is fully aware of his actions, including his rage against Yahweh, which is manifest in his move against Judah, Jerusalem, and Hezekiah.

The divine judgment against Sennacherib (and a statement of promise to Hezekiah) is given in verse 29. Yahweh will treat Sennacherib as a wild beast or a dangerous animal, putting a ring in his nose and a hook in his lip. (Assyrians and others may have treated captive prisoners and exiles this way; see Amos 4:2.) The Assyrian will then be made to depart by the same road he had taken to arrive. As often in his preaching, Isaiah here proclaims the destruction of the enemy through supernatural intervention on behalf of the Deity.

In verses 30-32, there is a promise of salvation originally addressed as an assurance to King Hezekiah. The reference to the content of the address as a sign probably represents not the words of the prophet but the popular depiction of the prophet as a sign-giver (see the discussion of 7:14, above, pp. 131-33).

The statements in verse 30 imply a time of shortage followed by a return to normalcy while verses 31-32*a* describe severe destruction through which however a remnant will survive from which new life will develop. Apparently, two conditions lie behind this prediction—namely, the approach of a sabbatical year (see Exod. 23:10-11; Lev. 25:1-7) and the presence of the Assyrian army in 701, each of which would make normal agricultural activity impossible during that year.

On the basis of Jeremiah 34 and 28:1 and the dating of the siege of Jerusalem by the Babylonians (assuming that Nebuchadrezzar captured the city in 586), it can be shown that the year 588–587 (an autumn to autumn year) was a sabbatical year. This would mean, calculating backward, that 700–699 was a sabbatical year. The following, then, would be the referents in Isaiah's statement: this year = 701–700; the second year = 700–699; and the third year = 699–698. Sennacherib's campaign in the west occurred in 701, probably in the summer. Apparently, his stay in the area extended beyond the autumn new year of 701 and thus the beginning of the year 701–700. Isaiah anticipated that plowing and sowing would be impossible in the fall of 701. Thus people would have to eat in this year what grew of itself. Since 700–699, the following year, would be a sabbatical year, people would have to eat what grew from the remains of the previous voluntary crop. Finally, and this constitutes the text's core and Isaiah's promise, in the third year, life would return to normal and the people would sow and reap and tend their vineyards and eat their fruits. Thus the prophet seems to have anticipated a fairly lengthy period of privation for the people, necessitated partly by Assyrian harassment and partly by the sabbatical year observances, which prohibited normal sowing and reaping. But beyond the privation, he promises a return to normal conditions. Clearly, the prophet recommended not only holding out against the Assyrians and refusing to surrender, but also the observance of the sabbatical year, even following the hardships of the temporary Assyrian occupation of much of the land.

In verses 31-32, the prophet promises that the people, like the crops, will survive and renew their life, again taking root downward and bearing fruit upward. He specifies those from whom new life would grow—namely, "the fugitives (fleeing to Jerusalem) from what remained of the house of Judah" and the inhabitants of Jerusalem itself. After the war, the remnant of Jerusalem and the fugitives who had found safety in Zion would go forth to be the stock of new growth. Isaiah thus seems to have anticipated the complete devastation of Judah with only the city of Jerusalem being spared and only its citizens and the fugitives taking refuge there surviving.

As he had earlier proclaimed the divine protection of Jerusalem when Ahaz had broken with Israel and stood apart from the anti-Assyrian coalition, putting Jerusalem under the threat of enemy assault (see 8:21–9:7 and, above, chap. 4, sect. 11), so again he proclaimed "the zeal of Yahweh Sebaoth will accomplish this" (v. 32b; see 9:7; 26:11).

The material in 37:33-35 presents several structural and literary problems. First of all, the saying is twice attributed to the Deity, once at the beginning of verse 33 ("Therefore thus says Yahweh to [or perhaps "concerning"] the king of Assyria") and again at the end of verse 34 ("says [or "oracle of"] Yahweh"). Second, verse 35 stands outside the material designated as a quotation of divine speech. In addition, the reference to "my servant David" in verse 35 has no parallel in the words of Isaiah, who speaks instead of "the house of David" (7:13; 22:22), "the throne of David" (9:7), "the city of David" (22:9) "tabernacle of David" (16:5), or just "David" (29:1). Third, the relationship between verses 30-32 and 33-35 is uncertain. Are the latter verses part of the same speech as the former? Some scholars argue that verses 33-35 should be considered the continuation of verse 21 with verses 22-32 considered an interpolation.

The following conclusions about this section seem most persuasive. (1) Verse 35 was not part of the original Isaianic saying but was added in the telling of the material or in its editing. (2) The opening statement of verse 33 also represents an editorial addition. The ascription of the words to the Deity originally occurred only at the end of the saying—that is, at the end of verse 34. (3) Like 22*b*-29 and 30-32, this material once formed an independent saying, probably addressed to Hezekiah in the midst of the crisis to assure him of the divine deliverance of Jerusalem.

The speech makes two points. First, Jerusalem will not be taken:

> He shall not enter this city;
>   and he shall not shoot an arrow there,
> or advance against it with shield,
>   or pile up against it a siege mound.

Second, the Assyrian monarch will be forced to retreat and return home (see 37:29*b*):

> By the road which he came,
>   by it he shall return;
> and into this city,
>   he shall not enter.

As he had throughout his career, Isaiah proclaimed the sufficiency of Yahweh's protection of Jerusalem and the city's ultimate inviolability.

What influence Isaiah's preaching had during the Sennacherib crisis remains unknown. Both II Kings 18:14-16 and the inscriptions of Sennacherib indicate that the Judean king paid the Assyrian monarch a heavy indemnity for his involvement and leadership in the revolt. But the conditions under which he paid his penalty remain hidden. Several historical scenarios are possible. (1) The Egyptian-Assyrian battle at Eltekeh may have been less of an Assyrian success than Sennacherib indicates. Assyrian rulers often claimed victory on the battlefield when the outcome was less than a glorious triumph, if not defeat itself. In this instance, the Egyptians also claimed the battle as a victory for themselves. Under conditions less than triumphant, Sennacherib may have withdrawn from the field, accepting Hezekiah's payment as evidence of sufficient repentance. (2) Sennacherib may have been as successful as he claimed, defeating local forces and the Egyptians and subsequently rearranging political conditions in the area before returning home. Under these circumstances, Hezekiah may have been convinced that surrender was the best policy. Sennacherib may have been willing to accept such submission from Judah since few states had shown as much loyalty as had Jerusalem over the years. (3) Sennacherib may have been reasonably successful in the west and, therefore, poised to place Jerusalem under what might have been a protracted siege when troubles in Babylonia seemed more pressing. (In 700, Sennacherib had to remove from the Babylonian throne Bel-ibni, his puppet king, whom he had enthroned in 704 or 703.) Even under these circumstances, Hezekiah may have been willing to settle matters with the Assyrians, sending payment to Nineveh that included among other things his own daughters (*ANET* 288) and "all the silver that was found in the temple of Yahweh, and in the treasuries of the king's house" and the gold stripped "from the doors of the temple of Yahweh, and from the doorposts which Hezekiah king of Judah had overlaid" (II Kings 18:15-16).

In any event, Judah survived, Jerusalem was not entered by Sennacherib, and the temple remained intact. During the process, Hezekiah apparently showed less confidence in Isaiah's promises than had Ahaz during the Syro-Ephraimitic crisis. In popular tradition, the outcome was nonetheless recalled as the result of divine deliverance.

35. HEZEKIAH'S SICKNESS (38:1-22)

P. R. **Ackroyd**, "An Interpretation of the Babylonian Exile: A Study of 2 Kings 20, Isaiah 38-39," *SJT* 27(1974)329-52; **Ackroyd**, "The Death of Hezekiah—A Pointer to the Future," *De la Torah au Messie. Mélanges Henri Cazelles* (ed. M. Carrez et al.; Paris: Desclée, 1981)219-25; J. **Barton**, *Oracles of God: Perceptions of Ancient Prophecy in Israel After the Exile* (London: Darton, Longman and Todd, 1986); A. K. **Jenkins**, "Hezekiah's Fourteenth Year: A New Interpretation of 2 Kings xviii 13–xix 37," *VT* 26(1976)289-94.

Earlier, we argued that the sickness of Hezekiah and the visit of Babylonian ambassadors to Jerusalem occurred at the time of the Ashdod-led revolt against Assyria (see above, chap. 4, sects. 22 and 24). If Hezekiah assumed the throne in 727, his fourteenth year would have been 713. Isaiah's denunciation of Jerusalemite leadership, especially Shebna and Eliakim, in chapter 22 and his symbolic action in chapter 20 are best understood in the light of popularly inspired Judean participation in the Ashdod-led revolt at a time when Hezekiah was at the point of death. In addition, the depiction of Hezekiah in Isaiah 36–37 nowhere assumes the king's illness during the Sennacherib invasion; thus another situation was probably the occasion for the events in chapters 38–39.

The Babylonian embassy to Jerusalem is more likely to have occurred during the reign of Sargon than during that of Sennacherib. Merodach-baladan was an important figure in Babylonia throughout much of Sargon's reign (see, above, chap. 4, sect. 23). The Babylonian Chronicles notes the following about Sargon's and Merodach-baladan's assumption of power:

The fifth year: Shalmaneser died in the month Tebet. For five years Shalmaneser ruled Akkad and Assyria. On the twelfth day of the month Tebet Sargon ascended the throne in Assyria. In the month Nisan Merodach-baladan ascended the throne in Babylon. (*ABC* 73)

Competition continued between the two for over a decade and reached its apex in 712. In 711/10, Sargon marched into Babylonia in strength and forced the retreat of Merodach-baladan into Elam (*ABC* 75). In the turmoil that plagued Babylonia early in the reign of Sennacherib, Merodach-baladan again seized the throne of Babylon in 704 or 703 but was in power for only a few months. Thus 704 or 703 hardly suggests itself as the time when Merodach-baladan would have been sending envoys to Jerusalem. Clearly the period following Sennacherib's western campaign in 702, suggested by the present placement of Isaiah 39, would have been no occasion for Babylonian ambassadorial visits to Jerusalem. Thus we are left with a time during the reign of Sargon, and most likely the period prior to the outbreak of rebellion against Sargon in 714/13, for the Babylonian visit to Jerusalem.

The narratives in chapters 38–39 are late and have been shaped by the experience of the Babylonian exile. They not only point explicitly to the exile (39:5-8), but also do so implicitly since Hezekiah's illness and recovery model the pattern of exilic distress and restoration, the community's experience of death, and the hope of new life. A date of composition after the death of Hezekiah is indicated by the author's knowledge that he lived fifteen years after the illness.

The Isaiah of these chapters is not the historical Isaiah but the prophet of popular imagination and legend. He is depicted as a wonder worker imbued with the power to perform or enlist divine miracles. In addition, he is a prognosticator, foreseeing the exact details of future events.

What aspects of chapter 38 may go back to events in the relationship of Hezekiah and Isaiah remain uncertain. The king's sickness and an Assyrian threat to Judah and Jerusalem may have coincided. Isaiah may have counseled and even medically treated the Judean king. The general tenor of the chapter, however, makes very tenuous any historical conclusions based on such evidence.

36. VISITING AMBASSADORS FROM BABYLON
(39:1-8)

J. A. **Brinkman**, "Merodach-Baladan II," *Studies Presented to A. L. Oppenheim* (ed. R. D. Briggs and J. A. Brinkman; Chicago: Oriental Institute, 1964)6-53; **Brinkman**, "Elamite Military Aid to Merodach-Baladan II," *JNES* 24(1965)161-66; L. D. **Levine**, "Sennacherib's Southern Front: 704-689 B.C.," *JCS* 34(1982)28-58.

In its present form, chapter 39 is preparatory to the preaching of Second Isaiah in chapter 40 and following. The latter proclaims an imminent return from Babylonian exile. Isaiah 39 declares that exile to Babylon was already predicted by Isaiah and set in motion by Hezekiah. According to the word attributed to Isaiah, Judean royal possessions will enrich the coffers of the Babylonian monarchy, and male Davidic descendants will serve as eunuchs at the Babylonian court.

The grounds for such a gloomy verdict on the future of the Davidic house would appear to be nothing more than a slightly over-enthusiastic friendliness toward Babylonia on Hezekiah's part. Responding to the courtesy of a royal greeting accompanied by a gift, Hezekiah is said to have shown the Babylonian guests all the royal treasuries and arms throughout the realm. To such disclosure, Isaiah responds that the Babylonians, having seen, will someday possess.

In spite of the special and legendary character of chapter 39, it is possible to hypothesize some of the events that may lie behind the present narrative. Given what we know from non-biblical texts about ancient Near Eastern history for the time, the following scenario can be reconstructed, even though the biblical materials have been significantly slanted.

(1) The most likely setting for a Babylonian embassy to the west was during Merodach-baladan's reign over Babylon between 721 and 710 (see *ABC* 73-75). He had siezed the

throne in Babylon almost simultaneous to Sargon's accession to the throne in Assyria (see, above, chap. 4, sect. 23). After having been forced to flee the region in 710, Merodach-baladan was able, in either 704 or 703, to regain the throne of Babylon for a few months before being driven out of the city by Sennacherib. This latter short reign hardly seems the occasion for an embassy to the west, although coordinated rebellions may have broken out throughout the empire at the death of Sargon.

(2) If Hezekiah's sickness were somehow related to his fourteenth year, this date (713) would have coincided with Merodach-baladan's rule. In fact, Babylonian texts report that the Babylonian monarch took the offensive against Assyria at about this time (see *ABC* 75). This was also the time political changes were occurring in Egypt and the Ethiopians were moving into the Delta, thus a time when exploratory Babylonian embassies may have visited the west.

(3) The revolt by Ashdod in about 714/13 may have been encouraged by Babylon. Since neither the Delta princes nor the Ethiopians offered Yamani aid or refuge, it seems doubtful that Egyptian influence would have been the prime or only stimulus for a western revolt.

(4) The fact that Isaiah proclaims the fall of Babylon (Isaiah 21) in connection with the Ashdod revolt, in which Judah participated (Isaiah 20; 22), would suggest a connection between Babylon and events in the west.

(5) Special Babylonian ambassadors visiting the west in about 714–713 may have visited Jerusalem and sought to enlist the participation of Judah in an anti-Assyrian rebellion. Such a visit may have preceded or coincided with Hezekiah's illness. Isaiah, deeming the time not appropriate for rebellion, may have criticized any collusion, actual or suspected, with Merodach-baladan. Only when Hezekiah became incapacitated did Judean leaders join in the anti-Assyrian rebellion (see Isa. 22, and above, chap. 4, sects. 24–25).

Appendix: The History of the Interpretation of Isaiah 1–39

P. R. **Ackroyd**, "Isaiah I–XII: Presentation of a Prophet," *SVT* 29(1978)16-48; L. **Alonso-Schökel**, "Isaïe," *SDB* 7(1971)2060-79; A. G. **Auld**, "Poetry, Prophecy, Hermeneutic: Recent Studies in Isaiah," *SJT* 32(1980)567-81; H. **Barth**, *Die Jesaja-Wörte in der Josiazeit: Israel und Assur als Thema einer Produktiven Neuinterpretation der Jesajaüberlieferung* (Neukirchen-Vluyn: Neukirchener Verlag, 1977); J. **Becker**, *Isaias— der Prophet und sein Buch* (Stuttgart: Katholisches Bibelwerk, 1968); G. L. **Berlin**, *The Major Prophets in Talmudic and Midrashic Literature* (dissertation, St. Mary's Seminary and University, 1976)118-68; C. **Boutflower**, *The Book of Isaiah Chapters [I-XXXIX] in the Light of Assyrian Monuments* (London/New York: Society for Promoting Christian Knowledge, 1930); L. **Brodie**, "The Children and the Prince: The Structure, Nature and Date of Isaiah 6–12," *BTB* 9(1979)27-31; G. **Brunet**, *Essai zur l'Isaïe de l'histoire. Etude de quelques textes notamment dans Isa. VII, VIII & XXII* (Paris: A & J. Picard, 1975); T. K. **Cheyne**, *The Book of Isaiah Chronologically Arranged* (London: Macmillan & Co., 1870); **Cheyne**, "Isaiah," *EB* 13(9th ed.; 1880) 377-84; **Cheyne**, "Isaiah and His Commentators," in his *The Prophecies of Isaiah* (2 vols.; C. Kegan Paul & Co., 1880-81)2.244-64; **Cheyne**, *Introduction to the Book of Isaiah* (London: A. & C. Black, 895); B. S. **Childs**, *Isaiah and the Assyrian Crisis* (London: SCM Press, 1967); R. E. **Clements**, *Isaiah and the Deliverance of Jerusalem: A Study in the Interpretation of Prophecy in the Old Testament* (Sheffield: JSOT Press, 1980); **Clements**, "The Unity of the Book of Isaiah," *Int* 36(1982)117-29; W. H. **Cobb**, "On Integrating the Book of Isaiah," *JBL* 20(1901)77-100; C. H. **Cornill**, "Die Composition des Buches Jesaja," *ZAW* 4(1884)83-105; V. A. **Dearing**, "A New Explanation for the Discontinuities in the Text of Isaiah," *The Critical Study of Sacred Texts* (ed. W. D. Q'Flaherty; Berkeley: Graduate Theological Union, 1979)77-93; W. **Dietrich**, *Jesaja und die Politik* (Munich: Chr. Kaiser, 1976); S. R. **Driver**, *Isaiah: His Life and Times, and the Writings Which Bear His Name* (London/New York: James Nisbet and Co./Fleming H. Revell, 1888); B. **Duhm**, *Das Buch Jesaja* (Göttingen: Vandenhoeck & Ruprecht, 1892); J. H. **Eaton**, "The Origin of the Book of Isaiah," *VT* 9(1959)138-57; G. **Fohrer**, "The Origin, Composition and Tradition of Isaiah I-XXXIV," *ALUOS* 3(1962)3-38 (= *BZAW* 99 [1967]113-47); K. **Fullerton**, "The Book of Isaiah: Critical Problems and a New Commentary," *HTR* 6(1913)478-520; **Fullerton** "Viewpoints in the Discussion of Isaiah's Hopes for the Future," *JBL* 41(1922)1-101; F. **Giesebrecht**, *Beiträge zur Jesajakritik* (Göttingen: Vandenhoeck & Ruprecht, 1890); H. L. **Ginsberg**, "First Isaiah," *EJ* 9(1971)49-60; **Ginsberg**, *The Supernatural in the Prophets with Special Reference to Isaiah* (Cincinnati: Hebrew University Press, 1979); H. **Gressmann**, "Amos," in *SAT* II/1 (Göttingen: Vandenhoeck & Ruprecht, 1910)322-29; **Gressmann**, "Die literarische Analyse Deuterojesajas," *ZAW* 34(1914)254-97; H. **Gunkel**, "Die israelitische Literatur," *Kultur der Gegenwart* (ed. P. Hinneberg; Berlin: B. G. Teubner, 1906)I/7.51-102; **Gunkel**, "Propheten II seit Amos," *RGG* 4(1913)1866-86 (= "IIB. The Israelite Prophecy from the Time of Amos," in *Twentieth-Century Theology in the Making, Volume I: Themes of Biblical Theology* [ed. J. Pelikan; New York: Harper & Row, 1969]48-75); E. W. **Hengstenberg**, *Christology of the Old Testament* (2 vols.; Edinburgh: T. & T. Clark, 1872); **Hengstenberg**, "Isaiah," *CBL*, 2.33-50; H. W. **Hoffmann**, *Die Intention der Verkündigung Jesajas* (Berlin: Walter de Gruyter, 1974); W. L. **Holladay**, *Isaiah: Scroll of a Prophetic Heritage* (Grand Rapids: William B. Eerdmans, 1978); F. **Huber**, *Jahwe, Juda und die anderen Völken beim Propheten Jesaja* (Berlin: Walter de Gruyter, 1976); D. R. **Jones**, "The Traditio of the Oracles of Isaiah of Jerusalem," *ZAW* 67(1955)226-46; Y. **Kaufmann**, *The Religion of Israel: From Its Beginnings to the Babylonian Exile* (Chicago: University of Chicago Press, 1960)378-95; R. **Kennett**, *The Composition of the Book of Isaiah* (London: British Academy, 1910); R. **Kilian**, *Jesaja 1-39* (Darmstadt: Wissenchaftliche Buchgesellschaft, 1983); L. J. **Liebreich**, "The Compilation of the Book of Isaiah," *JQR* 46(1955-56)259-77; 47(1956-57)114-38; R. J. **Marshall**, "The Structure of Isaiah 1-12," *BR* 7(1962)19-32; **Marshall** "The Unity of Isaiah 1-12," *LQ* 14(1962)21-38; S. **Mowinckel**, "Die Komposition des Jesajabuches Kap. I-XXXIX," *AO* 11(1933)267-92; **Mowinckel**, *Prophecy and Tradition: The Prophetic Books in the Light of the Study of the Growth and History of the Tradition* (Oslo: Jacob Dybwad, 1946); W. **Popper**, "A Suggestion as to the Sequence of Some Prophecies in First Isaiah," *HUCA* 1(1924)79-96; R. **Rendtorff**, "Zur Komposition des Buches Jesaja," *VT* 34(1984)295-320; A. H. **Sayce**, *The Life and Times of Isaiah as Illustrated by Contemporary Monuments* (London: Religious Tract Society, 1889); W. H. **Schmidt**, "Die Einheit der Verkündigung Jesajas. Versuch einer Zusammenschau," *EvTh* 37(1977)260-72; J. J. **Schmitt**, *Isaiah and His Interpreters* (Mahwah, NJ: Paulist Press, 1986); G. T. **Sheppard**, "The Anti-Assyrian Redaction and the Canonical Context of Isaiah 1-39," *JBL* 104(1985)193-216; U. **Simon**, "Ibn Ezra between Medievalism and Modernism: The Case of Isaiah x1-1xvi," *SVT* 36(1985)257-71; G. **Smith**, "On a New Fragment of the Assyrian Canon Belonging to the Reigns of Tiglath-pileser and Shalmaneser," *TSBA* 2(1873)321-32; G. A. **Smith**, "Isaiah," *HDB* 2(1900)485-99; J. **Steinmann**, *Le prophete Isaïe. Sa vie, son oeuvre et son temps* (Paris: Cerf, 1955); D. C. **Steinmetz**, "John Calvin on Isaiah 6: A Problem in the History of Exegesis," *Int* 36(1982)156-70; E. **Strachey**, *Jewish History and Politics in the Times of Sargon and Sennacherib: An Inquiry into the Historical Meaning and Purpose of the Prophecies of Isaiah* (2d ed.; London: W. Isbister & Co., 1874 [1st ed. 1853]); B. **Uffenheimer**, "The Consecration of Isaiah in Rabbinic Exegesis," *SI* 22(1971)233-46; J. **Vermeylen**, *Du Prophète Isaïe à l'Apocalyptique, Isaie, I–XXXV, miroir d'un demi-millénarie d'experience religieuse en Israel* (2 vols.; Paris: J. Gabalda, 1977-78); C. **Westermann**, *Basic Forms of Prophetic Speech* (Philadelphia: Westminster Press, 1967); E. J. **Young**, "The Study of Isaiah Since the Time of Joseph Addison Alexander," *Studies in Isaiah* (Grand Rapids/London: William B. Eerdmans/Tyndale Press, 1954)9-101; **Young**, *The Book of Isaiah* (3 vols.; Grand Rapids: William B. Eerdmans, 1965-72)1.487-93.

Most contemporary scholarship on Isaiah 1–39 is based on a number of domain assumptions, among which are the following. (1) These chapters are the product of a process of exegetical supplementation, editorial redaction, expansive interpolation, and creative reinterpretation that extended over centuries (see the subtitle of the book by Vermeylen). (2) This material is reflective of the religious and theological developments of the Judean people throughout the period in which the work was being produced and thus is a theological anthology of the monarchical period, late first temple times, the exile, and the second temple era. (3) As the material was in transmission and the process of formation, it was added to and edited to reflect practically every significant event in Judean history. (4) The successive phases through which the material has passed can, in general, be isolated, and the literary elements from the various phases can be related to particular historical and sociological contexts. Thus it is possible to outline the general process by which Isaiah 1–39 came into being and thereby to decompose the collection. (5) The process of decomposing the material leaves a deposit of isolated units and fragments that may be considered the original preaching of the eighth-century prophet and reflective of his views and thought.

How has scholarship arrived at this stage of affairs? Certain features in the book of Isaiah have required explanation and thus have eventually led to some form of decomposition and fragmentation.

First of all, there is the matter of Isaiah's vision in chapter 6, which many ancients and practically all modern interpreters have taken to be the prophet's inaugural call (see Berlin and Uffenheimer; note the comments in the *Mekilta* on Exod. 15:9-10 [vol. 2, p. 54 of Lauterbach's English translation]). The twelfth-century C.E. Jewish scholar Rabbi Eliezer of Beaugency and John Calvin, among others, doubted that chapter six was such a narrative about how Isaiah's prophetic career began (see Ginsberg, 1979, and Steinmetz). If Isaiah's call to prophetic office occurs in chapter 6, then this clearly indicates that the materials have not been ordered chronologically, for if they had the call narrative should open the book (see Jer. 1 and Ezek. 1–3). This peculiarity of the book of Isaiah encouraged decomposing the canonical Isaiah and placing the material in chapters 1–5 at some point or points after chapter 6.

In the second place, the radical change in language and style in chapters 40 and following, the exilic conditions presupposed, and the explicit references to the Persian king Cyrus (44:28; 45:1) raised questions about the unity of the work. Cyrus did not appear on the scene until 150 years after the end of Isaiah's ministry. The Jewish scholar Ibn Ezra (1089–1164) had doubts about whether the eighth-century prophet spoke so explicitly about matters so long after his time. Calvin knew of those he called infidels who argued that the references to Cyrus were written after the events had transpired. (Commenting on Isa. 55:3, however, he wrote as if texts like Isa. 55 were written during the Babylonian captivity.)

The differences—historical, theological, literary, poetical —between chapters 1–39 and 40–66 forced the decomposition of the canonical version of the book. The concept of an exilic Second Isaiah, beginning with chapter 40, gained a position in the mainstream of Old Testament scholarship in the last quarter of the eighteenth century. Influential in this regard were J. C. Döderlein, in his annotated translation of Isaiah (1775), J. B. Koppe, in his comments in the German edition of Bishop Robert Lowth's commentary on Isaiah (1779–1781), and J. G. Eichhorn, in his *Einleitung* (volume III [1783] 83-97).

If Isaiah 40 and following originated over a century later than the lifetime of the prophet Isaiah, then two positions are arguable: (1) the canonical book of Isaiah is more an anthology than a literary entity from a single historical figure and (2) study of the historical Isaiah must be disassociated from the material in Isaiah 40 and following.

The debate over the "Isaianic problem," as it came to be designated in the nineteenth century, assumed two concentric forms. The larger, or outer, circle in the debate concerned whether all of Isaiah 1–66 could be attributed to the eighth-century prophet. A majority of scholars gradually accepted a two Isaiah theory—an eighth-century pre-exilic Isaiah and a sixth-century exilic Isaiah. This view found expression in the commentaries on Isaiah by W. Gesenius (1820–1821) and F. Hitzig (1833) and in the general handbooks on the prophets by J. G. Eichhorn (1816–1819) and H. Ewald (1840–1841). The integrity and unity of the book were defended by conservative scholars, such as E. W. Hengstenberg (especially in his *Christologie des Alten Testaments* [2 vols. 1829–1835; 4 vols 1854–1857]), J. A. Alexander (in his commentary, 1846–1847), and F. Delitzsch (in the first three editions of his commentary, from 1866). By the time S. R. Driver published *An Introduction to the Literature of the Old Testament* in 1891, however, only a small minority of scholars were continuing to defend the authenticity and single authorship of the entire book (as is still the case).

The inner circle of the debate concerned a set of issues focused more narrowly on the authenticity and structure of Isaiah 1–39. If the location of the "call narrative" indicated some form of anthological rather than chronological arrangement of the materials, and if a late date for chapters 40–66 indicated the possibility that passages in 1–39 might also be late, then three major questions arose: Which texts derived from the eighth-century prophet? From what historical periods and social contexts did the inauthentic material derive? On what principles were chapters 1–39 presently arranged?

Scholars felt that the authenticity of many texts in Isaiah 1–39 was questionable and suggested more plausible settings for the material than the eighth century B.C.E. By about 1890, the following texts in chapters 1–39 were widely regarded as non-Isaianic: 12:1-6 (a thanksgiving psalm assumed to have been added after the exile); 13:1–14:23 (oracles on the fall of Babylon, presumably deriving from near the end of the exile); 15:1–16:12 (an older poem reused by Isaiah to which he added 16:13-14); 21:1-10 (a speech, presumably from the time when Babylon was the world power); 24:1–27:13 (eschatological texts assigned to the post-exilic period); and 34:1–35:10 (from a time late in the exilic period). The remainder of the material was generally considered authentic but was dated to various periods in the prophet's career. Several authentic texts were considered to have suffered from secondary dislocation. For example, that 9:8–10:4 and 5:25-30 originally belonged together and shared a common refrain was widely assumed. One scheme argued that the original order of this material was 5:25; 9:8–10:4; 5:26-30.

The organizational principles by which the material was structured and given canonical shape were not of primary concern in nineteenth-century scholarship. Most scholars pointed to the scheme of judgment speeches concerning Israel and Judah (chaps. 1–12), speeches related to foreign nations (chaps. 13–23), and speeches mostly concerning a future salvation (chaps. 28–35) as the basic organizing scheme. Such a scheme is found also in the book of Ezekiel (1–24, 25–32, 33–48).

A chronological ordering of the material of the entire book was advocated by such conservative scholars as Hengstenberg.

Chronology is, throughout, the principle according to which the prophecies of Isaiah are arranged. In the first six chapters, we obtain a survey of the Prophet's ministry under Uzziah and Jotham. Chap. vii. to x. 4 belongs to the time of Ahaz. From chap. x .4 to the close of chap. xxxv every thing belongs to the time of the Assyrian invasion in the fourteenth year of Hezekiah; in the face of which invasion the prophetic gift of Isaiah was displayed as it had never been before. The section, chap. xxxvi-xxxix, furnishes us with the historical commentary on the preceding prophecies from the Assyrian period, and forms, at the same time, the transition to the Second part [Isaiah 40-66], which still belongs to the same period. (*Christology*, 2. 2-3)

Correlations between the preaching of Isaiah and ancient Near Eastern history were of special concern for most nineteenth-century interpreters, both traditional and innovative. As a rule, however, attempts to make close correlations between text and event produced more and more material considered inauthentic to the prophet Isaiah, since what were believed to be correlatable events tended to date from periods later than the eighth century B.C.E. Strachey and Sayce appealed to Assyrian history and literary evidence to substantiate the genuineness of various Isaianic texts. The Assyriologist George Smith proposed, but never pursued, the close chronological correlation between the material in Isaiah 1–37 and Assyrian history. He noted the following parallels, which assume a chronological ordering of the Isaianic materials (pp. 328-39). He admitted that "in the passages relating to Babylon and in some others, later events are mentioned," and he does not consider some chapters in Isaiah, since "they have no relation to known Assyrian events of the period" (p. 329).

ISAIAH	ASSYRIAN ANNALS
Ch. i to vi.—During the time of Uzziah king of Judah.	B.C. 738. Tiglath-Pileser mentions Azariah (Uzziah) king of Judah.
Ch. vii to x—Relate to the expedition of Tiglath-Pileser, king of Assyria, against Syria and Israel, in the reign of Ahaz.	B.C. 734–732. Expedition of Tiglath-Pileser against Damascus, Israel, and Philistia, tribute of Yauḥazi (Ahaz), king of Judah.
Ch. xiii and first half of xiv.—Against Babylon.	B.C. 731. Tiglath-Pileser conquers Babylon and annexes it to Assyria.
Ch. xiv, *v.* 28 to 32.—In the year of death of Ahaz, rod of smiter broken.	B.C. 727.—Death of Tiglath-Pileser.
Ch. xv and xvi.—Against Moab.	B.C. 725.—Reign of Shalmaneser; details unknown
Ch. xvii—Against Damascus, Aroer and Israel.	B.C. 720.—Expedition of Sargon king of Assyria against Qarqar (Aroer), Damascus, and Samaria.
	B.C. 715.—Egypt makes alliance with Assyria.
Ch. xviii and xix.—Against Egypt.	B.C. 712.—Egypt stirs up revolt in Palestine against Assyria.
Ch. xx.—In the year of capture of Ashdod, prophecy against Egypt.	B.C. 711.—Sargon takes Ashdod; king of Egypt abandons his allies.
Ch. xxi, *v.* 1 to 10.—Against Babylon.	B.C. 710.—Sargon conquers Babylon.
Ch. xxiii—Against Tyre.	B.C. 702–1.—Phoenicia attacked by Sennacherib king of Assyria; the king flies from Tyre to Cyprus.
Ch. xxiv to xxix.—Sennacherib's invasion.	B.C. 702–1.—Sennacherib marches through Palestine.

Ch. xxx and xxxi.—Against rely- | B.C. 702.1.—Sennacherib de-
ing on Egypt. | feats the Egyptian army at Eltekeh.

Ch. xxxii to xxxvii, *v.* 36. | B.C. 702–1.—Sennacherib attacks Judah.

Ch. xxxvii, *v.* 37 and 38.—Murder of Sennacherib and accession of Esarhaddon. | B.C. 681.—Murder of Sennacherib and accession of Esarhaddon.

The work of C. H. Cornill in 1884 sought to move beyond analysis to synthesis and proposed not only that the material was put together along very general chronological lines, but also that texts were frequently connected along catch-word associations. No explanation of the ordering of the material reached anything like universal acceptance.

The interests and approaches current in Old Testament scholarship at the end of the last century furthered the decomposition and fragmentation of Isaiah 1–39. Several basic hypotheses can be isolated as foundational in the various methodologies that came to dominate twentieth-century Old Testament study. Each methodology has contributed to the development of Isaianic studies.

(1) Historical-critical interpretations of Old Testament literature has argued (a) that texts were produced within particular ancient historical-sociological contexts, (b) that these contexts must be recovered and reconstructed through literary-historical methods so that texts may be "reread" in their original contexts, and (c) that the basic meaning of a text is the ancient meaning it had for the one who uttered or wrote it and for the one who originally heard or read it. (These emphases had first led to the conception of a second Isaiah, to the idea that the book in final form is a post-exilic compilation, and to the post–eighth-century dating of some of the material in Isaiah 1–39.)

(2) Historical-critical interpretations of ancient Israelite religious life and thought came to conclude (a) that the prophets' range of vision was the present or immediately future life of their contemporaries rather than the distant future and eschatological matters (they were more *forth*tellers than *fore*tellers), (b) that prophets were concerned fundamentally with the ethical and social-historical life of their

times, (c) that the prophets were basically anti-establishment and thus were the opponents of the monarchs, their policies, and their ministers, and (d) that certain theological concepts—such as messianism, the inviolability of Zion, many a surviving remnant, and so forth—were late developments from post-exilic or subsequent times. The prophet Isaiah and the authenticity of the Isaianic traditions came to be assessed in light of these propositions.

(3) Form-critical and traditional-historical methodologies reached a number of widely shared conclusions regarding the original nature of prophetic speech and the process of tradition transmission, and these, also, greatly influenced research on Isaiah (see Gunkel; Gressmann; Mowinckel, 1946; Westermann). (a) Prophetic speech was brief, oracular, to the point, and consisted of sayings generally marked off by introductory and/or concluding formulae: "The prophets did not act as 'orators' with long speeches with a connected development of ideas according to modern logical rules; they were Yahweh's 'messengers' who stood forth with concise, spontaneous, topical, quite brief messages from Yahweh in the concrete situation" (Mowinckel, 1946, 40). (b) Prophetic oracles were concerned with the (immediate) future and thus were future oriented in their content. (This point was stressed in the form-critical, history-of-religions approach over the scholarship that sought to take prediction out of prophecy.) (c) Oracles could be either promises (announcements of salvation) or threats (announcements of disaster). (d) Prophetic oracles were both delivered and transmitted orally before being shaped and edited into written form.

The relatively brief, in itself, complete and concluded, independent separate saying ("oracle") is the original and real form of prophet "speech", his message, and that this is also largely the case with the historically known prophets, "the scripture prophets" as they are generally and misleadingly, termed.—These separate sayings have been transmitted by oral tradition in the prophet circles, partly unchanged, partly adapted to and revived in the new situations of new times; they have been living a *life* in tradition and have been serving a religious purpose within the circle; the tradition has not been static. In the course of the history of the tradition there have arisen greater "tradition complexes" and collections out of these separate sayings, which again in their turn have been joined together to final collections of tradition. The latter may also have been handed on by word of mouth. Finally, however they have been recorded; they have become "books." This written fixing may have started earlier, with the separate minor "complexes", and the oral tradition may have continued side by side with the written one. (Mowinckel, 1946, 60)

In 1892, Duhm published his landmark commentary on Isaiah in the *Handkommentar zum Alten Testament* series. His work, based on historical-critical procedures, challenged most of the assumptions held about the book of Isaiah and set the agenda for all subsequent Isaianic research. Duhm proposed not only a Deutero-Isaiah (chaps. 40–55), but also a Trito-Isaiah (chaps. 56–66) as well as an early post-exilic author of the special isolatable Servant Songs (42:1-4; 49:1-6; 50:4-9; 52:13–53:12). He distributed material now found in First Isaiah over a period of seven centuries, the earliest material going back to Isaiah and the latest coming from the first century B.C.E. According to Duhm, the genuine Isaianic materials formed the nucleus of what grew into three separate collections (chaps. 1–12; 13–23; 28–32). In addition to the materials that originated with the historical Isaiah (only 14:24-27; 17:1-6, 9-14; 18:1-6; 20; 22:1-9*a*, 11*b*-24, for example, are considered genuine in chaps. 13–23), other independent collections (chaps. 24–27, 36–39) eventually became part of the larger "Isaianic" collection. Even as late as the second century B.C.E., substantial material was being produced that was attached to or was used to expand the Isaianic traditions: chapter 33 (from 162 B.C.E.), 19:16-24 (from 150 B.C.E.), 29:15-24 and 30:18-25 (from Maccabean times), 24–27 (from 128 B.C.E.), 34–35 (before the days of John Hyrcanus[135–104 B.C.E.]), and 15:1-9*a* and 16:7-11 (from the reign of John Hyrcanus).

Since the turn of the century, research on Isaiah has labored under the shadow of Duhm's towering figure. More often than not, scholars have reacted to Duhm's theories and conclusions rather than to the text of Isaiah. A representative sample of theories about the authenticity and redactional history of the material in 1–33 (35 or 39) will be noted here (for a much fuller presentation of critical theories, see Vermeylen, 1-31 and Hans Wildberger's commentary, 1529-76; anti-critical approaches of recent vintage [see Young as representative] have added no new considerations to the debate).

One of the most complicated theories is that of Fohrer. He argues for seven small collections, each containing a corpus composed of some Isaianic material to which were appended various and diverse fragments and inauthentic promises deriving from periods later than the eighth century B.C.E. The following is his reconstruction of the process:

Corpus	Fragments	Promises
(A) 1:2-26(28)	1:29-31	2:2-4(5)
(b) 2:6–4:1	(3:25–4:1?)	4:2-6
(C) 5:1-23; 10:1-3(4)	5:14-17, 24	
(D) 6:1–8:18	8:19, 21-22	(8:23b); 9:1-6
(E) 9:7-20; 5:25-29(30); 10:5-15	10:27b-32	11:1-9(10, 11-16)
(F) 13-22; 28:1-4		28:5-6;(32:17-18)
(G) 28:7–32:14		32:15-20

In line with form-critical analysis, Fohrer argued that each corpus was composed of varous smaller units; for example, 1:2-26 contains five originally independent oracles (vv. 2-3, 4-9, 10-17, 18-20, 21-26).

In addition to these seven entities containing at least a few words of Isaianic materials, four other tradition complexes found their way into the book. These are:

(H) originally containing (a) 13:2-22; (b) 14:4b-21; (c) 15:1-9; 16:2; (d) 16:1, 3-5; (e) 16:6-12; (f) 19:1-15; (g) 21:1-10; (h) 21:11-12; (i) 21:13-15; (j) 23:1-14 to which were added later (k) 16:13-14; (l) 19:16-17, 18, 19-22, 23, 24-25; (m) 21:16-17; (n) 23:15-16, 17-18; (o) 17:7-8; (p) 17:9-11; and (q) 17:12-14. This material (a–j) was broken up and added to F and then further supplemented with k–q.

(I) 24–27, composed of five independent pieces (24:1-20; 24:21–25:12; 26:1-6, 7-21; 27:1-6, 12-13; 27:7-11) (no J follows)

(K) 33:1-6; 33:7-24; 34-35

(L) 36–39

This material was all combined in seven stages:

(1) juxtaposition of C and E (exilic period)
(2) insertion of D (exilic period)

(3) prefixing of B (exilic period)
(4) prefixing of A (post-exilic period)
(5) addition of F & H (5th century B.C.E.)
(6) addition of G with I and K (5th century B.C.E.)
(7) addition of L (5th or 4th century B.C.E.)

Vermeylen sets as his goal the elucidation of how Isaiah
1–35 evolved over a period of half a millennium. Here it is
sufficient to note the seven stages through which he saw the
material developing: (1) the preaching of Isaiah and the
formation of the first collection of his oracles; (2) enrich-
ments, additions, transformations, and so on, from the
period from Manasseh to the exile; (3) a Deuteronomistic
rereading from the time of the exile; (4) an eschatological
rereading and editing during the fifth century; (5) a redaction
stressing the conversion of the infidels; (6) a rereading by the
Jewish community to stress revenge on the impious; and (7)
late editorial touches relating to missionary concerns,
conversion of pagans, anti-Samaritan polemic, the gathering
of the dispersed, and the apocalyptic drama.

The historical contexts in which the Isaianic materials
presumably underwent reinterpretation and redaction vary
from scholar to scholar. A recent influential position has been
advocated by Barth. According to him, the traditions of First
Isaiah were subjected to an extensive redaction during the
reign of King Josiah (640–609) as the demise of Assyria
became obvious. Texts in Isaiah—such as 8:9-10; 8:23b–9:6;
10:16-19; 14:24-27; 30:27-33; 31:5, 8b-9—were added in this
Assyrian redaction to reflect the coming downfall of Assyria,
to praise Josiah, and to anticipate the coming salvation of
Judah.

Although recent scholarship has tended to doubt the
authenticity of much of Isaiah 1–33 (see Kilian), a few
scholars in the history of research have assigned large
portions of the material to the eighth-century prophet. The
older work by Boutflower sought to interpret many Isaianic
texts in the light of the events known from Assyrian history
and in doing so was following the nineteenth-century work
of Strachey, Smith, and Sayce. Ginsberg has argued for the
general authenticity and the chronological arrangement of
the materials in chapters 1–12.

Kaufmann has argued that all of chapters 1–33 are genuine ("not one non-Isaianic verse has penetrated Isaiah 1–33" [p. 382]) and that the Isaianic traditions in chapters 1–33 are organized in a general chronological fashion. (Kaufmann's proposals, which, however, are often more concerned with providing "a fundamental critique of classical criticism" than with positive constructions, are very similar in their broad conclusions to the present work.) Kaufmann offers several arguments for his critique of those who regard the book of Isaiah "as the most composite and disordered of the prophetic books" (p. 379). Against the idea that the book is a composite of materials from various periods, he offers a number of arguments. (1) Had material from the Babylonian period been incorporated into Isaiah 1–33, then the true nature of Assyria's collapse would be evident in the materials. However, the prophecies of Assyria's fall (10:5-34; 14:24-25; 30:27-31:9) foresee the collapse of the empire in the land of Israel. (2) None of the oracles about Zion and the Davidic monarch reflect the destruction of Jerusalem or the cessation of the monarchy. (3) Oracles universally accepted as Isaianic demonstrate that already in the prophet's own lifetime there was a rift between prophecy and history/reality. Prophecies about Damascus and Samaria and other powers were not fulfilled as the prophet had predicted. Had the book undergone extensive editing, surely these discrepancies would have been corrected. (4) Unlike many of the other Old Testament prophetic materials, Isaiah 1–33 contains no trace of national revenge. If the book had been produced by "an ages-long accretion of diverse prophecies and prophetic fragments" (p. 382), then this uniqueness remains incredible.

General Index

Adad-nirari III, 265
Ahab, 21, 39, 44, 136, 245
Ahaz (Jehoahaz I), 23, 24, 34, 35, 42-46, 48, 63, 68, 109, 112, 116, 122-36, 144, 148-76, 179, 182-83, 192, 212-14, 227, 236, 238, 256, 297, 352, 354, 375, 380-81
Ahaziah, 44, 155
Amalekites, 265
Amaziah, 27, 39, 44, 80, 155, 156, 328
Ammon, 23, 38, 39, 45, 177, 207, 216, 218, 246, 250
Amon, 35
Amos, 37, 38, 40, 52, 136, 177, 188, 238
Anatolia, 21, 22, 23, 26, 127, 228, 268, 272, 288, 295
Arabia (Arabs), 17, 21, 23, 27, 31, 39, 125, 218, 239, 258, 274, 276, 295, 374
Arpad, 22, 197-98
Ashdod, 17, 32, 39, 48, 58, 64, 131, 267-71, 273, 278, 297, 372, 375, 383, 386
Ashur-nasir-pal II, 20, 21, 31, 198, 199, 278
Athaliah, 44, 80, 81, 127, 155
Azriyau, 22

Babylon (Babylonia), 21, 24, 25, 27, 28, 34, 46, 63, 64, 220-34, 268, 272-75, 288, 290, 302, 372, 375, 382, 385-86
Bocchoris, 32, 262
Brook of Egypt, 23, 30, 31, 265, 298, 305, 319

Calno, (Kullani) 22, 197-98
Carchemish, 26, 197-98, 272, 278

Cimmerians, 27, 28, 295
Covenant, 53, 58, 89, 325-26, 329
Cult, 48, 70, 74-77, 97, 218-19, 251, 265, 297-98, 307-8, 315, 318, 332, 344-45, 362-70, 377
Cyprus, 27, 32, 259, 288, 292-93, 295, 302, 306

Damascus, 21, 24, 25, 26, 37, 38, 42, 43, 45, 46, 47, 64, 104, 128, 187, 197-98, 204, 228-29, 240, 247-49, 256, 263, 321
David (house of), 54, 56, 63, 80, 81, 83, 96, 100, 109-10, 112-13, 116-17, 121-36, 146, 149-52, 156-60, 164-66 176, 179-84, 202, 206-20, 245, 285, 286, 298, 316, 320, 332-33, 354-55, 360, 365, 367, 381
Deuteronomic Theology, 257, 265
Diviners, 85, 161, 166-67
Dumah, 274, 276

Earthquake, 62, 69-78, 83-87, 104-5, 185
Edom, 23, 27, 38, 43, 44, 45, 121, 151, 178, 207, 216, 218, 238, 269, 279
Egypt (Egyptians), 21, 25, 26, 27, 64, 131, 253, 257-67, 291, 306, 322-23, 336-51, 373-75, 377-78, 382
El Gibbor, 181, 197, 202
Elam, 25, 274, 281, 295, 331, 384
Elath, 37, 39, 42, 44, 87, 121, 190, 239
Elephantine, 265
Eliakim, 277, 284, 286-87, 296, 318, 383
Ephraim, 24, 41, 43, 64, 120, 121, 123, 149, 179, 186, 188-89, 191,

401

Author Index

Scripture Index

Scripture Index